# Kosher Jammers
## Jewish connections in jazz
### Volume 1 – the USA

Mike Gerber

# Table of Contents

*To Ruth, Lillian and Max*

*We're not always in harmony, but there's not another combo I'd rather be in*

# Preface: A stormy introduction

The denunciation of my proposed theme came like a bolt of lightning from God; or rather, Jim Godbolt, who as editor of *Jazz At Ronnie Scott's* magazine mocked the very idea that anyone would want to write about jazz and Jews.

But that is getting somewhat ahead of myself. The genesis of this book dates back several years earlier, to when I was approached to write a feature on the same theme for *Jewish Socialist*. Previously the only related article I had written was inspired by black clarinetist Don Byron's Mickey Katz tribute CD. That too was for *Jewish Socialist*, so when the magazine's editorial committee wanted a jazz Jews feature, they asked me. I phoned Godbolt hoping he would give me some leads. After all, the late Ronnie Scott had been Jewish, an award-winning tenor saxophonist, his club an international institution, and many of his jazz associates had been Jews too. Godbolt, as editor of the club's magazine, knew him and would have known others.

Our conversation lasted barely half a minute, I didn't even get a chance to give my name; Godbolt muttered some excuse and the call ended. A month later a friend phoned. Had I seen the latest edition of *JARS*? It contained a Godbolt editorial headed 'Jews and Jazz' that obviously alluded to my call. Strip away Godbolt's sarky witticisms and his editorial undoubtedly makes a telling point, a serious questioning of my whole enterprise. Referring to me, he says: "What findings could possibly result from his investigations? All I could think of was that Jewish guys played jazz because they wanted to – as simple as that... Jewish people were attracted to jazz in the same way as were indigenous Scandinavians, British, French, Swiss, Italians and Russians."

Godbolt was not alone in questioning the jazz and Jews theme. Another strongly opposed was the legendary Jewish jazz musician

Artie Shaw, though I am thankful that he granted me one of his last interviews. What I told Artie was that his misgivings, and those of the others, would be faithfully represented in this book.

And as I discovered in researching it, the Jewish input in jazz has been extensive, and fascinating.

*The above is an abridged version of the original introduction.*

# Introduction to the 2nd edition

This book was originally published in 2010 as *Jazz Jews* in a single volume, Part 1 dealing with the United States, Part 2 with the rest of the world. Running to 654 pages, it was a chunky tome. For this second edition, as it now includes substantial additional US related material, I have decided to separate those parts into two volumes – volume 2 to follow in due course. This first volume, then, focuses on the connections between Jews and jazz in the country where jazz originated.

The book's new title, *Kosher Jammers*, takes its name after Mickey Katz's jazzy-comedic klezmer band of the 1950s. I've altered the title for no other reason than that I prefer it to the old one.

For this new re-titled edition, I have updated, and inserted newly discovered information, where appropriate. And I've added an extensive chapter on the vital role that Jewish jazz facilitators – managers, impresarios, venue owners, label founders, record producers and such – have played, a sub-theme that contributes substantially to the value of this study.

A few words are pertinent on what I mean by Jewish. I don't mean it in the religious sense: although Judaism, as a religion, is clearly a critical component of the Jewish story, the Jews have been around so long, dispersed so widely across the globe, that much of what can be defined as Jewish is not religious at all – Yiddish worker songs, for instance. Plenty of Jews, moreover, although identifying as Jews ethnically, have no genuine religious conviction. What I also do not necessarily mean by Jewish is what the Judaic authorities mean by it, as dependent on matrilineal descent. It depends on the individual concerned. Someone whose father, but not mother, is Jewish, may well have some Jewish ethnological sensibility, perhaps even profoundly so.

Clarification too on the following point: "Jewish-jazz", hyphenated, indicates the fusion of Jewish music with jazz, or otherwise Jewish themed jazz, whereas "Jewish jazz musician" simply means a jazz musician who happens be Jewish.

I have retained British spelling throughout except when mentioning American institutions, or when directly quoting from American publications.

• • • •

Mike Gerber, London, December 2023

# Acknowledgements

This book has obviously benefited hugely from interviews and correspondence with jazz musicians and facilitators covered in these pages, and I am grateful to them all.

Here therefore is an opportunity to thank others who have helped the book along, starting with the Jewish Music Institute in London whose grant enabled me to research in the United States. And to Ross Bradshaw of my original publisher Five Leaves, whose suggestion it was that I apply for that grant. Without it, this book wouldn't be half what it is.

Alan, Carol and Rachel Cooper accommodated me in their home while I was researching in New York and New Jersey, then when I shifted base to Los Angeles I stayed with Anne Zimmerman, whom my friend Karen Merkel put me in touch with — so a big hug to them all; also to Anne's friend Judy for accommodating me for one night. Without their hospitality and companionship, and the home comforts, facilities, and conveniences I enjoyed, my US research would have been far less successful.

I must also mention my son Max whose musical knowledge informed a passage of this book; my wife Ruth, for her feedback and forbearance; and my friend Simon Lynn who read though the initial draft of this second edition and offered his comments. Gratitude too to Dave Richardson for his realisation of the concept for the cover design.

Finally, I wish to set on record my appreciation for the support of David Morrow, senior editor of Chicago University Press. I was sad to learn of his passing.

# Chapter 1: Whose music is it anyway?

In the beginning, Jews came to the promising land and saw that it was good. Or rather, they envisaged how good it could be if they worked hard, got the breaks, and surmounted the hurdles of establishing themselves in the New World, the United States of America.

Between 1881 and 1920, roughly two million Jews landed on America's shores and as their presence became more pronounced, Jews were debarred from admittance to certain industries, academies, institutions and localities, conditions that prevailed until well into the twentieth century. Still, as Americans, Jews had much to be grateful for, whatever the initial privations. No longer could they be singled out as readily as they had in Europe; now they took their place alongside the patchwork of minorities that so invigorated America's creative life. Whatever impediments were put in the way of their aspirations, America was ripe with opportunity for Jews that had the wit and drive to seize it.

Popular entertainment was a wide open and fast developing field where Jews rapidly made inroads as creators, performers and entrepreneurs. In popular music, Jews like many others found inspiration in the sounds of black America. Black composers and performers at the end of the nineteenth century and the early decades of the next pioneered the idioms that rapidly revolutionised America's, and ultimately the world's, cultural landscape – most significantly, jazz.

A generation after the abolition of slavery, Black people remained at the bottom of the social-economic order, yet their music was rhythmically and sonically so defiantly life affirming and emotionally sincere that it simply could not be ghettoised.

Few black musicians, composers and singers attained anything like the lucrative rewards pocketed by the most successful participants from the other groups, including Jews, that were heavily represented among the popularisers of music indebted in some way to African American idioms. Even today, when we've progressed to the point where some black artists are among the wealthiest musicians on the planet, one still occasionally hears the charge that black music has been stolen by the whites that most profited from it.

Before I embark on the story of Jews in jazz, a few words about the identity of this music. We have no trouble defining klezmer as Jewish, rembetika as Greek, blues as black – even if others perform them. Jazz? Well, a fundamental – *the* fundamental – part of what we think of as jazz is African American in inspiration. But we cannot just leave it at that. Jazz, in the way it developed, had highly complex musical and social origins. New Orleans, usually ascribed as its birthplace, was an ethno-cultural gumbo. And jazz rapidly became more multicultural as the music spread north to Chicago and New York and other large cities. By the 1920s jazz was catching on in the rest of the world where, in time, musicians would gain the confidence to incorporate indigenous elements.

If jazz then is a coat of many colours, that does not diminish an essential truth: that until comparatively recently the contribution of the foremost black musicians has outweighed that of any other group. Every jazz musician, every fan, everywhere, has drawn sustenance from their artistry.

So much so that there is a danger of undervaluing the influence that non-black musicians have had. Time to meet a Jewish musician and jazz historian who took tremendous flak for claiming as much.

• • • •

The late Richard Sudhalter spent ten years writing *Lost Chords*, which documents the contributions that white musicians made to jazz in the formative 1915-1945 period. His writings were informed by his many years' experience as a jazz musician, performing on trumpet and flugelhorn as Dick Sudhalter.

What leaps out is how prominently America's other, non-black, minorities were also represented in the music's first four decades. *Lost Chords* however struck a discord with some commentators. In an email to me, Sudhalter said: "Perhaps the best summation of the hostility came from the usually quite temperate [African American professor] Gerald Early, who in a moment of – inadvertent? – honesty, called it 'a long mess of a book that is neither serviceable nor kind to its reader... To write a book such as Sudhalter's, that is a defence of white people in their whiteness, is, for many, racism trying to disguise itself as an exploration of diversity.' In other words, whites should be content to be failed blacks where jazz is concerned, and not get any uppity notions about their own creativity or originality."

Incendiary stuff, and for some, the controversy has soured relations. Here is what one Jewish jazz musician, whom I will not identify, said to me: "We were bleeding heart liberals, really tried to help black people. I got on well with black musicians. The Jews were like blacks, suffered persecution, to survive they'd do anything. I marched in '62 for civil rights and all of a sudden, people being bulldozed by black militant bullshit. Jazz was not that kind of music. Benny Carter [saxophonist, arranger, bandleader] was colour-blind. He didn't like a racial slant on anything, dealt with everyone one to one. We played jazz because it was fuck-you music. We played their music because we despised the social thing. It was a way out. I might just as well have been black. I've stopped hiring blacks. They live in ghettos by choice, I'm sick of them." This, now deceased, musician's embittered pessimism notwithstanding, there is today perhaps a greater degree of ethnic collaboration in jazz than ever.

Aware of the feelings aroused by *Lost Chords*, I asked Dan Morgenstern, before he retired as Institute of Jazz Studies director, for his view. Munich-born Dan, former editor of *DownBeat*, settled in America in his teens after he, a Jew, fled from Nazi-occupied Europe where Danish Christians sheltered him and his mother until they made their escape. Dan is upfront about the debt Americans owe their black compatriots; his essay *Jazz – The Jewish-Black Connection* concurs with Albert Murray's thesis that "Blacks, in a sense, are the OmniAmericans because so many characteristics that we tend to think of as typically American are typically black American". 1

Dan defended Sudhalter: "He did a remarkable job on that book. It was something that deserved to be done. It's controversial of course, and a lot of people jumped on it, but I think it was very worthwhile to do, he did a tremendous amount of research and it'll stand when all this racial business dies down as a very valuable contribution to jazz history."

Strongly opposed though was Loren Schoenberg, a Jewish jazz musician who, although Sudhalter was a close friend, told me: "About *Lost Chords*, we could not disagree more strongly. It's revisionist."

Loren rightly insisted on the overriding importance of the black American in jazz but endorsed my attempt to document the Jewish contribution: "Jews have a part of jazz, as does anyone else whose ethnic background is part of the United States. Jazz music is the ultimate expression of the American culture and the American identity, almost in a utopian sense, as De Tocqueville hoped for in the sense of the potential for an American race. And certainly, the Jewish contribution to America has been wonderful.

"Jazz music," continued Loren, "has become a catalyst for expression in cultures all over the world, like any fine art, and in terms of Jews and their place in the jazz world, I think it's high time for someone to really take a serious look at it and to try and figure out exactly what's going on because it's a situation fraught with so many misunderstandings and so much super-sensitivity. First you have relationships between African Americans and Jews, which was one based in many senses in exploitation. It was a relationship in that they both seemed to be outsiders. It was forged in so many different ways, it's a complicated topic, but maybe you, like De Tocqueville, will come over from another country and take a look at what's going on here and bring to it a fresh perspective that we can't see because we're much too much a part of it. The Jewish involvement in jazz music has not adequately been looked at."

# Chapter 2: Jazz Age conundrum

Although few of the very earliest jazz players were Jewish, a widespread perception took hold that closely associated Jews with the new music. New Orleans, its birthplace, had a substantial Jewish population, but notes Dr Bruce Raeburn in his essay *Jewish Jazzmen in New Orleans, 1890-1940*: "Among the competing ethnic claims to priority in the 'creation' of jazz in the Crescent City, Jews are conspicuous by their absence." 1

Raeburn proceeds to show that "Jews did make their presence felt, as musicians, dance hall composers, song pluggers, and fans". The most famous white New Orleans outfit was the Original Dixieland Jazz Band that in 1917 cut the world's first jazz record. Raeburn makes no mention that any ODJB founding member was Jewish. Dan Morgenstern informed me that he believes the band's original pianist, Henry Ragas, was Jewish but was unable to recall where he had read this, or how good the source was. I contacted Dr Raeburn, curator of the Hogan Jazz Archives at New Orleans' Tulane University, but he could throw no conclusive light on Ragas' ethnicity.

Jews, anyway, were active in New Orleans jazz before the ODJB, Raeburn shows. He quotes ODJB's trombonist Edwin Edwards, who, in a 1959 interview about his favourite jazz experience, recalled a pre-ODJB outfit, "the best... jazz band I... was connected with was, Achille Baquet, clarinet; Mike Caplan was the cornet player; Bob Stein was the drummer; Joe Wolfe, pianist; and myself on trombone". The band, Edwards said, could "read music, improvise and play jazz too". Edwards and Baquet became jazz stars but not the three Jewish members, Caplan, Stein and Wolfe. Why not? Raeburn speculates: "It is likely that they inhabited a world of 'legitimate' music-making in New Orleans (such as theater work) which enabled them to make excursions into jazz without actually having to rely upon it." 2

Raeburn also mentions drummer John Kornfeld who, when learning his instrument, shared that knowledge with a "Creole of colour", Louis 'Old Man' Cottrell – an early example here of a black-Jewish alliance. Clarinetist Louis Cottrell, Old Man's son, recalled: "My father, being poor in his youth, was not able to afford any music lessons, but... Kornfeld, who was taking drum lessons, would come from his lesson and teach him all he had learned... The two were close all their lives; Kornfeld... became a good professional drummer." 3

As for Meyer Weinberg and Johnny Wiggs, they enjoyed long careers. Cornetist Wiggs was inspired to become a musician after hearing black cornetist King Oliver. Weinberg, aka Gene Meyer, a clarinetist, was active well into the swing era, recording with Louis Prima, and with Santo Pecora who testified to Weinberg's originality: "He didn't sound like anybody but himself... He didn't sound like Artie Shaw or Benny Goodman." 4

By comparison the Korn brothers, trombonist Marcus and clarinetist Monty, sons of an itinerant German rabbi, are obscure. Charles Edward Smith, surveying white New Orleans jazz, noted that the "era produced a 'crying' clarinet player whose name was Monty Korn". 5 Is that an allusion to klezmer style clarinet, feeding into jazz in its infant stage? Dr Raeburn believes the "possible connection of a 'crying' clarinet style to a klezmer source in the Old World is enticing and deserving of further investigation". 6

Dr Raeburn unearthed several other early Jewish jazzmen but concludes: "Too much emphasis on their Jewish connection is unwarranted. What is significant... is the similarity of their experiences to those of non-Jewish musicians – Italians, Irish, Germans, Greeks, and so on. The jazz community was multicultural in New Orleans, and we do not see reference to klezmer or other tangible ethnic traits appearing in the accounts of these musicians. Instead, we note musicians of diverse backgrounds coming together as Americans in their commitment to jazz. Indeed, the Jewish community in New Orleans had undergone a remarkable degree of assimilation even before the advent of jazz... the success of several Jewish jazzmen locally may be interpreted as a continuation of that process." 7

Whatever the ethnicity of the ODJB's Henry Ragas, the band, once relocated to New York, would have some Jewish influence with the pianist that succeeded him, J Russel Robinson. He had a Jewish grandmother and according to Hankus Netsky, Klezmer Conservatory Band director and chair of the New England Conservatory of Music's Contemporary Improvisation Department, Robinson did "occasional explorations of Jewish roots". Hankus directed my attention to Robinson's 'Lena From Palesteena', recorded with the ODJB in 1919. Seth Rogovoy, author of *The Essential Klezmer*, identifies the bridge as *Ma Yofus* – "the very DNA of old-time Yiddish music". 8

The Jewish New Orleans input could not possibly account for the strong tie in people's minds between jazz and Jews. In the early decades of the twentieth century however, ideas about what jazz was had not solidified in the public's or cultural commentators' minds and that is where we must start for our explanation. Famous Jewish music figures emerged that were influenced by jazz and its antecedents, and that although not today thought of in jazz terms, undoubtedly played a part in broadening public tastes. These include Irving Berlin, Sophie Tucker and Al Jolson, three talents I will now consider, and George Gershwin, with whom I conclude this chapter.

As early as 1911, Berlin, a Russian-born New York-raised Jew, was hailed as the 'King of Ragtime', the idiom that was the immediate forerunner of jazz, because of his massive hit

'Alexander's Ragtime Band'. Alec Wilder, in *American Popular Song: The Great Innovators 1900-1950*, comparing Berlin with the contemporaneous Jewish American songwriter Jerome Kern, said: "One sees how... Berlin, a product of Lower East Side poverty, could have arrived at an American sound much sooner than Kern, simply because he was directly exposed to it in all its rawness. There was no sophisticated home life, no money for study, no time for anything but work... Berlin was at least out in the street where it was all happening. 'Alexander's Ragtime Band' was no accident. He'd heard what was in ferment around him and used what came naturally." 9

Music historians correctly insist that the real ragtime king was Scott Joplin. While several of Berlin's early compositions refer to ragtime in title and lyrics, musicologists discern little trace of the syncopated 'ragged' rhythms that characterise the real thing. Yet as ragtime expert Max Morath has observed: "It may be hard to find syncopation in Berlin's music at this stage, but he had become a wizard at devising lyrics in syncopated slang... And in 1917, when a new label for American popular music finally surfaced, it was Berlin who led the pack with the neatly syncopating 'Mr Jazz Himself'." 10

'Alexander's Ragtime Band' in any case became a staple of early jazz bands. And 'Mr Jazz Himself' may indeed have led the pack because by the 1920s, many Tin Pan Alley songs were widely thought of as 'jazz songs' and some of the most enduring were written by Jews.

A further connection brings us to one of the most contentious manifestations in American culture, the blackface entertainer. Among the most famous were Jewish singers Sophie Tucker and Al Jolson.

Unlike Jolson, Tucker left blackface behind by the time she attained worldwide fame. Remembered now as a vaudeville singer, back then she was variously billed as 'The Queen of Ragtime' and the 'Queen of Jazz'. And Tucker collaborated with some of the hottest white jazz musicians in her Five Kings of Syncopation.

Tucker was also billed as a 'coon shouter'. Repugnant as the latter terminology is, it was part of showbiz vernacular back then. If by it we understand bastardised mimicry of black song, then it fails to do her justice. Tucker's delivery, if at times schmaltzy, is heavily blues inflected and she often used material written by black songwriters. 'Crazy Blues', penned by Perry Bradford, which in 1921 caused a sensation as the first recorded 'race' song when Mamie Smith covered it, was originally earmarked for Tucker who was no mere mimic of blues singers. When she sang, the emotions seemed to well up from her hard experience of life, at her best a truly affecting vocalist. Billie Holiday for one admired her. 11

Al Jolson, America's most popular singer of the era, starred as *The Jazz Singer* in the 1927 first talkie movie. Oceans of ink have been printed about the heavy symbolism inherent in that film, a tale about Jewish assimilation in Jazz Age urban America adapted from Samuel Raphaelson's novel. All I wish to add is how relevant it is that jazz, if in name only, is the medium through which the character Jolson depicts transcends the *shtetl* mentality of his fictional cantor father. This portrayal would have resonated with the experience of any number of young Jews growing up in America's cities who, like Jolson whose real father was a Lithuanian cantor, embraced the spirit of the age that jazz did so much to create. Against them you had the Jewish establishment personified by New York Rabbi Stephen Wise who, with biblical certitude, proclaimed that when America "regained its lost soul... jazz would be relegated to the dark and scarlet haunts whence it came" – that is, brothels. 12

Jolson is ignored by jazz historians as even in the film so titled, he does not come over as what people today would understand as a jazz singer. But it reinforced the belief that jazz and Jews were, somehow, intimately entwined. And Jolson is still turning people onto jazz; I know that because that is what happened to two musicians I interviewed, including Loren Schoenberg.

"But that's no reason to include him," Loren said, when we discussed whether Jolson should have a place in my book. Then Loren relented: "Okay, why do we include him? Dan Morgenstern feels Louis Armstrong had five records... which define the jazz language that everybody speaks to this day. And one of those recordings, 'Big Butter and Egg Man', Dan feels that Louis Armstrong was doing a little Al Jolson there for a couple of measures. I agree with him. Jolson was doing things in a very swinging way before there really was even something called jazz music. That means that Jolson listened very carefully to the African American idiom and its bastardisation and distortion in minstrel terms and used it in his own natural style to become a great entertainer and a great singer." London-based saxophonist Jeremy Shoham also got into jazz through Jolson.

It was in London too that I had an interesting exchange with saxophonist Bobby Wellins, whose Jewish father was a Glaswegian bandleader. Jolson was "brilliant", said Bobby. Yes, I said, but obviously no jazz singer. "Oh, I think he *was*," Bobby insisted. "I think he was so influenced by the black music. And he had all that phrasing, didn't he? It just came naturally. He may have sung things that we would call cheesy now but when you hear him sing other things, when he had gone away and come back and made that movie, his voice was beautiful. I think it was jazz of that era, absolutely."

Blackface unequivocally demeaned black people but it is misleading to load today's ethical values onto the past. *The Jazz Singer* was favourably reviewed in black journals the *New York Amsterdam News* and Baltimore's *Afro-American*, and black musicians Ethel Waters, Cab Calloway, Eubie Blake and Alberta Hunter, Jolson's contemporaries, spoke well of him.

. . . .

Motoring mogul Henry Ford, in his *Dearborn Independent* article 'Jewish Jazz Becomes our National Music', pre-figured Hitler's poisonous rants about Jews and jazz. Ford's Jews were seen as cultural middlemen, popularising and profiting from African American forms adapted for and contaminating white tastes. If we discount antisemitic paranoia about cultural corruption, this perception had considerable grounding in truth. Jews, as musicians and facilitators, did figure prominently as a conduit between black and white cultural worlds.

In the sprawling American cities that most Jews settled in, they regularly encountered and often shared neighbourhoods with black communities. So first-hand contact with their culture was always within reach. The cultural exchange was not all one way. Louis Armstrong, as an orphan growing up in New Orleans, was so affected by the warmth with which the Karnofsky family he worked for treated him that he sported a star of David for the rest of his life and fondly remembered singing Jewish songs with them. The family helped him acquire his first cornet. Armstrong related his astonishment that "other white folks... felt that they were better than the Jewish race. I was only seven years old but I could easily see the ungodly treatment that the White Folks were handing the poor Jewish family whom I worked for". 13

Some black people saw Jews as not quite white. A revealing anecdote is recounted by the wife of modern jazz pioneer Charlie Parker, aka Bird. Chan Parker, whose Jewish father had produced vaudeville shows and run a speakeasy in Jazz-Age New York, was "having another scene" with her husband in which "even Georgia the maid got involved... Bird, who was full of pills and whiskey, had become abusive. When Georgia tried to intervene on my behalf, Bird informed her that I was not white, I was a Jew." 14

Some Jews saw it that way too. Tenor saxophonist and journalist James McBride has written a touching book in tribute to his white Jewish mother who "never spoke about Jewish people as white. She spoke about them as Jews, which made them somehow different ... Later, when as an adult I heard folks talk about the love/hate relationship between blacks and Jews, I understood it to the bone". 15

Yes, and a relationship of enormous significance in American history. Through Old Testament spirituals, religious blacks tacitly acknowledged a kinship of suffering with the ancient Hebrews, with the hope of eventual deliverance. Jewish newspapers drew parallels between physical attacks on southern blacks and pogroms. Alliances were forged between Jews and the black community through the National Association for the Advancement of Colored People, which Jews helped found in 1909 and supported organisationally, financially and politically. 16

Harvard academic Jeffrey Melnick has written a study about the black/Jewish relationship in popular music, recording that: "By the 1920s it was obvious... that not only had popular music become the special purview of Jews and African Americans, but also within this sphere members of the two groups came into frequent and significant contact." 17

His emphasis is on how Jews used and adapted black music for purposes that had a great deal to do with their own ambivalent identity as Americanising Jews: "From the blackface of Al Jolson and Irving Berlin's early attempts to translate minstrelsy into sound, through George Gershwin's high-art aspirations to the white Negro of Mezz Mezzrow and Artie Shaw, Jews were holding an intra-group conversation about their status in America." 18

And in Melnick's understanding, the interrelationship between blacks and Jews has been mythologised with Jews "using music to establish black/Jewish relations as a healthy and necessary component of the American melting pot." 19 His portrayal is essentially unflattering: "Among the large number of Jews who had enormous success in the music industry during the first few decades of the twentieth century, perhaps none were so successful as those who traded in a Blackness which did not benefit African Americans and often worked to exclude them from centers of cultural power." 20

Nevertheless, we will see plenty of instances in these pages of Jews doing their utmost to elevate black musicians. Sure, there were inevitable tensions, including those arising from the economic relationship entrepreneurial Jews had with black people in popular music as in other fields, which was often paternalistic and at worst crassly exploitative. One should not however discount the liberal, humanitarian, and left-wing inclinations that motivated many Jews to support the underdog.

And there remained an underlying empathy that spilled into culture among those Jews that responded to the bittersweet blues strain so pervasive in black music. Gerald Early, the black cultural commentator, picks up on this in his essay Pulp and Circumstance about the white perception and intervention in 1920s jazz yet comes to the wrong conclusion: "If the uncultivated Protestant heard jazz with disgust, the more intellectual Jews of the period heard it as despair." 21 Did they? Those Jews that took to jazz, I would counter, embraced the joyous release inherent in this music. Early's essay is subtitled The Story of Jazz in High Places, a theme that obviously takes in Gershwin, and whatever Gershwin's music was, it was emphatically not a music of despair.

Somewhere in the whole above-stated complex of reasons, then, is the clue to why musically talented Jews have proved adept at harnessing African American idioms, in combination with other influences, to produce works of universal appeal. In 1847, half a century before the first stirrings of jazz, New Orleans Jew Louis Moreau Gottschalk composed *La Bomboula-Danse Negre*, thought to be the earliest example of an attempt to marry black rhythms with classical music. Gottschalk grew up in New Orleans' French Quarter near Congo Square, witnessing the weekly bouts of voodoo drumming and dancing.

Jews have produced several famous musical works that have – however imperfectly – grappled with African American themes, notably Jerome Kern's *Showboat* and George Gershwin's *Porgy and Bess*. Paul Robeson Jr, reminiscing about his father, the star of the original stage and film productions of *Showboat,* said: "He seemed to have an affinity to Jews and Jewish culture. They were the best friends we had, compared to other white folks. Jews weren't the ones lynching blacks." 22 The senior Paul Robeson's affinity for Jewish culture included his renditions of Yiddish songs.

Some pundits claim that *Porgy* and *Showboat* demeaned black people; Melnick cites a 1993 Toronto protest against the restaging of *Showboat,* "...according to the leaders one of the many works created by Jews which malign African Americans". 23 Mark the date though, 1993, a retrospective judgment, and one conditioned by recent black/Jewish tensions; it was hardly the composers' intention to slight their black compatriots.

*Showboat*'s – and Robeson's – most famous song, 'Ol' Man River', became part of the Duke Ellington band's repertoire in the 1930s after he first played it on request at the Cotton Club. What Duke thought about *Showboat* I have no idea, but we do know his take on *Porgy*. Pressed by a *New Theatre* journalist, Ellington said the depiction of blacks was not true to life. He thought the music "grand" but "did not fit use of the Negro musical idiom". 24 Yet jazz musicians of all backgrounds have made rich use of the songs from *Porgy*, as they have of Gershwin's Broadway songs.

. . . .

The impact of George Gershwin's songs on jazz I consider in Chapter 8 but there is much to debate, from a jazz perspective, about his orchestral works, notably *Rhapsody in Blue* (1924), *Piano Concerto in F* (1925), *American in Paris* (1928) and *Second Rhapsody* (1931). Invariably filed under classical in record stores, these compositions when discussed by jazz writers are presented as part of the phenomenon that in the 1920s was dubbed 'symphonic jazz'.

Jazz writer Max Harrison defined symphonic jazz as attempts to "fuse jazz with classical forms, and therefore a predecessor of the short-lived Third Stream movement" that surfaced in jazz in the late 1950s. 25 Idiomatic purists disparage symphonic jazz as attempts to dilute real jazz by 'bleaching' it. Whatever terminology one uses for efforts by composers, some from classical backgrounds, others like black jazz stride pianist James P Johnson, to synchronise these forms, such works pre-date Gershwin and continue being composed.

Invariably though, Gershwin's is the name most invoked. Modern listeners would accept that however jazz influenced his instrumental compositions are, they are not jazz. Even towards the end of Gershwin's short life – he died in 1937 – when the success of the big swing bands had dispelled earlier popular confusion about jazz, there were pundits that cited him as the man who elevated jazz to some higher realm, producing works worthy of the concert hall.

The misconception stems from 'King of Jazz' white bandleader Paul Whiteman, who commissioned Gershwin's *Rhapsody in Blue* for a 1924 concert at New York's Aeolian Hall and hyped the piece as having "made a lady out of jazz". Gershwin's piano accompaniments at Aeolian "made an unforgettable impression," notes music historian Richard Crawford. "Rather than reading fixed musical texts, he elaborated them freely... Later commentators would question the 'jazz' label for this kind of music making. Yet Gershwin's freewheeling approach to performance – he played in the style of an improvisation, though most details were planned – owed much of its spontaneity to jazz." 26

After Gershwin's success, we see an escalation in the trend for classical composers to utilise jazz elements, among them a striking number of Jews including Aaron Copland with *Music for the Theater* (1925) and *Piano Concerto* (1926). Although Copland perceived jazz as having a "narrow range of emotion", it remained an element in his Americanisation of classical music. 27 As Jewish composer Leonard Bernstein observed, Copland's mid-forties *Third Symphony* was "*very* symphonic and *very* jazzy". 28

Bernstein's feeling for jazz was unequivocal. It fed squarely into his works: his 1944 ballet *Fancy Free* is heavily based on jazz and blues themes, and a movement in *Symphony No 2 'The Age of Anxiety'* contains a moody late night, Art Tatum-ish passage. And Bernstein's 1950's album *What is Jazz?* employs his gifts as a charismatic educator to explain jazz concepts and heroes.

In Bernstein's essay *Jazz in Serious Music*, he contrasts the attempts of Gershwin and French Jew Darius Milhaud, composers from opposite ends of the Atlantic and different sides of the track, to blend classical music with jazz. Bernstein focuses on *Rhapsody in Blue* and Milhaud's 1923 'jazz ballet' *La création du monde*. While Milhaud was borrowing "foreign jazz elements", Gershwin was borrowing European symphonic techniques "to have a soil in which to plant his natural bursting seeds of jazz... Hearing Gershwin's piece is like biting into a fine, big, juicy apple and letting the juice trickle freely down your chin, while hearing Milhaud's is more like taking to the same apple with an elegant fruit knife and fork, carefully peeling it, and savoring one proper bite at a time". 29

Symphonic jazz is a thread that leads to Duke Ellington's extended works, beginning with 'Creole Rhapsody' (1930), the jazz component in Ellington's piece indisputable. Ellington, we know, was influenced by black predecessors that had experimented with similar generic cross-dressing – James P Johnson, Will Marion Cook, James Reese Europe, WC Handy. Melnick argues that "a major difference between Gershwin and, say, the African American composer and pianist James P Johnson is that, while both desired to write 'great' music built on American themes, only Gershwin had the institutional support". 30

Yes, but not *the* major difference. What set Gershwin's orchestral confections apart was his genius, his instrumental compositions distillations of all his cosmopolitan influences. Without conservatory training, Gershwin had, in 1924, only partly digested formal harmonic construction but with his intuitive feel for American idioms, Gershwin gets away with it. *Rhapsody in Blue* is definitive twentieth century music.

"It helped jazz, composition-wise, the fact that you could write it down and have an extended song form, and you could have avenues of expression other than just small groups in a club. That was fascinating, that someone would be able to compose something like that," jazz trumpeter Randy Brecker told me. Another jazz musician I interviewed, Terry Gibbs, observed: "All those blue notes that he used in those things – it's like, say, if you're playing in the major key, using the minor third – those are the blue notes. Nowadays we all use them, but he started to play those things. I don't know where he found them, it was a jazz feel compared with what was going on in those days in symphonic music. To me he was the greatest living composer."

Black jazz contemporaries were admirers. Fletcher Henderson, asked about his band's arrangements of *Rhapsody in Blue*, said he thought Gershwin's piece "outstanding". 31 From Fats Waller's son Maurice we know that by the late thirties, Fats "constantly talked about his admiration for Gershwin's *Rhapsody in Blue* and *Concerto in F*. He was introducing more and more classical themes into his music". 32 And Billy Strayhorn, Duke Ellington's arranger, wrote several pieces as a tyro composer inspired by the symphonic Gershwin, whom Strayhorn idolised. 33

Can it though be argued that Gershwin was an influence on Ellington himself? Mark Tucker's scholarly *Ellington: The Early Years* references symphonic jazz yet there's nothing on Gershwin. When I raised the question of the possible impact of *Rhapsody in Blue* on Ellington with Dan Morgenstern, he responded: "I'm glad you mentioned Ellington. *Rhapsody in Blue* did not have an immediate impact on jazz per se. It was a piece of very fine borderline popular music; *Concerto in F* is more of a legitimate classical piece with string jazz elements. But *Rhapsody* did have an influence on Ellington. And I think Ellington's first extended composition that was recorded, which was about the same length as *Rhapsody in Blue*, is called 'Creole Rhapsody'. Two versions – it was recorded for Brunswick on a 10-inch version, and for Victor on a 12-inch version which has a whole theme that wasn't included on the shorter one. And if you listen to that, and in my liner notes I say, you can certainly hear that influence, although Ellington might deny it."

Jazz writer Gary Giddins, like Morgenstern Jewish, told an interviewer: "My favorite of Ellington's extended pieces, the one that strikes me as most nearly flawless was originally called 'A Tone Parallel to Harlem'... It's a piece that I've always thought, and this is my opinion and speculation, I can't prove it, but it's a piece that I think is Ellington's response to... *Rhapsody in Blue*... look at the comparisons. They are the same length to begin with... *Rhapsody in Blue* begins with a clarinet in an ascending arpeggio. Harlem is built on a descending trumpet arpeggio. *Rhapsody in Blue* has a series of, as a rhapsody would... rhythmic and thematic figures that finally, about two-thirds through hits on one gorgeous Gershwin melody that... becomes the theme for all the variations that follow through to the end of the piece. That's exactly the way 'Harlem' is constructed."

Barney Bigard, Ellington's clarinetist, has left us a tantalising glimpse of what might have been: "Gershwin wanted to collaborate with Duke years ago in the Cotton Club. *George Gershwin*! Duke didn't want to. Duke wanted to do it all by himself, but Gershwin wanted to be a partner with Duke. And that would have been terrific." 34 Would it though? Ellington's instinct was surely justified; far better musically that each followed his distinctive muse.

# Chapter 3: 'White Negroes', black Jew

During the 'Roaring Twenties', the centre of the jazz world shifted from New Orleans to Chicago and New York. Around these loci of mass Jewish immigration emerged a loose fraternity of young whites who began to grasp what this music was about.

Several developed into jazz musicians, including the first truly significant figures of Jewish origin. From Chicago came pianist Art Hodes, clarinetists Benny Goodman and Mezz Mezzrow, drummers Ben Pollack and Vic Berton; from New York, trumpeters Max Kaminsky, Manny Klein, Henry 'Hot Lips' Levine, who replaced Nick LaRocca in the Original Dixieland Jazz Band, and pianist, arranger, composer Rube Bloom; from Indiana, clarinetist Izzy Friedman; while Artie Shaw got his start in Jewish bandleader Irving Aaronson's New Haven, Connecticut band.

Most would make their main impact come the 1930s but the twenties is the decade with which we most associate Pollack and Berton. Ben Pollack first surfaces around 1923 as drummer in the New Orleans Rhythm Kings, a white Chicago combo of considerable importance as for many white jazz aficionados, it was their point of entry. "They played not in the zany, tongue-in-cheek spirit of the white bands... but *seriously*, mean and low down... always *for real*. As we said in those days – there was no higher praise – *they played like niggers*," wrote Ralph Berton – Vic Berton's brother and one of the first jazz writers. 1

From 1926, Pollack fronted a large ensemble of glittering young talent – Benny Goodman, Jimmy Dorsey, Glenn Miller, Gene Krupa, Jack Teagarden, Harry James, Jimmy McPartland, Muggsy Spanier, and tenor saxophonist Bud Freeman whose father was a Jewish tailor. All would desert him and there are names there that set the world ablaze come the swing era. Pollack slid into chronic depression as he watched one after another of his protégés outgun him. He formed other bands, launched the Jewel record label, owned restaurants at which he performed, but hanged himself in 1971.

Pollack's importance in Benny Goodman's early career prompted me to seek Goodman authority Loren Schoenberg's verdict: "One of the great drummers of the early 1920s – his work with the New Orleans Rhythm Kings... you can hear him playing extraordinarily marvellous ensemble drumming. 2 Unfortunately, he got stars in his eyes and wanted to become like a Rudy Vallée, a singing bandleader, and Benny told me many times that it was a real shame, he should have stayed playing the drums and been a jazz drummer. But you see at the time that Ben Pollack wanted to be famous, which was 1928, 1929, they didn't have the swing bands. If you were a commercial bandleader, you were a frontman with a baton and so he stopped playing the drums. A tragic figure."

If Pollack compromised his art, we must perhaps allow for the commercial constraints that 1920s white jazz bands were under because of racial stereotyping. According to Richard Sudhalter, the recorded output of white bands, such as Pollack's, often offers only tantalising glimpses of the hot licks their star personnel were capable of because the record companies reigned them in. Stereotyping worked contrariwise for black bands; they were encouraged to play sensual, 'hot', not 'sweet'. 3

Vic Berton – real name Cohen – abandoned jazz by the thirties to take up more lucrative work in Hollywood, so today is little remembered. Burt Korall, in a book about the art of jazz drumming, recognised his contribution: "Berton's admirable facility served the music. Very skilful in the playing, accenting and manipulating of triplets... a relaxed, swinging free ensemble player and soloist." Jazz posterity owes Berton a considerable debt for his invention of what became known as the hi-hat. It comprises two small spring-connected facing cymbals allowing drummers to maintain the steady, propulsive accompaniment that we now take for granted. It made the drummer's job easier," said Korall. 4 Berton became buddies with Louis Armstrong, a friendship, says Armstrong biographer Laurence Bergreen, that was sealed by sharing a joint outside a Los Angeles club, an episode that nearly led to Armstrong's arrest: a jazz-loving detective let him off.

Chicago Jew Mezz Mezzrow was so in thrall to the music that he considered himself black. Mezzrow was a jazz clarinetist of relatively modest abilities but as Dan Morgenstern informed me: "Because Panassié [French jazz writer] championed him to such a degree, calling him not just the greatest white clarinetist but almost the greatest jazz clarinetist ever, and because Mezzrow was a polemical and cantankerous person, he suffered from being overpraised and underpraised. Mezz did have a great feeling for the blues, he was a great blues player, limited in technique, but he had something." Benny Carter, one of the most revered African American jazz musicians, was, said Dan, "very fond of him; Benny defended Mezz". Mezzrow moreover was instrumental in the revival of his idol, clarinetist and soprano saxophonist Sidney Bechet's career. When jazz became part of the cultural mainstream from the mid 1930s, many black originators got overlooked, whereupon Mezzrow "hustled gigs. He broke down the 'colored' line in more than one place", as Art Hodes attested. 5

Mezzrow's passion for jazz and blues was underpinned by his deep affection for the urban black way of life, such that in Mezzrow we have surely history's first instance of the 'white Negro', some quarter-century before Jewish novelist Norman Mailer adopted the term for the beatnik generation.

In Mezzrow's autobiography *Really the Blues* we learn that when he was jailed for peddling marijuana – an activity so associated with him that 'mezz' became street slang for a joint – he insisted on being classified a 'Negro' and was thrown in with the black inmates.

Mezzrow hated being reminded of his Jewish roots: "I didn't go for that jive at all; being a Jew didn't mean a thing to me. Around the pool-table I defended the guys I felt were my real brothers, the coloured musicians." 6 If Mezz took things to extremes, other white jazz contemporaries exhibited white Negro characteristics, including Benny Goodman though, unlike Mezzrow, Goodman didn't reject his Jewish identity.

One who did, for reasons that ostensibly differ from Mezzrow's, was Artie Shaw. Shaw changed his surname from Arshawsky to camouflage his Jewishness, about which he was first made to feel uncomfortably aware by boys that taunted him during childhood. Was that so different from Mezzrow? Sure, like many whites since, Mezz was captivated by the vibrancy of black culture. 7 But denial of one's Jewish roots, whatever reason one gives for it, is rarely a positive action; it is I suspect like someone who has severed a limb – psychologically, the limb is still there. If you happen to be a creative person, that may well come out in your art if it is sincere, however you couch it.

Shaw wrote memorably about the period before he became famous when he sought out the company of black musicians in Harlem: "I was actually living the life of a Negro musician, adopting Negro values and attitudes, and accepting the Negro out-group point of view not only about music but life in general." 8

A black jazz musician who had a profound impact on the young Shaw during this period, stride piano maestro Willie The Lion Smith, proclaimed adherence to Judaism: "You could say I am Jewish partly by origin and partly by association." The origin part possibly stems from his father, Frank Bertlehoff, "a light skinned playboy" whom Lion's mother kicked out before marrying his stepfather, John Smith. Lion, growing up Presbyterian, accompanied his stepfather selling hogs off a wagon. Some of their best customers, by Lion's account, were Jews. While making deliveries to a family named Rothschild, he would hear a rabbi teaching the children Hebrew: "The chanting sounds coming out of the parlour during the lessons fascinated me from the beginning, and Mrs Rothschild... permitted me to... sit in and listen. It didn't take much time before I began to learn the meanings of the Hebraic words. When the rabbi saw how well I was doing, he took special pains to teach me." 9

Lion says he was bar mitzvahed in a Newark synagogue and served as cantor to a black Jewish congregation in Harlem: "A lot of people are unable to understand my wanting to be Jewish. One said, 'Lion, you stepped up to the plate with one strike against you – and now you take a second one right down the middle.' They can't seem to realise I have a Jewish soul and belong to that faith." 10 Some Jews are uncomfortable about Lion's claim to kinship. A short Lion biography I found on a Jewish website ends: "We realise this entry is problematic because opinions differ on the 'Jewishness' of certain mostly black Jewish congregations."

However that may be, Lion – his nickname an allusion to the Lion of Judah – felt an attachment not just to the religion: "The people with whom I have had the least trouble in my life have been the Jews." 11 His jazz though was grounded in the African American tradition. Lion cited ragtime pianist One-Leg Willie Joseph as an early influence: "His ragging of the 'The Stars and Stripes Forever' beat out the phoney Mike Bernard, the Jewish ragtime kid, who copied the great ragtime originator Ben Harney's style." 12

About Lion, pianist Dick Wellstood told jazz writer Whitney Balliett: "I heard him sing 'Alexander's Ragtime Band' in Yiddish, or what he claimed was Yiddish." 13 Jazz musician and film composer John Altman related a similar story to me. John, who performed in Jewish musician Conrad Janis's California-based jazz band, told me: "His band in the forties included Willie The Lion Smith, and we did a number which was 'I Wish You Could Shimmy Like My Sister Kate', and the guitar player, Sheldon Keller, who was one of the comedy writers of the Sid Caesar show, sings a chorus in Yiddish, which is what Willie The Lion Smith used to do."

Lion took a shine to Artie Shaw when the teenage clarinetist was trying to establish himself in New York. Shaw, interviewed in a radio tribute to Lion, said: "He didn't know that I was Jewish. I didn't tell him that. But I was very surprised because his [business] card was in Yiddish characters." Known by friends by his Yiddish name, Velvala, Lion wrote with considerable affection about his early relationship with Artie, recollecting how the young clarinetist impressed Sidney Bechet: "My boy Artie was a good student and the Lion was proud of him when he went out to jam after finishing our nightly stint at P's &J's... One morning at Goldgraben's... Pops Bechet, who was particular about clarinet players, came up to ask about Shaw. 'Lion, who is the musicianer?'" When Lion told him, Bechet praised Shaw, declaring him "a good blues man". Shaw in turn helped Lion: "Artie used to encourage me to get my tunes written down and published. While at P's & J's I started to compose in earnest... Later when Artie had his first band, he recorded some of my numbers." 14

And Lion once jammed with Benny Goodman when the clarinetist was still with Ben Pollack: "Goodman met the test once when he played 'I Got Rhythm' to my accompaniment in the key of E major – I got him into a tough key just for the hell of it." 15

The swing craze was about sweep Goodman and Shaw, the sons of poor Russian Jewish immigrants, to riches and world fame.

# Chapter 4: Swing high, sweet clarinet

Radio came into its own as free entertainment in the thirties' economic depression when record sales declined, and the coverage that Benny Goodman's swing band received on America's airwaves propelled him to super-stardom.

Goodman inadvertently launched the 'Big Band Era' when a 1935 cross-country tour of gigs – some so dispiriting that he thought of disbanding – culminated that August in astounding scenes of youthful public acclamation at Los Angeles' Palomar Ballroom.

A massive following had built up in California owing to the band's Let's Dance radio shows. Broadcast simultaneously coast-to-coast, it hit the Pacific at peak listening hours and unbeknown to Goodman's New York-based band, an audience hungry to see them awaited out west. An augury of Palomar came at a one-nighter in Oakland. Frustrated by the compromises forced on them during the tour – including a Denver gig where the crowd demanded their money back and were appeased with waltzes – in Oakland Goodman's men let rip and the patrons loved it.

Then the band stepped out at Palomar "and boom – that was the real beginning", as Benny put it. Palomar was followed by a successful concert series at the Congress Hotel, Chicago and a nation succumbed. It could all so easily have been otherwise, said Goodman's drummer Gene Krupa: "Had Benny thrown in the towel before his first great triumphs... many of us who have enjoyed success... would never have attained these heights... Benny built himself a band playing musicians' music but didn't shoot over the head of the public." [1]

In New York a month earlier, Goodman set in train a development whose implications would resonate well beyond the world of popular music. After jamming with black pianist Teddy Wilson, Goodman invited him to record in a trio. Comprising Goodman, Wilson and Krupa, it cut four memorable sides. In later sessions another black musician, vibraphonist Lionel Hampton, was added. Inter-racial recording was not a complete novelty. As early as 1931, Jewish clarinetist Ted Lewis included Fats Waller on a session – Lewis not himself a jazz musician but he employed jazz talent. Mezz Mezzrow was another who played integrated sessions, while Eddie Condon "insisted on using Negro musicians". And in 1933, Goodman backed Billie Holiday on her first, and Bessie Smith her last, recording. 2 But as Goodman's mentor John Hammond, a wealthy white record producer and critic committed to jazz and black civil rights, made plain, until the Goodman trio recordings, integrated records were all "done very secretly because the public wasn't ready to see black and white together". 3

Goodman's next move was daring in the racial climate of the time. Prompted by Hammond, he took Wilson and Hampton on the road, beginning with an Easter 1936 gig. They were not integrated into Goodman's big band but the small group became a regular side-feature at gigs.

Soon, other major bands launched satellite groups as vehicles for star soloists. "Chamber jazz," said Teddy Wilson, "originated with Benny Goodman."

Dan Morgenstern underlined how significant was Goodman's racial breakthrough: "Jazz was the first publicly integrated sector of American life. Jackie Robinson went to the Dodgers [baseball team] in 1946-47 and that was a big deal. But in the jazz world, Teddy Wilson and Lionel Hampton had been performing publicly with Benny Goodman." 4 Hampton, interviewed in 1970, said Goodman did "something great for humanity. Civil rights really came about through music like the Goodman Quartet. I mean, everybody else was scared... Here's a guy that did, and he's got to have credit for it… He protected Teddy and I at all times… He's one of the finest guys I know." 5

When Goodman took Wilson and Hampton down south, Hammond, in an October 1937 *DownBeat* article headed 'Predicted race riot fades as Dallas applauds quartet', reported: "A minor revolution took place in deepest and darkest Dixie early in September when Benny Goodman's boys invaded the South for the first time… All along I had the suspicion that if the trio and quartet made excellent music the crowd would swallow its prejudices and acclaim the artists."

How much credit does Hammond deserve? "No, it wasn't John Hammond," Goodman biographer James Lincoln Collier told me. "He would always claim that, but the person really involved was Helen Dance. She came from a wealthy family in Canada. They had a jazz club in Chicago and they would hire top talent. And they had the Benny Goodman band when he was at the Congress Hotel, and Helen said, 'Why don't you bring on a trio, what do you think?' and she paid for Teddy Wilson to come to Chicago, and they played and the important point about that was that nobody cared – *DownBeat* didn't even make a big story out of it. And you have to give Goodman an enormous amount of credit. His band wasn't very old, he'd had his first taste of success, the depression was on, twenty-five per cent of Americans were out of work, you had kids getting up in the morning and having coffee for breakfast. And here he made a breakthrough, it looked like he might be able to make some money. Now the question was, would he be able to play in the south? So he took the gamble. It was no gamble for Helen Dance, she had money, what was it going to cost her? Goodman had come out of the gutter but he took the chance and nobody cared."

Black pundit Stanley Crouch, when I asked him, agreed: "Hammond always credits himself with that, but I'm not sure that you could take a guy who was standing on the line and have him risk his career because of your politics, and you already rich anyway. So I don't buy that. In other words, if Goodman really didn't want to do it, they wouldn't be in his band. He didn't have them in his band for some social purpose. If Lionel Hampton didn't play better than anyone he could get on the vibes at a time when he could have gotten anybody he wanted to get, he wouldn't have had him up there. It's the same thing with Teddy Wilson. That way that Teddy Wilson played, you couldn't play better than Teddy Wilson. So I don't buy any John Hammond made him do that; suggested it, yes, perhaps encouraged him to take the risk, yes. But that's like somebody talking to you in your corner in a boxing match; you don't have to take the blows when the bell rings, right?" 6

All the jazz big bands relied on intricate arrangements that left ample room for solo improvisation, and Goodman hired black arrangers, notably Fletcher Henderson whose charts contributed greatly to the Goodman sound. Retrospectively, this has provoked some outrageous slurs. When the band broke big, it was Fletcher's charts Goodman was mainly using and so, his critics charge, he was stealing black music. "I could walk into the Goodman band and play every arrangement they had, because Smack [Henderson] did it," said drummer Art Blakey. "It's Smack's music. He didn't get the credit for it." 7

Charges of exploitation overlook the barriers that stood in the path of a Goodman-like ascent for black artists in 1930s America, and the fact that, as Lionel Hampton testified, Goodman paid his black collaborators well. 8

His acquisition of black trumpeter Cootie Williams highlights the issues. The ability of white bandleaders, following Goodman's lead, to pay black musicians better salaries led to a drain of top talent from black bands. This generated resentment that white bandleaders "stole our players". Williams was lured from Duke

Ellington's peerless band to work for Goodman, predominantly in a sextet formation. *DownBeat* received a hefty mailbag from Ellington aficionados criticising the move. Raymond Scott, an idiosyncratic Jewish bandleader and composer, even wrote a mournful tune about it, 'When Cootie Left the Duke'. Scott was a composer of quirkily original, jazzy compositions who, though he packed his bands with jazz talent, pretty much eschewed improvisation, but he admired Ellington.

Goodman paid Cootie $200 a week, a hefty salary, but by Cootie's account money wasn't necessarily the main motivation. He adored Goodman's clarinet playing, and his band: "I loved it. It had a beat and there was something there that I wanted to play with." 9

· · · ·

As a young saxophonist, arranger and big bandleader, Loren Schoenberg became closely associated with Benny Goodman, who appointed him his archivist and personal manager and hired Loren's band at concerts. The relationship prevailed until Goodman's death in 1986. I interviewed Loren at the National Jazz Museum in Harlem shortly after his appointment as its executive director. 10

"Let me," began Loren, "talk about jazz and Jews in a way that I think might be helpful here, my attitude about it. I think that if you go back to the early years of the twentieth century, there were many populations that felt marginalised to a greater or lesser degree. If you read [Artie] Shaw's book, *The Trouble With Cinderella*, he's very eloquent, I can't add anything to that. Benny Goodman was really not that eloquent, he didn't talk that much about it, but if you read the standard biography by Ross Firestone, which is very good, there's good detail about how poor Benny was when he grew up. And I think that there was a definite feeling among people who were excluded from the mainstream of American society, some kind of kinship, and on that level, I think that the early Jewish jazz musicians could probably empathise with the plight of African Americans maybe to a greater degree than some others could."

Did Loren agree that the greatest black musicians of the big band era had more long-term influence than Goodman or Shaw?

"Of course, to this day the great majority of the icons of the music, the masters so to speak – a loaded term in this context – are without a doubt African Americans. That's who you emulate, and you learn from them to be yourself. You ultimately learn that race is all important and that race is non-important, there's no simple answer to it... No one played the clarinet better than Benny Goodman – I heard that from Roy Eldridge and I heard that from John Lewis [that is, from black jazz musicians] ... If we were to talk about the definitive influence on jazz, of course Lester Young's influence far trumps Benny Goodman's. But on the other hand, because of the inherently racist structure of the music of the great swing era, the black bands never had a chance of becoming cultural icons like Benny Goodman. Benny deserved everything he got but there were other people who also deserved it, that's the difference. People say that Benny Goodman didn't; I don't say he didn't, but Chick Webb deserved it, Don Redman deserved it, Benny Carter."

Loren scorned allegations that Goodman stole the music: "Benny Goodman was, as far as I can tell, the first major bandleader that went out of his way to credit the arrangers on the record. Fletcher Henderson got a lot of credit for music he didn't write. Benny Carter and John Nesbitt, Horace Henderson and Don Redman and Bill Challis also were writing music for the Fletcher Henderson band throughout the 1920s; Fletcher Henderson didn't say that this was so and so's arrangement on the record. When Goodman started recording the Fletcher Henderson arrangements, he went out of his way to credit Fletcher on the record labels and to hire Fletcher to play piano. Benny did everything that he could for Fletcher Henderson. He never for a moment thought that he was riding on Fletcher's coattails, except for the fact that to the public at large, yes of course he was. The public didn't care what was on the label, they didn't pay attention to those things. And part of the tragedy is that even when you read *Metronome* magazine and *DownBeat* and all the press of the day, even the press that was written by very, very sympathetic people like George T Simon, there's still this underlying perception it's like a white music, and yes, early on there were some black folks involved and they were good too."

In the pantheon of Jewish jazz greats, Loren felt Goodman stood out: "I don't believe in the best of anything, but if you're forced down that road talking about the best, I don't think you'd get an argument from anyone saying that Benny Goodman was the definitive jazz clarinetist of his time... The way that Benny was improvising on the clarinet in Ben Pollack's band, 1926 to 1930-31, he brought something new to jazz improvisation, he redefined the instrument, he took it beyond what his mentors did, Jimmy Noone and Johnny Dodds and Barney Bigard, he could improvise at tempos with a certain fluidity and coherence and a melodic sense that transcended all of his peers.

"He became a cultural icon, in the same way that Elvis Presley did, putting to the great American public a white face on a music that really came out of the African American community. The problem is that because we don't talk about race, we're so super-sensitive about this stuff, that many times they throw the baby out with the bath water in the sense that because Benny came to fame with a music that came for the most part out of the black bands, therefore he's suspect, it was horrible what he did, Fletcher Henderson's band should have been the famous one and we just forget about Benny Goodman. Benny Goodman did have a great band, did do things that the other bands couldn't do. Was the idiom absolutely African American? Of course. So what should Benny Goodman have done, not become famous? Of course not. Benny Goodman gave credit to Fletcher Henderson, and he insisted on putting their names on the record labels and talking about them in interviews and on the radio in a way that virtually no other bandleader, black or white, ever did. And then of course he integrated his band with Lionel Hampton and Teddy Wilson and Charlie Christian and Cootie Williams and Sid Catlett and others. So he was really someone who was very much concerned with showing the public, who might have had the misunderstanding that it was a white thing that they were doing, that African Americans are part of my band and not only that, but he will show them a respect that will start to raise questions in people's mind who'd just assumed that Benny Goodman, Artie Shaw, Paul Whiteman, that they were really the people who'd 'made a lady out of jazz', which is so demeaning and insulting."

• • • •

Artie Shaw, the other most celebrated swing era clarinetist, didn't publicly disclose his Jewish ethnicity until years later.

During the formative phase of his career, when Shaw was jamming around Harlem with black musicians, he befriended Billie Holiday. Some years later, in 1938 when Shaw had attained fame as a bandleader, he hired her for an opening night at Boston's Roseland State ballroom. She was nervous about the racial repercussions, as was Sy Schribman, a Jew who ran a Boston booking agency with his brother Charlie, and who was being called upon to underwrite the gig. 11 As Billie remembered it: "The sight of sixteen men on a bandstand with a Negro girl singer had never been seen before... Naturally Sy Schribman was worried. But Artie was a guy who never thought in terms of white or colored." 12 The job went ahead.

Shaw went one better than Goodman, integrating black artists into his full band. Drummer Zutty Singleton joined his first ensemble as early as 1936. By recruiting a black singer, Artie further upped the stakes. And with Billie, he was the first white bandleader to tour south with a black vocalist. 13 Billie remembered: "The hills were full of white crackers." Thanks to Shaw, the hills were alive with the sound of music too, as Billie's performances charmed white southerners.

There occurred however one nerve-racking incident. Artie recounted what happened at the International Association of Jazz Education's 2002 conference. As the band entered the deep south, Billie asked him, "Do you think I should do this?" Artie, by his account, replied: "I think it's important that you break that line." The first night went off fine but the next night, said Artie, "she finished singing a song... some redneck in front of the band hollered, 'Have the nigger wench sing another song'... Billie was a short-tempered lady... she was mouthing at him, 'You...' – you know what she was saying... Some angry noises came up; people gathered in knots on the floor... I had it all set; I had the cops out in the wings and they grabbed her and put her in the bus and drove her away... But the rest of the tour was pretty good... Billie was tremendous, the people loved her". 14

It was back in New York that the explosion came. Hotel Lincoln management insisted that Billie use the backdoor entrance where she faced the indignity of riding the goods elevator. Old Gold, the cigarette firm that sponsored radio broadcasts from the hotel, prohibited her from singing on air. She quit, just when the band's popularity soared after Shaw's instrumental interpretation of Cole Porter's 'Begin the Beguine' became a nationwide hit. A year later, Holiday told *DownBeat* she would never sing in a dance band again, accusing Shaw of not standing up to the Lincoln management and of not paying her for a recording of 'Any Old Time'. Shaw, in the same issue, said that was ridiculous: "If it were true, would she have waited a year before saying anything?" 15 Shaw later explained: "Nobody would let me record her. People were uptight about that stuff then. The vice presidents didn't want the band to play too much jazz, either. Dance music was what was selling."

Whatever the truth – and in her fury Billie missed out on a five-year contract – Shaw and Holiday patched it up. 16

"The singer Shaw replaced Billie with was Helen Forrest, who was Jewish and sharing the bandstand when Billie quit. Shaw has said they "were the only singers I could relate to musically. We had fourteen singers in and out of that band, I don't even remember most of them. But you had to have a female singer if you wanted to work." 17

About Forrest, Artie told me: "She was the best of all band singers. A lot of people don't give her credit for that." But there was a fundamental difference, he said, between Billie and Helen: "Helen sang the song; Billie made the song hers. It's a whole different feel... If you wanted just to hear the melody, played with some rhythm, with a beat, and with some understanding of the lyrics, do something with it, Helen was very good. I'd have kept her as long as I had a band. I did, then I quit the music business for a while. I couldn't find a singer until I found Helen Forrest who could manage to sing with a band. Billie I knew was not going to last because she had a hot temper and it didn't work." 18

• • • •

Richard Sudhalter confessed to me that in his study *Lost Chords*, a Jewish musician who should have had a place of honour was Mel

Powell: "By any standard a towering figure. His omission was a major oversight on my part, one I deeply regret."

When Benny Goodman hired him as pianist and arranger, Powell was only seventeen but impressed in the big band and side group. For Powell, it was a dream engagement and logical from Goodman's standpoint as his young prodigy was influenced stylistically by Goodman's former pianist. Powell, aged thirteen, had seen Goodman perform at the Paramount theatre and Teddy Wilson's improvisations made such an impact that Powell was inspired to jazz up Beethoven at his next classical lesson, provoking his teacher to rap his hands with a ruler. 19

Shortly after, a friend took Powell to a Greenwich Village jam and Powell worked up the courage to ask to sit in. After he did so, a man sitting by the piano told him, "You're going to be a real one." That happened to be Art Tatum – the greatest jazz pianist of them all. 20

Powell's instrumental prowess captivated a young André Previn, destined to become one of the world's leading classical conductors, and no mean jazz pianist himself: "I was still a teenager and he was Benny Goodman's famous pianist. I idolised his playing and tried copying his inventions." 21

No less inventive was Powell's arrangements. He was one of those who, like Eddie Sauter who preceded him in Goodman's band, took the art to new dimensions in the 1940s. In 1941, the year he joined Goodman, Powell had written scores for black pianist Earl Hines; a composition Powell subsequently wrote for Goodman was titled 'The Earl' in tribute to Hines. 22 Goodman, separate from his jazz activities, was involved in performances and recordings of challenging classical music, such was his facility on clarinet, and by using arrangers as musically ambitious as Powell and Sauter, he was attempting to up the ante in jazz. Max Harrison, citing Powell in an overview on jazz arranging, observed: "In his and Sauter's hands, and elsewhere, jazz arranging was turning into composition." 23

The tension between jazz and contemporary classical music shaped Powell's career, ultimately in favour of the latter. By the 1950s, Powell had abandoned jazz, bar occasional reappearances, to pursue an acclaimed career as a modern classical composer. He explained that as a youngster, jazz signified to him "the bordello. sex, fallen women and drugs. How was I, who had grown up with a Talmudic grandfather... supposed to relate to that?" 24

I asked Loren Schoenberg, who knew Powell, about him. "Talk about people who've not received their due in jazz, Mel Powell is one of them. Mel Powell got his due in classical music, he won the Pulitzer prize, and he was very involved in electronic music, and in the late twentieth century he studied with Paul Hindemith... Mel Powell adopted a Germanic accent after he studied with Hindemith, he really was a little bit of a chameleon there and took on, to the great amusement of his old friends, a little bit of a pompous Germanic way of talking that had nothing to do with his background... But a great pianist, derivative, like ninety-nine per cent of jazz pianists, with his own little streak of individuality in there. Very forward looking, very creative, and ultimately found that jazz was not large enough to express his musical vision. But he did some recordings for Capitol, incredible sessions, from 1947, extraordinarily creative and wonderful and he's been really forgotten about. His best records were two trio records he did in the early 1950s for the Vanguard label, one with Ruby Braff and one with Paul Quinichette – absolutely brilliant. But he left jazz."

A reason Powell gave for doing so was that "the endless repetition of material in the Goodman band – playing the same tunes day after day – got to me. That repetition tended to kill spontaneity, which is at the heart of jazz". 25

Within jazz, a twofold rebellion took place – one that looked forward to the innovations of bebop; the other looked back, a revival movement that fetishised the rootsy, spontaneous 'pure jazz' of the New Orleans pioneers and small-group Chicagoans of the previous decade, and several Jews were involved. Critic Rudi Blesh – who championed black music – was one. "Blesh claimed that swing was a corruption of jazz, that jazz was this wonderful naive African American music," Dan Morgenstern told me. Other Jewish revivalists included Mezz Mezzrow, trumpeter Max Kaminsky, singer Stella Brooks, drummers Morey Feld and Buzzy Drootin, and pianist Art Hodes.

Hodes was a passionate champion of old-school jazz. As a young musician he befriended Louis Armstrong in Chicago in the 1920s. "Louis, knowing I loved the blues, took me and [trumpeter] Wingy [Manone]... to a barbecue place where... the pianists that came up from the south, hung out... That's when my real jazz education started... That place and its people taught me the blues," Hodes recalled. 26

Throughout his career, Hodes was committed to mixed-race, blues-infused small group jazz, and not just as a musician, as Dan Morgenstern explained to me. Hodes, who in 1938 moved to New York, the hub of the revival movement, holds an especially fond place in Morgenstern's memory. "He was one of the first jazz musicians who ever talked to me, just fresh from Europe," from where, readers will recall, Morgenstern had taken flight from the Nazis. "He was very nice to me," continued Morgenstern, "a great blues piano player, and he was the first, for a long time the only, white musician recorded by Blue Note. Art brought in a few people, like Max Kaminsky and Mezz Mezzrow. Art, because he was a real jazz lover too, was a great proselytiser," including, Morgenstern said, as one of the first jazz disc jockeys on non-commercial public service radio WNYC – so non-commercial that Hodes worked for no pay, for love of jazz. Additionally, said Morgenstern, Hodes was among the first jazz musicians to start his own record label, Jazz Records: "And he added a magazine *Jazz Records* which lasted a little over three years; it was nicely done but of course it didn't make money." The magazine pioneered publication of oral history accounts of the jazz musicians it celebrated, many of whom had become overlooked as traditional jazz gave way to the big swing bands.

In later years, his close friend, clarinetist Barney Bigard, suggested Hodes join him in Louis Armstrong's All-Stars. Hodes spurned the chance as, weary of the road, he now mainly gigged around his native Chicago. "A great symphony orchestra," Hodes bemoaned, "is able to work in their hometown, but not a great jazz band. To the very last, Armstrong had to hit the road constantly in order to ply his trade. Ellington the same. Think of it. Both around seventy, still having to make the road scene. Same... with the Count [Basie]." 27

One of the most forceful proponents of jazz revivalism was a Jewish jazz musician who had been a beneficiary of big band swing – Max Kaminsky. Following his years as trumpet lynchpin in Artie Shaw's band, he became a founding member of small revivalist combo the Summa Cum Laude Orchestra. The musicians involved, Kaminsky averred, "were of a different breed from the swing kings. Now I was with a band composed of dedicated jazz musicians who never wanted to play in a commercial band ... Jazz was their sincerest belief – their whole life – not money, fame or glory". 28

Yet as we have seen, the money, fame and glory that particularly the white-led big bands enjoyed was totally unforeseen, triggered by the ballyhoo that ensued following the rapturous reception conferred on Goodman at the culmination of that gruelling cross-country tour.

# Chapter 5: The Chant

January 16<sup>th</sup> 1938 was the evening Ziggy Elman, trumpet dynamo in the Goodman band, dared make a mainstream musical declaration asserting his Jewishness. Or should I say *their* Jewishness, because Elman's showpiece swing rendition of the Yiddish refrain 'Bei Mir Bist Du Schoen' ('To me you are beautiful'), replete with emphatic klezmer *freilach* phrasing, took place during Benny Goodman's famous Carnegie Hall jazz concert.

The event, organised by Goodman mentor John Hammond, was historic for other reasons. It embedded jazz as an art worthy of presentation in America's most prestigious temple of classical music; paraded jazz on its own terms; and was a homage to, rather than Whitemanesque side-lining of, the centrality of black America in the jazz story. Besides the small group sections that featured Goodman's black stars Lionel Hampton and Teddy Wilson, Goodman devoted a portion of the evening to a 'Spirituals to swing' evolutionary overview of jazz development, bringing in guests from the Ellington and Basie bands.

The concert put a marker down for Jewish music, jazz the permissive medium facilitating Elman's interpolation of shtetl strains into the idiom most expressive of the twentieth century American metropolis. 'Bei Mir Bist Du Schoen' was actually Sholem Secunda's composition for a Yiddish Second Avenue musical. 1 Elman's jazz-klezmer solo was the highlight of the Goodman band's version, sung by white vocalist Martha Tilton, while arranger Jimmy Mundy was black. After Elman rendered 'Bei Mir' Yiddish-swing style at Carnegie Hall, it became a jazz standard, and Elman cashed in with follow-ups 'Fralich In Swing (And the Angels Sing)', with Johnny Mercer lyrics, and 'Bublitchki'.

'Bei Mir' was initially popularised by the non-Jewish Andrews Sisters whose rendition featured Anglicised lyrics by Sammy Cahn, a Jewish songwriter who later contributed the words to Frank Sinatra songs. There are two different accounts about 'Bei Mir''s popularisation, as chronicled by Kenneth Aaron Kanter: "One has it that the agent Lou Levy, thinking that an all-Yiddish song sung by three gentile girls would be an amusing hit... brought the song to the attention of the Andrews Sisters... Another story told by Sammy Cahn... says that he heard two black performers singing the song in Yiddish at the Apollo theatre in Harlem. 2 Though the audience couldn't understand a single word, they seemed to enjoy the song, Cahn was impressed so went out and bought the sheet music. He aroused the interest of the Andrews sisters." 3 The Andrews' 'Bei Mir' swept the world.

Then the decidedly Jewish Barry Sisters – originally the Bagelman Sisters – scored with it, resuscitating the Yiddish lyrics. The Barrys became mainstays of the Yiddish Melodies in Swing programme on the New York-based Jewish radio station WHN from the late 1930s to the 1950s, with pianist and arranger Sam Medoff and his Yiddish Swingtette laying down a toe-tapping groove.

Elman's klez-inflected trumpet style may well have influenced Harry James, Goodman's other featured trumpeter. Many people mistakenly thought that James was Jewish too, a view probably reinforced when he recorded a 1941 jazz version of 'Eli Eli', a Yiddish folk song composed in 1898 by Jacob K Sandler as a lament about Jews' millennial suffering. James wore a skullcap during the recording to get in the mood and was photographed with a rabbi to publicise the track. 4

Peter Sokolow, a veteran klezmer-jazz musician, agreed with me that there was probably something of the Elman *schtick* in James' style: "Ziggy of course was very well known, 'And All The

Angels Sing' and all these things, he really tried to make a commercial basis for this, possibly to make himself into a jazz-Jewish personality. He was the only one that could do that. Harry James, certainly he was influenced very much because he played that 'Trumpet Blues', all that stuff, he sounds almost like Ziggy. Yes, Harry James definitely did have a Jewish influence into that. The funny thing is, that's an anomaly. Most of the real Jewish trumpet players [klezmer musicians] played like brass band players, and they didn't ornament very much. Ziggy imitated a cantor on his trumpet – he was the first one to do that, and I think Harry James caught some of that stuff, he just applied it to American music."

Randy Brecker, one of today's leading jazz trumpeters, told me, about Ziggy: 'He was a great trumpet player with a great original sound, the fact that he was Jewish and the fact that he brought that element really to his music separated him from other trumpet players. And he became the type of standard, if you will, if there is such a thing, of the klezmer-type trumpet player. Harry James was probably heavily influenced by Ziggy, and he was just a great trumpet player and I hear I guess some influence there."

Dan Morgenstern related to me a story about black trumpeter Charlie Shavers: "Right that Harry picked up on Ziggy's *yiddishkeit*, but Charlie Shavers was an even better *freilach* trumpeter. At a wedding many years ago, a relative of the bride asked Charlie if he could play such a thing, and the response was so brilliant that it elicited a $100 bill – this was in the '60s so quite a tip." In Shavers' case, however, this wasn't integral to the way he played.

Could Ziggy's klez inflections also have influenced, in some degree, bebop trumpeter Dizzy Gillespie? Trumpeter and arranger Neil Hefti, interviewed for Ira Gitler's oral history *Swing to Bop*, made the following observation: "I heard Dizzy as a completely different soloist from anyone. As a matter of fact, I sort of strangely enough associated him with Ziggy Elman... Because up to that time, maybe Ziggy was the most different trumpet player I ever heard. Like maybe Dizzy Gillespie even sounded Jewish like Ziggy Elman in 'And the Angels Sing', and those kind of things he was doing with Tommy Dorsey. That he had sort of that ethnic flavor to his playing, and maybe Dizzy Gillespie had that too."

From Ziggy let us zag to more contentious ground – the argument that the way Benny Goodman and Artie Shaw played clarinet was also partly related to their Jewish roots.

I raised this with Loren Schoenberg, who was not buying it: "Take your great Jewish jazz musicians – Benny Goodman, Artie Shaw, Stan Getz and that list, what you're hearing them all do is express themselves in an African American idiom. When Benny Goodman plays the clarinet you're very well aware of the fact that what he's doing is expressing himself in an American idiom, sub-set African American. There's no Jewishness in Benny Goodman at all, except when he plays tongue-in-cheek – 'And The Angels Sing' or something like that. So I think that that's what you're hearing. I hear nothing Jewish in Artie Shaw."

Loren augmented his point with an observation about Goodman's speech patterns: "Benny Goodman could sound extraordinarily African American. When you listen to him talk on a radio broadcast of the 1930s he sounds like a black man, he does not sound like a Jewish man, ever. You never hear any Yiddish or Jewish inflection in his voice. You hear a ton of a black inflection. It was just natural, how he identified himself."

Stanley Crouch concurred: "One of the things that's most interesting about a guy like Benny Goodman, if you listen to some of his early recordings, he sounds like a black guy playing with the white guys, because he had been in the music playing at such an early age, he really had what you might call a natural affinity for it... And the other thing about Goodman, I made a case that if you listened to him on the radio in the 1930s, he sounds like a guy from the south side of Chicago... After he married into the Vanderbilt [Hammond's] family he starts speaking differently. What I'm saying is all of that was natural to him... he grew up in Chicago and spent a lot of time with the black people of Chicago when he was learning how to play and all of this stuff was second nature to him. Later on he changed the way that he spoke, but I think that was when he married upward and started travelling round the country with millionaires, mansions and all of that. But the other Goodman was a different kind of a guy."

Was Goodman being tongue-in-cheek though, when he played anything Jewish? Vibraphonist Terry Gibbs, who comes from a klezmer family background and worked with Goodman, told me that Goodman greatly admired klezmer clarinetist Naftule Brandwein: "I have a letter that Benny Goodman wrote me, and Benny signed it Naftule, because I used to call Benny Naftule. And Naftule was in that class, in his field."

There's recorded evidence of what may be a Jewish feel seeping into Benny's music early in his career – Goodman's fiery clarinet playing on 'That's A-Plenty', recorded in Chicago in January 1928. Goodman, with piano and drum accompaniment, takes off at a searing clip and doesn't let up for the entire three or so minutes the track lasts. I played it to a violinist at the Jewish Music Institute in London and, although 'That's A-Plenty' is unmistakeably jazz, she immediately, without promoting, picked up the underlying klezmer feel.

Clarinetist Dan Levinson emailed me: "I know the Goodman recording of 'That's A-Plenty' well – in fact I played a note-for-note recreation of it a few years ago with Dick Hyman for a Goodman tribute as part of his Jazz in July festival at the 92nd St Y in Manhattan... What probably makes it sound Jewish is the fact that

(1) the 'A' theme is in a minor key, and (2) Goodman plays it in the upper register of the clarinet, giving it that 'klezmer' sound. I think a lot of the early klezmer clarinetists played Eb clarinet, which is pitched higher than the standard Bb clarinet."

'That's A Plenty' was written by a Jew, Lew Pollack, and became a big thing for traditional jazz musicians to play. Pollack did not write it as a klezmer tune but there's that feel about it and perhaps Goodman just ran with it. Goodman had learned to play clarinet in a synagogue band and even if it only played a non-Jewish repertoire – which seems highly improbable – Goodman by hanging around the synagogue would have been familiar with Jewish music. Could it be that this had some effect on what came out of his bell when Goodman became a jazz musician?

Klezmer musician Peter Sokolow was not persuaded: "When he tried to play phrases on the later records he sounded as if it was learned, it didn't sound natural to him. Whereas Artie Shaw I think, did, because when Shaw played some of these phrases, it has a more Jewish texture. There's a record called 'Prosschai', one of these folk dances, it really has a nice feel – a swing arrangement of not a Jewish song but a Russian song. But you could see that Shaw had heard and knew, even though Shaw was a Goodman clone. He sounded just like Goodman – I'm talking about 1934, before he made his style more kind of a singing style. Goodman never really sang, but Goodman played biting, swing jazz, he was just incredible, he had a jazz thing in him, and I don't know how much of his Jewishness came out into that, I don't think very much."

Shaw, unlike Goodman, for years concealed his ethnicity, yet, said Peter: "In the back of his head someplace, when he used this singing approach on the clarinet, there had to be some chazzan [cantor]. There *had* to be, the chazzan was a major influence on all Jewish music; klezmer music is strongly, strongly chazzan-ic because the first music that a Jew heard was usually in shul with the chazzan. Some people were turned off by it, I don't think that Goodman reacted particularly well to it, but I would say that Shaw was more interested in singing on his instrument; this is the klezmer approach, even though he didn't go out of his way to play Jewish. It may not have been direct, but I think there was a little indirect influence."

On at least one track, the influence is direct, as Shaw disclosed: "I did it once at the end of a piece called 'Dr Livingstone, I Presume'. It had an African sound. At a certain point, I decided I would play it as a sort of Jewish piece; a *hora* it's called. It's a Yiddish piece of music and I went *rah rah rah-rah-rah-rah-rah did-da-dit-da-dit-da*, and the drummer went with me." 5

Richard Sudhalter detected Jewish strains in three other tracks, including a mid-forties Shaw recording of 'My Heart Belongs to Daddy' – an "intentionally 'Jewish' reading", wrote Sudhalter, "of this Cole Porter standard". 6 Another recording Sudhalter highlighted was 'Concerto for Clarinet', which he said reflects Shaw's cantorial side: "The opening especially... is in attitude and effect a *Doina*, the heavily embellished minor-key lament common in the folk music of... east European countries and in their Ashkenazi Jewish populations". 7 Finally, Sudhalter cited 'Nightmare', Shaw's dramatic signature tune: "Call it a Jewish flavour, an emotional predisposition, something cantorial: the catch in the voice, the certain keening, grieving, quality that distinguishes the *Kaddish* and *Kol Nidre* in Jewish liturgy." 8

'Nightmare' had a life-defining impact on Nat Hentoff, as revealed in his *JazzTimes* Shaw obituary: "If it hadn't been for Artie Shaw, I might not be writing about jazz... When I was eleven years old, walking down a street in Boston, I heard music coming out of a record store that made me shout aloud in excited pleasure. I rushed in, demanding, 'What is that?' Artie Shaw's 'Nightmare', I was told. Before then, the only music that had affected me so viscerally was the passionate, mesmerizing, often improvisatory singing of... the cantor in Orthodox synagogues on the High Holiday days. The *hazzan* sounded at times as if he was arguing with God, and the depth of his witnessing to the human condition later connected me with black blues."

Besides the Shaw tracks just mentioned, there was also his 1939 air check of a tune titled 'The Chant' which klezmer musician Hankus Netsky says goes as far as any recording from that era towards a Jewish-jazz fusion: "The tune itself plays on the close, and presumably incidental, relationship between the 'St James Infirmary Blues' and *Khosen Kale, Mazeltov*'... a popular Jewish wedding recessional." By Netsky's account, Shaw also quotes from "Bei Mir Bist Du Schoen', 'Yossel Yossel' and "such relatively obscure klezmer tunes such as *Patsh Tants*'... and the Ukrainian *Kamarinska*'". 9 Was the relationship between klezmer and the jazz standard 'St James Infirmary Blues' merely coincidental? We'll probably never know but on an Artie Shaw LP in my collection, I've noticed his band plays up the similarities again in a November 1941 rendition, Max Kaminsky coming in on trumpet Ziggy style.

Sudhalter quoted Shaw, thus: 'Often I was trying to sound like a violin, especially like Heifetz [the Lithuanian-Jewish classical violinist]. He had a quality apart... the best way to explain it is that what you play is what you are. Certainly I can't deny the influence of my Russian-Jewish-Austrian ancestry. But how it comes out, how it makes itself felt – that's a mystery." 10

As we'll see next, when I met Shaw, he was evasive about any Jewish influence on his music.

Before I come to my interview with Artie Shaw, I want to dive into the debate about who was the greater clarinetist – Goodman or Shaw. Musicians are divided. Clarinetist Kenny Davern, when I asked him, rated both above all other pre-war jazz clarinetists but plumped for Goodman: "A far superior jazz soloist and a better clarinet player. Shaw was linear; to some degree he was a genius. Shaw played sax-style clarinet, Goodman played clarinet-style clarinet. Shaw did start off on the sax." Duke Ellington's clarinetist Barney Bigard however rated Shaw "the greatest clarinetist who ever lived." And Jerome Richardson, a Benny Goodman fan until he heard Shaw, said: "He would get up to Bs and Cs and made not notes but... melodies. He must have worked out his own fingering for the high notes, because they weren't in the books... Artie Shaw was at that time... to clarinetists what Art Tatum was to pianists."

It is instructive to hear what a jazz modernist had to say on this issue. Saxophonist Herb Geller, who played with Goodman, appreciated his technique and swing but told me: "Artie's playing had a broader aspect for me because he was playing very interesting things harmonically. Benny never did too much harmonically. I never heard him play wrong notes, but he always played it rather safe. Benny knew harmony too, but not to the degree that Artie knew it. Artie was already into substitute chord changes." Geller felt Shaw's neglect by younger jazz musicians unfortunate: "The amazing thing about Shaw – he still sounds very fresh today. The band doesn't sound so fresh, that rhythm section was not the best by today's standards, but his playing is still just incredible." Even among avant-jazz improvisers, Shaw has had admirers; clarinetist John Carter named him as a primary influence, while Hal Russell recorded a tribute, 'Artie Shaw Suite'.

• • • •

I interviewed Artie Shaw in November 2002. Earlier that year he made the following unambiguous statement on NPR radio: "Jewish people were looked down on. I was ashamed of being a Jew; I'm no longer ashamed of that. It's the way it was. People ask if being Jewish has anything to do with your playing. If you listen to 'Nightmare', my theme, and listen to what the clarinet plays, there's an awful lot of Yiddish influence in that. You're what you are. In music it is very revealing. Someone pointed out the two great exponents of this kind of music during my period were me and Goodman. We were both Jewish by Russian background. It's not some accident that we both did what we did."

I brought that statement to the interview, aware that Artie disapproved of this book's theme. We met in the house Artie had lived in for several decades in Thousand Oaks, California.

He opened by asserting his opposition to my book, listing jazz players who weren't Jews: "Jack Teagarden, Louis Armstrong... I don't know where to begin." I reminded him of his NPR comments.

"It was the society I grew up in, and I ran into a particularly virulent case of it in Catholic New Haven. I didn't know Catholic from Episcopal, but that's got nothing to do with jazz."

"On the same show, they asked if being Jewish has anything to do with your playing."

"Being Jewish has everything to do with everything you are, in a society that is very abhorrent of Jews."

"And if you listen to 'Nightmare'..."

"That has nothing to do with it, that's a minor [key] piece."

"But you said in the programme that 'if you listen to that, what the clarinet is saying, there's an awful lot of Yiddish influence in that.'"

"That's horseshit. That's nothing to do with Yiddish, any more than everything else I did had to do with being Yiddish. I was on the Carson show one time and we got into a discussion – 'What did you want to be when you grew up, when you was a kid?' I said, 'I want to grow up and be a gentile'. The band started to laugh because there was a lot of Jews in there and they recognised it, and then after the laughter died down I said, 'And I made it'. Artie Shaw's not Jewish, Artie Shaw's a gentile icon. It has nothing to do with jazz. It's as if you're an Abyssinian with white skin or a Shiite. I was a foreigner in New Haven."

"But you're on record as saying that 'Nightmare' had this Jewish influence."

"Not that I know of. It was in the minor key – how many songs are minor key? 'Yesterdays' by Jerome Kern – you might say he was Jewish."

"Well he was."

"But that didn't have anything to do with 'Yesterdays'."

"Where did the idea for 'Nightmare' come from then?"

"I had to have a theme song and I was going on the air the next night, my first jazz band appearance as a leader. What is a theme song? It was late in the evening, 10 o'clock, so I had to sit down and write something that we could stretch. So it's a large, long background for a solo, with an introduction and an ending. When I played a certain theme [Artie hummed the first few notes], that told the damn comment on the next [a few more notes]; that had nothing to do with being Jewish."

"Did any of your music?"

"I never thought in those terms. This whole klezmer bullshit, it's such crap. Someone once said that the piece on which I played ending on a small group thing called 'Mr Livingstone, I Presume', that I went to do a long dance because Mr Livingstone and Mr Stanley met and they went into a... that's bullshit, someone romanticising. I just felt like doing that. So I (hums a few notes) ... it's sort of a Jewish kind of feeling, but I was thinking then that I was doing what Jews calls a *freilach* or a *hora*, I wasn't thinking in terms of Jewish, I was thinking that's a piece of music played by a certain kind of people. Had nothing to do with me. I was executing something, and I played it in a very difficult key."

"In that NPR programme, you said, 'Someone pointed out that the two great exponents of this kind of music during my period were me and Goodman. We were both Jewish by Russian background. It's not some accident that we both did what we did.' Can you discuss that?"

"Again, it had nothing to do with being Jewish. We both happened to be Jewish. Louis Armstrong happened not to be Jewish – he was one of the great exponents. No, it's not an accident, we played the clarinet and we both played superlatively well but Goodman was a technician, primarily, he had a limited vocabulary musically. He heard me later with my small group, he said, 'Man, where did you get that harmonic sense?' Well, I was listening to Bartok, before [jazz modernist Charlie] Parker came along. I could sing you the entire [Stravinsky] symphony called *La Mer* and *Firebird* and *Petrushka* – I listened to that music."

Artie, we have seen, gave a major profile to black artists during an era when this was a dangerous thing to do. I raised this with him.

"I just hired them because I wanted them in the band. Hot Lips Page, Billie Holiday – they sounded good." Artie hired musicians, he said, because he "liked them; period". Ethnicity had nothing to do with it.

"Can you talk about the complications of heading a band in American society then with these black artists in it? On the road, say?"

"The only way we could make a living with that band, we couldn't play in one place, one-night stands. We played in hotels during the winter because we couldn't travel in the winter, so we played in hotels and we'd take a little loss, and I would use the fact that I got paid for playing on the road to pay the men off. We got scale in the hotel. On the road I could afford to pay a little more, because we made a little more."

"But did you run into trouble with racial bigots."

"Sure, everybody knows that story about Billie Holiday, 'Have the nigger witch sing another song'; he didn't mean it badly, he was a southern cracker, that's how he talked about black women – 'nigger witch'. He liked her singing, he wanted her to sing another tune. She obviously didn't like the term. It wasn't bigotry, it's the way it was. If you want to say racial bigotry, go back to Gone With The Wind. Terror is racial bigotry, if you want to call it that, they built a society on it. General Lee is regarded as a great general and he was a bigot – hundreds of thousands of men were killed because he fought for what he believed in."

"Roy Eldridge, after he played with you, said he'd never play again in a white band."

"I don't blame him, I told him to get out. He had a very bad case of it. He didn't show up when the band did with the bus. He tried to go in the front way later and he was late – they wouldn't let him in, they thought he was a black guy trying to crash the dance. When he finally got in – because I heard he was out there and sent my band manager out and got him in, by that time he was mad, his playing was mad, and I didn't like any of it. So I said to my band manager, 'Give him his two weeks' notice.' I knew Roy was going to come in, and he came in – 'Motherfucker' – and he pulled a knife on me, and I said, 'But Roy, if I'm your enemy, who are your friends?' He started to cry. So I put my arm around him, I said, 'Why don't you get out of this country? You don't belong here. Go to Europe, make a life'. He did, came back, he didn't like Europe, he was an American. But we didn't regard black people as fully American at that time. So what you gonna do? You know, you did the best you could – there was a bad scene all the way round."

"Was you at all aware of any kind of social mission?"

"Roy Eldridge I hired because he was a trumpet player."

"But you must have known that you might take some flak for that."

"I didn't; he did. I made a deal with him, I said, 'I'll pay you more than anybody in the band; I'm going to expect more of you'. And when he didn't deliver I told him, 'Better get out of here.' I didn't think in terms of colour, race, creed, religion."

"No but a lot of the rest of society did."

"Well, fuck them. What came out of the horn is what I was interested in."

I asked Artie about the *DownBeat* spat he had with Billie Holiday, where he had to refute her allegation that she hadn't been paid for a recording.

"They thought I fired her because she was black. Wasn't she coloured when I hired her? So it doesn't make sense, it's all nuts. She got paid as much as everybody in the band including me."

"Really?"

"Until we succeeded. Then overnight I became an instant celebrity – I could do nothing without getting paid a lot of money, much more than I ever missed or saw."

"Looking back," I asked Artie, "how would you critically assess the big band era now?"

"Then it was kind of primitive. It's developed complexity since then. More and more complex, like human beings are – when they get into painting, we certainly don't do things that we used to do. Nobody's going round painting like Stubbs anymore." He pointed to a high-quality repro of a Stubbs hanging on his wall.

"Artie, I'm going to fire another label at you – bebop. Before you stopped playing, you were starting to get into it quite seriously."

"It was the music of the day I was playing. I liked it as much as I liked any music – the good I liked and the bad I didn't like. I liked Tadd Dameron's arrangements, I liked Al Cohn, George Russell. Miles was nowhere near the trumpet player that Dizzy was but who's listening to Dizzy? Dizzy took pride and left his audience. He made a record with Oscar Peterson – I defy anybody to tell me what that was all about except each one trying to play more than the other. It isn't a question of how fast and how proficient you are, the word musical is not there. I don't know why people have forsaken that idea. Music should be musical, no reason why it should be disagreeable or honking or unpleasant. Mahler, that's a good musician, he's musical. Chopin's musical – no mistaking what it was, he would go on and on and on with little filigrees, but they were musical. Getz has a good sound, Scott Hamilton, Chet Baker when he was good, when he was young, before he threw his life away. Harry James was a God-talented guy, he threw his life away too, went for MGM stardom and all that bullshit. Guy named Brad Mehldau, started out as a hell of a piano player, made a record called *Elegiac Cycle*, interesting record. He was doing what I recommended; if you're going to do music that's going to be imperceptible to most people, do your own, and that *Elegiac Cycle's* a series of pieces, they were very good. But then he got caught in the hands of a corporate producer, and they made a thing called *Largo* which is so overproduced, so overdone, he got too pompous for himself; hard to resist, success."

"You resisted it, in the end."

"Well, I walked away from it, I couldn't stand what was going on, it was too stupid for words."

Artie groaned about the venues he played in and the audiences: "The places we played in were bloody incredible. One we played, there was a carousel right down the block – wang, wang, wang – while we're trying to play pretty sophisticated music.

"Have you ever played before an audience that you thought really was appreciating what you was doing?"

"Blue Note in Chicago, one week, 1949, I had the best band I'd ever had, and the band could not play anywhere else because the beat wasn't oom-pah, oom-pah, it was very light. They couldn't dance to it, they wanted to dance. It's not dance music – dumb, stupid bastards. That 1949 band could have been, if it continued, one of the great bands of all time."

After renouncing his music career in 1954, Artie turned to writing, producing several short semi-autobiographical novels.

I steered the interview towards politics. In 1953, Artie got dragged before the House Un-American Activities Committee, a product of Senator Joseph McCarthy's political ambitions and post-war anti-communist paranoia. Jews active in the film, entertainment and music industries were prominent among those subpoenaed.

Any attempt to brand Artie as subversive fell flat, even though he informed on nobody and confessed to having attended a Communist Party meeting under a fictitious name, Witherspoon, at which, as he later informed *New Yorker*: "I asked so many impertinent questions that they told me, 'Witherspoon, you aren't Communist material.'" 1

Looking back from the perspective of his ninth decade, Artie seemed unbowed, telling me: "My political sympathies were with the underdog and they always are. I think we should live in a society in which everybody has what he needs. We give some people such a preponderance that there isn't enough left over. My sympathies are not with those people."

Marx, he said, made sense within limits: "He didn't make as much sense as Plato, but pretty good. So why pick on me? Because I was a name and they got press out of that. In some ways I agreed with many of the things that the Communists said, but we weren't up to it as a species."

I asked if he had accomplished everything in his life that he had wanted: "Is there anything that you wish you had done that you haven't?"

"No. I think I've led a good life, an interesting one. I could wish for a better world, more understanding in the world, but it isn't there, it's not going to be there. At least I didn't end up like Mozart, impoverished and disgraced. So, yeah, I'll take it as it comes, and it comes all right."

Artie concluded the interview with a reprise of how he started it: "I've got no patience with the premise of your book." Nevertheless, he'd given me nearly three hours of his time, having only booked me in for an hour, at a point in his life when time was running out for him. Artie told his assistant to show me up into his cavernous loft-study, the walls lined with a municipal library's worth of books, indicative of the breadth of Artie's intellectual interests. He died two years later, in December 2004, aged ninety-four.

# Chapter 7: Fruit of a different tree

In 1938, the year Billie Holiday quit Artie Shaw's band, she debuted at a jazz and cabaret club that had just opened in downtown Manhattan. Café Society, in Greenwich Village, with its colour-blind admission policy was committed to racial desegregation – a revolutionary development in 1930s America.

The club, its founder Barney Josephson a left-wing Jew, treated black clients and performers on an equal footing to whites. The roots of Josephson's stance on race – he even refused to hire black waiters as he did not want to put them in service positions – stemmed from his schooldays in Trenton, New Jersey. Josephson related the story, when interviewed for a British television documentary about Billie Holiday, about stepping into the classroom when he joined junior high school and "... there was a black youngster sitting at his desk in the direct centre of the classroom... you had the boys sitting all the way round the periphery... and this poor little kid was on a little island all by himself. I don't know what prompted me... I said, 'Er, do you mind if I sit next to you?' He looked surprised and said, 'Sure, go right ahead'... There were all these white students... and you could feel the resentment... a month or two later in the gymnasium... five or six of these boys worked me into a corner... they said 'only a Jew would love a Nigger'... and began pummelling me".

In the 'red scare' years of the late 1940s, Josephson came under FBI scrutiny because of the principles by which he ran his clubs, his support for progressive causes, and just guilt by association with his Marxist lawyer brother Leon whose activities included defending communist trade union organisers, and involvement in an alleged Soviet spy ring suspected of plotting to assassinate Hitler, for which he was arrested in Denmark in 1935.

Barney Josephson was blacklisted by the McCarthyites, effectively forcing him out of business. Not though before he opened a second Café Society in uptown New York, operating on the same principles. By the late forties, both clubs shutdown: "There was no let up for me," Josephson recalled. In 1955, "bloody but unbowed", he established a new club/restaurant in Greenwich Village, The Cookery, enabling him to give regular work to such musicians as R&B and jazz singer and pianist Nellie Lutcher and veteran blues singer Alberta Hunter, during the difficult years they endured following the advance of rock and roll. The Cookery closed in 1984 and Josephson died four years later.

Café Society was not the first jazz club where white and black patrons mingled but, as Dan Morgenstern advised me, it was the first intentionally desegregated club: "There were other places, in Harlem, they couldn't rule out white folks. But there were ways of doing that by making them feel uncomfortable. Harlem was pretty open." There was also, he said, the jazz scene in midtown 52nd Street: "But 52nd Street, although there's a lot of black musicians working there, it was primarily a white clientele. Most clubs would not refuse black people coming in but they would certainly not be particularly excited about it or interested in encouraging them. Café Society wanted black people to come and wanted an integrated audience. Everybody was welcome, they made sure that was understood." [1]

There is a wonderful anecdote, in Ted Vincent's *Keep Cool: The Black Activists Who Built the Jazz Age*, that captures the spirit of Josephson's club. Eddie South, a black, blind violinist, was performing there: "One night, the club seemed surprisingly empty to Barney, who notwithstanding his Jewish background had forgotten that it was Yom Kippur eve. But Eddie hadn't, and stopped a particular 'hot' set to play 'Kol Nidre' for the boss so sensitively that both of them openly wept. When Barney went over to embrace South, the violinist blurted out for the first time that one of his grandfathers had been white and Jewish."

One investor in Café Society was Benny Goodman, who evidently made an emphatic public gesture in support of the club's racial stand: "The white bandleader... routinely carried his own mouthpiece in his pocket. But he reportedly made a point of conspicuously popping into his mouth the instrument being played by the African American clarinetist Edmond Hall." 2

A Jewish Café Society patron of importance to this narrative was Bronx schoolteacher and poet Lewis Allen, real name Abel Meeropol, who composed the anti-lynching classic 'Strange Fruit'. It became so closely identified with Billie Holiday that people assumed she wrote it. When *DownBeat* repeated this assumption in 1965, Allen wrote to the magazine: "The song was not written by Billie Holiday at all. I wrote the words and music of 'Strange Fruit' as a protest against lynching. My name is on the copyright on file in Washington, on the song sheet published by Edward B Marks Music, and on the record labels, etc. The song was written a year or more before Billie Holiday ever heard it, and the first time she did was at Café Society, where I played it for her at the request of Barney Josephson, manager of the café, and Robert H Gordon, who directed the performers who appeared there in its early days. Billie did not even know what the word 'pastoral' in the song meant, and I had to explain it to her. She didn't dig the song at first because it was so different from all the other songs to which she was accustomed, and she was not particularly interested in it. It was only after she sang it at the opening of Café Society and got a tremendous ovation, and every night thereafter, that she got to really understand the song and appreciate how well it was suited to her. What she did contribute to the song was her own personal and strikingly original styling."

It is no coincidence that a Jew wrote that song, with its famous opening lines: *Southern trees bear a strange fruit/ Blood on the leaves and blood at the root/ Black body swinging on the southern breeze/ Strange Fruit hanging from the poplar trees.* Nor is it a coincidence that Billie first performed it at Café Society. Nor that it was Milt Gabler that released Billie's first recording of 'Strange Fruit' on his Commodore label. The song, the club, and Gabler, are fruit of a different tree – the bonds forged between African Americans and Jews in the first decades of the twentieth century.

'God Bless The Child', also associated with Billie Holiday, she is credited as co-writing with another Jewish Café Society patron, Arthur Herzog. The Herzog-Holiday partnership yielded other songs too, including 'Don't Explain'. Herzog's son Gregory gave me his understanding of the collaboration: 'The family story about 'God Bless The Child' is that Billie came over the house one night, Dad was there and a wonderful arranger, Danny Mendelsohn, and Billie came in and said she had an idea for a song. And it was 'God Bless The Child'. She came over to the house very often, I was told. This was in New York City; Billie and my dad I think met at Café Society and struck up a friendship. She came over, she had this idea for a song, so Dad said that he'd picked out a melody in short order, five or ten minutes. Then he wrote words for it. And Danny arranged it. There's no doubt that it was her recording of the song that made it as popular. And that's it; she certainly deserved credit for it."

# Chapter 8: Raising standards?

Jews have contributed prolifically to America's treasury of song, including such early twentieth century nuggets as 'After The Ball', 'Shine On, Harvest Moon', 'Let Me Call You Sweetheart', a great many pop and rock hits, and a surprising number of tunes popularised by black blues and R&B performers.

The songs that concern us here though are those that have attained the status of jazz standards, favoured as vehicles for improvisation. Most were composed between about 1925 to 1950 by songwriters of stage and screen, an astonishing number of which were written by Jews – so much so that you sometimes get rash overstatements. A *New York Times* article about Hoagy Carmichael said he was one of only three prominent non-Jewish popular songwriters of those years, prompting this reader's letter: "Meaning no disrespect to good ol' Hoagy, but for Mr Davis to say that Hoagy, Duke and Cole Porter were the only three composers in the 20s, 30s and 40s who were not Jewish tells me... that Mr Davis doesn't know a whole lot about great composers – and not just 'songwriters' – like my uncle, Walter Donaldson ('My Buddy', 'My Blue Heaven', 'Whoopee', 'Love Me or Leave Me'), George M Cohan, Jimmy McHugh, Johnny Mercer and so many other fine composers whose wonderful songs are still being sung and played all over the world." 1

Still, that does not invalidate the essential point Charles Hamm made in his history of American popular song: "The era marked off roughly by America's involvement in the two great world wars... was one of the peaks of the entire 200-year history of popular song in America... Most eras of popular song in America have been dominated by one or another of the national or ethnic groups making up the complex web of American society – the

English, the Irish, the Italians, the Germans, the Africans...The period... is no exception; it was dominated by Jewish Americans." 2

That includes lyricists: Lithuanian-born Mitchell Parish, for instance, who wrote the words to Hoagy Carmichael's 'Stardust', and Dorothy Fields, whose lyrics lit up such Jimmy McHugh delights as 'Sunny Side of the Street', 'I Can't Give You Anything But Love' and 'I'm in the Mood for Love'.

In my consideration of the Jewish contribution to song-based jazz standards I will however focus only on those who wrote the tunes, the component most critical for jazz instrumentalists. By the mid-1920s, writes Hamm, "such composers as Kern and Gershwin had pushed the harmonic bounds of popular songs immeasurably further, with much freer use of chromatic chords, anywhere in a song, non-dominant seventh and ninth chords, and a willingness to alter almost any note in a chord to a richer harmonic color... The source of this new harmonic richness and variety in popular song is hardly a secret... These men knew the music of the classical composers of the 18th and 19th centuries." 3 One reason Hamm says these songs "struck the ears of both Americans and Europeans as being distinctly and peculiarly American... was the frequent use of rhythmic patterns originating in ragtime, in the syncopated dance music played by early black jazz bands". 4

Composer Jack Gottlieb traced ways in which, he argued, Yiddish songs and synagogue melodies influenced the popular music of Tin Pan Alley, Broadway, and Hollywood. Take 'Summertime', from Gershwin's folk opera *Porgy and Bess*, a passage of which Gottlieb charted to support his point that the tune may be viewed as an amalgamation of Jewish and black based components. Gottlieb cites film composer Bernard Herrmann's conversation with Gershwin, who, said Herrmann, was anxious about the song: "'Do you think it sounds colored?' he asked me... I said, 'What difference does it make? Negro music, Jewish music, they're all quite alike.' George said, 'I'm still worried... People may think it sounds too Yiddish.'" 5

Gottlieb contended that there was the Jewish influence not only in Jewish composers' songs but also in those of some non-Jewish contemporaries, notably Harry Warren and Cole Porter. Richard Rodgers has left us with his account of an exchange he had with Porter, who, at a social event, "leaned over and confided, 'I'll write Jewish tunes.' I laughed at what I took to be a joke, but not only was Cole deadly serious, he eventually did exactly that. Just hum the melody that goes with 'Only you beneath the moon and under the sun...' from 'Night and Day', or any of 'Begin the Beguine', or 'Love for Sale', or 'My Heart Belongs to Daddy', or 'I Love Paris'". Rodgers thought Porter's songs sounded more Jewish than those by Jewish songwriters. 6

Whatever might, debatably, be musically Jewish about songbook jazz standards, one must keep in mind that Jewish songwriters were creative chameleons, bent on asserting themselves as modern Americans, integrating their multicultural influences into songs of mass appeal.

As many became hits, there was a sound commercial reason for jazz musicians to adapt them. Music publishers, as ever, simultaneously released populist trash too and jazz musicians made versions of such material, but generally, they spurned Tin Pan Alley's most banal outpourings. Jazz musicians took to the most musically challenging songs because the melodies and harmonies were dazzling and original. The songs, as products of the Jazz Age and swing era, lent themselves well to jazz adaptation. The symbiotic relationship with jazz began to develop from the mid-1920s; by 1930, Duke Ellington was predicting: "The future of music lies in the hands of those writers of Tin Pan Alley who see in popular songs and melodies of today the embodiment of the voice of the people." 7 As J Bradford Robinson noted, one characteristic of 1930s big band swing that distinguished it from the jazz of the early New Orleans pioneers was "a repertory based largely on Tin Pan Alley songs... The harmonic rhythm in swing was generally much faster than in New Orleans jazz, sometimes changing as often as twice in a bar, and soloists were expected to improvise melodies freely over these 'changes'". 8

Jazz musicians deploy these songs in two ways: 1) they play jazz versions of the actual compositions; 2) or they create their own compositions based on the chord changes. I will consider firstly the more obvious of these uses, jazz musicians performing interpretations of the actual songs, and pose the question: how many were composed by Jews? The most useful reference I have come across is *JazzStandards.com*, which features a top thousand listing, each standard's ranking determined by how frequently it has been recorded.

The compositions of Jewish composers constitute around a third of the thousand standards listed. Of the top ten standards, six were composed by Jews. These, their position indicated in brackets, are: 'Body and Soul' – composer Johnny Green (1); 'All the Things You Are' – Jerome Kern (2); 'Summertime' – George Gershwin (3); 'My Funny Valentine' – Richard Rodgers (5); 'Yesterdays' – Kern (9); and 'Stella by Starlight' – Victor Young (10).

Of the top hundred, Jewish composers account for forty-three, headed, predictably, by Gershwin. A measure of Gershwin's standing among jazz musicians is his eleven top hundred songs, more than any other composer. Besides 'Summertime', Gershwin's most popular songs with jazz musicians are: 'The Man I Love', 'Oh, Lady Be Good', 'Embraceable You', 'But Not For Me', 'Love Is Here to Stay', 'I Got Rhythm', 'Someone to Watch Over Me', 'They Can't Take That Away From Me', 'A Foggy Day' and 'S' Wonderful!'. In all Gershwin has twenty-nine top thousand entries – the same as Cole Porter and fewer only than Richard Rodgers and Duke Ellington.

Gershwin died when he was only thirty-nine, while Rodgers, Ellington and Porter enjoyed far longer creative lives.

Even lesser-known Gershwin songs have inspired jazz musicians. Bill Charlap, one of today's leading jazz pianists, who is Jewish, covered 'Lorelie' from the 1933 Gershwin brothers' musical *Pardon My English*, a song that doesn't make the *Jazzstandards* chart. "This is a unique tune," Charlap observed in a radio interview, "particularly how it comes out of the bridge... One of the things about George Gershwin is that there is always some little stroke of genius somewhere, where you think, 'My God, nobody else could possibly have thought how to get from there to there' – nobody would come up with anything as good, either, or with such a naturalness yet something so interesting."

The other Jewish songwriter most switched on to jazz was Harold Arlen. Twenty-two of his songs are top thousand standards, among them 'Come Rain or Come Shine', 'Over the Rainbow', 'Stormy Weather', 'It's Only a Paper Moon', 'Between the Devil and Deep Blue Sea', 'Get Happy!', 'That Old Black Magic', 'I've Got the World on a String', 'Blues in the Night', 'Ill Wind', 'I Gotta Right to Sing the Blues' and 'One for My Baby'. Some of the jazziest, bluesiest popular songs ever.

With Jewish lyricist Ted Koehler, the first of Arlen's three main collaborators, the pair produced 'Get Happy' for the 1930 show *9:15 Revue*. They then replaced the Jimmy McHugh-Dorothy Fields' songwriting partnership at the Cotton Club, the Harlem venue that showcased mainly black talent for a white clientele. Arlen had a long association with the Cotton Club, contributing material for eight revues. His songs were often premiered by the Ellington band with singer Ivie Anderson, and by other black artists. Jazz writer Ned Williams recalled "the unforgettable night when Ethel Waters stood in the spotlight with the Ellington band pulsating behind her, and sang, for the first time in public... 'Stormy Weather'", this for a 1933 revue. 9

Arlen's Jewish lyricist Yip Harburg, asked what made the music special, responded: "Harold doesn't use... anything that's recognizable as a cliché... he really uses the archaic theme and then develops it in his own individual way with great adroitness and beauty... Arlen background music is really Semitic plus Congo. It's the Negro music, the American Negro and the American rhythm and the American less sentimental, but a good deal of it is affected by... the southern blues, jazz, plus the melodic Hebrew... a terrific combination." 10

His feeling for the blues, Arlen believed, was linked in some elemental way to his upbringing as a cantor's son. Arlen's name came up when I interviewed Terry Gibbs, whose father, remember, was a klezmer musician. Terry hummed a few bars of 'Stormy Weather', clapping out a klez beat behind it, then declared: "It's almost a Jewish song. Harold Arlen's parents were probably born in Russia, were they? You know, it just comes out." 11

• • • •

What the *JazzStandards* chart doesn't tell us is the special status that George Gershwin's 'I Got Rhythm', from his 1930 show *Girl Crazy*, has attained in jazz. This brings us to the other way jazz musicians use songs – discarding the melody but improvising across the chord changes.

Thousands of jazz musicians' own compositions – including many that have become standards in their own right – are built on the harmonic foundations of Tin Pan Alley songs. Jazz performers were utilising such methods before the second world war but it was the beboppers that adopted this technique extensively. Many compositions by Dizzy Gillespie, Charlie Parker and other jazz modernists were radical transmutations of songs, including often extensive reworking of the harmonies. The resultant new compositions are called 'contrafacts' in jazz lingo. Many jazz standard songs have been transformed practically beyond recognition in this way. Professor Douglass Parker has defined contrafacts as "largely composed by working musicians in order to preserve familiar chord structures while avoiding the payment of royalties. Gershwin's 'I Got Rhythm' is the prize example, spawning numerous adumbrations". 12

When Leonard Feather described the contrafact phenomenon in *Inside Jazz*, he tabled a few outstanding examples, naming the title, the jazz musician that recorded it and the song on whose chords the contrafact was based. When Feather gets to 'I Got Rhythm', the way he puts it is that "Five Zillion" jazz compositions have been based on its chords, recorded by "Everyone" and on "All labels". *The New Grove Dictionary of Jazz* includes a list of contrafacts and confirms that 'I Got Rhythm' remains by far the most borrowed set of changes. So pervasive is this one song's influence that on Gershwin's centenary in 1996, Herbie Hancock, upon releasing a tribute album, *Gershwin's World*, said jazz was predicated on two things, the blues and 'I Got Rhythm'. Bassist Howard Rumsey concurred: "In all my years in the music business playing with so many jazz players... I never went to a concert in my whole life where no one played anything based on the 12-bar blues or anything based on 'I Got Rhythm' changes." 13

Richard Crawford dedicated an entire chapter of *The American Musical Landscape* to documenting this one song's impact since 1930. Dance and jazz band versions were recorded within days of the opening of *Girl Crazy*, and swing musicians were soon recording contrafact adaptations, Edgar Sampson and Benny Goodman's 'Don't Be That Way' (1934), and Duke Ellington's 'Cotton Tail' (1940) two noteworthy examples. Like other superior songs of the era, 'I Got Rhythm' was a link in the evolutionary chain between 1930s swing and 1940s bebop. Crawford notes: "Each of the most prominent black swing bands... had its own version of 'I Got Rhythm' as a standard vehicle for up-tempo blowing. So too did many bebop musicians. The reasons were partly artistic, partly social, but they were also economic." Crawford quotes bebop pioneer Max Roach, that: "Of course there are about ten million tunes written on the changes of 'I Got Rhythm'... This wasn't pilfering. In cases where we needed substitute chords for these tunes, we had to create new melodies to fit them. If you're gonna think up a new melody, you'd just as well copyright it as a new tune, and that's what we did." 14

What specifically is it about 'I Got Rhythm' that has even withstood attempts by post-bebop jazz experimenters to transcend chordal jazz? One musician I asked was Milcho Leviev, the Bulgarian-born, US-based pianist and composer whose father was Jewish. Milcho, I was sorry to learn, died in October 2019. I met him in Los Angeles where he was teaching masters students in jazz. When teaching, he said, he started with the blues, and with the 'Rhythm changes' about which he explained: "First there is such easy flow of the chord changes – I-vi-ii-IV; I-vi-ii-V; I-vi-ii-V – and then there is the bridge of this song, the middle part, that goes through the cycle of the fifths in such elegant and easy like a river way, that it's just perfect. And notably there's the melody: 'I Got Rhythm, da-da, da-da'. For the musician who is not educated, that doesn't mean anything but the educated musician hears (*Milcho scatted the first few notes*) this incredible poly-rhythm, which is in 3/8; (*Milcho in fast tempo*) 1-2-3, 1-2-3, 1-2-3; it's 4/4 – 1-2-3-4; 1-2-3-4; 'I've Got' 1-2-3, 1-2-3, 1-2-3, 1-2-3, 1... – it's equally 3/8, while still keeping the 4/4, 'da-da. da-da'. What is swinging really? Swinging is a syncopation based on a regular pulse, so that the melody naturally swings like hell. And then the harmony and everything that makes it a classic example of this form, 32-bar, AABA, and that's why it became such an ingredient of jazz."

Randy Brecker agreed: "Next to the blues it's the most important song form in American history. The chord changes – I-vi-ii-V and then going to the bridge which is all those dominant chords, just lends itself to great improvisation. And that's a very basic and hugely important piece, just that one thing alone, the fact that Charlie Parker – and he stated this in one of the books written about him – he learned to play by playing blues and 'I Got Rhythm' changes. And that's what I tell kids, a good place to start, those two forms are of the utmost importance."

• • • •

Whereas Gershwin and Harold Arlen were entranced by what jazz musicians did with their songs, another major Jewish songwriter, Richard Rodgers, disliked their messing around with his. Yet no fewer than thirty-five Rodgers songs make the *JazzStandards* thousand, second only to Ellington's forty-four. Alongside the sixth placed 'My Funny Valentine', Rodgers has three other top hundred titles, 'I Didn't Know What Time It Was', 'My Romance' and 'Blue Moon'. Other gems include 'Bewitched, Bothered and Bewildered', 'The Lady is a Tramp' and 'Manhattan'.

I phoned Dr Billy Taylor, jazz pianist and educator, after he had spoken about Rodgers on US national radio. He cited other Rodgers songs beloved by jazz musicians: "They interviewed me on several things being used by jazz musicians. I played 'Surrey with the Fringe on Top'. That was one of the tunes done by jazz musicians – why did we use it, why was it very influential? It worked for jazz. Basically, a lot of people played it, including Coltrane who used part of it on one of his tunes, the bridge to 'Giant Steps' uses chord changes that are the same as the bridge of 'Have You Met Miss Jones'. There were a lot of those songs where something was suggested to jazz musicians by the melody or the lyric. They would recast it as a jazz tune or play it relatively straight. Many Tin Pan Alley tunes were very well constructed. Because of the nature of performance, because of stage shows and revues, the music was varied. Sometimes the music was excellent."

Jerome Kern was not too fond of jazz interpretations either but twenty-one of his songs are top thousand standards. Gary Giddins, writing illuminatingly about how bebop musicians used contrafacts as springboards for creative expression, cited Kern's 'All The Things You Are' as a prime example: "It's challenging chords and key changes appealed to the modernists, and Gillespie turned it into a bop theme in a 1945 session with Parker, who played only the eight-bar release. The introductory vamp they fashioned is still standard in jazz versions of the tune. Parker performed the song often with his own quintet, and... affectionately called it 'Yatag,' an acronym of his favorite phrase from the lyric, 'You are the angel glow.'" 15

Irving Berlin is the other Jewish heavyweight, contributing twenty-four standards, including: 'How Deep is the Ocean?', 'Blue Skies', 'Cheek to Cheek', 'Always', 'Let's Face the Music and Dance', 'I'm Putting All My Eggs in One Basket', 'I've Got My Love to Keep Me Warm' and 'Heat Wave'. Many other Jewish songwriters' compositions also make the top thousand, among them Jule Styne with twelve songs, Vincent Youmans with nine, Arthur Schwartz and Victor Young with eight, Burton Lane, Frank Loesser, Saul Chaplin and Johnny Green, each with six. 16

Green's 'Body and Soul' is the most regularly covered of all jazz standards, and tenor saxophonist Coleman Hawkins' 1939 version is transcendent. 'Body and Soul' was already a staple of Hawkins' repertoire but that Victor label recording proved catalytic. It was a signature moment in the transition from swing to bebop because while stating the melody here and there. Hawkins launches into a series of virtuosic tangential variations on the harmonic underpinnings of Green's tune. Hawkins' shifting the focus so emphatically onto harmonic improvisation had a seismic impact on the young musicians that formed the modern jazz vanguard come the next decade. Yet Hawkins sketches in sufficient of Green's melody for the lay listener to readily identify the tune. Had he not done so, it is unlikely the record would have sold some 100,000 copies in the first six months.

Clearly then, the Jewish contribution to songbook standards has been enormous, but from the perspective of jazz historiography, is it valid to view them merely as raw material for jazz musicians' flights of inspiration?

Before I address that issue, I wish to share with readers a beautiful anecdote about one of the lesser known Jewish songwriters, Henry Nemo. About him, Kirk Silsbee told me: "Nemo wrote a couple of standards among other things; one is 'Don't Take Your Love From Me', which a lot of people have recorded, the other is 'Tis Autumn'. These are part of the Great American Songbook. He also wrote the words to 'I Let A Song Go Out of My Heart' by Ellington; he wrote an entire Cotton Club revue with Duke. I met him about five years before his passing. He died in his early nineties and he was a real larger than life character. I saw him when a very good jazz cabaret singer, Jane Harvey was performing in Santa Monica and she was kind of sniffy with the audience, which was a little chatty. And she said, 'I know this is a Hollywood audience with very important people but I'm going to acknowledge a real celebrity by singing this song and it's called 'Tis Autumn' and its composer is sitting over there in the corner – Henry Nemo.' After the performance, people came over to pay their respects to him. So, here is this big guy handling these people as though they were all friends and family. So I waited my turn and said to him, 'Mr Nemo, am I the only person here who's ever heard

'Ay Now' by Count Basie?' which he wrote, and sang on it with the Basie band, and it's an anomaly because in 1941-42 the Basie band had the great Jimmy Rushing so why are they giving a vocal spot to a guy who was just the songwriter? And he said, 'Hey, buddy, let me tell you about that, sit down.' Two hours later, we're standing out on the sidewalk, he's telling me about Ellington taking him home to meet his parents and Ellington in turn meeting Nemo's family and about the high respect that Ellington had for the family, and the conversation ended with Nemo saying, 'Love, baby, that's what it's all about, baby.'"

• • • •

Mindful of the prominence of Jewish songwriters, I decided to put the following question to several jazz artists: although the popular songs that became jazz standards were generally not written for jazz, did they influence its course?

"That's a loaded question," responded Billy Taylor. "You can say that there were things that changed jazz that weren't jazz and some things that were. It came from different sources."

"It's a 50:50 proposition," Loren Schoenberg replied. "The material was extraordinary. Also extraordinary was the way that this jazz music, this African American idiom, took it and used it. Take 'Body and Soul' – a wonderful song; it's 50:50. The material was first rate and what was done with it was first rate. What Louis Armstrong did with it was pretty radical, and then Coleman Hawkins. What Benny Goodman, Teddy Wilson, Henry Red Allen, Chu Berry and Roy Eldridge did with it, all before Coleman Hawkins recorded it. All kinds of composers were trying to write stuff at that time, great tunes, some Jews, some blacks, some Irish. Why did Jerome Kern have the ability to do what he did, Sigmund Romberg, George Gershwin, all these other people? Because Jewish people at that point were among the main producers and writers of the Broadway theatre, there's no doubt that all these Jewish Americans wrote this music and that's marvellous. They had the opportunity to do it and some great tunes came out of it. I think that if other groups had had the opportunity to participate in that, they too would have distinguished themselves. So I don't think it's a matter of any innate thing about it, but you're right, the fact was that the great majority of beautiful ballads of those days were written by blacks and by Jews. So what?"

A possible answer came from Richard Sudhalter: "Your point about the Tin Pan Alley men is exceptionally relevant. Their songs were the backbone of early jazz. Without the standards of Gershwin, Berlin, Kern and the rest – and an occasional *Goy* like Porter, the path might have been altogether different. This is one thread you can safely develop. Very important. Indispensable."

I also contacted Gunther Schuller whose *Jazz: Its Roots and Early Development* and *The Swing Era* are musicological studies of the way jazz progressed before the advent of bebop, but I could find nowhere in them any indication that the great songs might have played some part in that evolution. I asked him if that contribution had been underestimated?

He affirmed: "I think the great American songwriters contributed enormously, although, as you say, inadvertently to developments in jazz. Not so much in its sound, but in its harmonic and structural developments beyond and away from primarily the blues and simplistic early New Orleans and ragtime standards. Most of the songwriters you mention wrote harmonically quite sophisticated songs which in a way forced improvising jazz musicians to expand their ears to wider ranging harmonic, more modulating progressions, and in turn expanded their creative horizons."

Baltimore-born Jewish pianist Dick Katz shifted the emphasis back to what jazz musicians were doing: "What you have to factor into this is the learning and development of jazz musicians as jazz music progressed, as jazz musicians became more technically trained, even if they didn't go to school. The progress of the music that way is not to do with the songs. John Lewis [Modern Jazz Quartet pianist] used to say that the early jazz was like 'hunt and peck' – they played these little short phrases, they didn't know how to develop and sustain an improvisation over a long line. Louis Armstrong was ahead of his time doing that, the others just did this little choppy thing. When Coleman Hawkins came on the scene, Louis, and Red Allen, people started to play longer melodies, the music got more complex; the musicians made it more complex, not the songwriters. Some material was too sophisticated, jazz musicians wouldn't even play it – a lot of Cole Porter's music. First of all, the songs were too long, forty-bar songs; 'Begin the Beguine' was so long they could only get one chorus on the record. Then there are melodies – we talk about this – some melodies that are so strong, you don't want to improvise on them, you can't improve them. Thelonious [Monk, pianist and composer] told me that when you play a solo, after you've played the song once through, your solo's got to be at least as good as the song you've just played. And a lot of times it isn't. Great jazz musicians will play something even better than the song, should play something at least as good. You got to remember that there are many ways to approach improvisation. A complete musician knows how to play endless variations on the melody itself – Sonny Rollins, Louis Armstrong, James P Johnson, Art Tatum particularly, actually never losing sight of the melody. Then Coleman Hawkins came along, they became fascinated with the harmonic basis of the song, the chord changes. They loved Gershwin's chord changes. These chord sequences inspired them to come up with all kinds of stuff. They would take out songs with real simple folk type harmonies where there's only three chords over and over and they decided they would look for complicated chord progressions. Bebop really added so many chords, it got so thick, harmonically very dense, wherever there was one chord, they would add two in the same song. 'I Can't get Started' – there's a part there where they found where Dizzy Gillespie came up with this particular kind of progression and everybody jumped on the bandwagon and it was an exciting time. Then John Coltrane took it as far as humanly possible where there were so many chord progressions and it was so fast, that's as complicated as you can get.

"So they stopped at that point. And then there was a sea change, when the *Kind of Blue* Miles Davis album came out, it's the biggest selling [jazz] record of all time. It wasn't intended that way – all Bill Evans did was bring in a few scales and Miles, and they started playing on the modes, and they produced just a few chords. 'So What' is just two chords in the whole piece, let some air in the music. And the challenge was to be able to invent some good melodies on this. Of course, they started to use all these scales. But it was another social angle, which was a number of blacks thinking, 'I'm tired of playing all this white music all the time, all these songs. Let's make up our own music, our own melodies.' And they started writing all these pieces, Coltrane particularly. All this music had nothing to do with Tin Pan Alley, all these modal pieces. And Coltrane came up with some beautiful melodies, and Miles, and all that music from the sixties, that music's totally original. And then there's Ornette Coleman, they didn't want to play songs anymore."

Coleman, the doyen of free jazz, did however sometimes play songbook standards, as with his 1960 recording of Gershwin's 'Embraceable You', though he with Don Cherry, Charlie Haden and Ed Blackwell take it way out. And Coleman compositions 'Chippie' and 'Angel Voice' are based on 'I Got Rhythm'.

Classical cellist John Koenig, who through Contemporary Records – the jazz label his father founded – knew Coleman well, gave me some valuable perspective: "Coltrane got into modes, but he was doing Tin Pan Alley songs with modes. He did a recording of 'Chim Chim Cherrie' – which isn't strictly Tin Pan Alley – from *Mary Poppins* – that's totally modal. 'Inch Worm' he did in a modal way. 'Every Time We Say Goodbye' he did with the changes. McCoy Tyner [Coltrane's pianist] altered the changes a little bit but it's still that song. When you talk about someone like Ornette, you have to look at him in the same way as Schöenberg. Ornette kept some things from the tradition and jettisoned others. His music is very blues oriented, his early music especially, and you can hear a lot of Charlie Parker in him, even though you're not hearing Charlie Parker playing chord changes, you're hearing Charlie Parker's sound and a lot of blues inflection. If you met Ornette, I don't think it was rejection of Tin Pan Alley as much as it was 'I want to go this way'."

I phoned alto saxophonist Phil Woods as I'd seen a *JazzTimes* feature in which he spoke about the influences on jazz of "the Jewish-European harmonic contribution". It turns out that Phil, who was not Jewish, was relaying a phrase first expressed by singer-songwriter and jazz pianist David Frishberg. "Frishberg's opinion," said Phil, "was that developments in jazz went hand in hand with theatre music and most of that happened to be written by Jews. Where would Charlie Parker be without Jerome Kern's 'All the Things You Are'?; it fed right into bebop. The majority of the composers were Jewish. The whole harmonic pathos which fits right in with the American thing – it's hardly addressed at all. 16 Jazz has always fed upon popular song for inspiration. All the New Orleans guys were playing simple music, it was only when jazz went to Chicago and New York that the best players spread their wings. The whole thing about America is this diversity and this all feeds into everything. Art Blakey said jazz is not African, it's American and that should be good enough. Once you change the harmonic scheme and go from 12 bars to 42 bars, that drastically changes the shape of it. It wasn't only Jews, Duke Ellington also."

Similar thoughts were expressed to me by jazz pianist and songwriter Ben Sidran, whose album *Life's A Lesson* modernises synagogue music, and by bassist Greg Cohen, long associated with Radical Jewish Culture music scene experimentation, also a frequent participant in mainstream and traditional jazz bands.

"Everybody who plays the music brings something to it. Certainly, the Jewish composers over the years, who pushed the harmony and restructured the popular song form, had a great influence on the progression of the music," said Sidran. "The harmonic and melodic structure of their songs played a great part in shaping jazz improvisation for several reasons. First, by defining the grammar of popular American music, Jewish composers established a set of ground rules which not only affected future jazz composition but established the harmonic conventions of jazz which lasted well into the sixties. The Jewish composers literally erected the harmonic latticework from which jazzmen swung. Second, by inculcating a 'Jewish' sense of melody into the American psyche the Jewish composers influenced the 'voice' of jazz improvisation; that is, the leading tone of any jazz solo is determined by the original melody and the melody was laid down in many cases by a Jewish composer."

Cohen, whose credits include recording with Ornette Coleman, agreed: "Before New Orleans there was a ragtime form, and then as show tunes became more complex the Tin Pan Alley songs were different. They had chord changes that moved in a different way – more flexible, more scope for jazz improvisation. Tin Pan Alley, you could call it Jewish music; they were Jewish because you can't say the first twenty to thirty years of their life meant nothing. These Jewish songwriters synthesised this with the sound and style of their new country, but their Jewish heritage couldn't help but filter into the music. I would have to say that most of the time it was not conscious that you would have Jewish elements in the music."

Paul Gilroy, a black British sociologist who has written about jazz in its social context, cautioned me against making the songbook Jews, and their relationship to the evolution of jazz, an ethnic proprietorship issue: "My problem about what you're describing to me is that, yes, I accept it as a description of what happened, but to then turn round and invest it as a sort of Jewish story. So the question is then, why does that get written out of the history of jazz? And what's at stake in putting it there? Because if you do that, then you're in danger of making culture back into property and that's what worries me. It doesn't just worry me when African Americans are doing it, it worries me whoever's doing it. Because the message that I hear, in all these different directions, is that culture goes its own way and that it's only in the telling of it, that the question of what its origins are, who it belongs to, who it then doesn't belong to, who's appropriating it legitimately, who's misappropriating it, all of that becomes an issue."

My intention was not to make it a proprietorship issue. It is a matter of historical record that Jews were disproportionately represented among the foremost songwriters, and that jazz originates with black Americans who have provided a disproportionate number of its greatest innovators. All this coalesced with all the other innovators in popular song and jazz who were neither black nor Jewish. Culture works exactly as Paul described it.

Sitting across from the outspoken black jazz commentator Stanley Crouch, in his Greenwich Village study, I anticipated an antipathetic reaction. Stanley, it turned out though, had also been mulling over the black/Jewish connection in jazz, and the relationship between popular song and jazz: "A very interesting phenomenon, that is difficult for most people to understand, and that I'm not sure has really been investigated – and I've only mentioned it a couple of times, I've been thinking about it for a number of years. The thing is, if you and I go to Africa, and we go to a place where there's a great deal of tribal enmity, now even though we go from one ethnic group to another and ask them about the different ethnic group, and each of them will explain how screwed up the other ethnic group beyond theirs are, you or I not being from that country, we could see how they seem more like each other to us than they seem to each other, no matter how intense the hostility is. I contend that because the Jews were not Christian, they existed in this area between black and white and could see an American connection that segregation and/or racial hostility may have made it difficult for both groups. And that when they wrote these tunes, I felt like they were writing American songs that spoke to Americans across race lines because they saw that thing, they heard that thing, they could tell that. And I'm not saying that Irving Berlin and George Gershwin and these people sat down and said, 'Okay, I'm going to write three bars of this and this is for the coloured folks and I'm going to write two more bars and this is for the white people in the mid-west and I'm going to write some more and that's going to be for the Italians over on so and so.' I don't mean that. I mean that they can hear through that, the thing that makes it an American song. And that's the reason why people like Gershwin and Berlin and Harold Arlen and – you know, the list is long – that these people wrote these songs. And let's not forget something, these people were in contact with that, that was part of their learning how to be American.

"See, most of these guys are from Russia and they grew up with Yiddish being spoken in the home, they heard it in the street, they saw people running around with palliasses, that whole thing. But when they get to something like ... [*Stanley scatted the first few lines of 'I Got Rhythm']* … see, that ain't about back home in Russia. So the fact is that these people got into the stuff. In fact, I submit that *Rhapsody in Blue* is a praise song about Harlem; see *Rhapsody in Blue* is about the Negro, it's not about anything other than that. Listen to it. Don't forget that Gershwin's first musical was called *Blue Monday* which was for an all black cast. See, and I'm not talking about a minstrel show; when you listen to *Rhapsody in Blue* there's not one condescending note in that, it's about him going uptown to Harlem and falling in love with that music and seeing the vitality of the people. It's not an argument for [*evangelical preacher voice*], 'Oh, we must go out here and enlighten these dark people.' That's not what he's saying. It's like you and I were born here in the US and you and I have grown up and we went to Paris and Paris just knocked us out – 'Wow, Paris is great', and we were musicians, and we came back and wrote music about Paris, because we really loved Paris, right? That's what *Rhapsody in Blue* is. [*Stanley hums the opening bars*] I mean that's the Negro, man."

For me, I told Stanley, *Rhapsody in Blue* evoked the streets, the rhythms of New York, its multicultural people, its optimism, the excitement of modernity. Stanley responded: "That doesn't make it not being about what you're talking about. It's like Shakespeare being about how the Elizabethans looked at the world and about how one genius, who was an Elizabethan, wrote. And at exactly the same time it's that, it also speaks to anybody else. And if it doesn't have that, then it's not art, what's the value of it? But all those guys, don't forget that they were around when Louis Armstrong and Jelly Roll Morton and all that stuff exploded, and all of these great black dancers, all this was going on, it was like a vital, vital period and one of the most important things is that both the Negro and the Jew had something very much in common which was that they tended to celebrate the city, which is very different from what you hear in a lot of European music about the city. Because the city was not seen as this big mechanical trap, like Fritz Lang's *Metropolis* where all of these people turn into robots. Russia, where you had fucking Cossacks; when they [Jews] get to a city like New York, where you can open a business, you could get a job, and some guys didn't just get drunk and crazy and periodically just murder people for fun. Exactly the same thing for black Americans. When they came to the great northern cities there was a great deal more latitude and so one of the things you get in the music is this celebratory sense of urban life, and that's a very important thing they had in common, I would say."

Whether the greatest jazz standard songs were composed by Jews or not, they are part of the DNA of jazz. Whether or not you agree they had a pivotal role in jazz evolution, jazz would be infinitely poorer, and definitely less popular, without this treasury of material to draw upon.

# Chapter 9: Bop, Beats ... and Braff

Jewish law student Jerry Newman in the early 1940s lugged his cumbersome portable recording equipment to Harlem clubs Minton's and Monroe's Uptown and captured the after-hours jams that culminated in bebop – 'modern jazz'. These recordings are priceless documents of the informal experiments in sound created by the young greats-to-be, Dizzy Gillespie, Thelonious Monk, Kenny Clarke and others, their jazz characterised by extended improvisations over the main theme's harmonics, underpinned by complex, often rapid rhythms.

The beboppers inspired creativity beyond jazz. Pianist and French horn player David Amram, one of the many Jewish bebop-oriented musicians emergent at the time – he would go on to compose jazz-accented classical music – recalled: "There was cross-pollination of music, painting, writing – an incredible world of painters, sculptors, musicians, writers and actors; enough so we could be each others' fans. When I had concerts, painters would come, and I'd go play jazz at their art gallery openings... while beats read their poetry." 1

It was the 'Beat Generation' of countercultural poets, writers and fellow spirits to which Jewish novelist Norman Mailer gave the appellation 'White Negroes'. Their emergence coincided with that of bebop, and literary figures associated with the movement, including Jewish beat poet Allen Ginsberg – whose epic 'Howl' was a condemnation of post-war American values – were inspired by the rhythms, imagery, terminology and spontaneity of jazz.

Also on the scene was Jewish comedian Lenny Bruce, greatly admired by the modernist jazz community for his improvised satirical attacks on the political establishment, on racial bigotry, on anything antithetical to the jazz sensibility. Saxophonist Herb

Geller, who became acquainted with Bruce around that time, told me: "I was working a lot of burlesque gigs around LA. Whenever I didn't have a jazz job, I could always work a job playing for striptease. And I worked with his mother first of all, Sally Marr [like Bruce, a comedian], and she kept telling me you've got to meet my son, he's very funny. Then we started working together and I knew he loved jazz, and jazz musicians. So we had a lot to talk about, I knew his wife very well, we were like a family. My wife played piano, I was the bandleader, and his wife was the stripper, and he was the comic, the MC. And there's a bit on a record of mine – what happened he did this thing 'Religions Incorporated', and that's my title incidentally. That's why he liked jazz music, because he improvised, and we improvised. He'd walk on stage with a newspaper and then start changing it, making every bit into a funny situation. He would do the intermissions.

"So one night he came up with the *Los Angeles Herald/Express* and said, 'Hey, look at this, there's a picture of Orel Roberts – a preacher – and Lenny says, 'What do you think this ad costs in the *Herald*? Maybe all these religious guys are all working together.' And he turned to me and said, 'What do you think Herb?' and I said, 'Yes, Religions Incorporated.' And he said, 'That's it. I can see it now. There's this board meeting with Billy Sunday' – and he does this cracker bit with this real southern accent – and he says, 'Well, religion is up a point and a half, and Judaism is so and so, and the big eights, the Hindus', and he says, 'How about this campaign, a combination cigarette lighter and cross?' Then every night, if he did something good, he'd keep it and keep taking it further and further out. All the comics used to come in and see him – Milton Berle would come in, Bob Hope – this really funky place, to hear him. Then he started using drugs, and kept getting arrested, and it was very, very tragic."

Jewish beat writer, essayist and literary critic Seymour Krim ended up critical of the white hipsters that adopted black music and lifestyle. In 1957, Krim wrote 'Anti-Jazz: Unless the Implications are Faced' in *Village Voice*, arguing that "the white jazz-lovers, hear only the extract of the kind of life that produced this music... It is especially attractive to young people who are disillusioned with the values of white society. But no matter how beat they are themselves, the majority have literally no idea of the conditions of life that lie behind this music". Krim was editor of *The Beats*, published in 1960, collating contributions from advocates and critics of the movement. Mark Cohen in his 2007 'Missing a Beat' article in *Zeek*, defines Krim as "an offbeat Beat: the bridge-burning, miserably Jewish, self-described failure". Cohen quotes a follow-up to 'Anti-Jazz' in which Krim, who had suffered mental illness, attributed his youthful admiration for black culture to "a defiant liberalism and sense of identification stemming in part from my being the unreligious modern American Jew who feels only the self-pitying sting of his identity without the faith". Cohen concludes: "Krim saw that many Jews experienced Jewish identity as a 'blotch of birth' they hoped 'brilliant individualism' would help them transcend." Krim committed suicide in 1989, OD-ing on drugs in his Manhattan apartment.

* * * *

Jazz historians wrangle over whether bebop was an evolution or revolution in the music. It was both. Bebop evolved out of swing in that it remained embedded in song form and many musicians had played in the swing bands; but the beboppers reconstructed these formats so radically, in ways that made such formidable technical demands on the players, that – to most people – it indeed constitutes a revolution. Revolutionary enough, anyhow, to rile traditionalists, some of whom never became reconciled to modern jazz. If bebop was a bid by musicians to widen the scope of creative self-expression, it was also a form of social expression, certainly so for the originators. Theirs was a music of declamatory change, urgent, restless, a rude challenge to the status quo, reflecting the growing militancy in African American society that would climax in the civil rights struggles of the sixties. Bebop developed in the decade of the Harlem race riots, as young blacks, the war economy having opened up greater income and educational possibilities for them, rebelled in frustration against the racial hostilities, indignities, constraints and inequalities.

What most yearned for was erasure of the remaining barriers to full citizenship, and for a fair share of the rewards as America emerged from world war the most prosperous nation on the planet. Jewish Marxist Sidney Finkelstein perceptively articulated this mood in his 1948 book *Jazz: A People's Music*: "Certainly the new jazz, like the old, is in great part a national music of the American Negro people, and expressed in it are not only the old experiences of exploitation, but the new ones; the Jim-Crow army, in the last war; the rising sharpness of the struggle for full citizenship."

Among black jazz musicians, there was a perception that whites had colonised African American music. Charles Mingus asserted that whites had no right to play jazz, and Lorenzo Thomas in The Bop Aesthetic and Black Intellectual Tradition, notes: "There's no doubt one might have heard similar sentiments in the 1930s when top African American bandsmen in Philadelphia were making $10 a night... Youngsters like Dizzy Gillespie earned $2 a gig, but the white commercial jazzmen... were paid like movie stars." 2 White bands' very success accentuated what Scott DeVeaux dubs the wages of discrimination: "... with the encroachment of white bands on their territory, blacks soon found that their race was a liability, not an asset. The first signs of difficulty began to appear as early as 1938... leading to a steady erosion of theater engagements and one-nighters available to black bands. As business conditions worsened" – as they did in the 1940s for bands of whatever hue, because of the war and a union-imposed recording ban – "black bands were inexorably squeezed to the margins". 3 Moreover, it was far easier for white bands to secure steady hotel engagements for a winter respite from the road. One could hardly blame black musicians for feeling bitter, and yes, this bred prejudice against white players, even those that fraternised with them. Still, DeVeaux points out: "Although the leaders of bebop were African Americans, it would be a mistake to view the movement as inspired by racial separatism. The general camaraderie among like-minded musicians ensured that musical experimentation unfolded in environments as free from racial hostility as was possible in America of the 1940s." 4

* * * *

"The critics who really supported bebop strongly were Jewish – Leonard Feather and Barry Ulanov," so bebop chronicler Ira Gitler told me. Ulanov, who converted to Catholicism in 1951, is credited, as *Metronome* editor, with coining the term 'moldy fig' – a modernist's put-down of trad-jazz revivalists that scorned bebop, provoking polemical exchanges. Co-editor Leonard Feather was a ready accomplice – which is possibly why old-school cornetist Muggsy Spanier flattened him with a punch. 5

Yet Feather had many admirers among jazz performers as he was a decent musician himself. He played jazz piano and clarinet, accompanied musicians on sessions, wrote arrangements for Count Basie, and composed instrumentals such as 'I Remember Bird' and songs recorded by leading jazz and blues musicians. Feather also facilitated jazz activities, but some musicians regarded him as too powerful. "He did a lot for bebop," Dan Morgenstern told me. "The only thing was, the way he went about doing things for bebop was one of the things that had a lot to do with this very intense and shrill dogfight between the traditionalists and beboppers, which was unnecessary. It did a lot of harm to the music, to relations between musicians, especially to people who were caught in the middle, which were all the people who were rescued by Norman Granz [the Jewish impresario] – the Roy Eldridges, the Lester Youngs, even Art Tatum, Teddy Wilson – people who were pushed to no man's land because the conflict was between Bunk Johnson and Charlie Parker, which was nonsensical." Feather nonetheless produced recordings by Louis Armstrong, Duke Ellington and Benny Carter; it was the revivalists Feather couldn't abide, deriding them as retrogressive when bebop was driving jazz forward.

Gwyneth Cannon, Feather's sister, whom I met in London where her brother grew up, told me he was left-wing but no party joiner. At the outset of his jazz-writing career, before moving to America in the mid-1930s, he addressed sex discrimination issues, said Gwyneth: "Leonard said to himself, 'I wonder why there are no women in the jazz scene?' and he wrote a letter to *Melody Maker* and created a furore, because a lot of women wrote in and said there were, and the editor asked Leonard to write an article, and then asked him to write another, and then he was away." Feather was turned off the Jewish religion because women were segregated in synagogue.

In America, he became active in the National Association for the Advancement of Colored People. "Anything he could do to lend a hand in that line, he did do," said Gwyneth. "For instance, he would write scathing articles when someone like Billie Holiday had to go in the back entrance to a hotel... He was absolutely incensed with the way she was treated. Any sort of prejudice against black people, he spoke out wildly against."

• • • •

As a proselytiser for modern jazz, the Runyonesque jive-talking radio DJ "Symphony Sid" Torin was in his way as important as Feather and Ulanov. With him we can embark on a trail of Jewish jazz facilitators, culminating with the reputedly mob-connected Morris Levy.

Torin, from New York's teeming lower east side, was an ardent promoter of black music. With a devoted following among Harlem's black population, he was able to resist advertisers' inducements to play pop. 6 Priding himself on his bantering relationship with musicians, he championed jazz, R&B, gospel and Latin music. 7

So when modern jazz arrived, Torin was right in the thick of it, spinning bebop discs issued by the newly independent labels, many founded by Jews. The new jazz was also given exposure at the Three Deuces club on Manhattan's 52$^{nd}$ Street, its Jewish owner Sammy Kaye engaging Dizzy Gillespie for an eight-week stint. "Many listeners admitted they didn't understand the new music... but they found it enticing all the same and came back for more," notes Gary Giddins. 8

When in 1947 Charlie Parker returned to New York after a troubled period trying to break the new jazz with west coast pickup groups – winding up in a state mental institution – his Jewish manager, booking agent Billy Shaw, arranged long residences with settled personnel, including Miles Davis and Max Roach, at Three Deuces, and at Royal Roost on Broadway. Shaw also set up tours to Chicago, Washington DC, Detroit and beyond. 'Shaw 'Nuff', one of Parker's compositions, is named after his manager. As Giddins observes however, critics continued to snipe at Parker: "Leonard Feather and Barry Ulanov were the notable exceptions." 9

The struggle for acceptance persisted; Torin re-entering the frame with two other Jewish bebop devotees, New Jazz Foundation promoter Monte Kay and publicist Mal Braveman. They organised

Parker/Gillespie concerts at New York's Town Hall and persuaded Ralph Watkins – again Jewish – to present modernist gigs at his Royal Roost club. "Watkins was skeptical about the modern stuff," said Kay. "But I managed to talk him in to letting me and Symphony Sid produce a concert on an off night... we did a concert with Bird, Tadd Dameron, Miles Davis, Fats Navarro and Dexter Gordon... Dameron took over the band on a regular basis and was soon making records with the Roost Sextet on Blue Note. Bop didn't make it in a big way until a year or two later, but the Roost and Tadd played a considerable part in helping develop an audience." 10 A Roost record label was founded, this bringing in another Jewish jazz-loving wheeler-dealer, Teddy Reig; he, Watkins and Torin committing $1,000 each. 11

A new Broadway modern jazz club, Birdland, opened in December 1949 and ran at the same location until 1965. Its co-owners included the brothers Morris and Irving Levy and its manager Oscar Goodstein, all Jewish *starkers* [tough guys]. 12 Involved too were Monty Kay, later to become manager of the Modern Jazz Quartet, and Torin. When Irving Levy was knifed to death outside Birdland, the press proclaimed it "the bebop murder". That left Morris Levy in control. He opened other clubs and took over the Roost label, which became Roulette Records, before his incarceration for extortion in 1968. 13

"I can't tell you much about Morris except that despite his underworld connections, he wasn't disliked inside the music business," Dan Morgenstern said, when I asked him. That is supported by what John Levy, who was black and not Jewish despite his surname, and who managed jazz pianist George Shearing, told me: "I knew Morris very well, close relationship; I made the deal for 'Lullaby of Birdland' with his publishing company for George Shearing, because he would use the song. He was hung up with gangsters, but I can't say anything bad about him. He produced a show called The Birdland Tour and George Shearing was on it and I asked for $6,000 or $7,000 a night for it. And he said, 'I'll give you five, John, but if it does good, I'll give you $1,000 a night more for each night that it's on.' So, the tour went all over the country. About eight months later, I came into his office, I said, 'Morris, you remember the deal for George Shearing?' He said 'Yeah, how many shows did we do?' I said, 'I think we did twelve.' He said, 'Give him $12,000,' so a cheque dropped out the night for George Shearing. That was just on a word, it weren't on no paper. I did business with him, whatever acts I had to put in Birdland. I had a real good relationship with them all, even his brother who got killed."

• • • •

Jazz superfan Baroness Pannonica de Koenigswarte of the Jewish Rothschild dynasty – known as Nica, the Jazz Baroness – settled in New York around the time that bebop was germinating and became a benefactor to the black artists whose music she adored. "Her story is our story. It has to be told," proclaimed tenorist Sonny Rollins.

And it starts in her native England, where her love of jazz bloomed, listening to her father's Louis Armstrong, Gershwin and suchlike records, and accompanying older brother Victor to Duke Ellington and Benny Goodman concerts in London. Victor even entertained notions of becoming a professional musician, taking piano lessons from the visiting Teddy Wilson, with Nica watching on. For his wartime activities Victor, who had left-wing sympathies, was awarded a George Medal for bomb disposal, "claiming that years of copying Teddy Wilson and Art Tatum's chords were an ideal preparation for such tricky work". 14 Nica, meanwhile, accompanied her husband to Africa where she enlisted in the French free army to fight Nazis. 15

Post-war, Nica split from her spouse and headed across the ocean, attracted moth-like to the bright lights of jazz mecca New York. Taking residence at the Stanhope Hotel, she frequented gigs, Ira Gitler remembered her impact: "I knew Nica from the time she arrived here because people in jazz started talking about this baroness who was driving around in a Rolls-Royce." 16

She befriended many musicians but developed a special relationship with Thelonious Monk, supporting him in innumerable ways before he attained the critical acclaim his unique talent merited. "Nica was there when the critics... and half the musicians didn't get it... He loved her for that," Monk's son told Hannah Rothschild, author of a biography on her jazz-besotted great-aunt. 17

With Monk, Nica acquired a Steinway that was installed following her move to the Bolivar Hotel. There Monk composed 'Pannonica' and other tunes for his album *Brilliant Corners*, in tribute to Nica. Rothschild's book lists a pageful of compositions, by Monk and other jazz musicians, written for or inspired by Nica.

*Brilliant Corners*, Monk's third Riverside LP but the first to include his own compositions, was hailed by Nat Hentoff in *DownBeat* as "Riverside's most important modern jazz LP to date." So, *Brilliant Corners*, a turning of the corner in Monk's career? It had certainly taken an upturn, as in the year it was released, 1957, Monk's New York cabaret card was returned to him. His card had been revoked in 1948, then again in 1951, following narcotics arrests. Nate Chinen in his *JazzTimes* article The Cabaret Card and Jazz explains that a card was "a license to work in city establishments serving alcohol and thus, for a jazz musician trying to make ends meet at the time, probably the most crucial piece of identification in his or her possession... As an embodiment of the institutional distrust stirred up by jazz musicians, especially

African Americans, it's a key to our understanding of the odds those musicians faced in civil society".

In 1958, Monk was travelling to a Baltimore gig, Nica among those in the car with him, when Delaware state troopers stopped them. Marijuana was found but Nica shouldered the blame, as Monk's Jewish manager, Harry Colomby, attested: "Because of all those years he'd been an artist who had never had his due in terms of recognition and that was changing... Then this happened... she took the rap." 18 Nica was sentenced to three years imprisonment, a $3,000 fine, deportation to England on her release, and prohibition from America. On appeal, the case collapsed on a technicality as the police had not followed correct procedures. Monk's card was revoked anyway, again prohibiting him from club work. Nica's reaction to Delaware was twofold: she painted an abstract artwork based on a photograph of the lynching of two black young men, the same image that had prompted Abel Meeropol to compose 'Strange Fruit'; and she stepped up efforts to aid the jazz community. 19

Nica was never as close to Charlie Parker – 'Bird' – as she was to Monk; they were friendly acquaintances. Yet Parker may well have perceived in Nica a depth of sensitivity rare among those that idolised him. "For all the adulation heaped upon him by fans and musicians, Bird was lonely... I saw him standing in front of Birdland in the pouring rain and I was horrified... he said he had no place to go. When this happened he'd ride the subways all night," Nica recollected in a piece written for Ross Russell's *Bird Lives!* 20

Then came the fateful night in March 1955 when Parker turned up unexpectedly at her apartment, clearly ill, un-customarily declining Nica's offer of a drink. She summoned her doctor who, as Nica recalled it, stipulated: "I have to warn you that this man may die at any moment. He has advanced cirrhosis and stomach ulcers and must not leave, except in an ambulance."

Parker refused to be hospitalised. Nursed by Nica and her daughter, he died three days later. 21

"After the funeral the Baroness was... harassed by a round of scurrilous articles in the now defunct gutter press... intimating 'fowl play', and a romantic liaison between the jazz musician and the descendant of the Rothschilds... A barrage of libel suits would soon account for their disappearance," wrote Russell, for whose Dial label Parker had recorded. Russell put things in a truer perspective: "Baroness de Koenigswarter was one of Charlie's very few true friends, perhaps the only one who had no personally possessive or mercenary interest in him. She was a patron of artists and the arts in the tradition of European women who had led the great salons of the nineteenth century." 22

The black media, Hannah Rothschild rues, could be just as unsympathetic: "The black journal The Liberator published a piece accusing money-hungry agents, club owners and women like the Baroness... of making ruthless demands of hapless musicians. Nica served as a 'bitter insinuation that a rich white woman is a black man's salvation.'" Rothschild quotes too Amiri Baraka, the poet formerly known as LeRoi Jones, who dismissed Nica as "a wealthy dilettante and a groupie.'" 23

Groupie, so again, smutty sexual innuendo, but Rothschild counters: "Gossip and speculation stalked Nica but there is no evidence that any of these relationships were consummated." Trombonist Curtis Fuller, in Rothschild's book, reflects: "Black man, white woman, it had to be all about sex didn't it? That's the normal, offensive, old prejudice coming out." In all his years of friendship with Nica, Fuller testifies that he "never saw any touchy-feely stuff". 24

Nica's motivation she expressed in *Esquire*: "The music is what moves me. It has something I also hear in the playing of the Hungarian Gypsies, something very sad and beautiful. It's everything that really matters, everything worth digging. It's a desire for freedom. And in all my life, I've never known any people who warmed me as much by their friendship as jazz musicians I've come to know."

• • • •

Among the white musicians that can claim involvement in bebop early on were two young Jewish Philadelphians closely associated with Charlie Parker: drummer Stan Levey and trumpeter Red Rodney, the latter so named because of his thatch of ginger hair and orange goatee.

Bird had lost the services of Miles Davis so needed a replacement and hired Rodney, about which Ross Russell recalled: "Many musicians wondered what a young man barely out of his teens, and a white man to boot, was doing in the most distinguished combo of the day. Rodney was Charlie's own choice. His trumpet style, with its broad, soft, clear tone and fluid legato phrasing, was similar to that of Miles." 25 Parker called his new trumpet man 'Chood', a joke, by Russell's reckoning, with "mild antisemitic overtones". 26

Rodney's first trumpet was a bar mitzvah gift. His father was a working-class tinsmith who had fought with the British in Palestine, and Red began bugling in a Jewish war veterans' youth band. It was in a trade school for delinquents that he started learning trumpet in earnest.

Bebop bewitched Rodney and when he got the call from Bird, that was it – he gladly assumed the role of sorcerer's apprentice, running errands for everything Parker wanted, narcotics included, and thus began his own descent to the junk pit. When touring south, Parker dubbed his protégé Albino Red, declaring that Rodney was a black albino to avoid redneck aggravation. Unlike his idol, Rodney survived his excesses though a sizeable chunk of his life was a creative write-off, spending lengthy spells in jail through getting entangled in ingenious scams to attain funds to purchase drugs. 27

During the bebop years, Rodney had felt much at home among black musicians, even those he competed with for work in 52nd Street clubs: "We were sort of rivals... there was Miles, Fats Navarro, myself and Kenny Dorham... and I was the only white trumpeter... back then there was no problem of being white or black, among us anyway." 28 Black trumpeter Clifford Brown even sought him out for tuition. But come the 1960s – when jazz work shrank because of pop – Rodney was one of several white musicians who quit because of 'reverse racism'. 29 The phrase was coined by Leonard Feather and Barry Ulanov in a *Metronome* attack on instances of, as they saw it, black racism in jazz. 30

Rodney resurfaced in the early seventies but was disabled for a while by a stroke, causing financial distress about which he lamented: "As jazz musicians... we've been cheated all along the line. We never had the benefits that other people in American life do, the hospital insurance, even social security." This was said in a 1981 interview, after Rodney had re-launched his career, co-leading a band with trumpeter, saxophonist and flautist Ira Sullivan, whose mother was Jewish. 31 And Rodney helped with research for *Bird*, the Clint Eastwood directed Charlie Parker biopic. One event Hollywoodised in the movie was when Rodney – played by Michael Zelniker – arranges for Parker to perform with Thelonious Monk and Art Blakey at a Chassidic wedding. 32

About the drug habit that wiped out a chunk of his career, Rodney was unapologetic: "I think a lot of the good things in the music were because of drug use... When a guy is loaded and at peace, he shuts everything else out except what he's interested in. Being interested in music, he could turn out the honking of the world." 33

By no means was that a sentiment shared by every jazz musician that succumbed, as I discovered when I interviewed Stan Levey.

• • • •

I met Stan at his home in Sherman Oaks, near Los Angeles. For a guy old enough to have played with Dizzy in 1942, he looked great, face a little lined, but tall, tanned, square shouldered, hands splaying out from shirt sleeves like mechanical grabs. Stan had at one time been a heavyweight boxer, and there was still something of that about him, his unselfconscious ease of movement, a hint of danger. He fetched us a couple of icy beers and we were off.

"You've certainly jumped around careers – you started off in boxing, didn't you?"

"No, I started off as a drummer, as a kid. My father, Abe, was a boxing manager, automobile place, just by osmosis I got involved in that too."

"When did you finish with music?"

"1973. I got tired of it. Last day I did was *Rosemary's Baby*." As with many California-based jazz musicians, when work became sparse because of rock, Stan picked up film studio commissions: "And it got redundant. Other people were coming in, which is as it should be, younger composers, and they don't want to see an older guy – that's how the world runs. I saw that coming and I just did what I did. The other thing I could do was photography."

Like Red Rodney, Stan went through a junkie phase.

"Drugs? Well, we all did, sure. It was the flavour of the day."

"How did you turn that round?"

"Just stopped, saw it for what it is."

"Is there anything in what people say, that some creative people use it because it enhances performance?"

"Absolutely none. Total crap. It's just self-indulgent, that's all it is."

So what was Stan's take on Red Rodney?

"I don't think he was as good as he thought he was; I mean I've known him since he was a kid and the only reason for his notoriety was because he worked with Parker. He wasn't a great like Clifford Brown or those guys. He always sounded flat to me. He never played through the changes properly, he never got the hooks. And then he'd have a dead end and start something else. I don't mean to deride him, but I think the fact that he played with Parker, and that Parker gave him a job, made people aware of him."

"How did he get to work with Parker if he wasn't of that standard?"

"Parker would send him out to get drugs or... God knows what was going on. He was a gopher – go do this, go get that, give me your money, whatever. Parker was a demon, boy!"

"What was your relationship with Parker then?"

"We were very good friends. He was probably schizophrenic paranoid. I was nuts too, but I wasn't as crazy as him. And we lived together for a couple of years. We played all over and it finally got where I had to move, back away. You'd be talking to a chair now, if I didn't."

Stan became an aide to mobsters during those years: "Parker and the lunatics that were around in those days, you get caught up in it, and my parents were not there, anywhere, never were, and you become an unguided missile, do things you wouldn't otherwise do. I was with the gangsters in New York, the fight promoters – throw fights, stuff like that, very tough guys. Used to drive for them, I didn't know what they were doing – 'Wait there. Keep the motor running', you know? 'Okay, get four hundred bucks for twenty minutes', what the hell was that? 'Yes sir, when do we go again?' He said, 'You have a driver's licence?' I said, 'No'. He said, 'You don't need one.' These guys were unreal." Stan gestured while telling me this – indicating that he had carried a pistol.

"How did you get involved with Parker et al?"

"Well, first it was Dizzy. Dizzy's from Philly and he was working at a little club; I went out to hear him, I was about sixteen and I asked, 'Can I sit in?' He said, 'Yeah, come on'. And he liked what I did and then later on I went to work with him there, about '42, '43. Dizzy was a great teacher, it was a learning experience, for real. And Parker I met in New York, Dizzy went to New York and I soon followed, and I met Parker right away and we just had an affinity with each other. And I just started playing with him and continued on."

Scott DeVeaux, referring to the earliest white bebop players, has asserted: "George Wallington, Stan Levey and Al Haig are peripheral figures, but their very presence in otherwise all-black bands was a powerful statement – a deliberate breaching of the artificial barriers imposed by segregation." 34 Whether that was a motive or not for hiring whites, Stan got in on talent – he wasn't some token white. Stan was indebted to Max Roach, who was black, for turning him on to bop drumming, and to Parker, about whom Levey once said: "I would have followed him anywhere... over the cliff, wherever." 35

I put it to Stan that if you look back at that era, it's often presented as if every innovator was black: "Take drummers, the names that get mentioned are black – Max Roach, Kenny Clarke..."

"I'm mentioned just as much as they are. There's a book come out by Burt Korall."

I have since read Korall's *Drummin' Men* on bebop drummers. Korall, a drummer himself, lists eight in the section titled 'The Innovators', three of them Jewish, Shelly Manne, Tiny Kahn and Stan, whom Phil Brown, another drummer of that era, sees as "the first white drummer who could really play modern jazz. He had that fluid, relaxed, new kind of time. I loved his time, maybe even more than Max Roach's. A pivotal figure, he just sat down and played, and pleased the musicians". 36

Ross Russell has left us a vivid vignette of Levey in performance with Dizzy at Billy Berg's club: "When Levey goes to the wire brushes he is the fastest drummer in jazz, with a widely admired technique... he wears a ready-to-spring look. The wrists which hold the wire brushes are loose. The brushes slide down over the snare drum... Levey's hands and wrists... become a blur of movement, too fast to see. The sound of the brushes on the stretched head of the snare drum is a monstrous scratching, as on coarse sandpaper, done at dazzling speed, so the sounds runs together. The pulse is a compelling four-four."

Stan supported many supreme jazz musicians, yet here is what he told me happened when Leonard Feather invited him to a session with a musician whose technical genius was known to induce debilitating awe in his peers. "In 1944, from New York, I got a call from Leonard, to do a record date on 52nd Street in Raymond Scott studios. I didn't ask who's on it, I said, 'Yeah, I'll be there, what time?' Two in the afternoon, I drive my drums up on the elevator, I walk in the studio, and I see Art Tatum sitting at the piano. I picked up the drums, I turned around, I headed right for the elevator. Leonard says, 'What you doing?' I says, 'I'm not playing with Art Tatum, no way in the world, I'm not ready for that.' He says, 'Come along back in there, get back in, you're hired.' And I did it, and Art came over after, put his arm around me and says, 'You did real good.' He could have destroyed me, because he was the king of kings."

Stan was buddies with many black musicians yet there were those who resented it: "I played with black players all my life, I was with every black player, I was the drummer of choice, flavour of the month, Dizzy, Charlie, Coleman Hawkins, Monk I played with, Art Tatum, on and on and on, they didn't care what the hell colour I was. I tell you, a black drummer came up to Dizzy when we were on 52nd Street – and the band was phenomenal, Parker, me, Dizzy, Al Haig and Curley Russell – and the guy said, 'Dizzy, how come you got that white boy on the drums?' And Dizzy said, 'Look, when you can play better than him – not as good, but *better* – you'll have the job.' That's the way he was. Okay, the man can do the job, got the job. You can play, you can't play – pick one. If you can play you gonna work, it doesn't matter who you work with, black, blue, green or Indian. If you can't play, you're not going to work anywhere."

"Did you ever, as a musician, come up against antisemitism?"

"I heard it said about some other guys but not about me."

"What did you hear about other guys?"

"That 'they stole my style'. Well everybody steals everybody's style. If we didn't we'd all be playing like Bix. Everybody steals a little bit. I stole from Max, Max stole from Sid Catlett, Sid Catlett stole from Jo Jones – not steal but you use, you build on their ability. That's a stupid way of talking – 'he stole my music'. Stole nothing – who'd *you* steal it from?"

Stan died in 2005, aged seventy-nine.

• • • •

Burt Korall has recorded in his book that, in the early to mid-forties, four young drummers "who happened to be white" were singled out and taught by Dizzy Gillespie in the ways of modern jazz. All four – Stan Levey, Shelly Manne, Irv Kluger and Jackie Mills – also happened to be Jewish.

If that says a great deal about Dizzy's generosity of spirit, so too does Jackie Mills' experience growing up in Harlem amid the black community: "I never lived with my parents. My father, Jay Mills, a bandleader, led a successful hotel band on the West Coast. My mother was a dancer in the musical theatre. Neither wanted anything to do with me." He was shuttled around between relatives and was finally looked after by a "warm and understanding" black family in Harlem, the Faceys: "In almost every way, the Faceys were a lifesaver. They were terrific to me. Stan, their son, shared my interest in music; he was a fine pianist who worked with a number of good jazz people. Violinist Eddie South was one of them." 37 By late 1942, writes Korrall, "Mills had become deeply involved in the new music emerging in Harlem. He looked to mentors Dizzy Gillespie and Max Roach for further education." 38 Mills recognised that Roach was the "perfect drummer for this music... Max made it possible for the drummer to be far a more expressive". 38 Mills clearly was a quick learner, as he replaced Roach in what Korrall says "was the first bebop group to play downtown on 52nd Street... That Mills had the wherewithal to sit in Roach's seat with the Gillespie group does him great credit". 39 Later he moved to the west coast, where, Kirk Silsbee tells me: "He was one of the best and most versatile of the white drummers in LA before Shelly (Manne) and Stan (Levey) came to town. Jackie could play with the swing era guys and the boppers. Later on he was a presence in the studios, playing a lot of pop – even rock – dates and, of course, jazz."

• • • •

So inspirational was the riveting new jazz whose luminary was Charlie Parker that, as related by saxophonist and oboist Frankie Socolow – whose Brooklyn cellar was a hangout for bebop-oriented Jewish musicians – it was not only their idols' music they sought to emulate: "To be like Bird you had to be a junkie..." said Socolow. "He had such a big influence on people because of his playing – naturally somebody that looked at him with the most adoring eyes... would try to do anything to be like him. The only thing they couldn't do was play like him." 40

Socolow exerted a charismatic pull on the youthful Jewish jazz posse because he was, in Terry Gibbs' recollection, ahead of the game, "big time for all of us 'cause he played with Boyd Raeburn's band" – a leading swing-to-bop orchestra. 41 Socolow had moreover backed Bud Powell, the founding father of bebop piano, on a 1944 recording session.

Drummer, also vibist, Irv Kluger, whose talent budded through participation in the gatherings of the Brooklyn Jewish hepcat set: "I was fourteen when jazz become one of my major interests. Guys like Tiny Kahn, Terry Gibbs, Al Epstein and Al Cohn used to hang out in the cellar of saxophonist Frank Socolow's house on Amboy Street. We listened to the Basie band, Lester Young, Duke Ellington, Lady Day and other bands and fine singers. We jammed and rehearsed at Frank's every day. It was a close circle. The music was our special secret. We felt we were involved in something very important." 42 Kluger would go to work with Raeburn and Dizzy Gillespie, also Artie Shaw who extolled him as "a spark plug" in his small groups, including his beboppish Gramercy Five. 43

The forties saw a proliferation of young Jewish jazz modernists, among them trumpeter Paul Cohen, who spoke about how the success of Jewish swing-era role models Benny Goodman and Ziggy Elman prompted him, as a boy, to take up jazz. As a motivational factor, that may well have impelled many of the other Jewish talents emergent at the time – from New York alone, besides Cohen and the above-mentioned players, some others include Al Cohn, Johnny Mandel, George Handy, Chubby Jackson, Allen Eager, Stan Kosow, Dave Schildkraut, Danny Bank, Ed Finkel, Jerry Lloyd, and Larry Rivers, a baritone saxophonist who would make his name as an abstract expressionist painter and sculptor.

Tiny Kahn, a drummer and inspirational composer-arranger, was another. As a drummer, Kahn transcended his relative lack of technical ability as his timing was so good and his approach was musical rather than showboating, dedicated to making those around him feel good. Testimony of this comes from tenorist Stan Getz: "Tiny was one of my favorite drummers of all time, the nearest thing to Sid Catlett. He would musically get underneath you and lift you up. Most drummers batten you down from the top. And he wrote as well as he played." 44

As a composer-arranger, Kahn impressed his peers. In his short career, Kahn arranged for several leading big bands, including Charlie Barnet's swing-to-bop ensemble. Barnet would recall Kahn's "particularly beautiful treatment" of 'Over the Rainbow', as also remarked upon by multi-instrumentalist, composer, arranger and fellow band member David Amram: "Very advanced harmonically. His arrangement of Harold Arlen's 'Over the Rainbow' indicates where he was going." 45 An obsessive eater, Kahn ballooned in size and died of heart failure aged twenty-nine.

His influence, particularly on Jewish composer-arrangers, outlived him. Al Cohn and Johnny Mandel were the two great flowerings of the Kahn compositional style, jazz writer Kirk Silsbee informed me: "Tiny was the stylistic source for Cohn's writing on the east coast and Mandel's on the west coast."

About Cohn, Kirk revealed something Phil Woods told him, that "the greatest music he ever heard was in Al Cohn's living room. All had this wonderful analytical knowledge of harmony and composition, and yet there was nothing academic about his playing or writing. All very organic and musical".

It has been said that Cohn gradually came to neglect his tenor playing to concentrate on orchestration. Yet musicians had enormous respect for his playing. In a BBC television documentary about Artie Shaw, whose mid-forties band Cohn played in and arranged for, Johnny Mandel noted: "Artie would not play after Al Cohn; he loved and respected Al so much." 46

Cohn's musicality was, in Herb Geller's opinion, comparable to Charlie Parker's; as Herb explained to me: "Parker would come up with very simple things, yet they were so deep; that's the trick, simple and yet profound – Al Cohn was a master of that." Cohn was not, said Herb, the virtuoso that Stan Getz was: "He didn't play the saxophone like that, but he had a profound sense of harmony, he was a self-taught arranger, where Stan wasn't an arranger. But Al was like a real composer-arranger, and his tunes are wonderful – I did an album, just wonderful songs. One of his songs is called 'Ah-Moore' – it was like a joke – his first wife was called Marilyn Moore, so it was written for her. As a jazz ballad it's just as good as 'Round About Midnight', which was the supreme jazz ballad composition." Herb gave me a copy of this album *Herb Geller Plays the Al Cohn Songbook*, recorded in 1994 with a small band in Hollywood. One track on it, titled 'Mr Music' is Herb's tribute to Cohn. The top early post-war arrangers were all from New York, said Herb, and Al Cohn was their "guru". Compared with Getz, Herb said, Cohn had a heavy tenor sound: "It was never that good. He was always a part-time saxophone player; he'd write scores for Broadway shows, television shows, and composing, writing for record dates for six months of a year, and then he'd play for six months. So you could hear that sometimes, he was never the finished product that Stan Getz was. But his music was in some ways deeper, because he was really composing. Stan Getz was playing and composing, Al was strictly composing."

Sonny Berman, who hailed from New Haven, Connecticut, was, like Cohn, one of the many Jewish jazz modernists that featured in Woody Herman's post-war bands. A precocious talent, his life was terminated by a drug related heart attack, aged twenty-one. It was tragedy on tragedy as Sonny had taken up trumpet in memory of his older brother, a promising musician killed aged seventeen in a diving accident. As a soloist, Sonny astonished seasoned musicians with his exuberant invention, such that guitarist Chuck Wayne wrote a 12-bar tune, 'Sonny' for the young prodigy. 47 One musician Berman influenced, jazz writer Kirk Silsbee told me, was the Frisco-based trumpeter Tom Harrell: "I asked Tom Harrell if Sonny was a factor in his playing and he said, 'As a matter of fact, Sonny was on the first album I ever had, which was an anthology, and Sonny had a great influence on me.'"

Was there anything Jewish about Berman's playing? Music and comic book writer Harvey Pekar, corresponding with Ira Gitler, prompted: "Listen to a good cantor and then listen to his solos on 'Introspection' and 'Pam'. Pay attention to his interval, inflections and the way he will trail notes off at the end of a phrase." Gitler referred to another Berman track: "'Nocturne' can justifiably be added to these." 48 A record was released, years after Berman's death and retrospectively titled *Sonny Berman – Beautiful Jewish Music*, capturing him jamming with mainly Jewish musicians, as recorded by Jerry Newman. Gitler wrote the sleeve and again points up the intervals and inflections in Berman's solos "moving more than one observer to draw analogies with Jewish liturgical music".

An album titled *Sonny Berman Jam Session – 1946* brings bassist Chubby Jackson – half-Jewish, but that a very Jewish half – into the frame. Jerry Newman, who released the album on Esoteric, explains on the sleeve: "The Herman band played at the Paramount theater. Before the last show... Chubby said, 'Hey man, how about me bringing up a bunch of guys tonight and we can have a session for kicks at your place, and you can record it? I'll bring some new cats along who can play real great – in fact, I'm trying to get them in the band right now." Seven musicians showed up, three of them Jewish – Sonny, Chubby, trumpeter Marky Markowitz, who were already with Herman, and Al Cohn, who would follow. 49

Chubby, the instigator of that jam, proved pivotal in the transformation of Herman's Herd from a straight swing outfit into one of the most celebrated swing-to-bop hybrids, encouraging the leader to bring in bebop besotted musicians like himself. Chubby revelled in building up the Herd's esprit de corps: "There was never any doubt that I had positioned myself to become the cheerleader that egged every member to openly scream congratulations to one another at the completion of their individual choruses." 50

"Not the greatest bass player in the world, but an enthusiastic catalyst for the music," said Kirk Silsbee. "And he had good bands, in particular Chubby Jackson and his Fifth Dimension Jazz Band with Conte Candoli on trumpet, Frank Socolow on tenor, Lou Levy at eighteen years old on piano, who played a tremendous solo on a recording called 'Dee Dee's Dance'."

Time, the fourth dimension, has erased memory of Chubby's Fifth Dimension; Kirk was "flabbergasted at how few people know of the music that this band made – two sessions that were comparable to the best black bebop bands that were extant at the time". It was Chubby's Fifth Dimension that introduced bebop to Sweden in 1947, recording in Stockholm for radio broadcast, two months before Dizzy Gillespie recorded there.

A humorous side-feature of Chubby's band was the scatting vocal group The Three Nudnicks, which had a hit with 'Lemon Drop' (*Nudnick*, Yiddish for fool). The 'Lemon Drop' recording involved an all-Jewish line-up – Chubby, Terry Gibbs and Shorty Rogers. How it came about was one of the topics in my interview with Gibbs.

• • • •

Terry Gibbs, Chubby Jackson once said, "learned how to put a grin on music" – a tribute to Terry's effervescent vibes playing. Like his late pal Stan Levey, Terry had a boxing background, in Terry's case strictly amateur when he served in the US army during world war two. Unlike Levey, who discounted any connection between his boxing prowess and drum speed, Terry thought his own ringcraft aided his musicianship.

"I was a very good athlete, I was a baseball player – if I'd stayed with it I could have probably made semi-pro, pro. And boxing, some of my very good friends were Sugar Ray Robinson and Joe Louis. I loved boxing, I hated street-fighting, I loved the art of boxing. There was a boxer called Willie Pep who was really a boxer, they called him Will o' the wisp. He didn't want to get hit and neither did I. When I boxed, I watched your legs, what you call peripheral vision, anticipate, if you're going to move your left foot, some part of your body's got to move with it, so I watched feet, that had something to do with it. And I used to teach that boxing had a lot to do with playing the vibes, when you move one part of your body, one stick, the other one has to go somewhere."

Terry hails from a Russian Jewish Brooklyn family steeped in klezmer: "My father was a bandleader in the Jewish business, played clubs dates, weddings, bar mitzvahs, banquets. When I was a kid I used to go out and play with him." One musician who worked in his father Abe Gubenko's band was the revered klezmer clarinetist Dave Tarras. Another was Terry's brother Sol Gubenko, who changed his name to Sol Gabe when he formed his own klezmer band, and who Terry told me was probably the best Jewish-style drummer he ever heard – "the Art Blakey of the Jewish circuit. He could play you off the stage and incidentally, played great xylophone. He could play Jewish things on xylophone, or on vibes when he came to visit me, and bent notes, I would always keep looking, *bent notes*, how do you bend notes [on vibes]? He would make it sound like a clarinet player would bend them, couldn't understand how he did it. But he had that feel. It's something you're born with, that whole Russian Jewish feel."

In the early sixties, Terry recorded a hybrid bebop and klezmer album, *Terry Gibbs Plays Jewish Melodies in Jazztime*. Two bands were involved, Terry's jazz quartet and Sol's klezmorim. The jazz band included pianist Alice McCord, soon to become Alice Coltrane, making her recording debut. Alice was black but as sleeve writer Les Davis disclosed: "Terry said the Jewish group was amazed with her comprehension and feeling for the rhythms of their music." The klezmer group comprised Sol on piano, trombonist Sam Kutcher and clarinetist Ray Musiker.

"That," said Terry, "is authentic Jewish band playing, my brother, a great trombone player from the old days, and a great clarinet player. What I did on this actually, just like you have Latin music using a conga drummer, well I had that [Terry claps out a snappy klez beat with his hands] behind me when I played the jazz thing. Alice played on this, and she sold the record dates for me. She was just getting into Coltrane before they got married – I was the matchmaker on the marriage."

I burst out laughing at this image of Terry as a *shadchen*

"Yes, she was in my band, she recorded four albums with me. Remember, a lot of these songs hadn't been put on paper, that traditional thing, but I wrote a few myself because I come from that whole kind of music. So we used the Jewish band playing the introductions sometimes, and the endings, and in the middle we just played straight-ahead jazz with that beat played behind me."

"This is the only album you did that? How did it come about?"

"I always wanted to do that kind of thing, these songs with the Jewish beat behind me. Quincy Jones happened to be the A&R man on that thing, he produced the album. Quincy sat in the booth, wearing a *yarmulke* [skullcap] and a *tallas* [prayer shawl], and in the middle of the date, Lalo Schifrin bought me a box of matzos. It was a funny, beautiful date."

McCord knocked everyone out, said Terry: "She actually plays all those middle eastern runs."

"How much preparation did she need, given that she had no grounding in Jewish music?"

"Very simple, she was playing that way anyhow, she was just getting into John Coltrane, at the end when he was just starting to get into all those runs, a lot of harmonic runs, minor runs. And she played the heck out of it, she played that way even when she played straight bebop."

I shifted the conversation to Terry's old employer Benny Goodman, who had a reputation as a difficult taskmaster.

"He loved me, he really did. He called everybody Pops, he couldn't remember everybody's name; he called me Gubenko, he loved that name, he loved my telling jokes and he had a lot of respect for me. These were my young cocky days, I was in my early twenties and I gave him the utmost respect because I was in awe just playing with him, but when he got out of hand, with me he couldn't because I almost hit him. I tell you one story. We had just put a little group together, we were going to open up in Halifax, Nova Scotia. And when we got there, there were ten thousand people squashed against the stage. Benny Goodman was out in left field at the time, he didn't know where he was that day, he was gazing out at the stage. And they put some mikes underneath my vibes kind of loud. When we finished playing the song, he waited till ten thousand people started applauding and he said, 'Goddamn it Gubenko, shut that mike off, that's too loud.' Now in my early days, that was a way you could embarrass me. When I got that burning feeling in my tummy, I would hit you – I would knock you out. And I got that burning feeling but thank goodness I had learnt the business from my father, that's not the thing you do.... So, I started to walk off the stage; he said, 'Where you going Gubenko?' I said, 'I want to talk to you Benny' – I was smiling through the whole thing. He called an intermission, we had just played one song. And I called him every dirty word then went back on stage and everything was okay. But he was afraid of me because of that, so he never picked on me."

Terry moved westward in 1957 and secured a weekly date at the Seville Club, Santa Monica, for his sixteen-piece Dream Band. I learned about the Dream Band through Kirk Silsbee: "It was a watershed for west coast jazz, great musicians, good charts, and a lot of the guys who came in and out of the group loved being there."

As west coast jazz historian Ted Gioia bemoaned however, the Dream Band was "virtually unknown, especially outside southern California, during its brief existence. It never went on the road... its most important recordings were not released commercially until almost thirty years after the band broke up". 51 That they were released at all, said Terry, was largely down to the persuasion of Buddy Rich, whose 1948 band he had worked in: "He and Shorty Rogers used to come over my house – I had the recordings on reel-to-reel – and say, 'Put those out, they're the greatest band in the world', and I'd say, 'No, nobody can hear them but you and I, my friends.' But they talked me into it."

Terry turned 98 in October 2022, and a Terry Gibbs Legacy Band with his son Gerry on drums was scheduled to perform music from his songbook in June 2023.

· · · ·

Mel Lewis, who played in Terry Gibbs' Dream Band, was a Tiny Kahn devotee who developed into what Connie Kay, drummer of the Modern Jazz Quartet, said was maybe the best big band drummer he ever heard. 52 His pedigree for that role could hardly be topped. His friend, trombonist Bob Brookmeyer, revealed that, "Basie hired him when Mel was sixteen but he couldn't take a white Jewish boy down South. Still might have trouble." 53

Kirk Silsbee pointed me in the direction of the Gerry Mulligan Concert Jazz Band recordings: "Lewis is just right on the money for those demanding charts, swinging all the time, shading just right, always stopping at the place he should stop, starting right – just phenomenal." And from Stan Levey I got a drummer's perspective on Lewis: "One of the most musical, fantastic, great ear, different side of the arrangements, really keeps it together."

Lewis, who grew up in Buffalo where his father was a drummer, in 1957 moved to Los Angeles and was a major figure west coast jazz before settling in New York. There, in the mid-sixties, he co-founded the Mel Lewis-Thad Jones Orchestra. It was, by Silsbee's reckoning, a leg-up for Jones: "Yes, he's writing an occasional chart for this band, for that band, but there's really no jazz business for him to showcase his great work. So he and Mel Lewis start this band. All the great players that are around in New York who want to play show up." That included Eddie Daniels, a Jewish clarinetist and tenor saxophonist, who enthused: "It showed there could be that kind of love in a... band that had whites and blacks and Jews and Catholics and every combination, but nothing that had any weight other than the way you played." 54

Such a large ensemble survived in the rock age because Max Gordon, a Jewish club owner with a music-first policy, gave it a Monday night residency at the Village Vanguard, and because it relied heavily on musicians prepared to play for fun or union scale. Judging by the the band's 1966 debut recordings, issued on the 2016 2-CD set *all my yesterdays* (Resonance HCD-2023), the musicians and audience are having a ball.

Silsbee informed me about an interview Lewis did on his relationship with Jones. "Thad had been gone some years when Mel gave this interview. Lewis was dwelling on their differences and difficulties. Lewis gave him a Jewish star, he never wore it. Thad thought [Ugandan dictator] Idi Amin was a great figure to be revered; this stuck in the craw of Lewis. Thad essentially just walked away from the band the two of them had given birth to, struggled with for over twenty years, this wonderful band... And Thad and Mel's perseverance, they willed this orchestra into life and keep it on its legs and make something of it and record and take it around the world. What a success story. And one day Thad just walks away from it, goes to Europe, moves in with some Scandinavian woman, leaves his family back in the US, doesn't say, 'Mel, I've got a problem, let's make a change,' nothing, and Mel Lewis had some great frustrations." Renamed as the Mel Lewis Jazz Orchestra, the Village Vanguard nights continued into the 1980s. Lewis died in 1990.

• • • •

If Charlie Christian's guitar playing anticipates bebop, Barney Kessel probably has as much claim as anyone to being acknowledged as the musician who picked up the stylistic plectrum that Christian ceded through death, by fully adapting the guitar for modern jazz. There is certainly historical logic to that as Christian was Kessel's mentor. Both hailed from Oklahoma and became buddies in defiance of segregation.

Kessel had grown up in Muskogee, a place "where jazzmen and cowboys lived side by side". 55 As Kessel recalled: "Where I was born, the guitar was called a 'starvation box'. My earliest recollection... was hearing it played by tramps, hoboes and wanderers. As I grew older, I became aware of the guitar being used by many amateur musicians as they played and sang western songs." Inspired by the local sounds, he began playing aged twelve and was undeterred when his father, a Russian Jewish bootmaker, busted Barney's first guitar arguing that his son should be spending more time on homework. Increasingly drawn to jazz, at fourteen Barney was performing professionally as "the only white guy in an all-black band ... They helped me to understand how to play jazz". 56

His bandmates urged him to play guitar "like a horn" the way Christian did but it wasn't until the two met and jammed in 1940 that the advice began to make sense to young Barney. Kessel said it was a black waiter at the club where he played three nights a week that tipped off Christian about him. With Christian's boss Benny Goodman out of action recovering from an accident, Christian headed back to Oklahoma and Kessel was elated when his idol turned up unexpectedly where he was gigging and "registered his approval of what we were doing". Christian sat in and "took some breathtaking solos" on Kessel's guitar. 57 Although several years senior and a major star, Christian invited Kessel out to share a meal, though because of segregation this proved difficult so, wrote Kessel, "We finally settled on some restaurant where we had to eat in the kitchen." Christian suggested they jam the next day and it was then Barney decided that no matter how much he admired Christian or other guitarists, they would "remain only influences" that he would absorb "rather than being absorbed by them". 58

He lit out for LA, subsisting for a while as a dishwasher, then got his break when Ben Pollack hired him for the Chico Marx band. 59 In 1944, Kessel was the only white musician in Norman Granz's award-winning documentary *Jammin' the Blues*. Warner Brothers, anxious about distributing the film down south, forced Granz to go to great lengths to disguise his using a white player. "They went into having me in the shadows," Kessel revealed. 60 Another expedient was staining Kessel's hands with berry juice. As Kessel noted, in the film he ends up looking darker than tenorist Lester Young. Kirk Silsbee described it to me as a wonderful film that Norman Granz produced for black audiences: "A black short film like this could only be shown in black theatres. Kessel plays this wonderful fast extension of Charlie Christian. He's showing in that movie that he clearly has digested the Charlie Christian legacy, the contribution to the jazz guitar and is proving to be one of the great emissaries of that style."

Guitarist Martin Taylor, who knew Kessel, proclaimed him the "true heir of Christian" who could "play harmony and the tune at the same time". 61 Humphrey Lyttelton, on BBC radio, contended that when Kessel was in rhythm guitar mode, he even surpassed Christian. Oscar Peterson, of whose trio Kessel was a founding member, said he "opened up new avenues of sound for us. His prodigious technique and harmonic sense allowed me to write arrangements which not only facilitated on flowing lines together, but also contrapuntal lines between which Barney would weave in and out". Jewish jazz guitarist Joshua Breakstone goes so far as to say: "Barney Kessel, when it comes down to it, was the greatest of all." 62

· · · ·

Ruby Braff, a Jewish cornetist from Boston, began his career when bebop was happening but largely eschewed post-Parker innovations, rooting his music in lovingly personal, beautifully sculpted adaptations of earlier styles, each note enunciated with bell-like clarity.

This brings us to 'mainstream jazz', a term coined by jazz writer Stanley Dance in the 1950s to describe musicians whose playing adhered to pre-war styles though increasingly incorporating modernist inflections. Over the years, what is understood as the mainstream has expanded to embrace facets from later developments in jazz and as such, any list of Jewish American musicians that have been mainly active in the jazz mainstream would be far too extensive to cover comprehensively in this book. Braff however was clearly one of the first.

A disciple of Louis Armstrong, Braff contributed little to the evolution of jazz but his was one of the most distinctive instrumental voices; you can tell within a bar or two that it's him. Braff was gigging in London, I had got hold of his hotel phone number and steeled myself for the interview before I dialled, well aware of Braff's reputation, having read his acerbic exchange with Jim Godbolt in *Jazz at Ronnie Scott's* magazine.

The interview began as I feared – myself awkward and on the defensive, while Braff sounded gruff, spiky, querulous across the receiver. "Nobody thinks about Jews," he growled.

I mentioned the considerable Jewish contribution to jazz not only in the US, but in countries such as Britain too.

"All the big bandleaders in Britain were trying to do was copy American bands. Jazz is an American language," he snapped back.

Safer, I thought, to ask him about the great songwriters, whose tunes formed a large part of Ruby's repertoire. His music, he once said, was simply an "adoration of the melody".

He told me how contemptuous he was of many jazz musicians' own compositions: "What can they play in jazz but songs by the great craftsmen. Who cares about the others? It was very, very healthy this, for music in America. They were all out there listening to Louis Armstrong and all kinds of people, they had European classical music to listen to. Many people who try to play music prefer to make up their own junk. There's no comparison."

"Ruby, despite your orientation to older forms of jazz, I note you played with bebop legends."

"I played with Bird and Gillespie; I don't call them more modern. There's nobody more modern than Armstrong."

What then did he think of the beboppers' subversions of the popular songs he loved?

"Legally they could do it because they were not playing the melody. 'How High the Moon' is a much better melody that be-do be-do be-do bebop. The best record Charlie Parker made was a Cole Porter tune." 63 Braff told Steve Voce: "I just looked at Dizzy and Charlie as guys that had their own wonderful styles… but I think that anyone else that tried to play like that always sounded silly to me."

Musically, Braff's sincerity was manifest in the way he shunned fashion, even though in the 1950s it periodically put him out of work. As he said then: "I can't get any bookings unless I change my style – lose my identity and play like Miles Davis." 64

Ruby told me he loathed all ethnic music: "I don't like Jewish music, I like American music." Yet, sometime after the interview, I acquired a 1956 Braff LP with Dave McKenna on piano, and there's a track, 'Blue Prelude', on which I swear Ruby's phrasing invokes the sound of a cantor.

We moved on to the racial tensions. Ruby had grown up in a black part of Boston. As a young man, it was black drummer Sid Catlett that brought him to New York in his band and helped open doors for him. 65 And Ruby told me: "There's very little antisemitism in my profession. There's always been some. When I first came to 52nd Street, black and white were always playing together and having a ball. Black people were given a harder time. Who can blame black people for the terrible resentment they have?"

When Ruby personally experienced instances of racial aggravation, he simply "took a left and went elsewhere. I've worked with black and white all my life. They're not making me guilty. I was a person always in the corner of people who suffer racially of any kind. Just as evil is reverse racism".

Ruby seemed to have warmed towards me by the close of the interview, giving me his Cape Cod number so I could call him when I got to America – "but make it in the early hours of the morning" – a jazz owl to the end.

By the time I made the States weeks later, Dan Morgenstern advised me that Ruby was in a bad way so not to try to contact him. "Ruby's one of a kind," said Dan, "a definite anachronism. Now we're so accustomed in the post-Wynton era to people who draw on the tradition but when Ruby came up in the early fifties – and a lot was made of that in the jazz press, more than was really called for – he was a young trumpet player that was playing in the mainstream tradition. He knew Charlie Parker and may have played with him in a jam session. But Ruby wasn't an anti-modernist, it was just that the way he wanted to play was like Bobby Hackett and Louis. Ruby was a curmudgeon – there was a tee-shirt out once, 'I had a beef with Braff'. A little bit of that has to do with his size – he's pugnacious. He grew up in a poor section of Boston. He was a professional very early, playing in not very friendly places, neighbourhood beer joints; he says that they tried to pass him off as a midget because it was illegal. He never went to college. He's very bright but I think he had a complex about not being educated. And I think he had the same thing about music; it was not until mid-life when he decided to finally learn to read and write music. It wasn't that anybody picked on him, but he had a bit of an inferiority complex." Dan contrasted Braff with another thorny Jewish jazzman, Stan Getz, "a much more complex character than Ruby". Once you had figured Ruby out, said Dan, "if you didn't take offence when he cursed you, he would turn around and be okay". Ruby died in February 2003, shortly after my return to England.

# Chapter 10: Blowing hot and 'cool'

Cool jazz, the *New Grove Dictionary of Jazz* tells us, is a term applied to "diverse styles of modern jazz variously perceived as subdued, understated, or emotionally cool". It is often derided as predominantly white and associated, not wholly accurately, with the 1950s west coast modern jazz scene. In considering the issues however, let us start there, as a considerable number of Jewish jazz musicians were involved.

Herb Geller, who grew up in Los Angeles, told me the other Jewish guys he played with there were mostly from Brooklyn: "Johnny Mandel, Shorty Rogers, Shelly Manne, there was a group of them. There was a joke. I was a Shelly Mannester and Shelly said, 'Are you from New York or LA, because he knew that I lived in New York for a couple of years, and I told him actually I was born in LA. Well, he said, 'Would you mind if when I announce you I say you're from New York?' I said, 'I don't care what you say'. So he goes, 'This is a typical west coast band – on piano from Chicago, Russ Freeman, on trumpet Conte Candoli from Indiana, on bass, Monty Budwig from Nebraska, on alto, Herb Geller from New York, and you can tell by the way I talk that I'm from Texas.' That was part of the joke because he was a New Yorker.

"What we were doing was making fun of this whole west coast thing that the record companies started. I was born in Los Angeles but almost everyone that I played with migrated to Los Angeles because it's a much better climate and not so much of a hustling scene. New York is really a rat race, especially with musicians or people in the entertainment industry. There's only so much work, and so many wanting the work, that they're fighting each other. So sometimes it becomes not so much how good you are, but how good is the business end of it. And if you don't have too much money, it's much better to be in Los Angeles."

Was there not a distinctive sound, though, prevalent on the west coast?

"Yeah, if you talk to the average person about what the west coast scene was in the fifties, they'd say the music from the east coast was harder because it was mostly black musicians. But what they'd do – say it was Miles Davis or Art Blakey – somebody'd say 'do a session', so they'd come to the studio with no idea what they're going to do, and somebody says, 'Do you know this tune?' and they'd say yeah and play it, and now and again there'd be a discrepancy, the bass player wouldn't play the right notes, or the piano player who had an idea for the bridge that was different from the horn player. But they'd get through it and some great music – if it was simple tunes – came from this. So the difference in Los Angeles is they'd prepare the music different. Before they'd call it and guys come to the studio and figure out what they're gonna play, they'd call an arranger or composer, or both together, and plan the thing and get on the record date and have a more finished product.'"

What must be considered is that the west coast lifestyle may have impacted on much jazz produced out there. For white jazz musicians that could compose, arrange, proficiently sight-read, play two or more instruments, Los Angeles provided an idyllic environment. Besides the climate and topography, there were lucrative work opportunities in the film, TV and recording studios.

"It would only make sense that the jazz many of us played would sound the way we felt," Dave Pell, a Jewish saxophonist and bass clarinetist who settled north of Los Angeles, told Marc Myers. "We were blessed. The musicians were all playing in harmony because we were having a great time. You could say that all of that spirit and feeling came out in the music that writers called West Coast jazz." 1.

Jewish composer, arranger and trombonist Johnny Mandel told Myers that, following his move west, "when I arrived in LA, I found that many of the tenor saxophonists were too laid back... My metabolism was West Coast but my sensibility was still East Coast... I spent a lot of time with the black players out here. I had just finished working with Basie... and the guys here were in awe and invited me right into their groups." But, he rued, "the segregation in Los Angeles was terrible". 2

As Myers makes clear, although black and white jazz musicians generally respected each other, and white players would patronise Central Avenue black clubs, racist cops frequently intervened. Progressively, the harassment and other institutional barriers made integration among jazz musicians more difficult, particularly after the clubs shut down and black musicians moved further out into the segregated suburbs. The city's spawling logistics alone, and the lack of a culturally booming downtown, were further impediments to black/white fraternisation. Additional factors then, that may well have affected the direction taken by jazz out west. "Most West Coast jazz sounded like the jazz in New York but with no balls," said Mandel. 3

Terry Gibbs however, when I showed him one New York critic's dismissal of this "west coast... mostly white" development in jazz, was typically forthright: "Full of shit! What would he say about Miles? Shorty Rogers played the Miles Davis kind of school way of playing. So what to call that, west coast jazz? These labels! It's all according to who you play with. Shelly Manne was a hard swing player, his groups were hard swinging groups."

Miles Davis goes to the core of this debate as he is the assertively black musician that headed up the 1948 Impressions in Modern Music nonet sessions retrospectively issued by Capitol as *The Birth of the Cool*. The sessions were recorded in New York and first publicly performed there. What brought these musicians together – several of them Jewish – was a desire for a more nuanced, structured and contemplative take on the bebop template, expanding the tonal palette by experimenting with instruments associated with orchestral music.

Miles had just left Charlie Parker and, establishing a pattern that would recur throughout his career, was looking to move things on. One Chicago Jewish musician he hired was Lee Konitz.

• • • •

"When I heard the black expression – anger for the past and so on – I felt the Jewish oppression, I'm sure. But basically, I just wanted to learn the music," Lee Konitz said about his formative years. 4 And he told *Crescendo*: "Benny Goodman had to be one of the first bands I identified with. Jewish and white – how could I miss?"

Initially, Konitz took up clarinet, presumably in emulation of Goodman, but switched to alto saxophone which he thought more suitable for the new jazz. Konitz was as beguiled by Charlie Parker as other young post-war jazz musicians but is recognised as the first modern jazz altoist bold and imaginative enough to shift the focus significantly.

He was in Claude Thornhill's band that prefigured the Birth of the Cool stylistic and instrumentation shifts, and in baritone saxophonist Gerry Mulligan's opinion, Konitz was a genius: "Lee had joined Claude's band in Chicago and knocked us all out, including Bird, with his originality." 5

Miles Davis, challenged by black contemporaries about hiring whites for the nonet, fired back: "If a guy could play as good as Lee Konitz played – that's who they were mad about most, because there were a lot of black alto players around – I would hire him every time, and I wouldn't give a damn if he was green with red breath." 6 Leonard Feather observed: "Konitz bore the same relationship to Parker and Miles Davis to Gillespie in bop's evolution to its cool phase... Davis was the counterpart in Konitz's tonal approach, smaller and more languid that that of the early boppers." 7

Konitz's playing was smoother than Parker's, more rhythmically even, vibrato-less, "much like the French classical approach to the instrument", notes musicologist J Bradford Robinson. 8 His sound evolved continuously over the years, by his own admission getting closer to Parker at times, at other times, as on *The Lee Konitz Duets* (Milestone, 1967) that captures him in duologues with sympatico collaborators, flirting with the avant-garde. One of Konitz's loveliest compositions, 'Kary's Theme', named after his daughter, was based on an old traditional Jewish tune and opened his 1956 album *Inside Hi-Fi*. It was reprised on the 2010 *Live At The Village Vanguard*, the Jewish strain accentuated by the bowed solo of Jeff Denson, the bassist in Konitz's Minsarah quartet (*Minsarah* – Hebrew for prism).

In *DownBeat*, Konitz contrasted the attributes of two saxophonists he admired, Parker and tenorist Warne Marsh, and in so doing revealed much about his own music philosophy: "Warne was one of the most real players in jazz. When he played, it was all substance and no attitude to speak of. I heard attitude in Charlie Parker, except that he was a genius so he could compensate for that – or cover it. Attitude meaning that there was something extra-musical involved... Over-dramatic emotionality. Coming from the cool system, you can take that with a grain of salt. I love passionate expression, but sometimes it felt that all the emphasis was on trying to emote on the sleeve... What really gets to me is hearing a straight reading with great notes, sound and rhythm feeling. Warne was capable of doing that more than anybody I know."

Marsh worked with Konitz in the forties Lennie Tristano sextet that anticipated the freer jazz of the sixties, the personnel also including Jewish drummer Arnold Fishkind. And the saxophonists collaborated in the ensuing decades. Stanley Crouch, when I met him, coupled his admiration of Konitz with that of Marsh. About Konitz, he said: "An original; during that period, I think he was the only guy who was playing in a style that was different from Charlie Parker who was out of that generation. Now he and Warne Marsh, both Jews, and they're both highly original players who were tutored by Lennie Tristano and whose influence was not really that big until the sixties when Wayne Shorter in particular became enamoured of both Warne Marsh and Lee Konitz."

"What did Shorter pick out in their music?"

"I think he picked up the playing through the bar lines, the tone freedom that they played with, a certain flexibility that they had, and so he put that together with what he got from Sonny Rollins and Coltrane and he had a whole bag that was very different from other people. I mean if you listen to him playing on those 'I Got Rhythm' changes at the Plug Nickel with Miles I think in 1966, the Warne Marsh influence is all over what he's playing. And the piano player Walter Davis told me that in the late fifties, Wayne Shorter was telling people they should listen to Lennie Tristano, Warne Marsh and Lee Konitz, those guys, yeah, definitely."

Others I asked about Konitz included Dan Morgenstern, Loren Schoenberg, and Dick Katz. Katz, who worked alongside Konitz, extolled him as "one of the greatest improvisers by far," and as a "free spirit who broke away from the domination of Lennie Tristano and constantly sought new people to play with, playing songs, and abstractions". It was, said Katz, "like a mental game" trying to figure out what Konitz was playing.

Morgenstern focused mainly on Konitz's impact in Europe: "When I was in the army, stationed in Germany in '51 to '53, everywhere I went there were German bands playing jazz, the saxophone players sounded like Lee. There was a very good Austrian tenor player in Germany, Hans Kollar, influenced by him. Some of the Poles like [Zbigniew] Namyslowski. He was a strong influence in post-war Europe. As for how strong an influence he was here, he was obviously an influence on Paul Desmond, although Paul – who was half Jewish – had something in common with Lee, they had a kind of sensitivity that they shared." About Desmond's ethnicity, I refer readers to information I have uncovered in the footnotes section of this book. 9

In Loren Schoenberg's estimation, Konitz was one of the most influential of all jazz altoists: "Maybe my example is representative. I'm only a tenor saxophone player but I play the alto on occasion, and the first time I went to play a job on the alto, I went to play a solo and what came out, totally unconsciously, was like a version of Lee Konitz – a very poor version of course. But it just came out, I never tried to sound like him, I'd hardly ever played the alto, but I loved his music, I studied with him. 10 All good young saxophone players would be foolish not to listen to him. He's one of the great originals on the alto saxophone... In my estimation every one of the current generation sounds like Benny Carter, Ornette Coleman, Charlie Parker or Lee Konitz."

Konitz died, aged 92, from pneumonia related to the Covid virus.

• • • •

Another all-time great Jewish jazz musician was Stan Getz, but before I come to him, some thoughts on the so-called cool school. The main inspiration, even before Miles and his nonet, was another African American, Lester Young. Tenor saxophonists in particular – Getz among them – can be said to be modernist descendants of Young, who made his name as a star soloist in the thirties' Count

Basie band. Some would take it even further back: Benny Goodman was convinced that Chicago tenorist Bud Freeman, who was half-Jewish and whose career began in the twenties, had influenced Young: "I always thought it was Bud Freeman. The triplets, you know. The way he used his vibrato... I loved playing with him: he was one with whom the chemistry was right." 11 Benny Green, the English and Jewish jazz pundit and baritone saxophonist, pointed out however that: "Young has denied ever being influenced by Freeman." Green did pick out striking concurrences in their styles but thought the likeliest explanation was that they may have independently worked towards identical ends. 12 However that may be, it is interesting that Miles Davis numbered "that white dude, Bud Freeman" among the musicians whose "running style of playing" he liked. 13

What seems clear from all this is that to portray cool as white in contradistinction to black is simplistic. And as seen with Miles, also Konitz, to depict it as west versus east coast is lazy thinking.

• • • •

Stan Getz resided only briefly in California in the 1950s but recorded there two albums that Verve issued as *West Coast Jazz* and *Getz and the Cool Sounds*. Marketed that way, Getz was often upheld as one of the leading exponents of cool jazz.

Which was probably what Cannonball Adderley was thinking when he observed, "you can certainly tell Stan Getz is white, as contrasted to say, Coltrane". 14 Yet Coltrane, who admired Getz, said: "Let's face it, we'd all like to sound like that – if we could."

I'm not sure anyway that cool ever adequately encapsulates the warmth of the sounds that outflowed from Getz's horn.

Dick Katz, who played with him, told me: "This guy had several different personalities. He could be evil beyond belief, and he could charm the birds out of the trees. He was a womaniser, a major drug addict, he was one of the greatest players jazz has ever produced, regardless of colour. And he was not somebody that I ever felt I could get close to."

Getz's music is what posterity must remember him for. "My life is music," he said. "And in some vague, mysterious way, I have always been driven by a taut inner spring that has propelled me to almost compulsively reach for perfection... mostly at the expense of everything else in my life". 15

Born to poor Russian Jewish parents, he grew up in the Bronx during the Depression. The family tried their luck in Los Angeles where Getz recalled: "They still had ads in the *LA Times* for renting apartments reading 'No children, no pets, no Jews'. We lived in the back of a barbershop until we found a Jewish building owner." 16 His father, who scavenged for work as a printer, found the cash to buy the youngster a "silver, going on green" alto sax when Stan turned thirteen. Graduating to tenor, Getz rapidly established himself in Woody Herman's band, winning fame for his lovely balladry on 'Early Autumn'. And Getz is the name most associated with the popularisation of bossa nova, beginning with *Jazz Samba*, Getz's blowing so sensual on this 1962 release.

Another milestone was the 1961 album *Focus*. Getz commissioned arranger Eddie Sauter to write and score an extended work for him and *Focus* was the outcome. In Sauter's words: "His only instruction was, 'Do what you think is right.'" 17 What Sauter, a devotee of twentieth century classical composers, conjured up was a forty-three minute seven-piece opus on which Getz improvised over a massive symphonic string orchestra, the only jazz accompaniment piano, bass, plus, on two tracks, drums. This ensemble, performing Sauter's intriguingly strange and somewhat filmic compositions, swings, Getz's tenor the cynosure or 'focus'.

"One of the greatest players ever," was Stanley Crouch's verdict, when I asked him. "*Focus*, that's one of the grand masterpieces of the post-Charlie Parker jazz. That's unbelievable – the level he's playing on there, not many saxophone players could have gone on after... Getz was such a good musician, and such an arsehole, that even the white guys don't speak up for him."

Stan Levey urged me to seek out another album, *For Musicians Only*, recorded in LA in 1956: "You've got to have it; forget the others. You never heard a record like this, I'm telling you – Dizzy, Stan Getz, Sonny Stitt, me, Ray Brown, Herb Ellis and John Lewis, and Stan wipes them all out. He puts them all to bed, turns the lights out. Every musician's got that album, guaranteed." Levey's jazz drummer son Bob remembered his father telling him: "It was virtually a live real bebop session, nothing worked out, just play by the seat of your pants."

What struck me when I asked saxophonists Herb Geller and Jeremy Shoham about Getz was just how unique was his talent. Herb, who did a couple of tours and a big band recording with Getz, said: "Really, he was probably the best saxophone player – well, Charlie Parker – but as the finished saxophone player, I think Stan Getz is just the most incredible – technically, his timing, his ear, he had a photographic memory, he knew so many songs and he could play them in any key. No other musician I can think of, not even Charlie Parker, could play so many songs and in any key."

No one but Getz could have pulled off the *Focus* album, Herb added: "He was playing without a rhythm section, he had to keep the timing and it was very demanding, very challenging music, and also he had to get a very pure classical sense, and most jazz musicians can't adapt to that, but he was a complete virtuoso, he could do anything. It's not just the technique, it's the sound, he had it all. Now he told me that he didn't know that much about harmony, and it's true, but his ear was such that he could just adapt to anything. A lot of musicians play by ear, but you can hear it because they'll make mistakes, and I never heard him make a harmonic mistake. Bossa nova he played in a very, very gentle way, a loving way; a lot of jazz musicians would have played it too heavily. He knew how to fit into every possible situation. A lot of bebop musicians could only really play bebop; put them in a situation where they had to play a little more discretely, or more finesse, or subdued, they'd be lost, they'd say, 'That's not me', and then they'd go off on their own thing, but it wouldn't fit. But Stan Getz could fit. He did the things with Chick Corea, which later on Corea had hits with, Getz did them better than the other guys."

Jeremy Shoham made a critical point, that Getz was a completely individual, underivative player, his selection of notes unique: "Although Parker influenced him a lot you can't necessarily hear that in his playing. But what was new in Getz was that he was not a formulaic player in any way. He didn't use typical ii-V-I structures in improvisation, he was a completely intuitive player, and startlingly original. His lines were just his lines. So many bebop players, you recognise the lines they've learnt from other players; it would be hard to analyse what Getz does and teach it, unlike Parker, Coltrane and Brecker – you could start to be academic about what they do. With Getz it was much less easy to do that. So I guess that's saying that he was less systematic in what he did."

Extraordinary as Getz was, Loren Schoenberg told me it was not like talking about an Ornette Coleman or Lester Young, musicians who influenced the whole way that the music was played, and everybody on every instrument reacting to what they did: "Getz was a marvellous tenor saxophone player; did everybody hear him? Yes. John Coltrane admired Stan Getz – that's in his own handwriting. I can't hear any influence of Stan Getz on John Coltrane. I know John Coltrane's records fore and after, I know Stan Getz's fore and after and there's no influence at all. I can hear what the young Coltrane would have found very attractive about Stan Getz's playing, a tremendous technique, as Sonny Stitt had, but where Stitt was king of the mechanistic and locked into licks, playing the same thing over and over with great ingenuity, with Stan Getz you always had a feeling of free-flowing spontaneity, and not only that but Stan Getz was a pioneer of a certain kind of overtone effect and fingering things which he adapted from Lester Young, which he did in a different way. I think some of those things, especially if you listen to some of the things that Stan Getz made at Storyville in 1951, '52, you can hear things that I think Coltrane picked up and used.

"But that," added Loren, "leads us to the very important question: what does an influence mean? It's a question of degree? Major figures can be influenced by lesser figures."

. . . .

"All the best jazz drummers are Jewish."

That's what a klezmer drummer I met at a Yiddish swing rehearsal in New York told me. Some days later, I mentioned it to Dick Katz; his response was pointed: "Garbage!"

Indubitably though, many top drummers in American jazz have been Jewish and Dick spoke in highest terms about two I now wish to juxtapose – Shelly Manne, who became a leading figure out west, and Buddy Rich. About Manne, he said: "One of the greatest jazz drummers in history and never got his due, maybe because he's white – that's possible. I regret that I never knew Shelly Manne better. I played with him only once, a gig with Stan Getz in a club called Basin Street West and somebody recorded it – there's a couple of tunes on some obscure CD from the broadcast."

Manne on the one hand and Rich on the other make a fascinating contrast that goes to the heart of conflicting philosophies about drumming.

Let me start with Rich, as he was pretty much my entrée to jazz, in 1970, when I caught his big band in a live broadcast from the London Palladium. Before that, my main exposure to jazz was listening to swing era hits on my dad's *Reader's Digest* sets. I liked this yesteryear jazz but it in no way rivalled my adoration of the great chart acts of my generation, the Beatles, Stones, Kinks, Animals and such. The clincher, that sold me on jazz, was seeing Buddy on telly. The Rich band performed 'West Side Story Suite', their medley adapted from the Bernstein musical and Buddy broke into one of his famous extended solos, a Niagara of sweat cascading down his face, endlessly inventive, self-indulgent, of course, but thrilling, an unforgettable experience. I subsequently attended his gigs in London, including one with the black Jewish singer and entertainer Sammy Davis Jr.

When I started this book, my conviction was that Rich had strong claim to recognition as the greatest ever jazz drummer. I was taken aback therefore by Loren Schoenberg telling me that Rich didn't even rate in his top ten: "Nowhere near. Buddy Rich's influence? No one had the technique that Buddy Rich had and Buddy Rich had the potential to be a great artist but he was almost like someone gifted with some great physical attribute, and people wanted to see him do that. He had the fastest hands, and he started in vaudeville, and people always wanted to see him play the drums so fast. To me that's the least valuable thing about Buddy Rich. The most valuable thing is that he could be at times an extraordinarily sensitive percussionist. A great drummer, there's no doubt about it, he could kick a band along. Is he in any sense an important figure in the evolution of the way the drums are played? No. Buddy Rich was gifted technically in such a way that nobody played the drum set better than him but anybody who says he was the greatest jazz drummer ever has their head stuck up their arse."

Yet it is instructive to hear what drummers say. "A maestro," Laurie Morgan told me. "His playing was incredible, impeccable. It wasn't just technique, not at all, Buddy Rich was a giant. For purity of form, for presentation, you can't go past Buddy Rich, his playing abilities, his skill, and his ability to render his ideas, are absolute. Then you have other people to consider, Art Blakey, Max Roach, Chick Webb, Chico Hamilton, loads of African American drummers who approached it slightly differently, they presented a looser, not quite so clinical approach; Buddy Rich was almost clinical, everything he did was so immaculate. You won't hear a single drummer of any quality who would put Buddy Rich down in any way. It's impossible, and if you did you would be ignorant; everything he played, every drummer would like to have that skill, they might not render it in the same way, but they would like to have the technique and facility to be able to render their ideas like that. I could play him alongside Max Roach and Art Blakey and they would not be diminished by the fact that they play differently. Their rendering is so great in what they do that it's not a question of technique. Buddy Rich within his parameters was a giant, and he influenced everybody. I've heard him play solos that, well, they just stand on their own."

Stan Levey told me it was important to make a distinction between Buddy as a young smartarse drummer employed by pre-war big bandleaders and Buddy fronting his own ensembles from the late 1940s onwards. Early on, said Levey, "Buddy was doing chick-y, chick-y, chick-y, played like a machine in those days."

"So he developed beyond that?"

"Oh, he sure did. Listen to his records, at Ronnie Scott's. Hey, come on, you can't play any better than that."

"So he was at his best, post-war, leading his own big bands?"

"Yes. He wasn't a small band drummer – he was okay. But with that band, with the great charts, forget about it, put the lights out and say goodnight."

"Where does he fit among the all-time greatest?"

"You say his name and then you don't talk for about half an hour – that's where he fits in. Mention hero drummers, he's top of that list."

Crucially though, given the instrument's supportive role, reverence for Rich is by no means restricted to drummers. John Chilton, in his biography of trumpeter Roy Eldridge revealed: "Although Eldridge and Rich often engaged in some very salty exchanges, Roy consistently cited Rich as being one of his favourite musicians." 18 Bassist John Levy said: "One of the greatest drummers in the business, even if he was arrogant and opinionated... Musically, you never had to worry about time." 19 Oscar Peterson, confessing there were occasions they did not see eye to eye musically, still added: "Whenever one comes across his kind of talent, one must honour it in full – and Buddy Rich belonged to that very select group of people that I would label genius." 20 Miles Davis, who always put musicality above virtuosity, "wanted any drummer to play like Buddy". 21 George T Simon wrote about what happened when Buddy deputised for Count Basie's drummer, Jo Jones, who took ill before a gig: "As the Count reported sometime later, 'We asked Buddy to play again the next night. And you know what happened? The entire band showed up *early* for work. Now, you know that was just about unheard of in that band.'" 22

Jazz vocalist Mel Tormé, who was Jewish, in his Buddy Rich biography, relates an anecdote the drummer told him. Buddy was playing to a black audience in Harlem's Apollo and stepped out for a breather only to find his new sports car stripped clean. The stage manager told an incredulous Rich not to worry about it. "Anyway,

I came out after the last show. That car was put back together... It was Simonised in the three hours since I reported the theft. What happened was, some of the cats did not know that the car belonged to Buddy Rich... I can remember going up to Harlem after that... I could leave a thousand dollars on the seat of the car, I could leave my wardrobe... my drums, and the word would get around, 'That's B's car,' and everything was safe. That was one of the greatest feelings, because I was accepted in Harlem, and to me that was the greatest acceptance of my career." 23

Shelly Manne exemplifies the other polarity in jazz drumming. André Previn, expressing his appreciation of Manne, put it this way: "I have always held the view that percussionists fall into two categories... those deeply involved in the music... others just hit whatever drum is in front." 24 Previn, whose Jewish family took flight from Nazifying Europe, though most remembered as a classical conductor, was also an excellent jazz pianist as on Manne's *Songs from My Fair Lady*.

Manne started out deputising for Dave Tough in Benny Goodman's band, then replaced Tough under Joe Marsala. That was the early 1940s and Manne, serving in the coastguard stationed off Manhattan Beach, had ready access to the New York clubs where bebop was happening, "one of the navy guys who would sit in with groups up and down the block". 25 Some historians have raised a question mark over whether Manne backed Dizzy Gillespie's first bebop recording sessions, in 1945; they now think it may have been another Jewish drummer, Irv Kluger. Once having absorbed the new jazz, Manne had the wit to individualise it. "Shelly was doing different things," testified black drummer Roy Haynes. 26

After moving to Los Angeles, so successfully did Manne accommodate himself to his surroundings that jazz historian Ted Gioia singles him out as the personification of the 1950s west coast percussion style. Gioia, in *West Coast Jazz*, dedicates a chapter to Manne titled 'The Anti-drummer', meaning it as a compliment in that he "viewed himself, perhaps more than any of his contemporaries, as a musician first and a drummer only second". As defined by Gioia, that is the embodiment of the west coast approach to drumming – one in which rhythmic drive is often secondary to contributing to the melodic continuity of the piece being performed. What matters is that the musicians Manne supported drooled about it. "When he was at his best, he was the most fun of any of the drummers I've ever played with," said pianist Russ Freeman, a highly empathetic. Jewish, collaborator. 27

Stan Levey gave me his drummer assessment of Manne: "Great innovator, did things that nobody ever thought of doing, great sensitivity when he played, a real team player, wonderful guy, wonderful player. Anybody that's playing today, you have a little of him in there."

Like Terry Gibbs, Manne cut an early sixties Jewish-jazz album. Whereas Gibbs alternated jazz and klezmer with some idiomatic interplay, Manne's *My Son the Jazz Drummer!* features peppy modern-mainstream interpretations of Jewish and Israeli tunes, also the *Exodus* film theme. To my ears, the album, later re-released as *Steps to the Desert*, is perhaps over-arranged for a smallish combo – a tad too 'cool' perhaps?

It all depends though what records you listen to. The finest representation of Manne is *Shelly Manne & His Men at The Black Hawk*, recorded live in San Francisco and released by Contemporary in 1960 as four separate LP volumes. With Manne inspirational, Joe Gordon on trumpet, Richie Kamuca, tenor sax, Monty Budwig, bass and the Jewish Victor Feldman on piano, they deliver some of the most irresistibly swinging mainstream jazz you will ever hear.

· · · ·

The east coast/west coast controversy manifests itself in sharpest relief in the career of Shorty Rogers, whose first trumpet was a bar mitzvah present. Born in 1924, he grew up in New York where he broke through into the professional ranks. Yet, as Robert Gordon says: "If any one musician was identified in the public's mind with the term West Coast jazz, it was certainly Shorty Rogers." 28

"Where did west coast jazz come from? Maybe Count Basie," Rogers once said, adding that when he was growing up, either his sister or brother brought a Basie record home "and I played it and fell madly in love with Sweets Edison's solo", which he practised along to. 29 One of Rogers' fifties west coast albums was *Shorty Courts the Count*, and Rogers would later hire trumpeter Harry Sweets Edison in one of his ensembles.

For Rogers, other chief inspirations were jazz modernist: "A lot of people asked me: was West Coast better than East Coast? But we weren't engaged in a battle – no way. I'm from the East Coast, anyhow, and as I think about the music that was labelled as West Coast Jazz… well, for instance, at that time I think Al Cohn was the strongest influence we had. I just loved and adored what Miles Davis did with his ten-piece band, and I wanted to do something that sounded that way. Why? Because it would be the most fun; I would enjoy it the most. Miles Davis, Al Cohn, Bud Powell were tremendous influences on me – maybe people couldn't hear it in the music, but I know the input that was going into my head, and the source of things I love. That's where it was from." 30

Rogers was a fluent trumpeter and one of the first jazz musicians to take up flugelhorn but it was his abilities as a composer-arranger for which he was most renowned. When Rogers' career took off, he so impressed Stravinsky that the Russian composer, the harbinger of classical modernism, wrote *Ebony Concerto* for the Woody Herman band with whom Rogers was then engaged. Work with Stan Kenton drew Rogers westward. He settled in Los Angeles, enamoured by the lifestyle and mindful of the proximity to the studios. Kenton gave arrangers plenty of scope and Rogers' leaning towards experimentation was reflected in his progressively ambitious charts. He had privately studied contemporary classical composition with Dr Wesley La Violette and proved adept at integrating that knowledge into jazz.

By no means was Rogers the only jazz musician so inclined. After the second world war, young jazz musicians that benefited from free tuition under the G.I. Bill often studied with leading exponents of modernist classicism among whom were the Jewish émigré composers Darius Milhaud and Stefan Wolpe. Dave Brubeck, the famous jazz pianist, looking back on his early career, said: "From Milhaud's compositions and his classes I became more aware of polytonality and polyrhythms and the usage of Bach-like counterpoint... I don't know what influence our octet's sound had on Gil Evans and Miles Davis's *Birth of the Cool*... I do know that Milhaud was the true father of my octet. His influence ranged widely, but at the same time there were other European refugees... that were influencing and teaching young musicians." 31

Shorty Rogers, then, was a forerunner in deploying elements, in jazz, gleaned from developments in twentieth century classical music. 32 He initiated, and collaborated in, a stream of projects for small and larger ensembles that anticipated innovations of the late fifties and sixties jazz avant-garde, such as the modal abandonment of chord changes, and free-ish explorations. He pioneered the integration into jazz of Arnold Schoenberg's twelve-note system, whereby the twelve chromatic notes of the octave are used on an equal basis without dependence on a particular key. All this accomplished without forfeiting a vibrant lightness of touch that gained Rogers a global following.

"Really melodic and he set a standard, wrote a style of music that became known as west coast style", said Randy Brecker, who as a trumpeter admired Rogers' playing too: "One of the very first records that both I and my brother [saxophonist Michael Brecker] listened to was *Martians Come Back* [Shorty Rogers And His Giants, 1956], and he was also one of the first people to popularise the use of the flugelhorn, and that fact that you didn't need an amazing amount of technique to play the trumpet and be able to communicate; you can communicate with less notes – Chet/Miles Davis style. He in his time was very influential; if you don't have a great technique you have to figure out a way round your limitations and he was able to do that and create something kind of unique."

Increasingly, Rogers was drawn to working for Hollywood when it became chic to incorporate modern jazz elements into movie scores, co-writing the music for *The Wild One* (1953) and *The Man with the Golden Arm* (1955). Herb Geller explained to me: "Shorty returned to the west coast from New York, and he called me – we'd play together. I was playing at the Lighthouse a couple of nights a week and they'd have these Sunday jam sessions which would go for twelve hours, three different groups, and my wife for a while was the house pianist. And Shorty was there, several of them were with the Stan Kenton band and they'd quit the band and start doing record work – timing was everything with the onset of long-playing records. And they started using jazz elements in movies as backgrounds for films, and Shorty, who was already an arranger, was part of that."

As rock and roll kicked in, west coast musicians relied increasingly on the movies for well-paid work, in some instances pretty much abandoning jazz. Access to such work was far easier for white jazz musicians.

# Chapter 11: Race for the studios

Many jazz musicians supplemented their income by doing film, television, radio and session work. Often there was little jazz involved but such employment was welcome, particularly after the arrival of rock, a means for musicians to subsidise their jazz if they did not give up altogether.

Even at the best of times, the jazz life was wearing; as André Previn observed: "Quite a number of illustrious players opted for a life less given to excessive strain and turned to the film studios for work... trading in a part of their previous existence for soft shirts, California sunshine and station wagons in the San Fernando valley." 1 Film composing was especially lucrative and Jewish jazz musicians were well represented – among them Shelly Manne, Shorty Rogers, Lennie Niehaus, Russ Freeman and Johnny Mandel.

David Raskin was another – he had a worldwide smash with 'Laura' from the 1944 movie of that name; it became a jazz standard. Raskin, who started out as a jazz arranger in the 1930s, scored the 1962 film *Too Late Blues*, marked out by Chuck Berg in his essay Jazz and Film and Television as particularly significant in the history of cinematic jazz "because the vocabulary of jazz was called upon to shade dramatic moments in which music itself was not an actual part of the scene". 2

If the studios enabled some jazz players to adopt Technicolor lifestyles, recruitment policy often seemed dictated along starkly monochromatic lines with few black artists hired. Given that Jewish moguls and executives were a heavy presence in the movie companies, they must presumably take their share of the blame. Jewish studio highfliers must also have been complicit in relegating black actors and musicians to typically demeaning stereotyped on-screen roles.

Let us – for argument's sake – assume that, in pandering to the white majority audience, it was moral cowardice on Hollywood's part, augmented by box-office calculation, that determined how black people were generally presented on screen. Let us assume that it was not outright racial prejudice. What about radio work, and soundtracks? The musicians employed are not visible to the public; how then to account for the studios' historic resistance to hiring black musicians? Trotskyist jazz writer Frank Kofsky alleged "ubiquitous discrimination against black artists and composers". 3

Might though there have been other factors holding back black musicians' access? Stan Levey, who benefited from studio work, thought so. "A lot of them," he told me, "couldn't read that well, for one thing. There's no room for mistakes in rehearsing. You come in eight in the morning, a guy gives the downbeat, it's got to be spot on. Time is money, and some of them are good – Bill Green, Buddy Collette, Earl Palmer, no problem. Like I say, if you can do the work, you'll have the job, just like Cozy Cole, the black drummer."

"You don't think it was discrimination?"

"No, hell, if you can do the work, you get the job, bingo."

I quizzed LA jazz expert Kirk Silsbee about this. Were reading skills really such an issue?

"It was an issue, but then the recording studios and in particular the movie studios, this was and is today a caste system, a fraternity, an organisation that nobody just walks into. You have to be led in by the hand by somebody who's in it. It's not easy for anybody to get into that because you're talking about very big budgets, you've got contractors with very big egos. They know what they like and if they find somebody they can depend on, who can show up at a moment's notice, who can execute something that's in a very difficult manner, but in many cases take something that's sloppily written and make music out of it and do it quickly because the contractor's under the gun, they are less likely to take chances and yes, it has worked to the detriment of black players."

Could this be perceived as racism?

"There certainly is a strong component of racism. Maybe it's racism driven by economics, maybe flat-out racism. But David Amram, in his autobiography *Vibrations*, talks about coming out here and working on movies – he wrote the music for *Splendour in the Grass* and a couple of other movies – and he talks about encountering a Jewish producer on the movie who recognised Amram as this wunderkind from New York. He said, 'We're going to give you the best treatment, we'll get all the best musicians out here.' And Amram said, 'Good, I know just who I want to use.' And this producer said, 'Who do you have in mind?' And Amram said, 'Harold Land and… I forget who else, black guys. And this producer said, 'I never heard of him.' And Amram said, 'Well, he lives over there in south Los Angeles.' And the producer fixes him and says, 'Schwartzers?' [Yiddish for black people – the producer clearly knew he was addressing a fellow Jew]. And he says, 'Yeah.' And the producer says, 'You don't want to do that. You don't want to bother with these people because they're going to hang you up, and you mark my words…'; that type of thing." In the autobiography, Amram does not name this producer but merely identifies him sardonically as Mr Integrity. 4

"Amram did use Harold Land and other black musicians on a movie called *The Young Savages*," said Kirk. "They were wonderful, they gave them exactly what they wanted, and I'd be surprised if Harold Land ever worked on movie soundtracks again. I have sympathy for the white jazz musicians who were able to find studio work in the sixties when rock and roll was king. These guys wanted nothing so much as to play jazz but did what they could do and worked in the studios. It was well paid work and sometimes, when they got a Johnny Mandel score, when they got a Henry Mancini movie to be on, they had a good time. But very often they were required to make silk purses out of sow's ears. They wanted to play jazz. Now black musicians didn't have the access to that studio work. If you've dedicated your life to playing jazz in a marketplace that says there is no place for jazz, what do you do? It was tough for people like Harold Land, but they kept going. Through no fault of their own, the white musicians had these studio jobs, but I imagine that there was a lot of enmity toward them from black musicians."

An additional factor Kirk suggested that probably prevented black musicians gaining studio openings was inability to play more than a single instrument: "Buddy Collette could play all the woodwinds, so he worked; Harold Land just played tenor saxophone."

Quincy Jones came to mind as a black musician who thrived in the studios – including writing the jazz soundtrack to Jewish director Sidney Lumet's psychological portrait of a Holocaust survivor, *The Pawnbroker*, the 1964 movie shot on location around Harlem. So, I put it to Kirk that perhaps it wasn't necessarily racism that was at play, or if it was, it derived from studio recruiters' perception of black musicians as unreliable.

"Yes, I think that played a part in it, and yet from 1945 on, as far as I know, when Benny Carter moved out here, the studios were using him. He might not get the credit. God knows how many movie scores, or how much movie work he ghosted, with no credited record. Another guy, Phil Moore, a gifted musician who did a lot of movie work, in fact we will never know how much movie work Phil Moore did."

"He wasn't credited?"

"The people in power in the studios were loath to admit what they farmed out to Phil Moore. And after that, Joe Wilson, who worked with Phil Moore and learned from him. He was called upon to ghost movie music and I think it was 1962 when he got his first movie credit when he did the music for a stupid movie called *Where The Boys Are*, with Connie Francis. But he had to wait that long to be credited. So the Hollywood studios are a system unto themselves."

Though many Hollywood studios were Jewish owned, one has to distinguish between the moguls there and the person whose decision it was to recruit musicians. That doesn't necessarily mean no Jews were involved in hiring, but it does mean the decisions were made at a much lower level.

The musician most responsible for overcoming Hollywood's resistance to hiring black players was Benny Carter. His own Hollywood studio breakthrough came in 1942 when he arranged and played for *Stormy Weather*. Jewish music director Alfred Newman was so impressed that he recruited Carter for many productions for various studios. By 1946, Carter was in such studio demand that he gave up leading his big band.

And Carter played a leading role in the racial integration of Los Angeles musicians' unions, known as locals, in the early 1950s, after which black artists began clinching more Hollywood studio work. 5 If integrating the unions began to prise open the studio doors, the way was prepared by a bold merger campaign tactic. What happened was that integrationists from both locals established the racially mixed Community Symphony Orchestra as a symbolic vehicle, a means whereby the white, mainly classical, musicians involved could pass on formal skills to black jazz musicians. This, it was reasoned, would help them gain studio work.

Most white musicians involved in this gesture of solidarity were Jews.

• • • •

It was Kirk Silsbee who tipped me off about the heavy Jewish participation in the Community Symphony Orchestra, which he had learned about through black alto saxophonist Buddy Collette. Buddy began diversifying on other instruments through involvement in the orchestra, which for him led to studio work. I arranged an interview.

On the buses out to the LA suburb of Ladera Heights to meet him, I was aware that Buddy lived not far from Watts, famous for race riots triggered when white cops beat up a black guy. Buddy had suffered a stroke, affecting his movement, speech, and, at times, memory, but he was coherent, hospitable, and came across as a warm, decent guy.

I got straight to the point: "You were involved in the campaign to integrate the musicians' locals out here, and you reached out to the white local. Is that right that a lot of the musicians supporting you were..."

Buddy anticipated me: "...were Jewish, right. In the beginning we did start to try to get the black and white unions together, the white union was Local 47 and the black union was Local 767. And we didn't know who would help us, so we started having little get-togethers. We weren't looking for any particular people except people from the white union that would see what we were talking about getting a union together to have one union that would support everybody. I met a gentleman who was probably most influential at the time, Milt Holland [jazz and studio drummer and percussionist], a Jewish guy, but there were others.

"Milt was the main standout guy. And he said, 'We like that idea and there's a bunch of us that feel the same way that you do, that there should be one union.' We said we'd like to establish a symphony orchestra with integration in the orchestra, then we'd try and get the unions later. So we said, 'You get as many guys as you can get for the symphony orchestra and we'll get the rest of them. We got the black musicians, about fifteen – Red Callender, Jimmy Cheatham, John Ewing, Bill Green, James McCullough, Vic Woodman. Milt filled out the rest which amounted to about a sixty-piece orchestra. He was very instrumental in helping us find the other guys. We went to a few rehearsals for what became the Community Symphony Orchestra. There were other Jewish people later on, like George Kast the violinist. He helped us to form the orchestra where we could meet people and also train black musicians who hadn't had this classical training. The main other guy from the rehearsal was Julie Kinsler, the flute player, and we played duets together, to show them I could read. We did duets in the theatre backroom, like Mozart and Bach. There were a bunch of Jewish people; I don't know if it was mixed with minorities of whites. So we had a lot of people who worked very hard."

"Which musicians were from a jazz background?"

"The black ones were, they were learning the classical side. The Jewish musicians – most of them were classical, so it was a good meeting. Then we had jam sessions on Sunday afternoon for everybody. So when we got to know people and what they played, what instruments and what they were interested in, one thing led to another, we got bigger every day. The more people that would hear about it, the more would show up. We finally got in the paper because they wanted to say, 'Hey, first interracial symphony orchestra with blacks, whites, Jews.' So it made the papers and people knew about it then. We invited one renowned conductor, Mr Isaac Solomon. He was in town and some of the people said, 'Hey, why don't you conduct us?' So we got better, we rehearsed every week, different conductors would come in. In the meantime, the record dates were producing more mixed players and after that people began to be aware than the blacks and whites played good together, they got along well and made good music. And they used more blacks on the record dates, on the movie calls. And of course, there were other Jewish contractors who hired the musicians on the movie calls. So that was the beginning."

One Jewish musician attracted to the rehearsals was Jerry Fielding, whose credits included arranging for the jazz bands of Claude Thornhill, Jimmie Lunceford, Tommy Dorsey and Charlie Barnet. Fielding was music director of Groucho Marx's TV show – a connection that proved fortuitous for Buddy: "We rehearsed in Hollywood at La Conte Junior High School and that's where I met Mr Jerry Fielding. He came down to see me one night and I was playing something from Bizet's Carmen and he come over after the concert and said, 'I liked the way your flute sounded' – I'd played a flute solo, I was trying to play classical, and I had had training in classical music, so I wasn't improvising, I was just reading the parts. Anyway, he said he was looking for Marshall Royal, a fine saxophone player who played with Count Basie. He said, 'Do you know him?' I said, 'Yeah, but he's out of town.' He said, 'I got a job for him on the Groucho Marx show; if you play saxophone, maybe you could do it.' I said, 'That's what I play. I just started playing flute two years ago.' So he said, 'You got the job then.' He said the contractor would call me in about a week, and he did."

Fielding became a McCarthyite target. Buddy in his autobiography recalls: "I saw the House Un-American Activities Committee topple Jerry Fielding from the Groucho Marx show... After I was hired he began to integrate all of his orchestras. Jerry hired Red Callender on The Life of Riley show. He also had a TV jazz show with Callender, George Wiggins and me... Jerry kept on and it got him into trouble." 6 The upshot was that Fielding did little work for several years, except anonymously. It was only after Betty Hutton, the actress and singer, insisted he score a show for her that his fortunes improved. "He got back in," Buddy observes in his book, "but was never the same after that. I used to see him and he was an angry man ... Jerry was the kind of fighter that we don't have around very often." 7

The orchestra, Buddy said, disseminated the fact that the black musicians could read. Was it the case, I asked him, that many of them could only previously play by ear?

"Not just by ear, but when you're playing jazz, maybe they didn't think you could read. When you read, they got to see you reading."

The community symphonic initiative was such a revelation that, besides opening doors to the studios, it knocked a chink in the barriers that blocked black musicians from classical work,

"After that, we did get Henry Lewis – I guess he was studying then – he came to our first rehearsal as a black bass player, he got to be conductor of many orchestras. He was probably one of the first to play in one of the major symphony orchestras. Later on, maybe over the next ten years, blacks were working in the major symphony orchestras."

I told Buddy that I understood there was opposition to integration from some black musicians.

"The blacks had experience where they hadn't been hired, and they might not have had any hope."

"So how did you overcome that opposition?"

"We had to vote in the black union to see if we wanted to go in the white union, and they had to vote to see what they wanted. So it was a process. We had a couple of years that it didn't work but people got more aware – Benny Carter came in, wonderful man, Gerald Wilson and others. Then people said, 'Benny's for it, Gerald's for it, it must be okay.'"

Did Buddy have any notion as to why there was so much support on the Jewish side?

"I didn't know the reason, but I think it was the way they looked at the whole situation. They had the days of Hitler and stuff where they felt persecuted. So they probably felt different about us as underdogs trying to do something, maybe they could understand the reasons we were trying to better ourselves. And they said, 'Yes, we'd like to help'. And they more or less dedicated themselves to making a better world, is what I'm saying... We sure got a lot of help from these Jewish people who understood, almost as much as we understood, that we have to move our race higher, we can't just be cleaning toilets, we can do other things. And it worked, as you can see from the black people on the TV now. At the times we're talking about there were no blacks on TV, except maybe a maid in the kitchen. But look at blacks now. They've got their own shows, and they're real people."

One musician Buddy collaborated with was jazz and classical cellist Fred Katz. They worked together in the Chico Hamilton Quintet, and Buddy participated on Katz's 1959 album *Folk Songs For Far Out Folk*, a musical triptych of orchestrated jazz based on Hebraic, African and American folk songs. 8

I wound up asking Buddy if – beyond jazz – he had any idea why the black/Jewish relationship had come under strain in recent years.

"I don't know why. You see it in the papers. I've got lots of Jewish friends I've known for thirty years, guys with whom I'm closer to than ever. Nobody writes about that; they [the media] put Jessie Jackson out there because he says, 'Hymie'."

Buddy died in 2010. I feel privileged to have heard the integration story directly from him.

• • • •

Sometime after that interview, I came across a *California History* article about Bop City, a 1940's San Francisco modern jazz club. In Carol P Chamberland's article, she records: "On some occasions, the white union picketed white musicians who played in black clubs, but no one I interviewed recalled the black union picketing black musicians who played in white clubs. Drummer Dick Berk has some thoughts on that period, from a Jewish perspective: 'I, at the time, didn't belong to any union. And I was playing at Bop City.' Independent musicians like Dick Berk were usually pressured to join the union. Sammy Simpson, tenor saxophone player and president of the black union, was a good friend of Dick. Sammy asked Dick to join the black union, even though Dick is Jewish. Feeling honored and surprised, Dick responded... "Well, can I?" He says, "I'm the president of the black union, so you can join it.'" And Berk did, possibly becoming the first white musician to join a black union."

# Chapter 12: 'New Thing', old sores

During the 1960's civil rights struggle, when jazz became more overtly politicised, black poet and jazz proselytiser LeRoi Jones, in his *Black Music* anthology, asserted that "black music should be played by black musicians".

Nat Hentoff, who produced Max Roach's *We Insist! Freedom Now Suite*, a seminal radical sixties' black jazz album, in a statement directed largely at other Jewish jazz critics, notably Leonard Feather, argued that it was "unrealistic not to expect a period of catharsis for the American Negro – a period where all the rage and bitterness and anger and torment has to get out". Feather had voiced concern about Jones' "Crow Jim" exclusivism.

One Jones' essay mocked the contribution that pianist Burton Greene made at a Newark gig where he shared the bandstand with black musicians, about whose abilities Jones was contrastingly effusive. Greene, a Jewish Chicagoan, may for all I know have been as execrable as Jones portrayed him. My suspicion from a more general reading of Amiri Baraka's (the name Jones later assumed) jazz writings is that this was a pundit who listened first with his eyes, only then trusting his ears.

I contacted Greene, whose memory was vivid: "When I met Leroi he was living above Archie Shepp in a loft near Cooper Square in New York in the mid-sixties. Lots of musicians dropped by and jammed there. We all hung out at Archie's pad and I assumed LeRoi was cool but then a short time later he divorced his white Jewish wife [beat poet Hettie Jones] and left her with the two or three kids, descended into the Newark, NJ black ghetto with his dashikis and shades and pretended he had always been there, another 'po underprivileged Afro-American', blah, blah. In point of fact he grew up in New England in an upper middle class family. In that Apple Cores series article he did in *DownBeat*... he made it sound like I barged in on that gig in Newark with my white stormtroops' attitude. He neglects to mention I was invited to play that gig by Marion Brown and Pharoah Sanders. As far as 'beating and pummelling' the piano ineffectively with my fists, he also neglects to mention there were about twenty-five keys missing or unplayable in the middle of the old upright piano so all I could do is take out the bottom of the piano and play the strings with mallets and a drumstick, etc. I sent this info into *DownBeat* as a protest to that article sometime later but they never printed it. I was not the only white musician attacked by black writers like LeRoi and AB Spellman in that time."

Greene added: "Other Jewish musicians on the scene were bassist Steve Tintweiss and drummer Shelly Rusten, both of whom worked with me and others. Steve was the last bass player with Albert Ayler, and Shelly worked with Sam Rivers and others. Gary Friedman was the saxophonist in my group with Alan Silva, the Freeform Improvisation Ensemble."

I wrote an obituary on Burton Greene for the Fall 2021 edition of *We Jazz* magazine. He died on his Amsterdam houseboat earlier that year.

It was black alto saxophonist Ornette Coleman with his free jazz innovations who ushered in the 'New Thing' that LeRoi Jones championed as an exclusively black movement. But it was a Jew, Lester Koenig, founder of Contemporary Records, who gave Coleman his first recording breaks with the 1958 release *Something Else!!!!* and the 1959 *Tomorrow Is The Question* – this when many black musicians spurned Coleman's experimentation.

As Kirk Silsbee put it to me: "There is no set key that the music is in, there is no specific time, it's all open to interpretation. Yes, there is a compositional line that the musicians are playing on, but it's up to them to interpret precisely how fast they want to play it and in what key. His music was never where the band could

look at each other and go one-two-three-four. They just took off
and somewhere along the line, reached a consensus pulse, or not
reached because it didn't work every time. So for Lester Koenig
to release two albums by a guy working in this amorphous system
showed a lot of guts."

Despite excellent reviews, and the enthusiasm of
avant-inclined listeners, not much happened after the release of
*Something Else!!!!*, rued Nat Hentoff in sleeve-notes for *Tomorrow
Is The Question*. Shelly Manne, who participated on the second
album, got the new shift in jazz immediately, telling Hentoff: "I've
always been bugged by having to stay within boundaries. Here is a
guy that came along that was able to free me... of all those things I
wanted to throw off. Meter structure, for example... Ornette does
something with his own tunes that makes you not only hear the
tunes but make you hear them like eighteen hundred thousand
different ways."

Coleman later recorded for ESP-Disk, whose Jewish founder
Bernard Stollman issued albums by just about every major figure
of the sixties jazz avant-garde, including Albert Ayler's earliest
releases. The label offered musicians maximum creative freedom,
its motto, printed on every release, was, "The artists alone decide
what you will hear on their ESP-Disk." As Valerie Wilmer observes:
"Stollman was the only person prepared to invest money in
recording what was, in truth, an unknown quantity." 1

Investment was no less critical in the public performance
sphere where opportunities were sparse for the jazz vanguardists.
Dan Morgenstern, writing in *DownBeat* after attending an event at
the Half Note in 1964, argued that jazz experimentalists deserved
governmental or institutional subsides as much as "painters, poets,
classical musicians and writers who are now among the recipients
of such aid". In Morgenstern then, we have another positive Jewish
intervention backing the New Thing musicians.

Ornette Coleman's bassist David Izenzon answered the racial challenge this way: "I have a few thousand years of tradition to contribute myself. Since I'm white and Jewish, perhaps a Jewish guy is going to realise when he sees me up on the stand with black musicians that this new music has something to do with him." For Izenzon, what united the jazz vanguard was more important than what divided it: "We're saying in our music that we want a society without classes." 2

Trumpeter Bill Dixon, as co-founder of the New York-based Jazz Composers' Guild established in 1965 to support avant-garde musicians, invited white artists, Burton Greene included, to join as he considered their position little better than that of blacks. 3 Dixon played on cornetist/flautist Marc Levin's Free Unit 1967 album, *The Dragon Suite*, all the personnel black bar the Jewish leader.

While it is true that the New Thing was never as ghettoised as its more blinkered champions would have liked, in Chicago, in 1965, the Association for the Advancement of Creative Musicians non-profit collective was formed, orientated towards experimentalist black players. At the inaugural meeting, co-founder Muhal Richard Abrams, responding to white pianist Bob Dogan, made the point: "Being frank about it, when we started we didn't intend to have an interracial group. Not as opposed to another race, but we made it a point that each has his own, up to a certain height. Then the collaboration and contact with the other races or body takes place." Dogan countered, "... that would throw some low blows to a lot of cats that might really be interested". Abrams accepted it was no fault of white players the way things were manipulated in the industry: "The musicians don't do it. It's the people that control the thing... We're not fighting a racial fight. We're promoting ourselves and helping ourselves." 4

Howard Mandel, today a leading jazz journalist, remembered those times. "The AACM arose during the middle of the civil rights era, and I was interested in the cause," he told Marc Myers. Although AACM artists did civil rights fundraisers, for the most part, as Mandel understood it, "AACM musicians were not associated with the rhetoric of black nationalists or separatism and were not confrontational, except aesthetically. Certainly, there were times when I was the only white kid at a performance... But no one ever looked at me and said, 'What are you doing here?' They said, 'Cool! We hope you like it.'" 5

These observations prompted me to contact Mandel: "I wasn't the only white – most often Jewish – teenager going to AACM musicians' gigs on the South Side, though I was sometimes the only one at a given gig. I recognised at that time, and still run into, a circle of attendees in my demographic. I was surprised a few years ago to learn how many students in the high school class I was in on the South Side before my parents moved to a north suburb had forged a serious interest in either black blues or the AACM music of the Art Ensemble, Anthony Braxton, Leo Smith, etc."

The largely Jewish, formerly Irish Catholic locale Mandel grew up in was immediately adjacent to the large middle-class African American, and Hyde Park, districts surrounding the University of Chicago: "Even in the forties that was the rare residential and business area – blacks, whites, Jewish, non-Jewish, foreign-born housing and working together, in large part due to the cosmopolitan nature of the university. Many of the first wave AACM musicians – Art Ensemble's [Lester] Bowie and [Joseph] Jarman, among others – lived in Hyde Park, and there were concerts there, but also in all-black neighborhoods, which I attended, sometimes with friends, sometimes alone. Tenor saxophonist Fred Anderson was at the other end of the city, in the also integrated suburban Evanston, home to Northwestern

University, and there was a population of Jewish kids my age whose parents had moved like mine from the South Side to those suburbs, and like me they kept following the music."

. . . .

Mandel subsequently emailed me about Chicago Jews supportive of AACM, and/or of jazz more generally, one a woman he knows that he preferred not to identify, "who went to my temple... She was involved with the Jazz Institute of Chicago then, as was I... This woman I'm referring to did a lot of work with [AACM-affiliated saxophonist] Fred Anderson during the late seventies... [and] still an activist keeper of the flame". Mandel cited others: "Lauren Deutsch, executive director of the Jazz Institute of Chicago for more than 20 years, retired in 2019, and an innovative photographer, has a South Side background similar to mine, and has been a staunch supporter of AACM and unaffiliated but fellow black jazz musicians in Chicago, those not focused on playing original music but rather work on conventional and standard repertoire, and also white, Asian, Latin-jazz players. Attny Steve Salzman, originally from Cleveland I think, was formerly president of the board of the Jazz Institute of Chicago, and now curates a series of summer performances at our Museum of Contemporary Art. My pal photo-journalist Marc PoKempner; Jazz Showcase club owner Joe Segal; many of the critics and editors at *DownBeat* and other publications, also those in NYC and SF Bay Area and LA and New Orleans, and I suppose elsewhere, are landsmen or women" – that is, Jewish jazz writers beyond just Chicago. Mandel added: "How about SFJazz founder Randall Kline, DC Jazz Fest founder Charlie Fischman, I think there are many examples of such engagement, so many I take it for granted."

. . . .

Prominent among Jewish participants in the sixties jazz avant-garde were two artists I will now consider, soprano saxophonist Steve Lacy and pianist Paul Bley.

Born in 1932, Bley grew up raised by adoptive parents in Montreal. He studied piano from age seven with a succession of classically oriented tutors, graduating from McGill Conservatory when only eleven, but as he approached adolescence Bley developed an ear for jazz: "I was beginning to study for my Bar Mitzvah, which required me to sing text in Hebrew. When I asked my Rabbi 'how does the melody go?' he said, 'you just make it up.' That was very easy for me to do. Since they neglected to translate any of the Hebrew text so that I could understand what I was singing, I could fully concentrate on making beautiful melodies as an improviser. Up to this time I could play by ear all the written music and the improvised music I had heard but I had not yet attempted to improvise at the piano. This Bar Mitzvah freed me by giving me permission to create spontaneous music in front of an audience." 6

Within four years he replaced Oscar Peterson at Montreal's Alberta Lounge in 1949, then founded the Montreal Jazz Workshop, opening up performance opportunities with the likes of Charlie Parker and Sonny Rollins. Bley headed for New York to study formal composition and conducting at Julliard, launched a band that included saxophonist Jackie McLean and trumpeter Donald Byrd, and toured with Lester Young, Roy Eldridge and Ben Webster. Charles Mingus hired him to conduct his ensemble, then through Mingus, Bley secured the sessions for his 1953 debut recording *Introducing Paul Bley*, Mingus producing and playing bass in a trio completed by Art Blakey.

And Bley, as he became progressively steeped in experimental jazz, was instrumental in elevating Ornette Coleman's career. The collaboration with Coleman came about following Bley's move to the west coast. Bley secured a regular spot at the Hillcrest Club in a black section of Los Angeles with a quartet that included bassist Charlie Haden, drummer Billy Higgins and Jewish vibraphonist Dave Pike, and as Pike remembered it, "We were the first ones, as far as I know, to play free improvisation, and time signatures such as 5/4, 11/8, 13/8, etc. We made an album called *Solemn Mediation*. Ornette Coleman and Don Cherry joined the band in 1958." 7

It was Higgins that introduced Coleman to Bley, suggesting that Coleman, and trumpeter Don Cherry who accompanied him, be allowed to sit in, and as Bley related it, "After playing one set with them Charlie and I went out into the back yard and had a confrontation. We said, 'Look, we have been working at this club for a long time and most probably could stay here as long as we wanted. If we fire Dave Pike and hire Don and Ornette, we probably won't last the week. We'll be lucky to last the night. What shall we do?' And we looked at each other and said, 'Fire Dave Pike.'" 8 Hillcrest duly ditched the band.

When Coleman recorded *Free Jazz* in 1960, Haden, Higgins and Cherry were core collaborators. Bley wasn't involved but established himself as one of the prime movers in the jazz avant-garde. His mid-sixties album *Ramblin'* features him in a trio with two other Jewish musicians, bassist Mark Levinson and drummer Barry Altschul and includes an invigoratingly blues-infused reading of Coleman's 'Ramblin'.

Come the seventies, Bley was pioneering the use of electronics in jazz. Outstanding in this vein, with Bley on synthesiser and electric piano, is *Dual Unity* (1972), with his second wife, electric bassist, pianist, vocalist and composer Annette Peacock in a line-up completed by bassist Mario Pavone and drummers Han Bennink and Laurence Cook – mind- and ear-expanding jazz-rock. Ultimately Bley abandoned electronics, favouring acoustic solo and trio formats. When the mood took him, Bley could play the most superlative chordal jazz – listen to the lovely title track on his 1988 trio album of standards, *The Nearness of You* – but he remained committed to exploratory, harmonically open-ended improvisation, as on *Play Blue: Oslo Concert*, his live solo recording issued by ECM in 2014, two years before he died.

Jazz historian and pianist Ted Gioia posits Bley as one of the three US-based pianists – the others being Steve Kuhn and Denny Zeitlin, both also Jewish – who comprise a stylistic bridge between Bill Evans and Keith Jarrett, less pronounced in Bley's case. Gioia sees them as "...missing links – rarely noted and insufficiently appreciated – between Evans' pioneering efforts and the classically tinged ECM sound that came to the fore during the 1970s". 9 Supporting Gioia's contention, Keith Jarrett – a musician much associated with the ECM label – spent "thousands of hours", he said, listening to Bley's 1963 album *Footloose-no Surprise*. 10 Perhaps it is no coincidence that Jarrett also picked up Bley's habit of chanting along to his keyboard improvisations – a habit Bley carried over from his bar mitzvah.

• • • •

I phoned soprano saxophonist Steve Lacy a couple of years before he died.

It was black pianist Cecil Taylor that prised Lacy out of Dick Wellstood's traditional jazz band; as Lacy related it, Taylor asked him: "How come a young fellow like you is playing Dixieland?" 11 Between 1955 and 1957, Lacy formed part of Taylor's quartet, and he participated on Taylor's first recording, *Jazz Advance* that presaged some of the developments that were to blossom in the sixties avant-garde. Lacy subsequently worked with Thelonious Monk and formed a quartet devoted to Monk's angular bebop. His involvement in the avant-garde deepened and in the late sixties Bley moved to Europe where he was variously engaged in meshing jazz with contemporary art music, electronica, rock, opera, poetry and dance.

Lacy offered me some insight into his musical journey: "I had the call when I was sixteen. I responded to that. Each move I made, each music I played, had a lot to do with circumstances. In New York in the fifties, everything was going on at once. All the giants were creating, so I didn't skip that, I zigzagged through everything. Jazz music is all one thing, I make no distinction. So I didn't switch, I just moved on, made progress to the next step. Bechet was in France when I caught up with him."

Sidney Bechet had used soprano sax for years, but in traditional jazz style; Lacy derived his initial inspiration from Bechet, then, after working with Taylor, took the instrument in new directions.

"I fell in love with the soprano. I realised that I was made for it, we were meant for each other. It's easy to make it wrong. My friend, Howard Johnson [tuba and baritone sax] said I was one of the few who 'got the weasel out of the horn'. I heard a record of Bechet playing an Ellington piece and that was it. There's maybe some kind of heat sometimes in my playing – Bechet was famous for his passion and maybe I have some of that fervour like him, but different style. I played clarinet for a while. It's different – I think of instruments as animals and they're different animals."

Lacy had come up in my conversation, a few weeks earlier, with clarinetist and soprano saxophonist Kenny Davern, whose jazz was largely rooted in the mainstream and traditional. Davern, whose mother was Jewish, knew Lacy whom he insisted had not been given sufficient credit for influencing developments in the United States.

"When I was growing up," said Davern, "no soprano was heard except for Benny Waters, Johnny Hodges. Steve Lacy, we were kids together, I was in the same band as his that went to Boston, 1951; I was a teenager. I can hear two bars of him and right away recognise it's him. He was a very major influence on that instrument. All the other guys sound like hell on fire. I used to hear Thelonious Monk in the late fifties and listen to the group [that included Lacy] and I noticed John Coltrane would come in and stand at the bar after his gig. This would happen nightly. I said to Steve, 'He's coming in every opportunity', and then Steve said he would buy a soprano sax, and shortly after Coltrane did 'My Favourite Things' [on soprano]. So what Steve said was very prophetic, even though he was joking."

• • • •

If you look at histories of the jazz avant-garde, Steve Lacy gets nowhere near as much mention as his black contemporaries. Neither does Paul Bley. Perhaps that is as it should be: but might it also have something to do with other people's preconceptions about the relative merits of black as against white artists? With Davern's revelation fresh in mind, I thought it was worth putting the question.

Trumpeter Frank London prefaced his answer by declaring Lacy a genius: "If you start thinking about why certain things are more written about than others, you're getting clearly into a political discussion about why certain things are privileged over others. And a lot of me tries to step outside of that and just kind of live in the music world. Perhaps because Lacy chose to be an expatriate – that maybe put him outside; he did his most influential work after he left Cecil, in France. America's kind of an interesting place in that classical music we've always been Eurocentric and with jazz and improvised music we've always been very nationalistic. So, I think that we – not me – de-emphasise European improvisers, so I think with Lacy."

"Yes, but do you get more credibility from critics, jazz historians, audiences, being black, even before blowing a note?"

"This is a big debate that people don't talk about all the time and as sort of a psychological defence mechanism, I've really chosen not to go to that place, not to get obsessed with that," returned Frank. "I think this has to do with my personal musical career. Some people would say yes, some no. The idealistic side of me would say that the music you make is what counts more than anything else. I have to believe that as an artist. The practical side of me knows that your appearance, white, black, male, female, straight, gay, whatever, certainly has an effect on how you're responded to.

"I was actually the first white guy to play with Lester's band [Lester Bowie's Brass Fantasy]. I know why I was there. It was a mixture of that I was into the music and could play well and knew him personally, I lived on the block and he needed a sub, and I was walking by and I said, 'Hey, Lester, what's happening?' and he said, 'Hey Frank...' And a lot of the racial cliquishness in a lot of the groups has been, if nothing else, a community thing. Every musician I know works with their friends and with the people they hang out with. And if you have more friends across racial or gender lines you tend to play more with that than if your friends tend to be within racial, gender or other lines. A lot of that is just human nature."

Frank flipped the argument around to his own experience as a Jewish musician in a genre-bending klezmer band: "The Klezmatics' first European tour was in 1988. We weren't that good at that time but immediately, because we were mostly Jews from New York, we were perceived as having an authenticity to European promoters, audiences, and critics, whether or not it was true. That got us a certain amount of credibility and therefore bookings that would not have happened at that point if we were a bunch of European non-Jews."

"If you were going to do an ethnicity-blind jazz history then, what would be Steve Lacy's real significance?"

"Oh my God, for me Lacy's total top echelon. His particular defining genius – okay, I have to make one defining clarification in terminology – the difference between the so-called free jazz and free improvisation. Free jazz tends to mean the gestures of jazz, the ontology, jazz phrases, bass on swing beat, structures based on jazz; as opposed to collective improvisation based on sonic models, like the Art Ensemble, they would do a collective improvisation that would sound like (Frank rattles some tins wildly, rhythmically, then screams) ... that's free improvisation, not free jazz. Free improvisation meant we're starting with a blank slate and we don't know what the sonic thing that will come out will be and anything is possible; formally, sonic-wise, free improvisation is different from free jazz. And I brought that up because one of the geniuses of Lacy is that he is really overlapping those two worlds. Lacy is clearly rooted in jazz – and by the way, in big Frank London's opinion, jazz is African American music – and he's clearly rooted in that, in the older forms of Dixieland, in Monk, he's got that, he's got the harmonic language, but he also goes to a place of theatre, in the same way the Art Ensemble went to theatre. I mean, you could say that Steve Lacy is much more a jazz player than anyone in the Art Ensemble was – except maybe Malachi [Favors, the bassist]. And it made sense that he moved to Europe because in general the European improvisers of free improvisation and free jazz were more tied to theatre in the way Willem Breuker's Kollektief is, in the way the Vienna Art Orchestra is. So Lacy is the one who for me puts together free jazz, free improvisation, the using of the multiple eras of jazz as a root for modern music." Frank also recognised Lacy as a major composer, citing his work with Brion Gysin, who invented the cut-up technique that William Burroughs used: "Lacy actually set Brion Gysin's text – so he was working with text. He really set standards as the kind of person who puts it all together."

Loren Schoenberg was another to whom I related Davern's story. Lacy, thought Loren, was influenced early on by Lee Konitz: "Steve Lacy came up the real traditional way and slowly broke away, and as we all know, he played the soprano saxophone before John Coltrane, made records on it before John Coltrane, a very important figure and like Lee, so freewheeling and so in love with improvisation that he never even tried to chase a commercial career like Getz did. Lee Konitz and Steve Lacy from the beginning just didn't give a damn about how many records they sold. What they really cared about was expressing themselves as great artists."

In Loren's perspective, Lacy was "like a snake shedding skin – not implying any pejorative sense to that – or like some butterfly that's forever re-cocooning."

"And did he get his fair due?"

"There have always been musicians who don't get their due, and there's always been a great deal more great black musicians who don't get their due… Did he have the kind of career and influence of an Eric Dolphy? I don't think so. Did he have the kind of career and influence of an Ornette Coleman? No way in hell… There's probably a whole group of avant-garde contemporary musicians in Europe who heard Steve Lacy for twenty, thirty years and sound like Steve Lacy Jr; I can't talk about that.

"But in terms of the mainstream development of the music here I don't hear a huge influence of Steve Lacy. Just because John Coltrane hung around listening to him playing the soprano and then came out with a record, it means absolutely zip in terms of influence, so you can't translate these things outside of the way that musicians react to each other and listen to everybody. It still doesn't elevate Steve Lacy to Coltrane's level as an influence or as a great jazz original. So what? Many times these discussions about influence are used as a sub-text for really addressing great issues of resentment, and addressing the complexity of race relations."

Loren's right: any influence Lacy may have had on Coltrane does not elevate him to Coltrane's level. To keep the debate open, however, I insert here a quote I came across from Wayne Shorter, one of the world's most revered soprano saxophonists since his emergence with Miles Davis in the 1960s: "Anyone who plays soprano orientates himself on Steve Lacy."

. . . .

"How long can something be avant-garde?" mused Dan Morgenstern when I met him. Indeed, jazz as exemplified by Ornette Coleman and contemporaries is now well over half a century old. Yet many jazz fans still find such music too difficult to comprehend; it therefore resists incorporation into the mainstream comfort zone. Moreover, the sixties avant-garde has continued to inform much experimental jazz, including the work of many Jewish musicians.

These include Steve Cohn, "the great hidden secret of American jazz" in the estimation of a collaborator in sonic adventurism, Carl Baugher. Playing off each other, these multi-instrumentalists conjure up dazzling electro-acoustic extemporisations on their duo albums, theirs a music that goes whither it will. Cohn, clearly an artist of boundless imagination, has been involved in avant-jazz spheres since the 1980s, playing piano, various keyboards, trumpet, trombone, harmonica, percussion, and an international array of instruments.

My reason for contacting him was because I was intrigued by the incorporation in his work, as on the 2020 Cohn-Baugher release *Echo*, of the shofar, the ram's horn blown since ancient times in synagogues to mark Rosh Hashanah. It adds a primal frisson to the recording. Steve explained to me: "In the early eighties I started to add ethnic instruments to my ensembles. The shofar was given to me by my aunt who visited Israel a few years earlier. I picked it up using my experience with trumpet playing and over time found that I could slide up and down, playing any tune I wanted like a kazoo. A few of my instruments like the shakuhachi and hichiriki are used in ceremonial or religious contexts. Using shofar in modern secular music is a statement that when searching for new sound, any source is viable even if it breaks the traditional view of how things should be done. The shofar also creates interesting overtones and percussive elements and used in context with western instruments like French horn, violin, etc, it expands sound again."

Steve loved "the soulful moan of the cantorial chanting" and said his Jewish background had definitely affected his work: "My first record *Sufi Dancers*, the title track had influences in it from the Jewish music I was playing. The scale I developed was an extended scale of nine tones and borrowed from both modal language and the Jewish scales. I also feel that the more mystical nature of Jews via Kaballah etc, and maybe being white and intellectually orientated, found me working with metaphysical concepts from visions I had and influences of the occult."

Although Jane Ira Bloom, a jazz musician whose music gently prods the boundaries, has not consciously sought to integrate Jewish elements, confronted with the theme of my book, she had some most arresting things to say.

. . . .

I met Jane at New York's New School University where she was teaching on the jazz and contemporary music program. She welcomed the chance to ponder where her Jewish side might fit in.

"Being Jewish is something that's very much a part of me. I only tend to go to temples on high holidays, I haven't made it the subject of my music, although I have many thoughts about how key it is

to my fundamental understanding of melody making. I think those
are my primary musical sounds, what I heard in temple. I *know* it's
a connection."

"With jazz?"

"With how I play. With how I write, how I think, how I make
music."

"Can you define that? One of your albums is *Chagall*, so there's
obviously some connection there."

"I'll try, it's something I haven't given an awful lot of conscious
thought to."

I related to Jane what other musicians had told me about their
advice to students – that to play jazz properly, it must be
autobiographical. "Part of that something inside you is that
background, isn't it?"

"Yes, those were some of the first musical sounds I heard,
Jewish songs in the temple, a cantor or a choir singing with an
organ. I think, because I feel something whenever I hear a cantor,
I think it's the same indefinable something that you feel when
you hear a blues singer – some tremendously important musical
connection is there for me that has informed how I think about
writing melody and how I think about invoking feeling, how I feel
with melodic line. I'm a saxophone player so I think in the world of
melodic line, that's what I do and I'm certain that that's where it's
come from. I think there's a bittersweet quality."

"To all Jewish music?"

"That comes to me through that music, that I don't even have
a doubt that that's where my feeling for that essence comes from,
darkness and light, all in one."

Was she aware of the klezmer revival when growing up?

"No. My contact with Jewish melody came from cantorial
singing and from listening to the great Jewish American
songwriters."

Ah, I told Jane, I was delighted that, unprompted, she had brought up the songwriters: "What part of what the Gershwins and the Arlens did, that has such universal appeal and that has fed into jazz, is Jewish? Can you nail it down?"

"Wow, a tough one. The answer maybe in something that's a little more abstract than something that's as concrete as saying 'this is klezmer music'. It may be more in the realm of thinking of the music like poetry because it's the template, it's the essence of understanding how the melodies move, where they peak and how they reach people. If you ever look at the structure of classic American songbook songs, there's always a standard place where the melody peaks, where the emotional and melodic peak of a song is, and it's usually preceded or followed by a little more melodic motion, which is a standard practice in melisma in the singing of Jewish song."

Melisma is the ululating sound that is very characteristic of Jewish and Arabic devotional chants, and other traditions, the quality, as Jane put it, that you could liken to blues and to the African music tradition, the timbre of a note, not just its pitch but how much you flatten or sharpen it: "In African singing it's the indication of how much emotion you put into that note, and if you take that and transpose it to a cantor singing you understand that immediately. You hear all the beautiful dips and swells that are part of human voice, the humanness of voice singing. And then you take the next step in how the songwriters took those concepts and mirrored them in their own melodic line writing, even though now it's on a piano, let's say, dividing the octave up into twelve equal pitches. But if you look at how they use pitches and how important they are, how they mean things, it's something I talk all about with my students when I teach them about ballad playing. Also, in terms of the music they write and the melodic lines that they write, how they have married those ideas to the placement of lyric. So it's all connected to the meaning of words. You can say you've taken away the idiomatic sound of cantorial singing but the concept's still the same. Someone is usually writing a song about a deep emotion, usually about love or loss, something deep felt, and they're doing it with words and melodic line. Music's an amalgam of so many influences, African included, and those composers would tell you that as well. But, you know, the connection's real plain to me."

So what about the jazz avant-garde – specifically the 1960s New Thing? "Weren't they turning their backs on song form?"

"All I can do is share with you my thoughts, that musicians never make a musical choice that's from the negative, in other words we don't do something because it's not something else. I've found that there isn't a note that I play in some of the most avant-garde writing and playing that I do" – she refers to her album *Chasing Paint* that is inspired by Jackson Pollack's paintings – "there's not a doubt in my mind that all those note choices, everything I do, is informed by my love of simple song. It informs every musical choice I make no matter what I do. It's in there, I can feel it, I can hear it, I can see it."

"Would the same be true then of someone like Cecil Taylor?"

"It's the impulse. If you stop thinking about musical sound and what note did he pick and start thinking about the shapes that they pick, oh God yes, I think Cecil Taylor's one of the most lyrical musicians I know. So's Albert Ayler."

"Still informed by the tradition that preceded them?"

"I don't know to what extent, but I feel song, from wherever it came from. Whether it came from a church, from something they heard when they were young, who knows? I hear it, it's just that you have to get by the surface level of only hearing the top layer of the sound."

My preference is for jazz where the melody is close to the surface; as such, on Jane's quartet album *like silver, like song*. I am particularly taken by her melancholically tuneful composition 'Singing in Stripes', which puts me in mind somewhat of early to mid-sixties' Coltrane. Happily, there are two versions of it on the album, Jane's playing full of enchanting nuance, colour and meaning.

Steve Lacy, under whom Jane had studied in Paris, told me this about his erstwhile pupil: "Bright and very far ranging – she's great." When I mentioned this to Jane, she said: "I don't know if you've noticed it, but I have, the large number of musicians on the roster who play soprano saxophones who are Jewish."

I wondered if, for Jewish jazz musicians, soprano saxophone might be a modern substitute for the clarinet, that mainstay of klezmer music and the instrument famously associated with Benny Goodman and Artie Shaw? Jane's riposte fair took my breath away.

"I'll go even further back – for the shofar, that's what I think. I have two thoughts about it; one is that it is connected to the shofar in some way. And the other is that I think something else that informs Jewish thought is gravitating towards innovation. I remember in high school learning who the great innovative Jewish painters were and, wow, there is a tradition among Jewish artists to be on the edge. So, I thought, wow, yeah, I could be part of this, that's the way I think. And the soprano saxophone being an instrument that hasn't enjoyed quantity of performance in the jazz tradition – it hasn't been played as much as the alto, tenor and even the baritone – so it's an instrument that, if you want to say something new, it's not a bad place to go."

Jews, reflected Jane, were historically a people who had frequently fled persecution and lived on the edge: "So why should their art not reflect their lives? If you ask yourself other questions about a culture, about when you have to travel, what do you take with you that's precious, that nobody can take away from you, it's your music, it's your song, that's what – Chagall, painting all those fiddlers. Life's as precarious as a fiddler on the roof."

# Chapter 13: The gender trap

"Women have been influential as singers but there have not been that many influential instrumentalists." Dan Morgenstern pointed up that obvious truth when I asked him about Jewish female jazz musicians.

Until musicians of Jane Ira Bloom's calibre emerged, hardly any of the few women instrumentalists that had made a significant impact in the male-dominated jazz world was Jewish. Then Dan suggested Barbara Carroll "because she was one of the early bebop pianists". Before we come to my interview with Barbara, a few reflections.

Historically, there has been a tendency for male jazz instrumentalists to regard jazz singing – a field where women have predominated – somewhat disdainfully, although the most revered vocalists – Bessie, Billie, Ella, some others – have won adoration for their contribution. Yet the human voice is by far the most distinctive musical instrument, and Helen Forrest, we have seen, was one of the most admired big band singers of the 1930s and forties. Jewish 'canaries' of the era also included Fran Warren, Kitty Kallen, Georgia Gibbs and Bea Wain.

Then came the jazzy cabaret singers that were popular in the decades following world war two. For rabbi's daughter Ruth Olay however, hers was a bumpy career. She was working as a secretary at Twentieth Century Fox where she befriended Duke Ellington vocalist Ivie Anderson. Olay, whose mother was a classical choral singer, had taken singing lessons and Anderson detected her talent and prompted the teenage Olay to stand in during an Ellington jam in north Hollywood. Impressed, the wife of Ellington lyricist Irving Gordon introduced her to saxophonist and arranger Benny Carter. Olay persuaded Carter to let her perform with his celebrated big band in San Diego. It was an all-black outfit but

Olay, performing as Rachel Davis, was able to pass as black: "In the summers I used to get very very dark. I had short dark curly hair and I could have been anything... I always felt very much a part of the black community. It just never occurred to me that there was going to be a problem. I know that we couldn't eat in certain restaurants. But I let Benny and the guys handle that." 1

The mid-fifties found her working as a waitress/singer at the Cabaret Concert Theater on Sunset Boulevard when she came to the notice of Zephyr Records arranger Bill Hitchcock and cut her first album, *It's About Time*. When African American singer Abbey Lincoln vacated a job at the Little Club, she recommended her friend Olay in her place. Olay worked a year there before taking a much higher paying residency at another LA club, the Avant Garde where she took over when Billie Holiday became ill. She played there to packed houses, sharing billing with Lenny Bruce. And she did TV work, including on the Jackie Gleason Timex jazz show where she sang with Duke Ellington. In a production of *Showboat*, she played Julie, a black woman trying to pass for white. During most of her career however she found it necessary to work in capacities other than singing. 2

Sylvia Syms, Teddi King and Frances Faye were other Jewish contemporaries that, like Olay, navigated the line between jazz and cabaret. Syms, about whom Count Basie once said, "That chick knows things that they don't teach in no school," was a main inspiration for one of today's top female Jewish jazz performers, Daryl Sherman.

Feted for her light and intimate vocal delivery of songbook standards and lesser-known material, and her supple, sensitive piano playing, Sherman, as daughter of the late swing-era trombonist Sammy Sherman, grew up steeped in jazz. When she was a rising presence in New York, Syms advised her to "Stop listening to the sound of your voice and think about the song and what the song is saying", which Sherman maintains is just as applicable to her as a pianist. I'm enjoying one of her albums as I write these words – *A Hundred Million Miracles: The Music of Richard Rodgers* – on which a guest performer is cornetist Ruby Braff, one of that shrinking breed of jazz instrumentalists for whom "adoration of the melody" was paramount. He admired Sherman's artistry, as did that other curmudgeon, Artie Shaw, with whose comeback band Sherman toured in 1983; Shaw praising her as a "first-rate singer/musician".

Chicago-based Spider Saloff is another whose repertoire draws heavily from the songbook, as on *Cole Porter Live at Maxim's* that captures her in performance with Chicago Jewish jazz pianist Jeremy Kahn on piano. Spider's sassy vocalisations, her droll introductions to the songs, and Kahn's adroit harmonising, has the audience purring. 3 I was present at Spider's first ever London gig, a Gershwin 115th birthday special at which she sang the obscure 'Vodka' with a touch of Jewish cantorial schtick, as too on her Gershwin centennial album *The Memory of All That*. "It came from a Broadway flop called *The Song of the Flame*, and in the 1920s and 30s if you had a flop show, many times the composers would bury the music but this one was so worth dusting off," Spider told me when I interviewed her for my radio show. "Bradley Williams, my arranger on my Gershwin album, added the klezmer riff." 4

Recent years have seen the emergence of any number of American Jewish female jazz vocalists: Linda Kosut, Lynette Margulies and Hillary Maroon I particularly admire. 5 Margulies, whose repertoire ranges from blues to R&B to jazz, has an unaffectedly honest, lived-in voice, the impact of which is especially compelling on her album *Love of Life* because the accompanying instrumentation is, as Margulies puts it, "kept to the bare necessities on piano and bass". She needs nothing more. Margulies, who grew up in a religiously Orthodox household in

Washington DC, also recorded *Look For the Silver Lining*, pouring her soul into renditions of mainly Jewish liturgical tunes, and songs by popular composers from Gershwin to Carole King.

Linda Kosut has done much to celebrate the memory of black singer-songwriter Oscar Brown Jr and his hip poetic songs. Her album *Long As You're Living* draws exclusively on his material, including the shocking 'Bid 'Em In' with its wordplay chillingly evoking a slave trade auction. Another Brown song, 'Dat Dere', which so acutely captures the relationship between a father and his inquisitive young son, features on my favourite Kosut recording, *Life is but a dream*. The standout track for me is the Bruce Springsteen/Craig Carnelia medley 'Factory/The Mason', Kosut's rendition of Springsteen's lyrics such a moving testament to blue collar working life that my eyes water listening to it as I contemplated my own years doing poorly paid, dispiriting non-union factory work.

Hillary Maroon, from mixed black and Jewish parentage, co-led the group Maroon with Benny Lackner, a pianist/keyboardist whose half-Jewish father fled Nazi Germany after publishing dissident articles. The albums *Migratory* and *Who the sky betrays* are post-millennial in their openness to the possibilities of inter-fusing jazz with inflections from rock, soul and electro, Maroon's vocals understatedly dramatic. Her renditions of Bob Dylan's 'Love Sick' on the first album, and John Lennon's 'Isolation' on the second, are riveting.

• • • •

Professional female instrumentalists there were even in the bad old days, usually in the patronisingly marketed 'girl bands', most famously the International Sweethearts of Rhythm that played solid big band swing. The Sweethearts, whose original members met in a Mississippi school for poor and black children, flourished during world war two when there was a shortage of male musicians on the home front. Jewish Sweethearts included lead alto saxophonist Roz Cron, one of the first whites to join the band. 6 And drummer, arranger and vocalist Fagle Liebman, whose professional career began as a member of an all-female quartet playing the 'borscht circuit' and who when growing up, "loved jazz... only jazz; this was the only thing I listened to. I knew everyone's solo, I knew everyone's licks, I knew all the lyrics. I was a real hip little kid". 7

Cron as a young musician in the thirties loved playing jazz but there were few opportunities so she was thrilled when, with a day's notice, she was summoned to tour with the Sweethearts. Having grown up in Boston she didn't realise Jim Crow was slang for Southern segregation, thinking "it was some gentleman we would meet in the South". 8 On the road Cron learned to "pass for black" to deceive Southern law enforcers, experimenting with dark makeup, permanents and just being as inconspicuous as possible. 9 She spent a night in an El Paso jail when police didn't buy her story that her mother was black, her father white. The next morning, the band's manager brought along two real mixed-marriage women posing as "cousins". "The sheriff said he knew that I was passing but he just wanted us to get out of town," recalled Cron. 10 The risks she ran, for love of jazz, were all the greater because, as Sherrie Tucker perceived, "she would have had a quite different relationship to white supremacist groups... while travelling in the South than would a white woman who was not Jewish". 11 Flo Dreyer, former Sweethearts leader, told me she thought that, besides Liebman and Cron, there might have been two other Jewish members: "I am pretty sure that the trombone player Helen Jones' mother was Jewish, also Toby (Pauline) Butler, trumpet player. Toby joined my first band as a bass player."

Music historian, record producer and feminist Rosetta Reitz, who grew up in a Jewish family in Utica, New York, was instrumental in reviving interest in the Sweethearts. As a lover of early jazz and blues, it struck her that recordings by 1920s and thirties women musicians in those genres, particularly black artists, had all but been forgotten – Bessie Smith, aficionados knew about but otherwise, not much else. Reitz borrowed money to found Rosetta Records in 1979 and re-issued, on an extensive series of LPs, such gems as *Georgia White Sings and Plays the Blues* with Reitz's historical research on the sleeves. Reitz collaborated with film-makers Greta Schiller and Andrew Weiss on a 1986 documentary about the Sweethearts, her label issuing a related album about which Nat Hentoff confessed in *Wall Street Journal*: "When I used to hear tales of the music created by these traveling ladies, I figured they couldn't have been that good. But *International Sweethearts of Rhythm* reveals... that they were better than their legend. So how come they're not even mentioned in 'definitive' histories of big band jazz? Maybe because no one believed that women could do such things."

Female jazz instrumentalists today find it easier to gain acceptance but there remains a need for all-women bands, of which Diva is the best known. Stanley Kay, Diva's Jewish founder and artistic director, formerly Buddy Rich's manager and back-up drummer, began assembling the personnel after being blown away by Sherrie Maricle's drumming. Through organising Diva, Kay discovered "how difficult the women's lives had been, how much dues they had paid, and how much they were put down". 12 He issued the challenge: "Turn around and tell me if women or men are playing." 13 Jewish Diva artists have included pianist Janice Friedman, trumpeter Jami Dauber, saxophonist and arranger Leigh Pilzer, saxophonist Carol Chaikin, clarinetist and saxophonist

Anat Cohen. and trombonists Lolly Bienenfeld and Deborah Weisz.

I asked ex-Diva pianist Roberta Piket if she thought female instrumentalists were still handicapped by male prejudice. "Not male prejudice. Just a socialised, buddy mentality that excludes women by default. It's changing among younger male players because they grew up in a different environment than players my age. They are more comfortable having women friends and colleagues." That would include drummer Billy Mintz and clarinetist and saxophonist Sam Sadigursky, Jewish collaborators on Roberta's enjoyably varied album *Sides, Colors* on which standards jostle with free, modal, and soul-jazz. Roberta's father Frederick Piket, originally from Vienna, was a composer of Jewish liturgical music, and she told me: "I did a concert at Free Synagogue of Flushing where my father was music director for many years from the '50s to the '70s. One of the things I did was to improvise on some of his choral pieces. This concert was the idea of the cantor."

One of the first female instrumentalists to gain widespread recognition before she died tragically young from heart failure in 1990 was guitarist Emily Remler. "I may look like a nice Jewish girl from New Jersey, but inside I'm a fifty-year-old, heavyset black man with a big thumb", was her way of acknowledging a musician that greatly inspired her, Wes Montgomery. 14 At eighteen, Remler graduated from Berklee alongside mostly much older male musicians – "forty men to each woman". She moved to New Orleans where a 1978 encounter with jazz guitarist Herb Ellis changed her life: "I had a Herb Ellis model guitar and he was in town. I called... and asked him to fix it. I'm very gutsy." Recognising her talent, Ellis invited her to perform at the Concord Jazz Festival in California: "And there I was on a 'Great Guitar' bill with Herb, Cal Collins, Barney Kessel and Tal Farlow – my heroes." 15

Whether using plectrum or thumb, Remler played mainstream jazz guitar with rippling fluidity, fronting her quartet with bassist Eddie Gomez, drummer Bob Moses and trumpeter John D'Earth, or recording with her favourite pianist, Hank Jones. She brought the same facility to bossa, spending three years as accompanist to Astrud Gilberto. Before switching to jazz, Remler had practised Jimi Hendrix and Johnny Winter licks and the mid-eighties found her in duo formation with jazz-rock guitarist Larry Coryell. "I've played so many different forms of music that it's unbelievable," she said in one of her last interviews. "I lived in New Orleans for three years and I played Dixieland... the only white person in the band and the only person under 65." 16 Asked what she would most like to be remembered for, her answer was: "Good compositions, memorable guitar playing, and my contribution as a woman to music." 17

Mimi Fox is a successor to Remler in that she's a guitarist with technique to burn but it's all about taste, about artistry, not pyrotechnics. Fox grew up in a Queens. NY Jewish family and "pretty much taught myself how to play guitar from listening to The Beatles' *Rubber Soul* album when I was 10". 18 Her older siblings were into rock and pop but mother Anne was a semi-professional jazz singer-songwriter while Fox's father had a large collection of jazz records and it was jazz to which she was increasingly drawn. In her teens she got involved in bands in various genres, on drums and guitar, but realised she couldn't keep growing unless she "started to get more harmonic information". 19 Her main focus from then on was jazz guitar. Although she studied classical guitar, she "found the lack of improvisation sort of stifling". 20 The turning point in her career came when she moved to California and took tuition from Jewish jazz guitarist Bruce Foreman. 21 Fox's playing is sensational whether performing solo, or in small groups such as on the San Francisco String Trio release

*May I Introduce To You*, a loving 60$^{th}$ anniversary reconfiguration of *Sgt Pepper*.

For flautist Jamie Baum, composing is as important as improvisation and she has earned the respect of her peers for both aspects of her art. Her main compositional vehicle is Septet+, whose album *In This Life* is informed by her travels in south Asia and includes two tracks composed by the late Pakistani Sufi vocalist Nusrat Fateh Ali Khan, about whom Baum said in a radio interview, "when I heard him, it reminded me of the first time I heard Coltrane or Miles Davis, you know, just something very visceral". Dan Weiss, who features on tabla, is like Baum a Jewish jazz musician that has immersed himself in south Asian music. The 2018 Septet+ album *Bridges* delves ever deeper into this orientalist well of musical influence. Baum, who in her travels collaborated with musicians she encountered, has found deep connections between certain types of Jewish music – her earliest musical influences – and Arabic, middle eastern and south Asian music. "They share some of the same scales and approach to melodic development," she told me. "In fact at various periods in history, they often commingled, for example, relations between the Islamic schools of tasawwuf and the Jewish mystical movement of Kabbalah have been discussed in numerous works and in the 13th century it is widely know that there were Sufi Rabbis." *Bridges*, on which Septet+ is expanded to a ten-piece – including three other Jewish musicians, Jeff Hirshfield, Sam Sadigursky and Zack Lober – includes Baum's 'Song Without Words (for S James Baum)', written to honour the passing of her father, and is influenced by Kol Nidre, the Aramaic synagogue recitation that forms part of the Yom Kippur service. 22

If there's one instrument on which female musicians have figured most prominently in jazz, I'm guessing it's the piano,

among them some fabulous Jewish players including Myra Melford
and Jessica Williams.

I've been listening to a wide representation of Melford's
recorded work, and for me she is one of the most inspirational
talents in vanguardist jazz: limitlessly inventive as a soloist,
accompanist and composer. It is a joy to listen to her in ensembles
with similarly inclined collaborators, as in Trio M with bassist
Mark Dresser and drummer Matt Wilson – their albums some
of the most satisfying avant-jazz, or indeed any jazz, that I have
encountered. She is involved in two all-female trios, having
explained: "I've always had this ambivalence about identifying as a
woman musician... But as I've gotten older and reflected a lot more,
I've felt this need or desire to nurture young women players. The
truth is there are still way more men playing this music, although
things are changing." 23

One of Melford's albums, *life carries me this way*, is her solo jazz
suite inspired by the powerful abstract paintings of the late Don
Reich, a close friend – Reich's vivid artwork displayed on the sleeve.
Melford, who "let them speak to me for months and months" in
conceiving the music, said they seem to dovetail "with my own
tendency towards lyricism, abstraction and rhythmic mobility".
Indeed, I would describe Melford as an expressionist improviser
whose keystrokes render intricate patterns of aural shape, tone and
colour. She actually grew up in a work of art, in a Frank Lloyd
Wright house near Chicago, and is yet another Jewish connection
to AACM that, as seen in the last chapter, was founded as an
African American avant-garde collective. She was never a member
but has collaborated with AACM veterans Henry Threadgill and,
in the Equal Interest cooperative trio, with Joseph Jarman and
Leroy Jenkins.

If one were to survey the greatest mainstream jazz pianists of
the last half-century, Jessica Williams should surely be up there.

Lamentable therefore her neglect in jazz bibliography. Conservatory trained but finding the classical repertoire too constraining, her career began in the sixties in her native Baltimore, mainly fronting Hammond organ trios. She joined ex-Miles Davis drummer Philly Jo Jones in Philadelphia, collaborated with Stan Getz and Dexter Gordon, and, following a move to north California, worked from then on mainly solo and leading trios, recording scores of albums. These are evidence of how endlessly, eloquently inventive she consistently was, whether performing standards, her own compositions, or her many interpretations of one of her chief inspirations, Thelonious Monk. Her last release, *With Love*, was in 2014, the music, all solo, all slow tempo, profoundly beautiful but heartrendingly melancholic. She had been wrestling with a serious medical condition and sold her beloved Yamaha piano to fund treatment.

My contact with her was before this sorry situation, after I found the following statement on her website: "I refuse to play with musicians who are anti-Semitic, xenophobic, non-inclusive, anti-woman or in any way racist or sexist."

I emailed Jessica and got back a wholly unexpected reply. Telling me she always wore a star of David and shin around her neck, and that her mother was Jewish, my dad Irish, she said: "Yes, there is a considerable degree of antisemitism in jazz, increasing over the last few years. I have gotten comments, from 'you killed Christ' to 'you don't look Jewish' to 'how much money are you going to Jew me out of?' Frightful, no? Jazz is a microcosm of our culture, and it is rife with prejudice against women, LGBT people, those who have physical differences, those in wheelchairs or otherwise physically challenged, and anyone that doesn't fit the stereotype du jour. 'Jazz is the music of freedom' – Art Blakey said that, Philly Joe said that, I say that. But if jazz continues being elitist, non-inclusive, cerebral, androcentric and ego-driven, it won't be with us for long except as a museum exhibition."

I subsequently learned that Jessica, who died in 2022, was transgender, having undergone the surgery in the seventies. 24

For all the progress then, women instrumentalists still often need to strive harder than male counterparts to gain visibility. As the late, Jewish, jazz writer Leslie Gourse, saw it, "Women have discovered that entrepreneurship is the only way they can showcase themselves and build careers when calls to play with established all male groups don't arrive. Deuce, a fusion group that was founded by saxophonist, flautist, drummer Jean Fineberg and trumpeter Ellen Seeling, is an excellent case in point." 25

Fineberg, who is Jewish, made her name in New York where, she informed me, she had much success with Deuce, as well as performing in concert with Dizzy Gillespie and Clark Terry and touring and recording with Laura Nyro, Chic, Sister Sledge, David Bowie and Melba Liston. She relocated to San Francisco and became involved in the Montclair Women's Big Band, formed in 1998 to spotlight the talents of Bay-area female musicians. 26 Her latest outfit, the swinging octet JAZZphoria, is all female other than the drummer.

Banjoist Cynthia Sayer, whom I contacted after seeing her perform with Woody Allen's New Orleans Jazz Band, told me that while it is true that women instrumentalists are gaining greater access, it is a far from uniform process. "I think gender diversity and acceptance varies within the different kinds of jazz. For example, there are far fewer women in early jazz than in mainstream jazz."

Gaining acceptance, she said, was not at first easy: "I've experienced *many* strong reactions to my gender and my instrument through the years; initially it was an issue but now that

I've been around for a while it has gone more to the other side and is more of a marketing perk."

Cynthia concluded though that women needed special determination to be able to evolve to their best due to various forms of non-inclusion as they learn and work: "Small things like not being invited along to listen and analyse jazz recordings, or not being invited to join in developmental jam sessions, to large things such as being hired or not for how it looks on stage instead of playing ability."

• • • •

Barbara Carroll penetrated the male-dominated jazz domain as a pianist in the 1940s when bebop was turning the music on its head. She died in 2017; what follows is my interview with her for the first edition of this book.

As I witnessed when I caught her gigging at Birdland in midtown Manhattan, prior to the interview, she now also sang; although hers was not a technically striking voice, it was an understatedly charming accompaniment to her elegant playing. Most of the material was standards that, played and sung the way Barbara did it, it sounded fresh as a spring morning.

Jazz pianist Dick Katz was glowing about her: "A wonderful player, particularly on ballads"; Carroll had a way, he said, "of reharmonising and reinterpreting songs like every real creative pianist does". Katz however regretted that she "had to keep that sort of under wraps" in her thirty-year engagement at New York's Carlyle Hotel, a job she had lost at the time I met her.

Would Carroll have been perceived more eminently had she been a man, I asked Katz.

"Absolutely. When she came up, Mary Lou Williams was about it, and Marian [McPartland] had a hard time because of that. Yes, of course her career suffered because she was a woman. No doubt about it. Although that's changing rapidly – there's some wonderful young women pianists now."

The critic Leonard Feather helped bolster Barbara's early career, hailing her as "among the most important pianists whose styles look to some degree in bop". 27 She was, said Feather "the first woman pianist to embrace the bebop style... the only woman instrumentalist whose picture I included in the book *Inside Bebop*". 28 Feather first hired her for a live 1948 bebop session broadcast over WMGM from the Royal Roost on Broadway. She was, said Feather, "in fast company" – Max Roach and Bud Powell among them – yet "made such a striking impression that evening with her incisive boppish lines that the following March she was included in a group I assembled for a date led by the multi-instrumentalist Eddie Shu, on Rainbow Records". 29

Complimentary too, although in terminology so patronising it is hilarious, was Savoy Records, who early in Barbara's career recorded her leading a trio with bassist Danny Martucci and drummer Herbie Wasserman. Savoy eventually issued this on the jazz women compilation *Looking For A Boy*; the liner notes refer to the "delightful man-sized pianistics of lovely Barbara Carroll".

With man-sized strides, I made my way to Barbara's apartment for our interview.

"I grew up in western Massachusetts and started playing the piano when I was very young, about four or five, and began studying classical piano when I was about eight. But I always wanted to play jazz and things that I heard on the radio or that I made up myself and was always interested in improvisation. And I studied classical music and a lot of the teachers were not sympathetic to playing jazz."

"Were your parents?"

"Yeah. They wanted me to do whatever I wanted to do musically. My mother was a housewife, and my father a plumber and electrician, but he could play the trumpet, though not professionally. And I heard people like Nat Cole and Teddy Wilson and Art Tatum, people who really opened my eyes to the way I wanted to play. I went to the New England Conservatory of Music and began playing in bands in Boston, working till two or three in the morning and then getting up to go to school. So I cut the school and concentrated on working, then came to New York. My first job in New York was with Chuck Wayne [guitar] and Clyde Lombardi [bass] and we were fortunate enough to get an engagement at the Down Beat Club on 52nd Street opposite Dizzy Gillespie's big band. So there I was on 52nd Street where all my idols were."

"At that stage would you say you were most heavily into bop?"

"Yeah, that was the music at the time. I played there for a month or two, then played various clubs in New York, all with my trio."

"What was your experience of being a female musician in a male dominated jazz world?"

"You were pre-judged because you were a female but if you could show that you could play, then musicians were not judgemental. The bias, the discrimination, was there but if you proved that you were on a par with them musically, you were less apt to be discriminated against."

"Can you talk about the part Leonard Feather played?"

"He made great efforts to involve female jazz musicians into the mainstream of jazz. My very first recording was for a group that Leonard Feather put together. He was very quiet. Leonard was not an easy man to get close to, although I respected his musical criticisms very much. I thought he was a very able jazz critic, his taste was good. And he was a champion of young musicians and tried to help other female musicians. He championed female jazz musicians before it was fashionable to do so. I was not a victim

of sex discrimination a lot, I never felt that I was. Here's what
happens; if you're a female jazz musician, they automatically think
that you're terrible before they hear you. But if they hear you and
they don't think you're so terrible, the discrimination lessens."

Barbara recalled the impact of another kind of discrimination,
involving a singer: "He came in on the wrong key, it was his fault
and he blamed me, and he said something about the Jews. I was a
kid and never forgot it – it was very hurtful."

The interview turned to Jewish songwriters. "Richard Rodgers
employed you in a show, didn't he?"

"Yes, I was in a show called *Me and Juliet* with my trio and
was on stage with a speaking part as well as playing. We played
at the beginning of the show, and Richard Rodgers allowed us
to improvise. It was a marvellous experience to get to know Mr
Rodgers and Mr Hammerstein and George Abbott. I never wanted
to do it, I didn't even want to go to the audition because I was
playing at the Embers which was a marvellous jazz club in New
York, and I was asked to audition for this thing and I thought,
'Why would I want to play for the theatre, I just want to play
bebop?' But this agent prevailed upon me to go to the audition,
so we went and auditioned for Rodgers and Hammerstein and
they seemed to like it. I wasn't even nervous because I didn't want
the job anyway. Very often that happens, if you want something
desperately you don't get it, but if you don't, you relax and get
it. And we were with the show for a year. It was a very gratifying
experience. Getting to know Richard Rodgers and Oscar
Hammerstein was thrilling. They were quite different. Rodgers was
a very interesting man. He was not all warm and fuzzy, he was a
little detached and withdrawn, but he was very nice to me. Usually,
he was very demanding that the songs in his show be sung and
played note for note the way he wrote them, he didn't want
anybody fooling around with his stuff the first time it was

presented. I was fortunate because the role which I had in his show, which was a show within a show, I took the part of a backstage pianist and the role allowed me to play the part of a jazz pianist and improvise. I think he respected the fact that we were jazz musicians and could improvise which doesn't happen much in the theatre. Hammerstein was an interesting and extremely warm and loveable man and he certainly was an enormous talent."

As vehicles for jazz, Barbara was dismissive of most songs written since the arrival of rock – some Beatles she liked, Paul Simon, but the main exception for her was Burt Bacharach, the Jewish songwriter of some of most sophisticated, most beautifully orchestrated pop songs, much covered by jazz musicians, the "Gershwin of the second half of the 20$^{th}$ century" as he was hailed.

Given her main career as a jazz instrumentalist, I wondered how important for Barbara were the lyrics of the songs she performed.

"If you're playing a ballad, it's very helpful to know the lyrics. I always know them, not that I have made a real effort to know them, it's just that I do. It's helpful in the way you phrase a song, and the way you improvise instrumentally. Naturally that's the case when you sing. But I've only begun singing more recently; when I began, I was just playing."

That took us to her more recent career. "Around 1978 I began playing solo piano at the Hotel Carlyle and I worked there for years." It was there that she started singing, though she took no lessons.

"And it was well received almost immediately?"

"People love the lyrics of the good songs, the standards. They love them for a variety of reasons, first of all because they're great lyrics and then because there's often a nostalgic reason involved."

Another songwriter Barbara knew was Harold Arlen.

"Oh, Harold Arlen was magnificent. As a personality he was a dapper, handsome man, always beautifully dressed and very attractive. And he sang – oh, he was a great singer. I had the great pleasure of recording a demo with him. When he was getting set to record, he wanted to do some demos of songs that he didn't want to record, and he asked me to help him out. It's a very nervous thing to play a composer's songs for him while he's singing. Anyway, he sang 'One For My Baby' and 'Come Rain, Come Shine', those wonderful songs, and he had a great voice because it was part cantor influenced and part black influenced, not jazzy but it was the perfect combination. It was fabulous. I never thought of him as a jazz musician, I know he played piano okay, but I never thought of him in that way... This all happened to me when I was very young and he was very encouraging."

"Arlen found some correlation between the way his cantor father sang in synagogue and jazz. Can you hear that too?"

"Definitely, and Harold Arlen was able to take that and incorporate that emotion into his songs and when you hear him sing, he's got that cantorial sound. In addition to that part of his music he was very influenced by the black musicians that he heard and was able to integrate the two, and he came out with this emotional thing that he was able to write. He wrote songs that just had that kind of feeling, they were different from the songs that Cole Porter was writing, or Richard Rodgers or Irving Berlin. His songs had a different emotional appeal. It was the Jewishness of Harold Arlen's songs."

"Are there any songs where this is particularly striking, where you can't miss it?"

"How about 'One for My Baby', huh? – *'It's quarter to three; No one in the place but you and me; One for my baby...'*; or 'Stormy Weather' is another perfect example, practically any Harold Arlen song – 'Over The Rainbow'. He had this gift for melody and harmony, and therefore, with those two things going, you're a great songwriter and of course he aligned himself with fabulous lyricists. 'Old Black Magic' was another one."

"When you led this small 1940s combo with Chuck Wayne, you, a woman, did you get immediate acceptance?"

"I didn't, but little by little I did. I was the leader and I asked these guys to play the job with me, and I had just come to New York, I was a kid."

"That took a lot of..."

"Chutzpah, yes. But being Jewish, I had a little of that. But Chuck was a wonderful influence, I admired him so much."

"Did he say yes immediately to working with you?"

"Yes, he said, 'Who is this chick?', but he wanted to work. The same with the bass player, but it worked out very well. I learned a lot."

"How long before you felt 'I am the leader'?"

"I never felt that way. It wasn't a female/male thing, it was an inexperienced musician, as opposed to a very experienced musician. I always felt that Chuck was such a superior musician that it was a privilege to be working with him, even though it was my trio. Unfortunately, it didn't last too long. We worked together for about six months then he went to George Shearing or Woody Herman."

"In that six months or so, how much do you think it improved you as a musician and your confidence?"

"Oh, greatly. Don't forget, I was thrust into this concentrated hodgepodge of musicians on 52nd Street; Charlie Parker was working the Down Beat, Miles Davis, Art Tatum, Billie, Dizzy, they were all right there, and there I was in the centre of this heaven which is what it was for me. Certainly, I had more confidence because I had been around for a while, I had been accepted to some degree. And you were talking about the advantage or disadvantage of being a female; if you were accepted musically, the female thing almost became a commercial advantage, the reason being that you were different, you were one in a field of many."

"Except that until comparatively recently, that really hasn't been the case, has it? There were exceptions like Mary Lou Williams, not counting singers."

"I don't feel that I was discriminated against a lot because I was a woman. At the beginning, probably."

"Of course, you had that grounding in classical training."

"I did, and also I wasn't working in big bands, I was either working solo or in my own small groups so it was my thing, I was in control, so I didn't feel they were putting me down because I was a chick piano player. I don't know, maybe they were. The truth of the matter is I wish I had more chutzpah because I may have been able to do a lot of things I was too timid to do."

Maybe so, but Barbara must have been tough to have stuck in there; a contemporary of Barbara's, vibraphonist Marjorie Hyams, quit because of rampant chauvinism.

"Let's turn things on their head a little bit – do you think you as a woman performer bring anything to the party that's different to a male performer?"

"How could I not? If I'm playing honestly, it's a self-expression, that's what we're doing. So how could I be expressing myself in the same way as a male musician? So naturally I'm bringing a female sensitivity to the piano."

"If you were to analyse one of your recordings alongside that of a male pianist that you admire, what would be different?"

"It's hard to dissect it in terms of sex. When I say that I'm bringing something of my own to it then I run the risk of the worst put-down in the world which is, 'You play great for a girl.' You know, that's what people used to say. But I play differently, I would have to, because I'm me."

"Most of the musicians you've played with have been men..."

"Yes – don't strain yourself with that, they have been."

"Any reason for that? Could you have brought on women musicians?"

At this, Barbara smiled: "I like men... no, the reason is that there are obviously more good male musicians than there are female; that's the way it's been."

She spoke about her first husband, the bassist Joe Shulman, also Jewish: "He was marvellous, he played with Miles Davis on some of his early records, and with the Glenn Miller army band, and with Peggy Lee. He died when he was thirty-three. We worked together."

"Didn't you play with Charlie Parker somewhere?"

"He used to come in where I was playing sometimes. He would sit in. I never played with him professionally."

"And you won handsome tribute from Duke Ellington."

"Oh, he was very charming, gallant, and it was very fine of him to say that."

"You once opened up for Art Tatum. That must have been fearsome."

"Yes, it was, like playing on the same piano. I played first – it was terrifying. At the same time, he was kind and complimentary and encouraging to me. But you can just imagine that feeling. I had just come to New York, it was terrifying and exhilarating all at the same time. I was working at the Embers and they always had two acts, and there was only one piano."

So, from impressing the likes of Ellington and Tatum early in her career, to a dismissal of her art as 'cocktail music' during her decades of solo gigging at the Carlyle.

Having witnessed that Birdland gig, and listened to the CD *One Morning in May* that Barbara gave me, I still get annoyed on her behalf when I think of that glib 'cocktail' put-down.

# Chapter 14: Between rock and a smooth place

"There was a decision quite a few years ago to try and treat jazz like pop music and raise the expectations of the record companies. That is when music started to become watered down."

So said tenor saxophonist and flautist Lew Tabackin in an interview with Fred Jung, his target 'fusion'. Plenty of jazz musicians and fans – particularly, but not only – of Tabackin's or earlier generations, feel the way he does about fusion, a generic term for those heavily electrified and amplified hybrids, jazz-rock and jazz-funk.

Before I delve into the Jewish input, some words about Tabackin whom Jung rightly described as "Criminally unheralded". 1 He grew up in a blue-collar Jewish family "just trying to survive" in Philadelphia where every morning "was a trauma because I had to get past a Catholic school to get to my public school". The Irish Catholic kids would bully minorities, especially Jews: "Those were the days when blacks and Jews kind of had a feeling of brotherhood out of necessity." 2 He became jazz smitten in the 1950s, his first major influence a Jewish tenorist: "Al Cohn had a big fan club among musicians in Philadelphia; he was like a hero to them, for some reason." 3 And as he told Jung, he had to stop himself from becoming another Coltrane clone. As with all truly significant artists however, Tabackin transcends his influences.

I only learned about him after discovering his seventies' LP *Tabackin* in a second-hand vinyl sale, Tabackin looking rabbinical with bushy beard on the cover. His tenor playing on *Tabackin*, supported by Bob Daugherty on bass and Bill Goodwin, drums, is sensational.

Tabackin is the husband of the Japanese American pianist, composer and arranger Toshiko Akiyoshi, and explains on the sleeve: "This album was recorded following a two-week tour of Japan by the Toshiko Akiyoshi Quartet. We taped the album in one evening in a very informal manner, once we got a workable set-up... Most of the tenor tracks are first takes."

'Come Rain or Come Shine' is the standout, Tabackin's tenor solo, sustained throughout, extraordinary, taking Arlen's melody as far out as it can possibly go without tipping over into avant terrain, a wildly inventive, rollercoaster ride. Humphrey Lyttelton, on BBC radio, played it and said it was one of the three times in his life he caught a performance by Tabackin and thought what "smashing playing... some of the most exciting music I had ever heard".

I could find no trace of the album online, not even second-hand so contacted Tabackin to ask if it had ever been released on CD.

"The album you are referring to is my first leader album, recorded in 1974, in Tokyo. Original title was *Let The Tape Roll*. There is no CD."

"Why ever not?"

"I have many recordings that have not been issued on CD. The jazz record biz is unfortunately controlled by market people, not artistic people."

And the record biz, in embracing fusion as it emerged in the late sixties and early seventies, tapped into what for jazz is a lucrative market, and commercial considerations certainly motivated, at least in part, most artists involved.

Miles Davis was the catalyst and Clive Davis, a Jew who rose from working class beginnings to head Columbia Records, played an underappreciated role in Miles' late sixties change of direction. "He started talking to me about this younger market and about changing," Miles disclosed in his autobiography. For Miles, it wasn't just the commercial imperative as he genuinely appreciated rock, soul and funk artists such as Hendrix and Sly Stone and his albums from the late sixties on reflected such influences. He shocked many devotees but gained far more and albums such as *Bitches Brew* appealed to progressive rock fans, leading some to a wider appreciation of jazz.

Fusion does not however start with Miles. In America a viable jazz-rock movement began budding around the mid-sixties. At weekly jams at New York's L'Intrigue there congregated a group of musicians who besides jazz dug the rock that was happening around that time, and they attempted synthesising these idioms. 4

Among the L'Intrigue participants was vibraphonist Mike Mainieri, founder of the fusion big band White Elephant, several of whose personnel were Jewish – trumpeter Randy Brecker and his tenor saxophonist younger brother Michael, salsa and jazz trombonist Barry Rogers, and drummer Tony Levin. Mainieri, whose father only was Jewish, was older than most jazz-rock pioneers, having worked professionally since the early fifties with Buddy Rich, Benny Goodman, Coleman Hawkins and Wes Montgomery, but he was in tune with the latest developments in popular culture: "Everyone had their hair long, everyone was into the Beatles, and later, who didn't have a Stevie Wonder album?" 5

Similar sentiments were expressed by Steve Marcus, Jewish leader of Count's Rock Band that included electric guitarist Larry Coryell, pianist Mike Nock, bassist Chris Hills and drummer Bob Moses. Their album, *Tomorrow Never Knows*, released in January 1968, weds the psychedelic kick of late sixties rock with the expansive possibilities of jazz improvisation, including bursts of free blowing. Marcus on overdubbed soprano and tenor is inspired, heavily indebted to Coltrane, extemporising on Beatles, Byrds and other epochal rock material, and complemented by Coryell's standout electric guitar and a rhythm section attuned to post-Ornette jazz and Hendrix impro-rock. It works so well because the musicians were fans of the great rock of the period; "The Beatles made kids of us all," said Marcus. 6

I heard about Marcus through Andy Simons, who as editor of the jazz record collectors' quarterly *IAJRC Journal* told me: "I was thrilled by Marcus bashing the three-chord guts out of the Troggs' hit 'Wild Thing' at Newport in 1969. He and other fusion players were hipper than the mostly adult jazz festival crowd because, although they were willing to be playful with rock music, they loved it anyway."

*Tomorrow Never Knows* and the Marcus-led releases that followed, *Count's Rock Band*, and *The Lord's Prayer* with Herbie Hancock on piano, came out on Vortex, a label founded by Herbie Mann who produced the records. Mann was a Jewish post-bop jazz flautist who championed various hybridisations of jazz. In fusion mode, Mann was involved not only as a facilitator but as a musician; his 1969 album *Memphis Underground*, on Atlantic is a coalescence of jazz and southern-fried sixties soul pairing Mann, guitarists Larry Coryell and Sonny Sharrock and vibraphonist Roy Ayers with a funky Memphis rhythm section.

As a producer, Mann could be, almost like George Martin with the Beatles, a significant creative influence, notably so on Dave Pike's *The Doors of Perception*. Although the instrumentation of the all-Jewish line-up is mostly conventional – Pike, vibes, marimba, Lee Konitz, alto sax, Eddie Daniels, tenor sax, clarinet, Don Friedman, piano, Chuck Israel, bass, fender bass, Arnie Wise, drums – the music comes over as free jazz-rock psychedelia, an impression augmented by Mann's sound effects and the sleeve design.

Pike, like Mann a Jewish post-bebopper, played a significant role in early US jazz-rock. Self-taught on vibes, his professional beginnings in the fifties owe much to the black Los Angeles jazz fraternity: "I started working clubs in Compton and Watts even though I was sometimes hustled out of joints because I was too young. I became a protégé of the black jazz scene in Los Angeles and quit school to go on the road with jazz groups." 7

Ousted from the Paul Bley band when Ornette Coleman joined, Pike nevertheless carried over an open-mindedness to jazz-rock music-making and was one of the first vibraphonists to experiment with electrifying the instrument though his playing deviated little from his bop roots. After a well-received gig at the Berliner Jazztage in West Germany, Pike with three German musicians founded the Dave Pike Set and relocated to Europe. The group was experimental in that it combined late sixties-inspired rock and free jazz with odd meters, the musicianship exemplary but nothing too heavy; that buzzword of the era, "groovy", somehow encapsulates the sound. "We did not want deadly serious music, but something light and bright... played for hedonistic high spirits," explained Volker Kriegel, whose spry electric guitar and sitar lines complemented Pike's zippy runs. 8

While jazz musicians incorporated elements from rock, rock musicians took inspiration from jazz. Lou Reed, the Jewish New Yorker who fronted Velvet Underground, spoke of his indebtedness to the sixties' avant-jazzers: "Take 'European Son', which came out of my listening to [Ornette Coleman's] *Free Jazz*... At one time I was listening to Ornette, Don Cherry, Pharoah Sanders, Albert Ayler... I always heard a lot of rock and roll in what Ornette was doing... Cecil Taylor too... I don't want to sound pretentious, but I wanted to play guitar like Ornette Coleman played sax. Distortion made your guitar sound like a sax. Or even like a sax section, with all the overtones." 9

The Doors' first album in 1967 was hailed by producer Michael Cuscuna as "the first successful synthesis of jazz and rock". 10 That is not the way I hear Doors music but Jewish lead guitarist Robbie

Krieger, who wrote some of the group's most enduring anthems, including 'Light My Fire' and 'Love Me Two Times', brought in a jazz sensibility. "I didn't plan on rock 'n' roll," he has revealed. "I wanted to learn jazz. I got to know some people doing rock 'n' roll with jazz, and I thought I could make money playing music. In rock 'n' roll you can realise anything that you can in jazz or anything. There's no limitation other than the beat. You have more freedom than you do in anything except jazz – which is dying – as far as making any money is concerned."

When Miles Davis performed his first concert in front of a rock crowd, at the Fillmore West in 1970, on the bill too was Blood, Sweat & Tears, a brassy band that heavily featured Jewish musicians from jazz or blues backgrounds. The initial impulse came from the blues side when keyboardist Al Kooper and drummer Bobby Colomby, both Jews, and other remnants of their group The Blues Project, sought out musicians schooled in jazz.

Blood, Sweat & Tears, featuring horns in the context of carefully structured extended songs, promoted itself as a jazz band that did rock-influenced material. Joining Kooper, Colomby and Blues Project guitarist Steve Katz, were saxophonist Fred Lipsius, the latter arranging and doubling on piano, and trumpeters Jerry Weiss and Randy Brecker – all Jewish. When Weiss, Kooper and Brecker quit, other Jewish musicians, trombonist Jerry Hyman and trumpeters Chuck Winfield and Lew Soloff stepped in.

Brecker's departure, following his participation in the group's 1967 first album *Child Is Father to the Man*, was prompted by his feeling that the jazz component was becoming compromised. Bringing in a lead singer, David Clayton-Thomas, while de-emphasising the instrumentalists' contributions was, Brecker felt, going too pop. The group hit with 'Spinning Wheel' by which time Brecker had joined Horace Silver's quintet. In 1968, he recorded the first album in his own name, *Score*, heading a sextet that included Michael Brecker, Larry Coryell, and pianist Hal Galper, the tracks alternating between hard bop, funky jazz-rock and a touch of bossa. The following year Randy and Michael Brecker were founding members of jazz-rock group Dreams that included Barry Rogers and another Jewish musician, bassist Don Grolnick. Randy drilled a hole in his trumpet mouthpiece and attached an electric pickup with a guitar jack plugged into a wah-wah pedal: "The pickup allowed me to make electric-guitar-like effects with my horn and we could also amp up the volume" – this before Miles Davis, who would drop in on Dreams' gigs, did likewise. 11

By the early seventies, Blood, Sweat & Tears, sans Randy Brecker, and bolstered by chart success, were eclipsing even Miles when booked with him at New York's Village Gate. Miles was perplexed, as Art D'Lugoff, the Gate's Jewish owner, who had founded the club in 1958, revealed: "I loved Miles dearly but he wasn't doing the kind of business that pop acts were doing... Miles felt that Blood, Sweat & Tears should open for him... Blood, Sweat & Tears drew the larger crowds. We didn't underpay Miles. Blood, Sweat & Tears got $25,000 for a week while Miles got $5,000. But that was based on box office." 12

Early seventies Miles' fusion groups featured Jewish saxophonists Steve Grossman and David Liebman. Grossman was a teenager when he replaced Miles' soprano saxophonist Wayne Shorter in 1970. Miles had courted him, turning up to watch a group Grossman played in, telling him how great he was. 13 Grossman came in for some critical barbs but Miles' biographer, trumpeter Ian Carr, defended him: "The new saxophonist... though much maligned by reviewers, was an excellent choice for this music, playing at white heat and creating a flow of interesting melodic lines." Carr, writing here about Miles' live albums recorded at Fillmore West and Fillmore East, adds: "Although he regarded himself primarily as a tenor saxophonist, all of Grossman's tenor solos were edited out, because Miles wanted only the soprano solos." 14

Liebman, primarily then a tenorist, joined Miles following Grossman's departure. He had been in the jazzy-rock group Ten Wheel Drive whose soulful singer was Polish-born Holocaust survivor Genya Ravan. Then Liebman linked with Grossman in jazz drummer Elvin Jones' band. "Grossman and I had been among the first of the post-Coltrane generation saxophonists to absorb some of his concepts. With Elvin's group we had established a way of playing that was already being emulated by others in the late seventies," Liebman has asserted.

I asked him if he could substantiate that claim, given that numerous saxophonists were Coltrane-inspired.

"Yes, there were a few other saxophonists 'chasin' the Trane'. But since Steve and I were fortunate enough to play with both Elvin Jones and Miles Davis as members of their groups, we had an opportunity and vantage point that was special. Musically, the use of pentatonic scales with chromatic side-slipping encapsulated the basic material we used. Of course, saxophonic techniques employed by Coltrane such as use of the altissimo register and multiphonic passages were also on the plate."

One resulting album from Liebman's time with Miles was *Dark Magus* recorded at Carnegie Hall; Liebman's sleeve-notes describe what was going on: "There was no direct harmony present, meaning chord changes... Although the bass lines were key-centred, the way Miles and myself played over them gave the music a distinct polytonal flavour. Melodically there were no extended lines... the few heads we played were basically two or four bar riffs and many of the tunes had no discernible melody."

When still with Davis, Liebman formed Lookout Farm that debuted with one of the most multi-hued fusion recordings of the seventies; Liebman on saxes and alto flute, John Abercrombie, guitars, bassist Frank Tusa, drummer Jeff Williams, and Jewish acoustic and electric pianist Richie Beirach, while tabla player Badal Roy and percussionist Armen Halburian reflected Liebman's interest in Indian music. Involved too was Liebman's girlfriend, Jewish vocalist Elena Sternberg. *Lookout Farm* is spiritual, passionate and wide-ranging, impelled by the shifting Latin, Indo, jazz and rock rhythms. In jazz-rock historian Stuart Nicholson's estimation, it combined jazz-rock and world music elements "in a lyrically convincing way that suggested, perhaps more than Davis or any other group of the time, an important new direction for the music". 15

Electric violinist Jerry Goodman is another Jewish figure of significance as a founder member in the early 1970s of the Mahavishnu Orchestra formed by ex-Miles guitarist John McLaughlin. Goodman had been in the psychedelic jazzy-rock band The Flock that included several other Jewish musicians – saxophonist Rick Canoff, guitarist, keyboardist and vocalist Fred Glickstein and drummer Ron Karpman. Reminiscent of Blood, Sweat & Tears in featuring horns, the album *Flock* was heralded by the rock and jazz press alike. 16 The music is somewhat overblown, redolent of the excesses of prog, but Goodman's violin stands out, notably his extended soloing on 'Introduction' on which he veers from folkish Gypsy/Jewish to avant-classicism. Impressed, McLaughlin hired him.

The Mahavishnu's *Inner Mounting Flame* – with its unusual time signatures and the virtuosity, cohesion and attack of McLaughlin, Goodman, keyboardist Jan Hammer, and Billy Cobham's seismic drumming – reached number 89 in the *Billboard* chart. It represented, by Stuart Nicholson's reckoning, the "next decisive step in the evolution of jazz-rock" following Miles' breakthrough success. 17 Miles had scored with the 1969 album

*Bitches Brew,* which was languid, diffuse and allusive in its effects. McLaughlin had been guitarist on that, but with Mahavishnu he shifted the emphasis towards a more upfront approach and extended improvisations based on jazz, heavy rock and Indian music.

There is a tributary of fusion marketed as 'smooth jazz', a field that emerged in the 1970s in which Jewish musicians are prominent, notably pianist Dave Grusin and drummer Larry Rosen, co-founders of the record label GRP, and saxophonist Kenny G whose work Artie Shaw dismissed as "elevator music". 18 Kenny G, real name Grolnick, struck back: "We've gotten terrible reviews from the purist critics who don't know anything about the style of contemporary jazz we play. I live that, I'm one of the creators of it... We're the young players who have created something new and different that's still called jazz." One of the most successful groups of this type, Spyro Gyra, was formed in the late seventies fronted by two Jewish musicians of considerable jazz pedigree, saxophonist Jay Beckenstein and vibraphonist Dave Samuels, a later line-up adding Jewish drummer Joel Rosenblatt. Beckenstein repulsed the critics: "If you define fusion as a previously existing jazz form that combines with outside musical influences to come up with a hybrid, you are talking about the history of jazz from day one... It's our music, we love to play." 19

Tenor saxophonist and arranger Bob Mintzer, also Jewish, argues that he should not be considered in smooth jazz terms at all. His association with the Yellowjackets is the reason he is. Mintzer joined Yellowjackets in 1991, on the back of a career working with leading jazz and Latin musicians. And Stuart Nicholson has acknowledged that after Mintzer joined Yellowjackets, the group "gradually changed their musical mandate, moving away from the smooth sounds to embrace a broad range of approaches". 20

Mintzer maintains however that Yellowjackets should never have been lumbered with the smooth tag in the first place, telling me: "Even the early Yellowjacket music had quite a bit more going on. I joined the band to make the recording called *Greenhouse*. This is anything but a smooth jazz recording. I wouldn't have joined a smooth jazz band to be away from home for half the year, with a one-year-old child at home. My roots were playing with people like Thad Jones, Mel Lewis, Jaco Pastorius, Randy Brecker, Buddy Rich. I have never had much interest in playing smooth jazz music, except as a freelance session musician on an infrequent basis."

Yellowjackets' music focused on doing interesting things with time and feel, as in odd meter compositions, and ways to obscure the time and a regular 4/4 groove, added Mintzer: "The forms in our compositions are generally fairly complex and extended. The solos go on for a while as well. The harmonic terrain in many of the tunes draw on twentieth century classical composition and more dissonant jazz harmony, a far cry from the very diatonic and 'happy' sounds found in most smooth jazz compositions."

Eclecticism is an attribute many of the post-eighties' generation of musicians contribute to fusion. Take Jewish drummer Ben Perowsky, whose album *Esopus Opus* is one of my favourite new millennium releases. 21 Perowsky, with quartet partners Chris Speed on tenor sax and clarinet, Drew Gress, bass, and accordionist Ted Reichman, concoct a folksy psychedelic smorgasbord of sonic delights, the material ranging from Perowsky originals to covers of Brazilian composers Hermeto Pascoal and Jacob do Bandolim, to renditions of Hendrix's 'Manic Depression' and the Beatles' 'Within You Without You' and 'Flying'. Perowsky's drumming is lissome and free-ish, while Reichman – whose résumé ranges from avant-garde jazz with Anthony Braxton to extensive involvement in the Radical Jewish music scene – adroitly interpolates east

European strains. The album, the happy outcome of all this generic intercourse, is a wondrous love child of jazz and rock.

Jake Hertzog – a "blazing wunderkind" as *Guitar Player* magazine acclaimed him – brings us full circle in that he has recorded a highly contemporary jazz-rock album that deploys the talents of one of the pioneers of the form. For *Throwback*, Hertzog, who is Jewish, bassist Harvie S, who is also Jewish, and drummer Victor Jones, are joined by first-wave fusionista Randy Brecker. Hertzog explained what he was seeking from Randy at the sessions: "I wanted him to be almost more like the lead singer in a rock band than a trumpet player, like Bono in U2, Kurt Cobain in Nirvana, Eddie Vedder in Pearl Jam or Chris Cornell in Soundgarden... I arranged it so he could just kind of float above and do whatever and it would sound great as long as the rhythm section is cooking." Rising to the brief, Brecker's blowing is inspirational, notably on the standout track, Hertzog's ballad 'Sending Home'; his empathy with the guitarist seemingly clairvoyant.

Hertzog was born four years after the break-up of the Brecker Brothers band that Randy formed with Michael Brecker. If Randy's impact still resonates across the generations, so too, very much so, does Michael's, even though he is no longer with us.

• • • •

Michael Brecker, who with Randy formed the popular jazz-funk outfit The Brecker Brothers, is often upheld as one of the most influential musicians in post-seventies jazz. Although he attained something of an iconic stature among the post-Coltrane generation of saxophonists, it took until 1987 before he released an album in his own name, *Michael Brecker*. On this, aside from playing his customary tenor horn, he utilises the sampled sounds emitted by an Akai EWI electronic wind instrument. He had tried various electronic devices hitched to the sax before but said, "I always felt it cheapened the sound to put a box on it" whereas the EWI was "an instrument unto itself, very different from taking a sax and electrifying it and expecting it to sound good". 22

Jeremy Shoham is one of the countless saxophonists that have taken inspiration from him. Shoham's jazz, with his London band Jazz East, is tinctured with traits from Jewish music and we were discussing this [to be covered in Volume 2 of *Kosher Jammers*], when he surprised me with the following observation: "One thing which makes me more confident and secure in making this link between Jews and jazz is the effect that Brecker had on me the first time I heard him, his tonality. People talk about Brecker as coming directly out of Coltrane... I never heard him talking about his Jewishness. I don't know anything about Brecker's background, whether he was brought up as a Jewish person at all. But I know that, for me, what he was doing connected not just from the point of view of jazz, but also from something that was fundamentally Jewish in me, and my Jewish musical identity, which I can kind of separate in me. I have two musical identities, one is Jewish and one is jazz, and that's how I write and that's how they come together. From the seventies, Brecker started a whole generation of improvisers. People described this thing as 'outside playing'... a complete master of fusion, but also the purest jazz musician. His influence has been enormous – the style of improvising. There's bebop and there's modal/outside playing, the two post-second world war styles of jazz improvisation; Brecker came out of Coltrane; what Coltrane was doing, experimenting with, and becoming an absolute genius at, he took further, and this might sound so trite, but this is what it feels like to me – there's something about Brecker's Jewishness which fused with his Coltrane-type ideas, created something that was uniquely him. Plus, Brecker's interest in R&B-soul which also comes through."

I asked Shoham if he could give me concrete examples of this Jewishness he hears in Brecker's music.

Shoham cited the first track he ever heard by Brecker, 'Pools' off jazz fusion band Steps Ahead's 1983 debut release: "It's slightly unusual for Brecker in that it isn't cascades of notes, it's quite cool. But the very first few lines are completely out of the chords – the notes don't fit in with the chords. But somehow, they work, and they work because of the way he resolves the line. And that for me is about angst, about pushing against something that doesn't quite fit and making it fit, about tension and release. And that's what I hear when I hear cantors singing, when I hear imams singing in mosques. You talk to any modern saxophone player now – not just saxophone players – there isn't any question, Brecker's been a key influence. Some people have stayed in the bebop or mainstream thing, but people who've gone a bit beyond certainly have been influenced by him."

In August 2006, months before Michael Brecker died from leukaemia, he recorded his last album, *Pilgrimage*, that included his poignantly titled composition 'Five Months from Midnight'.

• • • •

I told Dan Morgenstern I had an interview with Randy Brecker lined up, and as Dan, when editor of *DownBeat*, had known both Breckers since they were breaking through, I asked him to suggest a question. "Ask him if they disappointed their parents by not becoming lawyers." So I did.

Randy, sitting across from me in his Manhattan apartment overlooking the Chrysler building, responded: "My parents, recently deceased, were both major jazz fans. My father Bob Brecker was a semi-professional pianist and lawyer. He was a wonderful piano player, songwriter, singer, probably both my and Mike's biggest influence. He really taught us how to improvise when I was very young and had a great record collection, and we had jam sessions in our living room constantly. At first, although he loved music, he tried to dissuade us from going into it full-time and tried to explain what a difficult life it was, not much security etcetera. But he was so in love with music and so much wished that he had done it professionally full-time that he almost had no choice. And as soon as he started seeing our name in print he was thrilled, he was our biggest fan, and I can't tell you how many musicians in jazz and even the rock and roll world have come up to me and said, 'You know, I met your father.' I met Charlie Watts of the Rolling Stones a few years ago backstage in Tokyo; the first thing he said to me was, 'I met your father.'

Randy continues to work in both fusion and mainstream jazz settings, playing acoustic or electrified trumpet, whatever the situation demands.

How, I asked him, had his music evolved?

"Number one, the instrument that I constantly try to develop on... I just try to work at it every day to get better. But also, a big part of my musical day is composition and working on projects. And I continue to do that. My philosophy is to try to utilise technology and have that a part of what I do. So usually, my projects are oriented in that respect. And occasionally I'll do, for want of a better word, an acoustic project. But I was trying, even years ago when I did my first albums, to reflect whatever I'm hearing currently so I keep my projects current. And sometimes they're somewhat controversial, but that's my philosophy towards recording projects. And each one is different and each one might have a different theme, but I try to reinterpret what I'm hearing currently, which is a lot of different things."

"Randy, fusion was one way that musicians found they could make a few bucks, and some did very well out of it. But from a historical perspective, as you were very steeped in it, how should fusion be judged artistically?"

"It's like anything else, it was a product of the times, it was an exciting period and there was a lot of good music that came out of it and a lot of bad. Obviously if there's any success then a lot of people jump on the bandwagon, particularly record producers, and there was an inordinate amount of trash during that period. But there was some good music, the top five or six bands were heavily influential – among them Chick Corea's band, a lot of things Miles did, Mahavishnu, Herbie's [Hancock] stuff drew a lot of people into the music and you can't fight the fact that we need an audience out there. That's part of the problem today, we seem to be losing a lot of the older audience because they're passing away and a lot of the younger audience doesn't have any idea because they're not exposed to jazz at all so that's also an important consideration. I try to keep that in mind when I perform."

Several years after Michael Brecker's death, Randy was assembling a band for an engagement at New York's Blue Note club when he realised that the entire personnel had featured in the Brecker Brothers at various times. The upshot is that Randy entered a studio with these alumni, plus his wife, saxophonist Ada Rovatti, to record *The Brecker Brothers Band Reunion*, which was issued as a CD/DVD set, the DVD filmed live at the Blue Note. In contrast to all the funky tracks is Randy's brooding 'Elegy for Mike', in memory of his brother.

# Chapter 15: Hustlers and straightshooters

Jews have contributed heavily to jazz as facilitators; we saw an inspiring example earlier in this narrative in the highly conscientious role played by Café Society founder Barney Josephson in challenging discrimination against blacks in American society. I will now consider a few of the many other key facilitators.

As with their black compatriots, Jews were for many years restricted in the professions they could engage in and popular music was one area that was open to them. With Jews, it was not only as musicians that they made critical interventions in the development of American popular music.

Before the Jazz Age, Jews established a dominant position as music publishers clustered on Manhattan's 28th Street that, because of the conflicting musical sounds passers-by heard, became known as Tin Pan Alley. Few, by Hazel Meyer's account, were as scrupulous as Max Dreyfus, a Jewish publisher who "devoted his lifetime to befriending and understanding young composers and lyricists, in many instances out of his own pocket until they could support themselves... It was Dreyfus who first recognised creative genius in an eighteen-year-old... employed as a pianist by another firm and gave him a weekly salary and contract as a composer... The boy... was George Gershwin." 1 As Meyer documented however, often terms of payment in Tin Pan Alley "were so loose that several songwriters set up shops for themselves out of rebellion against publishers who haggled over price, drove sharp bargains and were vague about royalties". 2

One of America's earliest jazz and blues venues was Isadore Shor's Entertainer Café on Chicago's Southside. Shor was Jewish and his establishment ultimately became what was known as a 'slumming resort' in that it attracted white patrons to black gigs. Similarly, Connie's Inn in Harlem, founded by another Jew, Connie Immerman.

Ted Vincent, appraising this phenomenon, records: "The 'slumming resorts' were a flamboyant offshoot of the cabarets, which also spawned the less gaudy institution, the present days jazz and blues clubs. The resorts were known for their nasty doormen, who intimidated those prospecting African American customers not already dissuaded by the ridiculously high entrance fee... Perhaps the nationwide pioneer in the resorts was Isadore Shor's Entertainer Café... He had been involved in the jazz scene from as early as 1917, and Alberta Hunter [jazz blues singer] recalled Shor as being a hard worker who did everything at the Entertainer from taking the money at the door to sweeping up, Shor could be considered rather typical of that segment among the founders of jazz and blues clubs that comprised immigrant whites (largely Jewish or Italian) who lived and ran little businesses in the African American neighborhoods. These were Whites who shared with African Americans a loathing of the bigoted mean-spirited WASP culture but who were much closer to the WASP economically. Although Isadore Shor, and his counterparts such as Connie Immerman, clearly felt they had the interests of the black community at heart, they did much to turn jazz and blues clubs into a business of high-priced tourist traps." The Entertainer Café, said Vincent, became distanced from its roots. 3

For better or worse then, from the first decades of the twentieth century, Jews were acting as facilitators in popular music. One of the earliest involved jazz-wise was Irving Mills.

• • • •

"Mills was Jewish but he was a son of a bitch, he put his name on every tune that he recorded, he never wrote a note of music in his life, he made millions, major dollars, as a composer." Well, that's what Artie Shaw told me, repeating a commonly heard accusation.

Irving Mills grew up poor in New York, the more so after his immigrant father died when Mills was eleven. Like older brother Jack, who preceded him in the music business, Mills hustled to support the family and there was little chance of a decent education. Starting out as a song-plugger, Mills established himself as a music publisher, booking agent, and before the twenties were out, he managed several bands, among them Irving Mills and His Hotsy Totsy Gang, some of whose recordings featured him as vocalist. For these sessions, Mills assembled some of the hottest white jazz talent of the era, Benny Goodman included. In 1936 Mills founded the Master and Variety labels, mainly to issue recordings by his own stable of artists.

Most importantly from the historical perspective, he was Duke Ellington's personal manager from 1926 to around 1940, the years during which Ellington forged his international reputation for creative pre-eminence in big band jazz. Duke was establishing himself in New York when they first met. Mills, Duke recalled, "was known as the last resort for getting some money by those who had been peddling songs all day without success". 4 Blues songwriters, Duke said, would sell Mills "the same goddamned tune over and over so many times... Just change the name of it, switch the first line and the second line, the blues are all the same anyway! And a couple of times I would... get them recorded and they would make money". 5 In 1925 Ellington was involved in a recording session on which Mills sang and played kazoo on 'Everything Is Hotsy Totsy Now' that Mills is credited as having written with Jimmy McHugh. 6

Around this time Mills saw Duke's The Washingtonians perform at the Kentucky Club in New York where the band had a regular spot and where, in answering requests, as Duke remembered it, "we sang anything and everything – pop songs, jazz songs, dirty songs, torch songs, Jewish songs". 7 According to Ellington lyricist Don George: "Duke never forgot that summer evening in 1926 when Mills walked into the Kentucky Club... Duke played the 'Black and Tan Fantasy', and Mills said, 'This is it. This isn't just a Tin Pan Alley songwriter but a real composer at work, weaving different themes, creating compositions, not only thirty-two bar songs." 8

With Ellington, Mills launched a corporation in which they were equal partners to promote the band. 9 Besides songs, Mills encouraged Duke to write lengthier, loftier material: "Irving Mills came to me one day with an original idea. He was always reaching toward a higher plateau for our music... So I went out and wrote Creole Rhapsody." 10 Duke also acknowledged Mills' flair for filling in tricky or elusive passages in compositions. 11 Nonetheless, it does seem that Mills sometimes dubiously took author's credit and royalties as co-composer.

That was actually a widespread practice, as Leonard Feather observed: "Even Duke Ellington, who had to share credit with Irving Mills on countless works, was not above using this ploy himself when members of his orchestra, and a few outsiders, brought their original material to him. Like many others of the day, from Chick Webb to Benny Goodman, he felt it his right to participate in the profits to which he would give widespread exposure. The ethics are still being debated but the practice has never been dropped."

Feather was himself a victim: "Although, over the years, Irving Mills extended many favors to me and I eventually came to regard him as a friendly and gracious old man, there were moments when the necessity for caution became obvious. One such occasion was the day when I saw a proof of the copy Mills had sent to the printer of 'Mighty Like the Blues'. The credit line read: 'By Leonard Feather and Irving Mills'. My protests, loud and unsubtle, took immediate effect." 12

I contacted Mills' son Bob Mills, and also interviewed the man described as Ellington's greatest fan, Bob Udkoff, who was very close to Duke, about the Mills-Ellington relationship. Bob Mills emailed me as follows: "I'm happy to be of any help I can be to keep the record straight regarding my father's contribution to the development of jazz and his relationship with the black musicians he worked with... I did grow up to work at Mills Music for a number of years prior to and after WWII... While people loved and enjoyed black musicians and jazz music and would pay good money to see and hear them live, they wouldn't house them or allow them to eat where they were performing. That was the reason my father only booked black talent in cities along the railroad. He rented railroad cars so they would always have a place to sleep, eat and carry their gear. Maybe that is why he was called the Abraham Lincoln of the music industry. With regard to relations between Jews and blacks. I can only tell you that my dad apparently had good relations since a great deal of the talent in Mills Artists, Inc were black and their association lasted many years. Life isn't always a bowl of cherries – but problems are for solving and there was always respect... I'm aware of negative things that have been written regarding ownership of royalties. I'm sure you know it would be unlawful to put your name on another's property without consent. Everything published by Mills Music, Inc is by arrangement. I know of no lawsuits pending. Through the years people have worked 'for hire' in the industry. Even Dorothy Fields is quoted as saying she was a $50.00 a night girl for Mills – referring to material she wrote 'for hire'. That's the way it was in those days. Perhaps even today. If you're asking if my dad was a lyricist – he certainly was, but more than that, he was an idea man and really had his finger on the pulse of the time. Like Duke Ellington said in one of his books: 'When Irving Mills came into the studio and said, Duke, 'It Don't Mean A Thing If It Ain't Got That Swing', he's the writer." No, Irving Mills did not play an instrument but he certainly was a composer and performer."

I subsequently met Bob Mills for an LA café breakfast interview. When songwriters, such as Jewish lyricist Dorothy Fields, wrote for hire, it meant they sold the song outright to the publisher and the Mills company was established on that basis, said Bob: "Since they were a small company, they didn't have a staff of writers, so they got new writers and a lot of them turned out to be good, very popular writers. But they were nothing to begin with. They got them because nobody else was interested in them and they weren't assigned to some bigger publisher. It was like they do in the motion pictures, where the writer don't own it, they write for hire."

"So they would get a one-off fee for a song, or lyrics?"

"Yes."

"It would have been in their best interests, wouldn't it, to have insisted on royalties?"

"When people are new and hungry and haven't made it yet, their best interest is to get $50 to pay rent, buy food and clothes. So it's what the deals were of the time. It's like there was a time when a negro was called a nigger, and then that passed. Times change, so that's what writers did in the early days. The royalties would go to the publisher if it was outright. There were some things that were outright, but Irving Mills always said that, 'When things are good, it's good for everybody', and there were writers who had written things outright who would collect royalties because the money was there, but they didn't have to get paid royalties. So there were times when that's the way the business was, not just Mills but everybody."

I had come across evidence supporting what Bob was telling me; a quote suggesting that Juan Tizol, Ellington trombonist and arranger, sold the rights of 'Caravan' for $25, but Mills agreed to give the rights and royalties back once it became a success.

"Right," said Bob. "By arrangement. Whatever the deal was, it was a deal. Because Juan Tizol again did a lot of stuff with Ellington's name on it – it wasn't stealing, it was by arrangement. He was getting paid as an arranger."

I mentioned another snippet I had come across: Fats Waller claiming he sold Mills nineteen numbers including 'Ain't Misbehavin'' for $500, less than a week's salary.

Bob responded: "This might have been something where, if he bought tunes, if anything happened to it, he would pay them anyway, even though he owned them legally... You can pick up the ASCAP [the performing rights organisation] book that lists all of the tunes; ASCAP recognised him, and Ellington and everybody else whoever is in there don't question anything, that's the way it is and that's the way it's been for all these years. He didn't write everything, and he might not have written the whole lyrics on 'It Don't Mean A Thing If It Ain't Got That Swing', but there isn't much more in the lyric, but again, that's the way the arrangement was then, that he would be in on it, that they were partners. But he was, and the band and everybody else would admit it, an ideas man. You can have an idea to a title of a song and not write the whole thing, but you got the germ of it, you got it going and you're running the studio and you're part of it. So he didn't steal anything or there'd be problems."

Another cutting I brought along was a quote by Ellington drummer Sonny Greer, saying the orchestra had the same wages as the white orchestras.

That, by Bob's reckoning, would be a natural thing to do, "otherwise they'd go somewhere else. You see, that's another thing that Irving said, 'It's whatever the traffic will bear; when it's good, it's good for everybody'. If the guys weren't getting paid, they would never have stayed together all those years".

I showed him a November 1936 article in black newspaper the *New Amsterdam Press*. Headed 'Our Musicians Are Slaves Owned, Body and Soul Work for Massa Mills', its author A Clayton Powell, referring to Ellington's band, proclaims: "The boys in the band are just hired hands who haven't netted $3000 a year despite the fact that it is rumoured that Mills got $19,000 in 1934 alone... When they work, Mills gets $4000 to $6000 per week for the Ellington unit, he pays let us say 13 boys $100 each, Sonny Greer £150, Ivy Anderson $75 and Duke $300, that is less than $2000... The Broadway boys, without swinging the swivel chair, pocket 50 to 65 per cent of the intake."

Bob countered: "You know what the deal was with the Duke, 45 per cent each with 10 per cent going to Sam Buzzell, who was the attorney. They were equal partners in their association. So when somebody says this, it's out of context. They're not saying who paid for the travel, who paid for the clothing, for the train" – all of which, Bob informed me, was first-class and paid for by Mills – "they're not talking about that. But no, they were equal partners and $100 in those days was money. So when they write it that way, how is anybody else going to read it other than, this is in the papers, it's gotta be true? It doesn't make it true."

Some days later I interviewed Bob Udkoff, a Jewish guy who, in his youth, began what became a lifelong friendship with Ellington. My reasons for meeting him were to discover more about the Ellington-Mills relationship, but first I just had to ask how he came to befriend Ellington.

They first met in 1934: "My father had a cleaning store here in LA and I used to work after school, pick up clothes, deliver, and one day I saw a truck with some trunks on it, Duke Ellington Orchestra, and they were just coming in off a series of one-nighters and standing in an apartment building off South Central. So I followed them in and found that they had clothes that needed cleaning, laundry, so I went back to the store, talked my father out of his car, which wasn't easy because I just had a learner's permit, and I went back and picked up loads of clothes and, as a result, I became friendly with some of the band and started to drive Duke to the studio, to Paramount, he was making *Murder of the Vanities*, a movie with Mae West, and doing some recording. And we became simpatico. I was 15 and the band was here for, I guess, six or eight weeks, working at Frank Sebastian's Cotton Club, and when they got ready to leave, I went down to the railway station to say goodbye. One of the guys said, 'Hey, Bobby, why don't you come with us?' So I ditched my books at the Western Union stand and got on the train and, about three weeks later, in Salt Lake City, at a theatre, Duke woke up and said, 'Hey, shouldn't you be in school?' I said, 'I'm through with school'. He said, 'The hell you are. Grow up to be a bum or something?' He said, 'Jonesy' – who was his valet – 'send this kid home. We could get arrested for harbouring a minor.' So that was my introduction to the band. I did go home but shortly afterwards I got a job on a magazine crew [selling subscriptions], working my way through college, travelling all over the country. And I ran into the band from time to time and, I think it was in Pittsburgh, Duke said, 'Why don't you come to work for us?'

"Anyway, I became an advance man, I didn't know what I was doing but I would go into the town prior to the band coming in, contact the disc jockeys and push the date that they were performing, and line up accommodations. Because in those days, it was difficult for a black band to find. And Duke told me how to go about it, 'You go to a black undertaker – he's the most important guy in town, tell him that the Ellington band's coming in and we need places to stay.' In most cases there wasn't a hotel but you would wind up boarding in people's homes. Then somebody got the idea of getting a Pullman car and a diner and travelling that way and living in it and not having the hassle."

"Wasn't that Irving Mills?"

"Could have been. What you could say about Irving Mills is that he takes credit for a lot of things; Leonard Feather and I were associated in producing a [TV] series called Jazz Profiles, which never got off the ground, but we interviewed Irving Mills. Anyhow, then the band went to Europe, didn't take me, I went back selling magazines but over the years we developed a good friendship. And in 1958 – by this time I was married, had a family, had a business selling swimming pools – in '58, Duke called, spoke to my wife, in his charming way, he said, 'I'm going to Europe and I need some help and I wonder if you would loan me Bob for a few weeks?' She couldn't say no to anything he asked. As a result, I went to Europe for a little over three weeks on a whirlwind tour. I acted as a road manager, which wasn't very difficult because I knew all the guys. We had no problem, just a lot of fun. Then – skipping a lot of things – we were invited to the White House to his birthday party, 1969. And in '72 he invited us to go with him to Russia on a five-week tour, my wife and I. I learned a lot from him, he was like a father to me, and he was a very generous man. On my 50th birthday, he gave me the band for my birthday party. My wife had arranged it with him and I belonged to a country club and the band played."

"A relationship between a young Jewish boy and a black, world-class, famous musician, at that point in American history, with the segregation – it sounds astonishing. You need to explain the simpatico bit, how the hell did that come about?"

"Because Duke used to say, 'Someone's beyond category' – he hated to categorise, and the fact that you were white didn't automatically put you in the ofay category. One summer, when I was 16 or 17, I stayed at his apartment with his sister and mother and Mercer [Duke's musician son] in Harlem. I was there for about three weeks. And I never had any feeling that there was any differentiation. He just wasn't that way. I never felt it. I think Duke, if anything, probably had an affinity for Jewish people because he had worked for so many of them. As a matter of fact, I remember him telling me that he and Sonny Greer were working in a club, I think it may have been the Kentucky Club, where after the band did their thing, Sonny and Duke used to sing this song 'The Yiddle With the Fiddle' in Yiddish."

"So what can we say about Irving Mills? You met and heard stories about him."

"Irving Mills always treated Duke and the band with respect, but he was controlling, and maybe pretty good: they always dressed well, had good uniforms. But he made a lot of money out of them. Because he put his name on so many of Duke's songs; he'd say, 'Do you mind?', 'Okay', so he was on. He was called up before ASCAP once, and I don't know the circumstances, but he failed their tests to prove that he had written any of their songs." Which contradicts what Mills' son told me.

Mills, Udkoff continued, "was a hustler, a great promoter."

I put to him that no matter how great the Ellington band, Mills, because of the way he promoted them, raised them to a level that they probably would never on their own have reached; not that is in American society back then.

Udkoff agreed: "You can have all the talent in the world but if you're stuck in a sewer like the Kentucky Club, you're not going to expose yourself. Irving had the talent for exposing him. He auditioned at the Cotton Club, he got the gig, he was able to parlay that, through Irving to a great extent, into his career. The Cotton Club made him. Duke always said that 'without Irving Mills we might never have achieved it'. But it reached a point where he'd gone beyond that and felt that Irving was taking advantage of him financially."

Ellington was subsequently engaged with the William Morris entertainment agency that had been founded in 1898 by a German-Jewish immigrant. Beyond that he took up with various other Jewish facilitators, including Norman Granz and Joe Glaser.

As Udkoff observed: "It was almost required that a black entertainer needed a frontman, because without that white guy in front, he couldn't achieve. And of course, because the Jews were so prevalent in the entertainment industry, it was usually a Jew. Now after Duke took that jump-start, he took off, but he needed that jump-start."

Dan Morgenstern concurred, when I mentioned the trashing of Mills in that black newspaper: "Well, hey, you know, who else was going to do it, when you're better off than what there was of black management, and there was very little, it wasn't effective because in that world which was still very heavily segregated, run by white folks, what are you going to do? What's the alternative to Irving Mills? When Ellington broke up from Mills in 1939 he was big enough at that point in time to be able to function without an Irving Mills, but other people were of great help to him. There was Leonard Feather who did PR for him and worked on his recording sessions. So you always needed intermediaries and any artist in any field is going to need that."

On that note, let us consider another big-time Jewish jazz facilitator, Joe Glaser.

. . . .

A good place to start is what Bob Udkoff told me about Ellington's
relationship with Glaser: "Duke always had trouble dealing with
Joe Glaser, didn't like him. He had a deal at the Riviera where he
booked Duke and Louis Armstrong and they were each supposed
to get $20,000 a week but he set it up so Louis got $25,000 and
Duke $15.000. He pocketed the $25,000 and paid Louis, I think
his contract was $1,000 a week plus $100 a day spending money
plus all his expenses. Louis was very happy with it. And he tried to
make some sort of deal with Duke. And Duke said to him, 'Joe, I'm
not your kind of nigger.' But he had to use him; there was nobody
else."

Armstrong contracted Glaser as his manager in the 1930s in
a professional relationship that – though the allegedly
mob-connected Glaser was no angel, far from it – endured
throughout the rest of the great jazzman's life. So let us investigate
Glaser primarily via that relationship; Glaser went on to represent
many other black and other artists, but it began with Louis.

Glaser had grown up in a middle-class Chicago family but
loved hanging out with gangsters and the popular entertainers and
musicians who, in prohibition America, performed at mob-backed
establishments on Chicago's Southside, the "black and tan" venues
where blacks and whites mixed pretty freely. Glaser was involved
with several such nightclubs whose proprietors established these
venues on land his mother owned. He persuaded Armstrong,
whom he had seen perform with King Oliver's Creole Band, to lead
his own band at Dreamland, in front of which Glaser erected a
sign plugging Armstrong as "THE WORLD'S GREATEST JAZZ
CORNETIST". 13

Louis featured regularly at another club on premises Glaser's
mother owned, Sunset Café, whose lessees were a Jew, Ed Fox, and

his partner Sam Dreyfus, also by the name Jewish. Initially Louis performed there with the Carroll Dickerson band but Glaser, who had a managerial role at the club, realising that Louis was the main attraction, put him out front.

Under the direction of Tommy Rockwell, Armstrong's star continued to rise as a popular entertainer, including performing in the 1929 Broadway musical Hot Chocolates. With a new manager, Johnny Collins, Louis embarked on his first European tours. The second excursion ended badly, with Louis, his finances in disarray, unhappy about Collins' management: "Always something would be wrong, always in trouble with the promoters – trying to make me declare bankruptcy... I decided Joe Glaser was going to be my manager; had always admired the way he treated his help." 14

According to Ernie Anderson, who knew both men: "Louis told me, 'I could see he was down and out. He had always been a sharp cat but now he was a raggedy ass. I told him, 'I want you to be my manager.' He said, 'Oh, I couldn't do that. I'm stony broke.' 'That don't make no difference... You get me the jobs... You collect the money. You pay me $1000 every week free and clear. You pay off the band, the travel and hotel expenses, my income tax, and you take everything that's left.' They shook hands on this arrangement. There was no other contract." 15

Glaser swiftly repaid Armstrong's faith, securing a continual stream of work – venues, recording contracts, broadcasts, movie engagements. The payback for Glaser was immense, wrote Anderson: "As word of Louis's new manager spread through show business, other black attractions... also asked to be represented by Louis's manager... Joe had them all sign formal agency contracts and he took only the usual 10%. When some agencies began to take 15%, Joe raised his commission to 15%... Ultimately... Joe found he had 500 clients including such as Bob Hope... Louis was earning large sums of money for Joe Glaser who now operated as president of the Associated Booking Corporation [ABC, Glaser's agency] ... Commissions from his other 500 clients brought in tens of thousands of dollars more every week... Joe... was now, only a couple of years later, one of the most affluent agents in all show business." 16

Under Glaser's guidance Armstrong in turn enjoyed affluence, certainly by the standards of most black jazz musicians, and particularly when, in later life, he topped the global pop charts with hits such as 'What A Wonderful World'. 17 When Glaser was hospitalised following a massive stroke in 1969, Armstrong, himself ill in the same hospital, was shaken when he learned of his manager's ultimately fatal condition. From his hospital bed, Armstrong wrote an affecting memoir of his early years in New Orleans and his relationship with the Karnofskys, *LOUIS ARMSTRONG + THE JEWISH FAMILY IN NEW ORLEANS, LA., THE YEAR OF 1907*, dedicating it to Glaser, "the best friend that I've ever had... His boy and disciple who loved him dearly".

His describing himself as Glaser's "boy" gives the clue to the basis of their relationship. As a young musician in New Orleans, Louis, by Anderson's account, received the following advice from a black drummer before moving north: "You must find yourself a white man who will stand up for you and say, 'This is my nigger.'" 18 Glaser fulfilled that role.

His detractors claim he encouraged the commercialisation of Louis at the expense of artistic integrity, drove him too hard with bookings, and raked off a significant amount of Louis's legitimate earnings.

The first allegation is broadly true. Louis's 1920's sessions with his Hot Five and Hot Seven groups, which pre-date Glaser's management, rate as among the most influential bodies of recorded work in jazz history. 19 Whereas under Glaser, notes Armstrong biographer Laurence Bergreen, "Louis's ideas about music, jazz and performing were now fixed, and most nights he played tunes drawn from a repertoire of about two dozen jazz standards. This was fine with Glaser, who wanted his musicians to play nothing but hits." 20 Another biographer observed, Louis's "Uncle Tomming, so far as whites were concerned, was part of it. They liked the smiling, uncomplaining black man who was obviously trying hard to ingratiate himself... the first black to be featured in top-line movies". 21

If Armstrong still took up work that appealed to jazz purists, it was usually at the instigation of Armstrong devotees who persuaded Glaser – without whose say-so Louis would undertake no engagement – to acquiesce. Thus, Ernie Anderson overcame an initially frosty reception from Glaser to form, in 1947, what became known as Louis Armstrong and his All-Stars, Louis fronting a small group of top jazz disciples. 22 In 1960, with All-Stars personnel, Louis recorded with Duke Ellington, playing and singing Ellington's immortal songs. How this came about was indicative of Glaser's connections. Bergreen writes that Louis and Duke did not make the record for a major label, as might be expected given their celebrity: "Instead, they circumvented their contracts to record for tiny Roulette Records, a label whose boss, Morris Levy was later revealed to have strong ties to organised crime." Producer Bob Thiele recollected that the "miasmal hoodlum atmosphere at Roulette Records was so heavily oppressive that it was often difficult for me to concentrate on the musical matters". 23 Glaser allowed Louis just two days to complete the sessions before returning him to his relentless touring schedule.

"He was working 365 days a year, he was making records and on every day he was doing most of the playing, and his lip was a mess," Armstrong biographer James Lincoln Collier told me. "Glaser didn't pay any attention to the fact that he had nothing but scar tissue on his lip. He'd get him out there and Louis would go along with it because he wanted the audience, he wanted people applauding, he said that. And he shouldn't have been playing those high notes when his chops were in a mess." In Glaser's defense is what another Armstrong biographer, Ricky Riccardi, discovered: "When I asked five surviving members of the All Stars... if Glaser was at fault, they all said it couldn't be further from the truth. Armstrong was only happy when he was constantly working and was known to complain to Glaser if he had too many nights off in a row." 24

Crude and foul-mouthed though he could be, Glaser inspired trust in his dealings with black artists, many of whom had got burned in previous dealings with whites. "If he made you a promise that was it," said black bandleader Andy Kirk. 25 And Armstrong testified: "He just *impressed* me different than the other bosses I've worked for. He seemed to understand Colored people so much." 26

Glaser continually showered Armstrong with expensive gifts: the best suits, new cars, a gold ruby-encrusted star of David neck-chain. Armstrong's bills were regularly paid by Glaser's office with whom too he had an arrangement whereby his wife Lucille could spend $350 a month on a charge account at Saks' Fifth Avenue department store. 27 But, claimed Anderson, "the aggregate of these extraneous expenses hardly accounted for the large sums Joe Glaser was taking for the performances of Louis Armstrong". 28 That amounted to 50%, by Lucille's account. Dave Gold, ABC vice-president and treasurer, maintained however that the firm only took the standard 15% agent's fee and put the rest into Armstrong's account which paid his basic expenses, taxes, mortgage and his and Lucille's allowances, and into savings accounts and trust funds that were turned over to the Armstrongs following Glaser's death. 20

We do know that Armstrong, through generosity and carelessness, dissipated much of his wealth. Bergreen cites an instance: "Glaser usually kept Louis supplied with a $1000 monthly payroll as well as the occasional $2000 bonus, which Louis instantly sorted into envelopes and distributed to a large number of camp followers, needy cases and the occasional girlfriend. In one burst of generosity, he splurged on $500 television sets for various elderly acquaintances, and to pay for them he borrowed $2500 from a Broadway loan shark... and his finances, always casual, collapsed under the strain". After reprimanding Louis, Glaser paid off the loan shark and supplied the sets himself. 30

Ultimately, Louis was a major beneficiary of Glaser's will to the tune of more than $2 million, although Anderson believed this to be, under pressure from Lucille, the work of Glaser's protégé Oscar Cohen who was now president and 20% owner of ABC. 31 All the shares in Glaser's International Music, his music publishing company, he left to Louis. 32

Still the suspicion remains that Louis did not get his full due. Stanley Crouch, dismissing Glaser as a crook, told me that when Armstrong died, two years after Glaser's passing, there was far less money in his estate than might reasonably have been expected.

I related this to Dan Morgenstern, who defended Glaser: "A mysterious and I think very misunderstood figure. I'm not going to tell you that Glaser was a saint; he most certainly was not. But I don't think that Glaser was a crook and I don't think he cheated Louis Armstrong."

Dan addressed the Armstrong/Glaser issue in some depth, beginning with their nascent relationship at the Sunset Café: "Glaser was the manager of the room and of course, this being prohibition, this being Chicago, he was involved with gangsters where his family owned that property. He must have been pretty young then, in his twenties – he and Louis were about the same age – and that's how they first became acquainted, and Louis always said that he took a liking to him then. So he must have been treating the musicians right and they liked to work for him. He was not probably doing the booking, he was managing the room.

"What we know about Glaser is that, after prohibition ends, and the Sunset closes – the whole business changes when prohibition ends and the depression starts – he gets involved in boxing, the fight business." That, said Dan, was as a small-time booker. In the meantime, Louis's career was bedeviled by managerial troubles: "The people involved are Tommy Rockwell and Johnny Collins, this is Irish-run management. And eventually he goes to Europe, Johnny Collins is a pretty miserable person and Louis fires him. Collins takes Louis' passport as if he didn't think Louis could get his passport replaced and threatens that when Louis comes back to the United States he'll never work again. Louis then does come back, in early 1935. He also had trouble with his wife because Lil and he were not divorced yet and she was suing him for maintenance. And he was signing a contract with somebody and Collins scotched it, 'He can't sign a contract with anybody, he has a contract with me.' So Louis is in a bad situation. So what does he do, he says he remembers that Joe Glaser was a nice guy whom he liked and he gets in touch with him and then Joe fixes everything.

"Louis told me that he had trouble with gangsters and if it hadn't been for Joe Glaser, he really was afraid at the time that his career might be over – they threatened to do all sorts of things, to bust his chops. Joe straightened it up. So there's a handshake agreement kent with Louis... Glaser sets up a desk in the Rockwell office in Chicago. Rockwell by then is Rockwell-O'Keefe and they're in the booking business. And that's where Glaser begins his career as a booking agent for jazz, at first exclusively Louis and he then adds other clients. And when he comes to New York a little later he's also in the Rockwell office and then after that, around 1937, he becomes independent.

"So Joe and Louis had a handshake agreement, they never signed anything, it was based on trust. Louis says when they first started working together, Glaser went with him on the road, when they went down south he went with him, his presence was there to protect him against any unpleasantness in the segregated south. So it cemented the relationship that became very close until the very end."

Dan believed Glaser may have carried a gun when he toured south with Louis, and certainly had a relationship during the twenties with Al Capone's establishment, but that he was no gangster himself. And although he could be very intimidating, at other times, as Dan remembered him, Glaser could be as sweet as pie: "Joe was in many ways a crude guy. He used foul language long before that became fashionable, yet he wrote the most flowery letters, very old fashioned and very polite. A little bit of correspondence I had with him when I was editor of *DownBeat* was always very pleasant. He was a real hands-on person with his artists, took an interest in their personal lives to the extent where there might have been problems that might have interfered with them businesswise. There's a whole bunch of correspondence with Mary Lou Williams who became associated with him when she was still with Andy Kirk. Joe Glaser is the only person in his capacity who had a song written about him, 'Little Joe From Chicago' which is by Mary and which was recorded by Kirk's band."

"What about the allegation that Glaser pushed Louis too hard?"

"Joe had one weakness, which was that he could never turn down an offer of work. That went for any of his artists, but many of them were not as workaholic as Louis. So when he started getting all these offers of bookings for Louis, he took them all and he never really thought about the fact until much later in the game. Louis never complained that he was pushing too hard."

That was not, said Dan, down to lack of concern for Louis's welfare: "Glaser always said he had a doctor travelling with Louis, one of Glaser's cronies, Dr Schiff... he had been the doctor for the New York Boxing Commission sometime.

"It's a funny thing about Glaser, he was very concerned about Louis, they had an almost day- to-day relationship, but at the same time he got him far too much work. I always thought Joe should have had the sense when Louis had reached the peak of his profession, that he could book him in Las Vegas for six weeks at a big hotel and then give him some time off and get him some very good television deals. He did have a lot of movie work but he could have had more if he had been available. The thing was Joe always kept the All Stars on the road, and one of the things that irked me terribly and others too was that when it came to a recording session, this was something that didn't pay that much even when he could get top dollar for Louis, it didn't pay as much as a week at the Crescendo in LA. Joe didn't consider record dates to be that significant. Most of the time when Louis was recording in the fifties and sixties, he hadn't rested, the recording sessions were rushed, it's amazing that a lot of the stuff came out as well as it did."

Whatever may have been Glaser's shortcomings, he was a terrific booking agent, concluded Dan. "There was something about Joe that I found quite likeable, he was a character, totally outspoken. And the thing about taking money from Louis, that Stanley Crouch told you, Lucille Armstrong, a pretty smart businesswoman, she would not have suffered that gladly. And let's remember that Joe died before Louis. If there had been any suspicion, Lucille and Louis could have sued, so I don't buy that."

Dan lamented that very little work had been done on Glaser: "It's a pity that all this time has been wasted because everybody who's been involved with him is dead."

That now includes Phoebe Jacobs, who knew Armstrong and Glaser well. But she was a vivacious 84-year-old, when, at Dan's suggestion, I interviewed her, not only about Glaser but also about her life in jazz.

· · · ·

Phoebe Jacobs suggested we meet at the Blue Note jazz club in Greenwich Village, founded by Israeli Danny Bensusan. The Dizzy Gillespie Alumni Band that evening included Jewish pianist Benny Green. Before the music got underway, Phoebe arrived elegantly attired in greatcoat, hat, and scarf. When she removed them, she was wearing a smart black outfit and prominent necklace and ring. Very domineering, I thought, very New York. I interviewed her while we awaited her companions.

Phoebe was executive vice president of the Louis Armstrong Educational Foundation that Armstrong established in 1969 following Glaser's death: "Louis told me he was going to start a foundation. I said, 'What, you crazy?' He said, 'No, I want to give back to the world some of the goodness I got.' He put down the by-laws and stated the mission, 'I want this foundation to help kids that are talented and need music lessons to be taught music' – scholarships, support music programmes, and he put me in charge of the legacy and heritage. And the man who handled all his finances, who worked for Joe Glaser for 30 years, he made him the president, David Gold."

When Phoebe died, in 2012, the memorial concert featured a host of leading jazz musicians. The publicity notification listed her accomplishments. In her Foundation role, that included rousing support for and helping establish the Louis Armstrong Archives at

Queens College, the Louis Armstrong House Museum, the Louis Armstrong Center for Music and Medicine at Beth Israel Hospital, the Jazz for Young People Concert Series at Lincoln Center, the Duke Ellington Center, and the Jazz Foundation of America that aids jazz musicians fallen on hard times, lobbying for provision of high school and college jazz scholarships, and much else. But Phoebe was probably best known as a publicist, for Armstrong, Ella Fitzgerald, Sarah Vaughan, Duke Ellington, Della Reese, Peggy Lee and other artists. The memorial event accordingly was billed as a celebration of one of the most influential women in jazz history.

Born in 1918 to a Bronx Jewish family, Phoebe's passion for jazz was ignited by her Jewish uncle Ralph Watkins who had played saxophone in a Long Beach jazz orchestra then opened nightclubs on Manhattan's 52$^{nd}$ Street. In her teens Phoebe worked as hat-check girl at one of his clubs, Kelly's Stable: "We had Nat King Cole, Billie Holiday and people of that ilk." A club Watkins co-owned with another Jewish guy, Irving Alexander, proved a staging post in Frank Sinatra's career: "They took Sinatra from the Paramount when he was working with Benny Goodman after he left Tommy Dorsey, they hired him and took him into a club called Rio Grande and gave him his first in-person opportunity."

It was at Decca where Phoebe was contractor for recording sessions that she first met Louis Armstrong, and thereafter periodically at Basin Street: "My uncle named Basin Street for Louis Armstrong; he was mad about Louis and just couldn't do enough for him. Louis played the club at least twice a year. And I would do certain things for Louis, make him take his clothes to the laundry, tailor, and Mr Glaser would ask, to go on a trip with Louis for a couple of days, to take care of the money, or the press or interviews."

Phoebe became the club's publicist, and was later director of public relations, and producer of special events, at the Rainbow

Room and Rainbow Grill in New York where she was responsible for gigs by many prominent jazz musicians. It was as a PR specialist that she began her close association with Armstrong, which naturally brought Joe Glaser into the frame, "A diamond in the rough" in Phoebe's estimation.

"Joe was raised in an era of the survival of the fittest in Chicago. You had to be a tough man otherwise you couldn't make it at all because it was very competitive and very rocky with the roughnecks. It was a city of violence. So when you hear people say that Joe Glaser was a roughneck, was obnoxious, all I can tell you was that he never cheated anybody, he was the most honourable, honest gentleman."

"Some people allege that when Armstrong died and they totted up his estate, there wasn't as much in there as you might have expected for someone of his stature," I interjected.

"The estate was the estate. Who are they to assume anything? I can tell you there was nothing that Louis wanted, or Lucille wanted to buy or do, that Joe Glaser wouldn't pick up the tab. Louis chose to say to Joe, 'Take the money, hold it for me, give us allowances' – Louis chose to do that, otherwise he would have died a pauper like Lionel Hampton."

My interview with Phoebe terminated abruptly when her companions – a gospel singer and another black woman – arrived at our table prior to the gig. "Turn that off, now," said Phoebe, indicating my recorder, "I want to enjoy my friends." She introduced me, "This is Mike from England – he's writing about jazz and Jews." The singer – I won't name her – gave me her card but pretty much ignored me the rest of the evening. The other, younger, lady was chatty but there was an undertone. She said something along the lines that, "You'd better get this black-Jews thing right, and that it was black genius that was the important factor in business relationships." It wasn't exactly as emphatic as that, but that was what she meant, adding, "Get it right and you could do a lot of good." Then she said something like, "The young hip hoppers are now keeping the Jews out"; which is not wholly correct as hip hop is another field in which Jews – Rick Rubin, Jerry Heller, Lyor Cohen, Bill Adler – have facilitated black music.

• • • •

America's first dedicated jazz record label was started by Milt Gabler, a music business *mensch* if ever there was one.

Gabler was born in Harlem in 1911. His father worked in a hardware store and as a streetcar conductor before opening the Commodore radio shop. After handing over its management to his jazz-infatuated son, Gabler converted it into the world's first dedicated jazz record store. 33

This transformation he undertook with missionary zeal for which the jazz fraternity should sanctify him. The great depression was on, few people owned a phonograph, and radio was a free way to enjoy music. The Okeh company, that had issued most 1920s' 'race' records, collapsed by the early thirties and was taken over by Columbia, who, commercially driven, disdained the treasure trove of early jazz now in its possession. Columbia allowed Gabler to rake through hundreds of thousands of records at Okeh's Bridgeport plant to buy, for a dime apiece, pretty much all the "hot jazz" wasting away there. He also acquired records from warehouses and shops that were going out of business, and from the Salvation Army, and licensed out-of-print masters from major labels so he could reissue them via his – believed to be the first ever – mail-order record club. Sporting the venture's own United Hot Clubs of America label, these were the first reissues in jazz history.

The majors took note and began issuing their old or unused jazz masters themselves. Gabler was unfazed; if it was a jazz record, he'd sell it: "What's the difference if they make it or I do? It's jazz, isn't it?" 34 By early 1937 however, the shop had, as Gilbert Millstein in *New Yorker* learned, "piled up, for art's sake, debts to the amount of $20,000". 35 The store received a publicity boost when *March of Time* sent a newsreel crew to film the establishment. But with the majors now issuing vintage discs, Gabler realised, he told Dan Morgenstern, that, "The only way for the Commodore Music Shop to stay in business was to start my own label." 36 Another factor was Gabler's revulsion at how record companies had hitherto handled jazz musicians, if not neglecting them altogether.

So in 1938 he launched the Commodore label, almost but not quite the world's first dedicated jazz recording company. The French Swing label preceded it by a few months. Commodore was first, however, in listing full musician personnel details on record labels, including who took solos, and also the first to do liner-notes. "Milt was a saint, he loved the music, he loved the musicians, they hung out at his store, he helped them out when they were broke, he was just a great guy," Dan Morgenstern told me.

Among the musicians that frequented the store was Billie Holiday; the story of how the anti-lynching song 'Strange Fruit' came to be written for her I related earlier, but no major label would risk recording it. Billie turned to Gabler: "She said to me, Columbia won't record it because they're afraid of the content of the song – afraid, that is, about the southern record dealers and the adverse publicity. They also didn't think it was a pop hit. But it was a marvellous piece of music with a great message." 37 Provided Billie could get a one-session release, Gabler undertook to record her for Commodore.

That meant dealing with Vocalian, a predecessor of the Columbia label, to which Billie was contracted. Her recording director there was the jazz-loving anti-racist campaigner John Hammond, but Hammond, Morgenstern explained to me, had not wanted her to record 'Strange Fruit' as he felt it was a wrong career move: "But he allowed her to go to Gabler, who he knew – Gabler and Hammond were close." So, backed by Café Society's house band, she cut four sides, including 'Strange Fruit' in April 1939. Commodore was rewarded with its biggest seller but Millstein put that in perspective: "He has sold 50,000 copies... which is considerably more copies than he has sold of any other Commodore record. If a hot [jazz] record... goes over five or six thousand, it is considered a sensation. As a best seller, though 'Strange Fruit' scarcely ranks with Victor's 'Chattanooga Choo-Choo', which sold over a million copies in one year." 38

Billy Crystal, Gabler's nephew, made the point: "This wasn't about making a hit. This wasn't anything about capitalism. This was about humanism, this was about civil rights, this was about fairness, this was about an America that he would like to see. This was about an artist expressing herself in the best way she could. As a family member... we all feel so proud of the fact that here was this plump Jewish guy who saw the truth in those lyrics. And after everyone said they didn't want to record it... How proud I am that he had the guts to do that." 39 The B-side, 'Fine and Mellow', was also a hit. Gabler contributed greatly to the lyrics but credited Billie as sole composer enabling her to enjoy full royalties. 40

Between January 1938, when Commodore recorded Eddie Condon's revivalist jazz band, and the last Commodore session in 1954, more than one hundred and fifty musicians recorded for the label, its catalogue dominated by revivalist and swing music. No bebop, however; "Gabler is rueful about having missed them," jazz writer Whitney Balliett discovered. 41

Gabler also initiated a long-standing series of free-of-charge jam sessions at Jimmy Ryan's club on Manhattan's 52$^{nd}$ Street. These eventually included a band of Harlem-based black musicians. Although the street's clubs often featured black artists, the owners showed no inclination to attract integrated audiences, and uptown blacks were anyway chary of midtown socialising. The Harlem band was Gabler's bid to address this issue, the idea being, he hoped, that they would bring their wives, and that in time would create a racially more relaxed vibe so other black people would feel comfortable attending.

Another 52$^{nd}$ St club, Kelly's, following Gabler's lead, staged jams; this the club run by Pheobe Jacobs' uncle. These sessions ended in mid-1943 when police padlocked the door. "Naturally it had to do with the black-white thing... We drew an integrated crowd," said promoter Monte Kay. 42

In 1941, Decca recruited Gabler as a record producer but allowed him to continue producing records for Commodore, which he did until 1950. Gabler's brother-in-law Jack Crystal, Commodore's jazz promoter, ran the label after Gabler joined Decca. 43 Whereas Commodore's output remained hot jazz, including further Billy Holiday cuts after Columbia dropped her in 1944, Decca was a pop-oriented label with whom Gabler began engaging with musicians in diverse idioms, including Bill Haley whose Gabler-produced 'Rock Around the Clock' launched rock and roll, but Gabler ensured that jazz was not neglected. Billie Holiday signed a five-year Decca contract, claiming that at Columbia, she "didn't get a cent of royalties... The only royalties I get... are on my records after I signed with Decca". 44

Pheobe Jacobs, in my interview with her, said about Gabler, her Decca colleague: "A guy like Sy Oliver, who was a giant in the industry, Milt Gabler gave him the opportunity to be the first black man to be musical director of a major record company. Gabler started to buy old masters from a woman by the name of Bessie Berman; she inherited a record label from a cousin, race records, she had a lot of black stuff" – that would be Apollo Records, another Jewish-established independent label.

At Decca, Gabler was also responsible for persuading Joe Glaser to temporarily release Louis Armstrong from touring to record the series *Louis Armstrong: A Musical Autobiography*, on which Armstrong's All Stars covered material spanning his career. "When Milt Gabler wanted to do that autobiography with Louis, a major undertaking, four LPs worth, he made a deal with Joe; he paid enough for that to tell Joe to leave Louis alone for a week," Dan Morgenstern informed me. "And that's why those records came out so well."

• • • •

Following Gabler's breakthrough, other indie labels emerged that recorded jazz. That included Savoy and Prestige, founded respectively by Herman Lubinsky and Bob Weinstock, both Jews, both allegedly exploiters of jazz musicians.

"Miles Davis disliked the Savoy and Prestige record labels intensely," Ozzie Cadena, producer for both companies, informed me. "He thought that he and Charlie Parker were taken advantage of, especially when they were under the influence. Herman Lubinsky once told me that he would return all the songs that he controlled to their original writers' families; that should include me for 'The Right Time.'"

Savoy, founded in 1947 in a black district of Newark, started as an offshoot of Lubinsky's radio and electronic parts store. It was one of the small labels that came into existence following the foundation of BMI, the performing rights organisation established in 1939 to challenge the dominance of ASCAP. Whereas ASCAP largely represented the interests of Broadway and Hollywood composers and music publishers, BMI opened the path for musicians in genres that ASCAP overlooked, including black idioms such as R&B and gospel.

Remembered as a "tough talking, cigar-chewing record man", Lubinsky had no love of black music but scented the commercial possibilities and hired jazz fan Teddy Reig to scout talent. "Reig, who would go on to produce Charlie Parker and the hardcore boppers in the late forties for Savoy, said Lubinsky would go into a 52nd St bar, sit at a table all night long nursing a beer if he'd even buy that, and line up contracts on his table and expect the musicians to come to him to sign them," Kirk Silsbee told me. "He had no interpersonal skills, and somehow Reig was able to convince him that it was he who should be his interlocutor to the musicians because Reig knew the music and the musicians. He was a Jewish guy who lived black, lived in Harlem, had a black wife. So it was Reig who would take Charlie Parker into the studio and record him, and early Stan Getz, early Al Cohn and the like boppers."

Reig was a hustler – described himself as such – but was well regarded among musicians, said Silsbee: "He knew who should be on a particular session and who didn't belong there. He knew when a tape wasn't up to reasonable quality. You hear him on the Charlie Parker and Dexter Gordon alternate takes, yelling at Leo Parker when Leo Parker's not cutting it."

And Reig was proud at Savoy of giving Charlie Parker – whom he idolised musically and personally – his first recording dates as leader. He also arranged Miles Davis's first leader sessions, despite Lubinsky's opposition. "Miles hated Lubinsky with a vengeance," said Reig. 45

Miles' early career is illustrative of the dealings many jazz musicians had with certain labels. His cachet grew after the Capitol-issued *Birth of the Cool* recordings but he developed a serious drug habit and did little other commercial recording until his first session for Bob Weinstock's Prestige in 1951. Unlike Savoy, Prestige was a specialist jazz label and Weinstock adored the music. He knew and liked Miles and, he told jazz writer Joe Goldberg, sought him out: "Miles sort of disappeared from the scene, and I was on a business trip to St Louis... I made some calls [to Miles' home there]. They told me he was in Chicago... Finally he got in touch with me, and he came back east... though he still dug the cool music of Mulligan and Evans, some of the primitiveness in him started to come out ... On his first date, you can hear a very different Miles Davis than on the Capitols." 46

Between 1951 and 1956, Miles recorded for Prestige but, claimed jazz writer Frank Kofsky, the label's reputation was so odious in the way it did business "that Miles Davis, for one, advised younger musicians just arriving in New York to contract with any other company... It was notorious in jazz circles that Weinstock habitually took advantage of musicians who were desperate for money – often because of an addiction to heroin – by signing them to contracts that required them to record a huge number of selections in exchange for a minute advance against future royalty payments, with the latter set at an unconscionably low rate". By such means, alleged Kofsky, Prestige built up a priceless catalogue of recordings by Miles, Sonny Rollins, Charlie Parker, Coltrane and others. 47

Ira Gitler, who took over as producer at Prestige when Weinstock no longer wanted to do it, told me: "He was stressed out. I think he told me that musicians were always hitting on him for extra money – a ten here, a twenty there, a fiver, whatever. Being in the studio with them made him accessible. My first date as an A&R man was December 17, 1951, the eve of my 23rd birthday and Sonny Rollins first session as a leader."

Gitler, who in later years as a jazz writer came under fire from Kofsky for not supporting the black avant-garde, dismissed Kofsky as an extreme leftist with an agenda: "There were a lot of musicians who were junkies in those days but Weinstock didn't set out to deliberately exploit them because they were addicts; he recorded musicians because he dug the way they played. A standard record date in those days was four sides, three minutes or so each, in three hours of recording studio time. Sidemen got $41.25 and leaders $82.50 in the standard union contract. Of course, leaders usually got more than the minimum $82.50. The contracts also stipulated how many sessions were owed to the company during a three-year span."

Weinstock, Gitler said, "was just as tight about his money as any other independent record label producer. Probably had two sets of books like everyone else although I don't have first-hand knowledge of this. As for the drug thing, Gene Santoro in his book on Mingus quoted Mingus on a session that Weinstock supposedly offered Mingus as a leader that would have included cocaine, but Mingus turned down the session. I doubt this because in addition to the sessions I produced, I was in attendance as a listener at a lot of the other sessions for which I wrote the notes. I never saw Weinstock or anyone else from Prestige offer drugs to anyone. Sometimes we had a bottle of whatever and/or some beers but just as often or more often, sandwiches, coffee and Coca Cola".

Many Jews, said Gitler, gravitated towards the business because they were musically inclined and soulful and connected with black music: "The record business, even at the top, in those days was not run by lawyers and accountants. Many actually liked the music."

Dan Morgenstern gave me further valuable perspective: "I'm not privy to what people did in their business life. You hear all kinds of things, about how the record business always cheated musicians, and that goes for major labels, and it goes for Goyim too and Jews, so that has nothing to do with that. Individuals that I know about: Teddy Reig probably pulled some fast deals, everybody did – it was a business where, if you were Herman Lubinsky and running Savoy records, you didn't have a million-dollar budget so you cut corners. One of the things all these people did – Ross Russell who was not Jewish, with his Dial label, and Savoy, and Prestige, they all had their own publishing companies. In other words, when they recorded a musician like Charlie Parker or Gerry Mulligan – and they recorded a bunch of original compositions, which very often were not very original and not really compositions either, but they were copyrightable – they would be in the record company's publishing company. This enabled them, where if you signed with BMI, they would give you an advance on your original composition. If you were in BMI and you were Charlie Parker, you could get a couple of hundred bucks by writing a piece and having it published. So, this was a sweet set-up. Most of the time, during the bebop era, a lot of this money went right into the pocket of drug dealers.

"Let's say you're a small record label like those little jazz labels, say you're Prestige, Bob Weinstock, you've got a date set up with Charlie Parker, finally you get everybody together, which can be hard sometimes because somebody goofs off and doesn't show up and here you have a situation where somebody is so strung out, they can't do anything without getting a fix. So instead of which, what they also did, sending out for a bottle of booze, you'd give somebody an advance and they'd send their man out. So what are you doing? You've got this record date set up, you've got the studio booked, you don't own the studio, you've got to pay for studio time, you've got a bunch of musicians there, so you've got to do whatever you have to do. You're wasting half an hour, forty-five minutes on this deal anyway, but you do it."

Small labels were always juggling, said Dan. "Bob Weinstock made a lot of money at Prestige, but you know how he made it, by selling the label. While he was running it he really wasn't making the kind of money. I mean, after all, if you're in business, it's not a charity. You should pay people what their services are worth, you shouldn't cheat them out of royalties – that's one of the things that people get accused of. I think major labels, whether intentionally or unintentionally due to poor bookkeeping and sloppiness, do cheat artists out of royalties, rather than small labels. The small labels are an open book – you know, if you have any sense, that they're not pressing 200,000 copies of an album and then selling 150,000 and telling the artist that they've only sold 50,000. If that many records were selling all over the place, you'd know about it, you can't hide it. And we know that the jazz business is a very small business. In the days of the junkies, there were things that were done that were not ethical but then it was a temptation because musicians put themselves into that position because of what they were trapped in, to say, 'I'll do this for you, just give me this upfront, you can have the rights, no royalties.' People who accepted that, maybe they were wrong to do it, obviously a lot of things like that were done, but later on it didn't become possible to do things like that."

By 1970 Weinstock was so bugged by musicians demanding money that, in Prestige producer Bob Porter's recollection, "the delicate balance between fan and businessman had tipped completely". 48 Weinstock sold the label to Fantasy.

Miles Davis, having kicked his addiction and recorded increasingly impressive albums for Prestige, outgrew the independents. "As Weinstock well knew," Dan Morgenstern reflected in notes for the CD-boxset *Miles Davis Chronicles: The Complete Prestige Recordings*, "it was only a matter of time until a major label would become interested and make a contract offer he could not hope to match. It turned out to be Columbia."

Which brings us to another stratum in the story of Jewish jazz facilitators. William Paley, the son of a German Jewish cigar-maker, bought the CBS radio network in 1927 and under his ownership, CBS acquired Columbia Records in 1938. Under producer John Hammond, Columbia recorded Benny Goodman and Billie

Holiday and other important jazz artists as part of its genre diverse roster.

The appointments of German-Hungarian engineer Dr Peter Goldmark, and classical pianist and composer Goddard Lieberson, both Jewish, proved highly significant. Goldmark invented the LP – long-playing – vinyl record, while under Lieberson's artistic direction, Columbia grabbed the initiative in recording Broadway musicals. These developments, and Lieberson's successes in attracting mainstream pop talent, saw Columbia overtake RCA Victor as America's largest record company by the 1950s.

"There are people who had no direct relationship to jazz but who were important to the record business and who were Jewish," Dan Morgenstern explained to me. "An outstanding example of someone who had a very positive influence is Goddard Lieberson who was president of Columbia records in the early days of the LP era and who was an absolute contrast to people who have generally been in positions like that as he was a person with very well-developed aesthetic tastes. He had a windfall with *My Fair Lady*. It was his idea to record Broadway shows like that and *My Fair Lady* was a tremendous success. That made it possible for him to do a lot of things. Among the things he did, he made it possible for all these Miles Davis-Gil Evans ventures, which was expensive. An average jazz album would never have involved as high a cost because of the high instrumentation and, if it had been up to Gil, it would have taken up even more rehearsal time, and it took a good deal of rehearsal time. Goddard was a class act, involved in the world of commercial recording, able to make a success of it and not compromise his standards."

Miles Davis enjoyed his best years at Columbia, and his album *Someday My Prince Will Come* includes 'Drad-Dog' – Goddard spelled backwards – Miles' tribute to Lieberson for his support.

. . . .

Before his Columbia breakthrough, Miles recorded several sessions for Blue Note, the label founded in 1939 by Alfred Lion and run with Francis Wolff, both German Jews transplanted to American soil. They built Blue Note into the most iconic of all jazz labels.

"I dealt with those guys years ago," Randy Brecker told me, "particularly Francis who was a very sweet individual, and very well loved among all the musicians. As was Alfred Lion. They were both unique individuals and added quite a legacy to the music with all those great records. I did a lot of Horace Silver records and Francis Wolff was the producer and photographer – he took many great photos. He had a feel for the music, he knew what was good and what was bad. I remember him commenting on one of my solos that I thought was pretty good myself and he liked it too. He had a real natural feel for jazz, especially being from Germany, escaped the Holocaust – they just had a real natural feel and love for the music, and I think it was reciprocated. I never heard anything bad about them."

Stanley Crouch agreed: "I don't think I ever hear anyone accuse Lion or Wolff of being crooks."

Dan Morgenstern told me something else about them that perhaps bespoke their origins: "The thing about Alfred and Frank was that neither were very public figures. They were very private and even when Blue Note was at its height, Blue Note was unusual in that whereas most other labels I could walk in, like at Riverside I could see Orrin [Keepnews], it was wide open, Blue Note was like a bank, you came there, there was a door and then you came into this tiny little it wasn't even a room where there was a window which was closed; they wanted to know who you were and what did you want, it was kind of barricaded, it was weird."

Perhaps the Blue Note partners' German background had ingrained in them habits of formality, and, as Jews, of circumspection. Alfred Lion, born in Berlin in 1909, remembered as a youngster being taken to a resort hotel where he was sent to bed while his parents danced to the ballroom orchestra: "I'd get dressed and sneak down to the stage entrance... The musicians... put me in the orchestra pit and I sat for hours next to the drummer. It meant something, to feel that rhythm." 49 In 1925, Lion caught Sam Wooding's band in the Chocolate Dandies revue in Berlin, his first live exposure to black American music: "It registered with me right away." 50

He began collecting American records and made his first New York visit in 1928, working as a docker, enjoying the city's music, and returned again working for German exporters, each time collecting more records. Come 1933, the year of Hitler's power-grab, the family departed for Chile where Lion worked as a lobster fisherman. Once he settled in New York, again working in export, he gravitated to Gabler's Commodore store.

Then came the December 1938 concert, at Carnegie Hall, that changed Lion's life, as Dan Morgenstern told me: "He started Blue Note, inspired by John Hammond's Spirituals to Swing concert which he attended and heard the boogie-woogie guys there, Meade Lux Lewis and Pete Johnson and decided to record them, so booked a studio and recorded Albert Ammons and Lewis on 12-inch records. The usual 78rpm disc was a 10-inch; 12-inch 78s enabled the recording of longer pieces but there had been very few issued; Milt Gabler had made a few 12-inch records by then. And Alfred was an enthusiast and recorded the right things and Blue Note became a success. He starts out with piano boogie-woogie, and he really records a lot of that, he loved Meade Lux Lewis, and almost recorded in my opinion an overload of Lewis. I used to buy these records because I knew they had to be great, but three or four Meade Lux Lewis and then harpsichord, it gets awfully monotonous, but it certainly caught on, and then he branched out."

Much of the start-up funding was provided by Jewish left-wing writer Max Margulis, who contributed publicity and advertising material. In 1947, when the label began recording bebop, Margulis was uninterested in that so Lion bought him out. 51

Francis Wolff arrived in the States on one of the last boats out of Nazi Germany before the war. Wolff had become friends with Lion in the twenties, sharing the passion for jazz. About Blue Note, Wolff recalled: "People used to say, 'Alfred and Frank record only what they like.' That was true. If I may add only three words, we tried to record jazz 'with a feeling'." 52

As for example Sidney Bechet's 1939-1940 Blue Note sessions, which can be counted among Bechet's finest recordings, including his peerless take on 'Summertime'. Bechet was a New Orleans jazz pioneer but by the late thirties, as Leonard Feather noted, "The music business seemed to offer no substantial future; Sidney settled down with a small tailoring business in New York. Blue Note Records played a significant role in his slow but sure climb up the ladder from inactivity to newly found global fame. It was after a major record company had refused him permission to record a certain popular song that Sidney came to Albert Lion." 53

By the late forties, Lion and Wolff switched focus to the new jazz, bebop. "They were the first to give Monk a real chance, and totally honest," Nat Hentoff told me. "That was the only indie label that paid for rehearsals before the sessions." Thelonious Monk, as a pianist and composer, the most singularly leftfield bebop innovator, first recorded for Blue Note in 1947, this a decade before his full acceptance by the jazz public. 54

Blue Note was also the first to record pianist Bud Powell. That was in 1949, and further sessions were recorded over the next decade. "Just exactly why Alfred Lion routinely got great performances from Bud Powell when others got mediocrity is not known, but it is true," mused producer Bob Porter. 55 One reason would be Lion's and Wolff's empathy for the music, providing the most supportive environment and creative freedom for the artists.

The Blue Note partners cared about the musicians as individuals, as their relationship with the troubled Bud Powell illustrates. About Powell, Michael Cuscuna observed: "By the early to mid-fifties, the frustration of being black and an artist in one's own country, which has little use for either, compounded his longstanding mental problems and the effects of bad habits that he acquired to ease the pain." 56

Francis Paudras, an amateur French pianist who befriended Powell after Powell's move to Paris, interviewed in a documentary film about Blue Note, related a heart-rending story: "One night at Birdland Bud had outplayed them all, Charlie Parker, Fats Navarro, Max Roach, they didn't dare come back on to the stage, his music was so strong and exceptional. And then a strange thing happened – Bud was playing quite loudly when suddenly his fingers moved on without a sound being heard. He was always up to doing funny things that shocked the American audience or made fun of them. Soon two bouncers came and threw him out onto the pavement. Alfred Lion appeared on the scene. Bud was so frightened that he hid under a car, 'Like a cat,' as Alfred said later. For half an hour, he tried to get him to come out. And eventually he succeeded. He took him back to his place, let him have a bath, fed him and made him stay overnight." 57 Altoist Jackie McLean believed that "if Alfred Lion and Francis Wolff... had been able to handle Bud from the early part of his career, he would have turned out a much different person... They always treated him with the greatest respect". 58

The arrival of the vinyl LP nearly spelled the end for Blue Note. "Suddenly their whole catalogue that they had worked so hard to stay in business to generate was obsolete... and at this point, Alfred almost threw in the towel," revealed the label's discographer Michael Cuscuna. The difference, he pointed out, between a 78rpm disc and an LP is cover art: "You make a 78, you put it in a brown envelope... Once you come to the LP, even a 10-inch LP... not only do you have more recording costs but even if you're reissuing stuff that you already own, suddenly you have the art costs, you have to create a front cover, liner notes, back cover and it became a far more expensive business to be in." Lion seriously contemplated an offer to buy him out but it "was so embarrassingly low that Alfred decided to fight it out... And fortunately he did because two very important things happened, Art Blakey and the Jazz Messengers, and later the Horace Silver Quintet". 59

Blakey's *Moanin'* and Silver's *Song For My Father*, the title tracks from these albums among the most famous themes in jazz, are indicative of Blue Note's critical engagement, from the mid-fifties on, with recording 'hard bop'. It emerged largely in response to the R&B that was enjoying widespread popularity in black communities, diminishing the market for bebop. The earliest hard bop artists typically had bebop pedigree so found it limiting when, as many did, they took R&B jobs. Hard bop allowed greater scope for inventive solos, while retaining the earthy propulsive rhythm-and-blues and gospel influences. A related development was soul jazz, as exemplified by organist Jimmy Smith's Blue Note albums. In the sixties, Blue Note would issue releases too by jazz experimentalists Ornette Coleman and Cecil Taylor, but hard bop helped the label survive the onslaught of rock and roll.

Between the mid-fifties and the start of the seventies, Blue Note issued numerous LP albums, the musicianship consistently splendid, and recorded with impressive naturalness and clarity. 60

Blue Note LP sleeves, with the striking modern minimalist graphics and typography of Reid Miles and the photography of Francis Wolff, became bywords for hip design that remains widely imitated. What those covers impart to you is that the musicians are modernist masters, their music high art.

• • • •

The Village Vanguard, in downtown New York, run by Max Gordon until his death in 1989, when his wife Lorraine Gordon, also Jewish, took over, can probably claim to be the jazz club most revered by musicians.

What countless jazz performers appreciated was the Gordons' obvious passion for the music, their honest approach to business, and the venue's vibe; "Playing the Village Vanguard is like playing inside this strange, beautiful old instrument that all these amazing people have played before you," said guitarist Bill Frisell. 61

Born in a shtetl near Vilna in 1903, Max Gordon arrived in America in 1908, grew up mostly in Portland, Oregon, his father sustaining the family by peddling furs bought from trappers: "We were poor, and we hustled as children. I sold papers... Mark Rothko, the great painter, was related to us, and we sold papers together." 62 His family expected Gordon to become a lawyer but he abandoned college and between jobs, spent afternoons reading in New York Public Library, then hung out till the early hours in Greenwich Village poetry clubs with vague notions of becoming a writer. 63 A humorous piece he wrote about a *schnorrer* [sponger or beggar] was published in a Jewish journal but he struggled to get by: "Running a joint is tough, but my years in the Village before I opened one were tougher." 64 Luckily his landlord was lenient, "the kind of landlord you could owe a week's rent to, two week's, even a month's. A generation of Villagers owe their survival during the Depression to Strunsky". 65

A woman Gordon befriended at the poetry events convinced him that "you don't need any money" to open a venue. 66 So in 1932 he launched the Village Fair Coffee House where poets gave readings. Its success encouraged him to open the first Village Vanguard, in 1934. The room's limitations prevented his obtaining a cabaret license, so he shifted base to the triangular basement of a former speakeasy where the Vanguard remains to this day. The shows back then were varied – jazz, cabaret, poetry, folk music, comedy.

In 1943 Gordon established, further uptown, a swankier cabaret club, Blue Angel, in partnership with Herbert Jacoby, a French Jew who had managed Parisian venues. Acts that went down well at the Vanguard were then booked at the Angel. The partners' policy, like that of Barney Josephson's Café Society, was racially enlightened, with black folks welcomed as customers, not just as performers. 67

A few years later, Gordon and Jacoby bought Café Society Uptown from Josephson whose business had taken a dive following his brother's subpoena. The partners changed its name to Le Directoire, spent a fortune altering the decor, but the venture flopped and was sold back to Josephson at a huge loss. By the late fifties, television was increasingly impacting on the partners' ability to hire, at reasonable fees, such diverse talent as previously booked. Jacoby's suggestion of converting Blue Angel to a restaurant only was unwelcome to Gordon who bailed out.

Apart from a brief stab at establishing an ice cream parlour, Gordon's sole focus from then on was Village Vanguard, now primarily dedicated to jazz. In the early sixties, it nearly went under, Whitney Balliett learned: "Max had to sell his car, his house on Fire Island... borrowed £10,000... and by dint of shrewd booking... pulled the Vanguard through." 68 "I have never been much of a businessman," said Gordon, "but we've taken in some money at times. When I could still afford Miles Davis, he'd bring in nine thousand a week. Money is a funny thing. A lot of musicians have borrowed from me, twenty-five, fifty, a hundred – and most of them pay it back." 69

Under Gordon's charge, world leading jazz musicians performed at the Vanguard: "I admit it was tough during the early sixties. Kids who listened to music were on a rock 'n' roll binge... Then in the late sixties, early seventies things started to happen. I began to find jazz musicians who were going places: Chick Corea, Herbie Hancock, Keith Jarrett, others. Kids were growing up and graduating from rock 'n' roll." 70 Jarrett, once he'd attained global status, performed several nights at the Vanguard for well below what he could then charge, in gratitude that Gordon had booked him when no one else would. 71

Then in the 1980s, as his health began to falter, Gordon came close to selling the Vanguard, as recounted by Lorraine Gordon: "The Japanese finally put a deal on the table, and they weren't offering enough. I couldn't help myself. I said, 'Max! Hey! this is a big bunch of nothing.' And he listened... Max Gordon simply never dreamed of me, Lorraine Gordon, his wife, taking over his club. I know that... I don't know what he thought... That I wasn't capable? That I was a woman? Very old-fashioned man." 72

After Max died, Lorraine closed the Vanguard the following day, reopened the day after and ran the club, eventually involving her daughter Deborah, who became de facto owner following Lorraine's passing, aged 95, in 2018.

• • • •

My efforts to secure an interview with Orrin Keepnews proved unsuccessful, regretfully as he was one of the good guys, serving the music supremely well as founder and producer of three labels, and as a penetrating jazz writer.

Born into a New York Jewish family, he was studying for an English degree at Columbia when world war intervened. As an Air Corps navigator and radar operator he took part on bombing missions over Japan, then post-war continued his degree while writing jazz reviews for the college paper.

In 1948, ex-Columbia classmate Bill Grauer, having taken over *The Record Changer*, appointed Keepnews as managing editor, a "virtually non-paying" title, but, said Keepnews, it led to two developments "directly responsible for altering the entire direction of my life". 73 The first was an invite to Alfred Lion's house to hear test pressings of Thelonious Monk's debut recording. Keepnews met Monk there and wrote an essay on him. That meeting was a harbinger of their collaboration in years to come. The second was an investigatory report Keepnews wrote for the *Changer* on record bootlegging at RCA Victor's production plant, which had pressed pirated discs for an outfit having the chutzpah to brand itself Jolly Roger Records. RCA Victor claimed it was unaware of the scam and signaled its willingness to lease its old jazz masters to Grauer and Keepnews. 74

They formed Riverside Records but the reissues came out on a RCA subsidiary, not what the *Changer* partners had initially understood the deal to involve. They complied but began reissuing other companies' vintage jazz and blues on Riverside. From the mid-fifties, Riverside began making fresh recordings, initially sessions with Jewish pianist Dick Hyman, following which the label recorded its first jazz modernist, Randy Weston. Grauer took charge of the business end, Keepnews, learning on the job, assumed the role of record producer. 75

Their big break came with the signing of Thelonious Monk, following a tip off from young jazz writer Nat Hentoff that Monk was unhappy with Prestige. "We knew Prestige wouldn't get rid of him if another label was interested, so this had to be done deviously," said Keepnews. "A meeting was set up and when Monk shows up, to my incredible surprise he tells me that that article that I had written about him seven years ago was the first writing about him to appear in a national magazine. He decided to throw his lot in with us. Prestige had advanced him some money, something like $128 and odd cents, so I gave Monk $130... He went to Prestige and came back with a letter saying you are released of all your recording obligations." 76

That was fortuitous for Riverside, immediately boosting its standing in modern jazz, and for Monk who, as pianist and composer, was finally becoming appreciated as an outstanding jazz innovator. Between 1955 and 1960, he recorded some of his strongest albums, solo and in group contexts, for the label. 77 Keepnews found Monk to be "an erratic, basically intolerant personality" but "overwhelmingly talented". 78 After Monk took up a more lucrative deal with Columbia, Keepnews reflected: "Of my projects at Riverside, I am probably most proud of what I could help Monk to achieve." 79

Riverside developed an outstanding catalogue, benefitting from tip-offs by artists already signed up. Guitarist Mundell Lowe phoned Keepnews to play him a tape of a gig at which Bill Evans was pianist, whereupon Keepnews engaged Evans to record his first album, *New Jazz Conceptions*. Issued in 1956, featuring Evans with Teddy Kotick, bass and Paul Motian, drums, it sold poorly in its first year despite strong reviews. For two years, Evans resisted attempts to record him again. "He didn't think he had anything new to say," said Keepnews. 80 He persevered and *Everybody Digs Bill Evans*, with a trio completed by Sam Jones and Philly Joe Jones, came out in 1958. Introverted, meditative, and with Evans' haunting, almost classical 'Peace Piece', the album marked out Evans as a true original.

The label's greatest commercial success was with Cannonball Adderley. The alto saxophonist was struggling with his band when Riverside signed him on recommendation from trumpeter Clark Terry. With his soulful, driving hard bop, Cannonball rapidly rose to star ranking. His 1959 album, *Cannonball Adderley Quintet in San Francisco*, with brother Nat on cornet, sold 50,000 copies. In 1961, with Cannonball's contract about to expire, and Keepnews resigned to Riverside's hottest asset being seduced away, "We made our best gesture – and he took it, even though it turned out to be much less than at least one major label had offered. The reason he gave, that he felt comfortable and at home among friends with Riverside." 81 By 1964, Cannonball had recorded fifteen albums as leader for Riverside, and two – with Milt Jackson, and with Kenny Dorham – as co-leader.

His loyalty manifested itself in another way, by alerting Keepnews to another future star: "I found Wes Montgomery through Cannonball, who came bursting into my office one morning and said I just heard this guitar player in Indianapolis, we've gotta get him on the label... I flew out and listened to him play on his after-hours job. I spent the whole damned night, and then at six in the morning, dramatically whipped a union contract for him out of my pocket and he signed. I later discovered it wasn't that I was dramatic and impressed him. Cannonball had told him, I think I can get my label interested in you, so it was the other way around. The point is that one thing led to another. Riverside had an honest to God family feeling." 82

Following Grauer's death, Riverside folded and in 1968 Keepnews with pianist Dick Katz started another jazz label, Milestone. When in 1972 Milestone was acquired by Fantasy, Keepnews was installed to head its jazz division, entailing a move from New York to California. Fantasy, a Berkeley-based label, was founded in 1949 by Jewish brothers Max and Sol Weiss and recorded jazz musicians such as Dave Brubeck, Gerry Mulligan and Cal Tjader, and comedian Lenny Bruce. 83 In 1968 a group of investors led by Saul Zaentz, also Jewish, bought the company, after which Fantasy rapidly became a big-hitter thanks largely to the success of rockers Creedence Clearwater Revival. Zaentz is mainly remembered as a film producer, but he was passionate about jazz and under him Fantasy acquired a number of independent labels.

At Fantasy, Keepnews continued producing, including Cannonball Adderley's and Bill Evans' last albums. One Evans' album is *Re: Person I Knew*, which is the title track and an anagram of Keepnews, Evans acknowledging in this way his indebtedness to him.

• • • •

John Koenig, whom I interviewed about his late father Lester Koenig, the founder of LA-based jazz label Contemporary Records, compared him to Orrin Keepnews, some of whose sessions John attended: "Both felt it was incumbent on them to create a setting where people are comfortable in order to perform well. To that extent, their sessions were similar. I think it would probably be fair to say that my father had more of an interest in the technical side – he was always looking at what were the best microphones and the best signal path."

Lester Koenig's fascinating life and career, up to the point he formed Contemporary, John related to me in detail. Koenig grew up in a comfortable New York Jewish family, his father a judge whose brother was the Republican boss of New York State, then New York secretary of state. Yet Koenig became a left-winger: "My father came of age during the depression and that influenced a lot of people, particularly in the big cities, towards left-wing ideals. I suppose in his case it seemed inequitable that he was living comfortably because his father was a government employee, a well-paid one as a judge, whereas his neighbours were always hungry. They were living in the lower east side and very quickly moved up to 86th and Madison which is a very nice neighbourhood, but from his early childhood, that was something that was very apparent to him.

"His interest in jazz, he was just interested in records first, and then he hung out in record stores, the famous ones in New York, and was very good friends with John Hammond... I think he met John in one of the record stores... It was a very small circle of collectors and they all knew each other. John was a few years older than my father and had already begun producing sessions when my father was a teenager, and my father was invited to come along. So he got the bug. He graduated from Dartmouth, went to Yale law school at his father's insistence, he didn't want to go really. When my grandfather died, I think he left and went to work for a guy called Martin Block, on the radio programme *Make Believe Ballroom*."

A year later came the opening that would draw Lester Koenig westward. He received a telegram from BP Schulberg, head of production at Paramount, whose son Koenig had known at Dartmouth where Koenig had written film articles for the college publication. Schulberg offered to set him up as a Paramount writer.

"And the first really permanent place he lived was on Malibu; he rented a guest house from film composer Hans Eisler who eventually moved back to East Germany, and for a while was known as the composer of the East German national anthem. Through Eisler he was invited into the famous intellectual, mainly Jewish circle, which included such people as Thomas Mann and Arnold Schoenberg and Bertolt Brecht. That was a big influence on him.

"At the same time, there was a jazz presence in Los Angeles, the Jazz Man record shop that was started by David Stewart and his wife Marilyn Morgan: David was recording New Orleans-type music. And in the bay area of San Francisco, there was a New Orleans revival going on. My father, having the interest he had, knowing John Hammond, I guess approached David Stewart and said he'd be prepared to go to San Francisco and record things. I think 1941 was when he made his first recording for the Jazz Man label and the Crescent label.

"Then the war came and he hooked up with Willie Wyler because he was from the air force unit that made films, and Wyler took a liking to him and they worked together for nine years. There were two air force pictures, *The Memphis Belle* which my father wrote the narration for, and the other was *Thunderbolt*. After he worked on *Best Years of Our Lives* and *Carrie* and a detective story and *Roman Holiday*; his name was taken off several of them because of the blacklist. But while he was working with Wyler after the war, his interest in jazz hadn't gone away. And I think in the late forties, just before I was born, he bought the catalogue of The Jazz Man masters, and hired David. And Contemporary Records started out as a classical label; he'd gotten to know and recorded a lot of prominent classical composers who were doing film work, like Aaron Copland. So he had an interest in things new and novel.

"And Howard Rumsey, who told me this story, had a club with John Levine, the Lighthouse, and they started Lighthouse Records and recorded the Lighthouse All-Stars. And it quickly became apparent to them both that either they were going to run a bar or be in the record business, they couldn't do both and decided they liked running the bar better. They approached my father, that's how Contemporary Records became a jazz label."

His father, John continued, was hauled before the House Un-American Activities Committee, leading to his blacklisting by the film industry: "He testified but refused to respond to the questions. I heard a tape of his testimony and one of the inquisitors said after the preliminary polite questions, 'Are you associated with any red organisations?' and he said, 'Yes', and there was a hush in the courtroom, and they said, 'What red organisation was that?' and he said, 'The Firehouse Five Plus Two – the world's greatest jazz band, I record them.' My father never spoke about it to me, I just heard it from the tape." Koenig recorded The Firehouse Five for his first label, Good Time Jazz, which became a traditional jazz subsidiary of Contemporary Records.

Contemporary's focus was on modern jazz, including the 'cool school' variant, about which jazz historian Ted Gioia observed, "The West Coast jazz movement of the 1950s may have reflected, in some degree, the surrounding geographical and meteorological environment, but it also reflected the taste of producers Les Koenig at Contemporary and Richard Bock at Pacific, the two most influential West Coast jazz arbiters of the period." [85] We've seen, earlier in these pages, how disputatious this all became: California, sneered Frank Kofsky, was the "center for these bleaching efforts" – his prime target, Contemporary Records. [86]

What Kofsky omitted to say was that Contemporary recorded – again as we have seen – Ornette Coleman's first releases, so avant-garde that few of his peers wanted to know.

"My father came across Ornette because he had been playing in jam sessions around Los Angeles. He was working as an elevator operator at a department store, and he would try and sit in at clubs and sessions all around town, and people kept hearing him play three notes and throwing him off the bandstand. Finally Red Mitchell, the bassist, who was a very empathetic guy and very warm-hearted, and he had played on one of these jam sessions and Ornette said, 'Have you got any idea how I can get ahead in this business because I seem to be getting nowhere?' And Red said, 'You should call Lester Koenig, I don't think he'll be interested in recording you but you have some interesting tunes, he might be willing to publish them.' So Ornette and Don Cherry showed up at Contemporary and my father said, 'Can you play the tunes for me? Red told me you have some interesting tunes. The piano's back there.' Ornette said, 'I don't play the piano.' So my father said: 'Well, how can I hear them?' Ornette said, 'Don and I will play them for you.' So they played these tunes and they were all unison lines. My father was very interested in avant-garde stuff anyway. I remember as a small child being dragged off to avant-garde dance and theatre. So he was receptive. He heard Ornette and Don play these lines and thought, 'This is interesting.' It was during a period when he was doing a lot of recording and he thought, 'Perhaps I'll make a record.'"

Gioia prudently points out that jazz historians invariably write as though musicians are the only influencers, but often a single influential person – and Gioia cites Koenig – can make the difference. 87 And Koenig didn't stop with Ornette Coleman. Shortly after, Contemporary recorded another jazz radical, pianist Cecil Taylor's *Looking Ahead!* As this was done in New York, Koenig hired Nat Hentoff as producer. 88

Somewhat less leftfield than Coleman or Taylor, but in no sense dismissible as cool, was tenor saxophonist Sonny Rollins' 1957 Contemporary release *Way Out West*, so named because Rollins, a fan since childhood of westerns, made superlative jazz with 'Wagon Wheels', 'I'm an Old Cowhand' and suchlike corny material. For the sleeve, Koenig hired jazz photographer William Claxton to take Rollins to the desert, shooting him adorned in a cowboy hat and gun-belt.

"This blew people's minds," Kirk Silsbee told me. "This is a very distinctive album in the Sonny Rollins discography. And for Rollins to play 'I'm An Old Cowhand' – the Rollins discography is full of these sardonic vehicles – things that no other jazzman would even wipe his feet on, Rollins would do something with it. But even in that discography of Rollins, with all these wildcard choices, *Way Out West* is a distinctively wildcard album and it's got a distinctive wildcard look to it. This does not look in any way like a Blue Note, like a Prestige, like any of the east coast labels. So my gut feeling is that Koenig was after a quality product. He was involved in the film industry as I believe a film editor, giving him not only a visual sense but a sense of craft. And as much as any other label you can think of, Blue Note included, the Contemporary catalogue holds up, compares favourably in terms of quality, on every level."

Contemporary records, in Kirk's summation, was a class act: "The Contemporary records, down to the last one, the sound was good, you knew the artists were in the studio for something other than a pay cheque. This wasn't a junkie label like Prestige. You listen to an album on Contemporary, you know these are not just junkies who have stopped into the studio, who can throw together six tunes to jam on with no thought in terms of composition and arrangement, who just want to get this thing over with so they can get their money and go stick it in their arm. The Contemporary catalogue is no slipshod effort. As [saxophonist] Teddy Edwards told me, 'When I met Lester Koenig, I never met anybody in the music business who was that fair to work with.' He also said that he would take your tape and study it, sometimes for a whole month. And he would get the utmost out of that tape that was humanly possible. And then the covers of those albums were always so wonderful."

Contemporary's exemplary treatment of artists is evident in Koenig's relationship with alto saxophonist Art Pepper, whom he stuck by despite ongoing personal issues. "He was Pepper's good patron," said Kirk. "Pepper would fuck up and get thrown into the joint, and as soon as he got out, Koenig would have the studio going for him, advance him money to go get a horn, open the studio for him, 'You want to record with the Miles Davis rhythm section? Sure, go ahead'" – the album Kirk referring to here, the splendid *Art Pepper meets The Rhythm Section*. In his autobiography, Pepper was unstinting in his appreciation: "I had made albums for different companies but I'd never gotten the right shake on my royalties... I just figured that's how the record business was. Then I was approached by Les... his whole operation was different. I saw that here was an honest man, and I felt very safe with him, and so I signed... We developed a beautiful friendship... When I was really in trouble, I talked to him. He helped me a lot."

His father, John Koenig told me, was referred to as Saint Lester, such was he revered by musicians: "It was an idiosyncratic label, he was not interested in making big money, he would have probably liked it if he had made a little bit more money than he actually made but that wasn't why he was doing it. He was doing what he did because he felt he was doing something creative that would advance some aspect of the culture."

John took over at Contemporary after his father died in 1977. In 1984, the label was acquired by Fantasy, freeing John to pursue his career as a classical cellist.

• • • •

As impresario, label founder, and manager of Ella Fitzgerald, Oscar Peterson and other top-rank artists, Norman Granz was one of the foremost, and most generous, facilitators in jazz history. And courageously principled in defying racial bigotry.

The son of poor Jewish immigrants, Granz grew up in Los Angeles in the racially mixed Central Avenue area. Coleman Hawkins' celebrated 1939 rendition of 'Body and Soul' turned him on to jazz. He became close friends with Nat Cole who was developing his trio, and with local drummer Lee Young, hanging out with them around LA's black jazz scene.

From 1942, he began organising jams. The first was at Billy Berg's Trouville club, Granz insisting on stringent pre-conditions: that the gigs should be advertised ahead of time and the musicians paid at union scale or more, rather than expected to play for free as happened at drop-in jams; that tables be placed on the dancefloor because jazz is music to listen, not dance, to; and finally, Granz told Berg, "You have to admit everybody, black or white, or whatever... They sit wherever they want to sit, and if it works, then you have to admit them the whole week." Berg protested that he had nothing against black people but they would deter white patrons. Granz, who as his career developed would face down far more stubborn, indeed hostile, adversaries, persuaded Berg to try it and even waived any fee. 89 The jams were a success.

Then came the pivotal point in his career and fortunes, his first Jazz at the Philharmonic concert. This landmark event in jazz history, in July 1944, was a benefit in support of Chicanos arrested in LA's 'Zoot Suit' riots and convicted on trumped-up murder charges. The Chicanos were known as Zoot Suiters in reference to the hip loose clothing they wore, attire favoured by black boppers. Granz borrowed money to stage the benefit, at the Philharmonic Auditorium, LA's largest music venue. It sold out, Illinois Jacquet, Nat Cole and Buddy Rich among the performers. Encouraged, Granz began staging commercial JATP jams monthly, bringing more musicians onboard, among them Charlie Parker and Dizzy Gillespie, and the next step was taking these shows on the road, in America initially and eventually overseas.

Jazz at the Philharmonic went on to become the longest running, most successful series of jazz concerts in the music's history, Tad Hershorn, Granz's biographer, told me: "The black press of Los Angeles and sooner or later all over the country really were aware that he was doing business in a proper way. And a lot of that came down to the fact that he did a lot of his own advance work with JATP, it became a national thing, he would go to all the radio stations, he cultivated both the mainstream and the black press, he bought ads."

Tad gave me the benefit of his expertise before the publication of his book *Norman Granz: The Man Who Used Jazz for Justice*. I interviewed him at a café across the road from the Institute of Jazz Studies at Rutgers University, where he was an archivist.

Granz's stance was an audacious challenge to the discriminatory practices prevalent in American society. By Tad's reckoning, some of it came down to personal relationships: "He really had the interests of these musicians at heart and JATP was so successful, he could pay good fees for that and underwrite recording projects that maybe other recording producers could not afford to underwrite, certainly not on the scale that he did."

Some JATP concerts were taped, Granz discerning that live recordings could capture the spontaneity of the jams. Initially he sold or leased the recordings to Moses Asch, the Jewish founder of the Asch label. They were later leased to Mercury Records, and thereafter issued on Granz's Norgran and Clef labels which he ultimately amalgamated to form Verve Records in 1956.

By 1952 Granz was grossing $1,000,000 a year, his JATP venture a commercial rollercoaster. He rewarded the artists handsomely: "His salaries are probably the highest in the history of jazz," observed *Metronome*. "It's safe to say that his men average two and three times as much a week working for Granz as they would playing in nightclubs elsewhere. It's been said that one performer's nightly salary with Granz equaled one week's work at a top nightclub." Granz reasoned: "I figure you can live a lot longer with yourself if you share the gains with your people." 90

His troupe traveled first-class, often by chartered plane, and Granz demanded first-class treatment for the black artists no less than the whites, at hotels, restaurants and venues. He resisted attempts to segregate audiences, even removing signs that read 'White toilets' and 'Black toilets' 91 – explaining that: "The whole reason for JATP was to take it to places where I could break down segregation and discrimination... I insisted that my musicians were to be treated with the same respect as Leonard Bernstein or Heifetz because they were just as good, both as men and musicians." 92 *Negro Digest*, March 1948, reported: "Adhering strictly to his purpose, the leader had turned down requests of southern bookers to play engagements with an all-Negro or all-white group. He has refused bookings as far north as Detroit, and Flint, Michigan, for the same reason. Despite this loss of lucrative engagement, amounting on his last tour to a reported $40,000, Granz is one of the highest-paying leaders in the band business."

Naturally, conflicts ensued, particularly in southern states, including confrontations with police.

Might Granz's Jewish upbringing, I asked Tad, have influenced his stance on race?

"That's a very curious thing because Norman was extremely private. At one point he asked me to draw up a list of questions that gave him some idea of things I wanted to know. Some of the first questions were about his parents who both came from the Ukraine to the United States around the turn of the century, and if they had much of a social outlook. And it was not until about a year and a half later that I started to do some telephone interviews and those were among the first questions that I asked him. That made him very uptight and angry and ultimately he cut off the interviews and we didn't talk again for about eight months."

From Tad I learned that Granz had been in the Communist Party: "He was in the party I think somewhere around 1945 to 1947 and it was actually like a musicians' group. In 1956, the House Un-American Activities came to Los Angeles to focus in on party influence in the music business... He knew ahead of time that he was probably going to be subpoenaed. He told me that he had fled to Mexico for a while to avoid a subpoena with the idea that, even though he was self-employed, that kind of publicity might damage his business. In October '56 he called up the FBI office in Los Angeles and they sent agents and Norman offered information, answered all their questions except implicating other people, and they concluded that he was not worth putting on any security index. They did try and lift his passport. When he applied for a passport renewal in Geneva and checked the box stating that he had once been a member of the Communist Party, he went to the State Department with the general counsel of CBS and got the decision reversed."

About JATP, Tad said it was something of a revolution in jazz presentation: "It was like a brand. He took an idea and ultimately just turned it into a juggernaut, integrating it with management, recording, and he's the only one who did it quite that way. It was like Norman Granz's take on jazz."

Could Granz, I ventured, be criticised at times on qualitative terms in that there was a feeling that some JATP jams – assemblages of sometimes stylistically disparate musicians – were a bit over the top?

"Certainly there were musicians who felt that that was like a circus-like atmosphere, and maybe even a parody of jazz. Dizzy Gillespie said that JATP reflected Norman's weird sense of competition. A lot of critics panned it. There was a lot of very good music too. He had a reasonable idea of who might play well together."

I had read that Granz sometimes made and issued recordings for the historical record, by artists he knew were unlikely to return a quick buck, even when the music was more modernist – until his tastes caught up – than the pre-bebop jazz that had first enthusiasm him.

"Absolutely," Tad confirmed. "Like Lee Konitz, for example. And I called up Lee Konitz about it, and that music was a bit way out for Norman in terms of his particular taste. But he recorded him and actually kept him on a weekly salary, which Konitz said that he really appreciated from the standpoint that he was just beginning a family."

And Granz supported the careers of many older generation jazz musicians whose livelihoods were threatened first by bebop then rock and roll, among them Art Tatum, the phenomenal pianist who recorded a series of solo and small group albums for Granz's Pablo label.

That, Tad said, was Granz at his best: "He knew that Tatum was ill, that he probably didn't have a long time to live and felt that Tatum never really got his just dues. So the idea of taking him in a studio and saying just play whatever you want I think has pluses and minuses. Without Norman, there would not be that catalogue of Art Tatum. On the other hand, there are people" – Tad cites here pianist Hank Jones – "who say that one way you don't record Tatum is to just take him in a studio and run this through like sausage. It's an example of where Norman had a conviction about something, he could afford to do it, and there are just people who can be critical even of a fairly monumental project like that. He thought that jazz was in Tatum's debt, and that Tatum was such a unique player that he just didn't have the fame or the prospects."

That whole humanitarian side could, rued Tad, be "clobbered" by the fact that Granz could be such a bastard: "This is a guy when they wanted to give him a Lifetime Achievement Grammy, just said, 'I think you guys are a little late' and didn't take it. Not particularly helpful in documenting a lot of the history that he made. That is just part of the mystery of him. On the one hand you feel that he never really got his just desserts, on the other hand he never really made it easy for someone to do it."

. . . .

In building up his JATP empire, Granz undertook most core tasks himself but was assisted early on by Martha Glaser, who was hired in a promotional role. She eventually became manager of jazz pianist Erroll Garner. Dan Morgenstern described her to me as a unique individual, with a strong, not religious, Jewish identity, and a wonderful sense of humour: "Trummy Young [trombonist, singer] in an interview that we have here [at the Institute of Jazz Studies] said that Martha was very smart and that she taught Norman a lot about business. She also did PR work for Piano Playhouse, that's how I think she first became acquainted with Erroll. She took over Erroll's career, he had no kind of decent management, he was being exploited left and right and there would be an instance of people recording Erroll for small labels and paying him a pittance and later making lots of money off the records. She took Erroll on and from that moment devoted herself exclusively to managing him and she did a fantastic job. She did for Erroll what Norman did with Ella – the analogy would be perfect because they're really comparable. She raised Erroll to a level of income which was unheard of in the jazz field as an instrumentalist. Louis [Armstrong] made a lot of money but Louis had a band and he was a singer and entertainer; Erroll Garner didn't do anything except play the piano, and she managed to build him into a top notch, worldwide attraction."

. . . .

Kirk Silsbee made a case, when I interviewed him, for Los Angeles Jewish jazz facilitator Gene Norman – DJ, founder of the Crescendo nightclub and record label – as comparable, in some respects, to Granz: "Gene Norman, while not quite the social crusader that Granz was, did put a lot of black performers in highly visible places. You know the Crescendo on Central Blvd, his club, was really about as good a place as you could play in LA in the fifties." Subsequently Kirk emailed me about other LA Jewish facilitators: "The role of the entrepreneurs can't be underestimated in LA jazz. Norman Granz, disc jockey/impresario/label owner Gene Norman, and club owner Billy Berg all had an incalculable effect on access, presentation and racial integration. Lee Wilder bought the Tempo Music Shop on Hollywood Blvd from Ross Russell when the latter got so involved with Charlie Parker and his Dial label that he moved to New York. Under Wilder, Tempo was Bebop Central in LA – the one place where modern jazz records could consistently be had in southern California and a magnet for musicians and bebop-minded people – from March '47 to '51 when she sold it. She also spun bebop records on KFWB after Gene Norman's Sunday night show. It was the first exclusively modern jazz radio show in LA. Alex 'Sleepy' Stein started KNOB in Long Beach in the late '50s. It was the first all-jazz radio station anywhere and his live remotes, from the Lighthouse and The Strollers in Long Beach, disseminated jazz in general and, in the case of the latter, the music of the nascent Chico Hamilton Quintet. Ben Shapiro opened Club Renaissance on Sunset Blvd in 57/58. It was its own business model: informal setting (pillows on the floor), handmade crafts for sale, eclectic entertainment (Lord Buckley, lots of jazz from Miles to Getz to Mulligan/Webster to Paul Horn to Jimmy Witherspoon to King Pleasure to Jazz Messengers, folk music, gospel and even mime), unusual food and drink. Shapiro produced concerts (Miles, Getz, Dylan, Baez, Ravi Shankar) at larger venues like the Shrine, Hollywood Bowl and Santa Monica Civic. He was instrumental in the Byrds getting their record deal with Columbia and was in on the ground floor of the Monterey Pop Festival. Miles loved Ben – as did everyone in jazz – and asked him to manage."

• • • •

George Wein's innovations in jazz presentation can be seen as a
progression from what Norman Granz started several years earlier.
I arranged an interview.

Before we come to that, some insight from John Levy who,
to remind readers, wasn't Jewish but one of the very few black
facilitators, pre-Berry Gordy, to have enjoyed sustained music
business success. Starting out as a bassist in 1940s New York,
including in George Shearing's quintet, in 1951 he founded John
Levy Enterprises, Inc, becoming personal manager for Shearing
and eventually for a client-base that included Cannonball
Adderley, Joe Williams, Shirley Horn, Ramsey Lewis and Nancy
Wilson. Levy died in 2012 shortly before what would have been his
hundredth birthday but when I met him, at his home in Alta Vista,
Ca, he was ninety and still involved in the business.

Levy had many dealings with Wein and had no hesitation in
proclaiming him a straightshooter: "Oh, I've known him all my
life, his family, the whole thing. When he started out, he wanted to
be a piano player. But his doctor father used to tell me, 'Would you
come to Boston and have dinner with my family?' And his father
said, 'Can't you talk him into something else. He's running this
club and he's playing in it and they're not doing any business. I got
to pay the money to keep the damned thing going.' Until George
Shearing or Erroll Garner comes in, then he makes some money,
but other than that he's not making any money in that club. But
George was a believer, and finally when the Newport festival thing
started, then he got business."

Wein went on to become heralded as "the most important
non-player in jazz history". From 1950 to 1960, he ran the
Storyville jazz club in his native Boston where he also founded
the Mahogany Hall club run by his cousin Jolf Wolfson, and the

Storyville record label. In the 1970s he formed the New York Jazz Repertory Company so that older forms of jazz, and its precursors, could be cherished, performed, and reinterpreted. And as a pianist, he loved to play along with the stars at his jazz festivals.

But it was Wein's role as the originator of those festivals by which he merited that "most important" accolade. It all began in 1954 with the first Newport Jazz Festival [NJF], on Rhode Island, an annual event that celebrated its 60$^{th}$ birthday in 2014. As a brand, the concept proved transportable: so there have been NJF tours of Europe, the NJF in Mexico, the NJF at Madaro, Japan, the NJF at Saratoga Springs, the NJF-New York.

The financing of annual events mainly via ticket sales, perhaps augmented by some official subsidy, could be precarious, so from the mid-sixties, Wein's Festival Productions became increasingly reliant on sponsors. Brown & Williamson, the company that produced KOOL cigarettes, assumed particular importance, the KOOL brand-name thereby appended to festivals throughout the United States. Other Wein-produced jazz festivals included the Midwest, the Boston Globe, the Ohio Valley, the Hampton in Virginia, the White House, the Playboy, the Grande Parade du Jazz in Nice, the Capital Radio in London, and – in collaboration with Michael Dorf – the JVC-sponsored 'What Is Jazz?

Wein moreover founded the Newport Folk Festival, the Newport Opera Festival, the Essence soul music festival, and the New Orleans Jazz & Heritage festival (whose Jewish co-founder, Allison Miner, when she died in 1995 was honored with a traditional New Orleans jazz funeral for her work in promoting, managing and recording previously obscure artists such as Professor Longhair).

Wein's career was not devoid of controversy. In 1960, Charles Mingus, furious that Dizzy Gillespie and Dave Brubeck were offered larger purses for that year's Newport Jazz Festival, arranged

the Rebel Festival to run concurrently elsewhere in Newport. 93
And for the 1969 Newport festival Wein, fearing that "that the
jazz festival was becoming lost in... the media explosion of rock
and roll," included some rock acts. Although it yielded a record
attendance for Newport, Wein reflected: "The 1969 NJF had been
four of the worst days of my life. Jazz – the music I loved – was
being poisoned and stamped out, and I had served as an unwitting,
but willing, accomplice in the murder." 94

Yet, far from murdering jazz, it is the jazz festival, as conceived
by Wein, and now widely imitated by promoters globally, that is
perhaps more than anything else what has kept jazz alive over the
last seventy years.

My interview with Wein took place at his apartment near
Central Park. Given Jews' prominence among jazz facilitators, and
similarly in blues, R&B and related idioms, I asked if he could
discuss the "black music, white business" controversy.

"Everything is history. The Jews were entrepreneurial, they've
always been entrepreneurial. They went into the professions –
doctors, lawyers. Because other avenues were not open to them,
historically, from medieval times; you know these things, these
so-called lords who couldn't handle money. So the Jews handled
the money, you also had Jewish moneychangers, and being an
entrepreneur, as opposed to looking for a job or a civil service job.
The Irish want to go into city hall, so they take over city hall,
wherever there's an Irish population you have Irish mayors, Irish
governors. You don't have Jewish mayors or governors in most cases
because they don't control the popular vote in democratic societies.
So they become entrepreneurs unless they have a family business
to go into, but the family businesses started on an entrepreneurial
basis as opposed to just getting a job. And one of the reasons is they
couldn't get jobs in Gentile firms, so it's history.

"Blacks had no openings, nobody would hire them, they were just menial labourers, that was the future if you were black; maybe you could get a job as a teacher in a black school, maybe you'd have gone to the church, maybe as things got better, you could become a social worker, a technician. But if they were a doctor they couldn't get into a good hospital. So what could they do? They couldn't take part in sports because they were barred from sports. But they could play music, but they didn't know what to do – they just played. Entrepreneurs came along, some of them good, some bad, most of them just looking how they could make money and the musicians were looking how they could get paid. I don't think there is anything that is difficult to understand about that."

"What is clear from that description," I put it to Wein, "is that does leave the field open, through naivety on the part of some musicians, at least initially, to exploitation."

"Everybody's exploited to one degree or another. Sometimes it's good exploitation, that helps someone, sometimes it's evil exploitation. Being ripped off is part of our society. Nobody got ripped off like the immigrant workers when they came to America, by the robber barons, before they got unions. People had to get unionised to get something. I mean, ripping off is the American way, the European way that pointed through the domain of the lords and the serfs. The people here, the robber barons, they had people living, the steelworkers, in company houses and company stores, and every cent they earned had to go back to them for rent or buying things – that was real rip off. Things are a little better now. People would still rip off if they could. The only thing that keeps people from doing all the ripping off is 1) unions, 2) lawyers that protect people. Most black artists have Jewish lawyers to protect them, not rip them off. So history changes. But everything was part of a way of life at one time, Jews did not rip off blacks any more than whites ripped off whites, it was the American way."

"One thing you read about," I said, "is artists getting paid for the session, and not getting royalties."

"They probably wanted the cash because they thought that they would never get the royalties – they didn't know what they were doing, it takes education to learn these things. And the guy who paid money for it, in his day, might have made money, might not have made money. The record labels that ripped off R&B artists – you have a Rhythm & Blues Foundation now just for that reason. The foundation's there for one purpose, to see that all the R&B artists from the fifties that started to make money are recompensed. And when they were struggling in the record business, the reputations the artists made from the recordings that didn't give good royalty deals, they were making more money than the record company just from performance, not from the records. As the years went on, the record companies have made more money, naturally, if they stayed alive. But in the early days all those small record companies were struggling, they made the best deals they could. I'm talking about in the fifties when blacks first started to make hit records on their own. Before the fifties, no big label would touch a black artist. Think of a black artist that made a record with a big label with the exception of Harry Belafonte, Lena Horne. The jazz artists, Billie Holiday – do you think she got royalties for all her records? And the man who recorded her was John Hammond who's done more for race relations than anybody in the history of jazz. And I don't know if she got any royalties. It was a way of life; that's something you've got to understand. Now that way of life has changed. I never believed in that way of life; when I signed musicians to record, I gave them royalties, and asked them if they wanted me to publish their songs. If they said no, they had their own publisher, then I said fine. I never made it a condition that they would have to give me a song to publish. I didn't believe in that. That was a way of life. When Benny Goodman, or Tommy Dorsey who wasn't Jewish, if they had a song-plugger come to them who might have been a white or a black song-plugger – it didn't make any difference – they said, 'Well if I'm going to record this, I want a piece of the song.'"

Now, Wein pointed out, the families of musicians such as Miles Davis and Thelonious Monk were making more money than they did when the artists were still alive: "Miles' lawyer told me that the estate is making over $1,500,000 a year, $2,000,000; Miles never made that, and that money goes to the family."

"And most of the people representing them would be Jewish lawyers?"

"In most cases, although that's changing too. What's happened is as the years went on, more and more blacks went to college, got higher educations, masters degrees, became professionals. My friends in New York, most of them African Americans, most are very important people. They all had to work through a maze of things to get where they are, they had to overcome the fact that they were African Americans in a white society. My wife Joyce's aunts were born in slavery. She had two aunts. Her mother was one of thirteen children and the two oldest ones were born in slavery. So there was this gradual evolution of things. You think today the blacks are getting an equal play in our society? They're not. Go to these inner cities and see the schools and then go downtown and see the schools. And you talk about rip-offs in the entertainment business; you ought to do an article about society and rip-offs, not Jews and rip-offs."

As the reader will realise, my intent is to give a rounded account of the Jewish role in jazz business; Wein's reaction to my questioning was defensive, when all I was seeking was his perspective on the issues.

"The concept of what you're talking about is historic," he repeated. "And anything historic has to be much deeper than the surface of what it is. And that's what I'm trying to tell you. I'm not defending anybody – if a guy's a crook he's a crook. When you look at the paper and see the Wall Street rip-offs – we don't know what rip-offs are – a hundred million dollars, a billion dollars from everyone that's investing in that company, rip-offs that didn't exist before, Brink's robberies – a billion dollars of petty cash. And you look at the papers and you say, 'All these guys are Irish that did it, thank God they're not Jews. Oh, there's no blacks, oh there's a black.' You look at the charities in New York, look at the people on the lists of the people that give to the arts and to cancer, in New York which is forty per cent Jews, or maybe a third Jews, seventy-five per cent of the money given to charity is Jewish money."

Whereas, said Wein, most American corporations were not Jewish controlled: "Very few of them are. Wall Street has a fairly big Jewish influence but not the major companies – corporate America is not Jewish."

Despite Wein's reputation for straight dealing, inevitably there were occasional fractious exchanges with musicians who, like Charles Mingus in 1960, believed they merited a bigger cut than he could necessarily pay them. In 1981, Wein was able to offer Miles Davis $70,000 for a double concert at Avery Fisher Hall at Lincoln Center, taking a chance on Miles' continuing allure as he sought to re-launch his career following a six-year hiatus. Few if any musicians in jazz history have had the pull of Miles.

"In my case, the music was the raison d'etre because I played it, but I found I had a better head for organizing," said Wein. "If I was working with a band and there wasn't a gig, I found a way of getting a gig, I did that naturally, I don't know why. I wasn't trained that way, I never had any business training. I know one thing, you spend $10 you gotta take in $11 or you don't stay in business long. I got paid finally for my visibility that I created, but I was 48 before I was out of debt. But I just kept doing things. I could have been the biggest rock and roll promoter in America, in '69 I played every rock group at Newport. Jimi Hendrix called me up, he wanted to be in the festival. I said, 'Jimi, I haven't got room for you.' I had Led Zeppelin, Jeff Beck. And after that I said I don't want this, I'd never seen so many people in my life, I said that's not my life, that's not what I want."

His proudest achievement, Wein told me, was that through all the years he'd remained number one in his field – toasted as the "granddaddy" by other festival promoters the world over: "The importance of festivals was the greatest single public relations that jazz ever had. Because when a festival comes to town, that's all they talk about is jazz – the newspapers and reviews. Before it never happened, it was all spread out. But when Newport came along, all of a sudden it was in the national magazines, everything jazz, jazz, jazz. So now, when you go to New Orleans, the Jazz & Heritage Festival, it's in the paper. In Europe now, there are a hundred festivals, thirty festivals, I don't know how many, you lose count. The greatest source of well-paying income, gigs, jobs, is at the festivals. The musician gets on the circuit in the summer and plays twelve, fifteen festivals – that's the biggest money he'll make all year."

Even though he died in September 2021, historically, George Wein remains the granddaddy.

# Chapter 16: Rooted cosmopolitans

Jewish-jazz – jazz that can deemed musically and thematically Jewish in some way – has proliferated in recent decades, but we must go back to when jazz was in its infancy for the earliest attempts to mesh jazz and Jewish.

Immigrant klezmorim – Jewish folk musicians from eastern Europe – that settled in America early in the last century, such as the celebrated clarinetists Dave Tarras and Naftule Brandwein, could not easily translate their talents into a facility for jazz, but for commercial reasons few could ignore it. Under the impulse first of ragtime then jazz, the US klezmer repertoire, from about 1920, starts becoming jazzier – the 'jazz' content dubious, though no more so than a lot of stuff so branded back then. Thus, in the early twenties, Julian Rose recorded the jokey 'Yiddisher Jazz'. 1 There was Joseph Cherniavsky's Yiddish-American Jazz Band with Dave Tarras on the vaudeville circuit. 2 And the Abe Schwartz Orchestra's 1927 recordings 'Lebedik', 'Un Freylekh (Tants), and 'Rusishe Sher'. As for the Harry Kandel's Jazz Orchestra's 'Jakie Jazz 'Em Up', klezmer musician-historian Henry Sapoznik asserts: "It's only 'jazz' element is a do-wacka-do trumpet break – already hopelessly out of date given the brilliant trumpet solos then being recorded by jazz greats like King Oliver, Louis Armstrong and Bix Beiderbecke." 3

I arranged an interview with klezmer and jazz musician Peter Sokolow. Born in Brooklyn in 1940, he was hired by veteran klezmer players because of his jazz savvy, starting with clarinetist Dave Tarras who came to America from the Ukraine: "I got to know Dave and his spiritual followers because I played with Dave, first when I was nineteen, 1959. Then I became his last regular keyboard player back in the seventies."

The interview took place after I watched Peter perform with a Dixieland band in a downtown Manhattan jazz bar. He introduced himself as "an old-time klezmer and old-time stride Dixieland piano player, ex-reed player, and jazz historian", then offered me his insights on klezmer and its relation to jazz in the United States.

"Both were dance musics to start with, essentially ensemble musics, the tones of the various musicians were fairly similar. If you listen to a New Orleans clarinet player and a klezmer clarinet player, the sound was fairly similar, both using Albert-system fingering. And the earliest jazz bands, before recording, used violins; if you see pictures of some of the early New Orleans bands, Morton's band has a violin. The violinist was often the leader, he would teach some of the other guys who couldn't read the tune, because he was some time classically trained. With klezmer a lot of them didn't read music either. If you listen to the Dixieland trombone, and the brum/brum-brum/brum-brum-brum-brum, klezmer used to play very similar, it was like a Jewish tailgate – tailgate meaning the old New Orleans jazz style. And they all played the tuba, boom-boom-boom, the old klezmer bass players used to boom, so did the old jazz players – that was the old recordings. The tuba was used because you could get a definite bass tone which was limited in sustain. Sustain was the worst thing [to record]. When you listen to the old jazz recordings you hear very little in the way of drums [again because of the primitive recording equipment], and all you'll hear on [twenties] klezmer records are blocks, sometimes sleighbells, and snare drums. There was something called the pook, a small bass drum on its side with a little cymbal, and the player used to use a little mallet in his right hand and on the cymbal and drums they'd go tinka-tinka-tinka-tinka. It was almost like a march beat. The early jazz drummers, very similar, but the difference between the klezmer and jazz drumming was that the jazz was essentially 2/4 – this was like an offbeat."

Another essential difference Peter pinpointed was in the melodic approach. Whereas the clarinetist in early jazz records was improvising on the tune, this was unknown in klezmer: "They played the melody, over and over again, melodic embellishments, ornamentation, not improvising."

Which conflicts with the following extract, from the erudite sleevenotes that accompany the vinyl record *Klezmer Music 1910-1942* (Folkways FSS 34021), that: "In the late 1920s, Tarras rose to great popularity as the originator and foremost exponent of the 'hot' clarinet style heard in Yiddish theatre. The great composers of the theatre would often leave open sections in their scores for Tarras to improvise freely." I had not come across that LP when I interviewed Peter, otherwise I would have read out that passage to him. Even if I had, given that Peter knew Dave Tarras musically and personally so well, my feeling is that he would have responded that Tarras's 'improvisations' were indeed little more than embellishments, whether spontaneous or written by Tarras for those open sections.

What about the minor modes in klezmer music, I asked Peter, any parallels with jazz as some claim?

"It's a false lead – take it from one who knows. Because the music follows cantorial modes, modes that people are used to hearing from music in the synagogue, middle eastern things. Let me tell you about the modes of Jewish music. There is a mode called freygish. Freygish follows the phrygian but with a major third – it's a middle eastern mode. So very often there will be so-called blue notes in these things because they're in the scale. It's got nothing to do with bending the note – in jazz, yes, in klezmer, no, because it's in the actual scale, in the actual mode."

On the bar piano, Peter demonstrated the difference: "They do share a kind of a blue tonality, but Jewish musicians did not hear, like, blues in particular. There was a similarity in feeling between the blues singer, to an extent, and the chazzan."

Peter singled out trombonist Harry Raderman as a 1920s Jewish musician who, in Ted Lewis' band, did exhibit genuine jazz and klezmer credentials: "Raderman was a real crossover, he played the Dixieland trombone style, he played some with mutes."

It was not though until the late thirties swing-era that a true Jewish-jazz hybrid began to emerge: "The major thing in mixing the two were first generation Americans, musicians born in the US of Jewish extraction. The one you could think of immediately was obviously Ziggy Elman – he actually played some Jewish jobs. Elman played several instruments including clarinet and violin, he played Jewish weddings on trumpet, clarinet and violin, bags of them. And he really found not only a spiritual but a commercial basis for mixing the two during the thirties. When 'Bei Mir Bist Du Schoen' became popular, everybody started doing Jewish stuff."

Then came Sam Musiker, who had worked with jazz drummer Gene Krupa and was, said Peter, key to the jazzification of Tarras' repertoire: "Tarras was not in any way a jazz player, played clarinet Jewish style, an amalgam of European influences, Hungarian, Romanian, Bessarabian, Russian and Polish. Sammy sort of pulled Dave into the crossover camp but Dave certainly never mastered it. Sam was a marvellous saxophone and clarinet player, a good arranger. He did a lot of klezmer when he was a kid, I don't know how old he was when he started. He did some things which were nothing less than amazing, when he played the jazz solos in Krupa's band between 1938 and '40, '41 in New York. He does a very good solo on the Goodman-Krupa version of 'Tuxedo Junction'. Sammy only soloed on clarinet in the Krupa band. He did however something that was never released, 'Jungle Madness' and he plays real honest-to-goodness klezmer; while Krupa is playing the tom-toms line, the 'Sing Sing Sing' bit, Sammy plays Jewish. I also have Sammy with a studio band that played Latin music after the war and Sammy plays honest-to-God Jewish, like a slow rumba or cha-cha, one of the Jewish theatre tunes, and he plays wow!

"Then he did the *Tanz!* album with Dave Tarras, 1955, and put all of that together; he was the arranger, he got a band of trumpet and three reeds – Dave, Sammy and Ray Musiker, saxophone, clarinet. He also had some studio players, one was Phil Bodner, the jazz alto player, also Jewish. He had a couple of other double-reed guys and he used the accordion imaginatively like a tertiary soloist on the horn with the accordionist playing soloist by himself and with the ensemble. He also arranged a record session in the late forties between Dave Tarras and a small band, trumpet and three saxes and Dave and a rhythm section on the Savoy label. Dave would play Jewish solos and then would come back to the jazz again, and Dave did a cadenza at the end of the thing which was out of Artie Shaw but it was written – Dave was the only one out of those real klezmorim who could read music well. Sammy did not play solos on those things at all. There were about eight tracks, very good but they were all the same thing, it went nowhere. Dave had a recording session of Jewish music where Sammy played nothing but jazz tenor, he sounds just like Stan Getz. So, Sammy started at the Jewish end and ended up more at the Jewish end, but in the middle he was really a very capable jazz player. Klezmer is essentially a melodic music without too much harmony – the harmony is implied. Sammy Musiker was big on having what we would call hip American-type harmony. A lot of people didn't like what he did; when you listen to a bulgar that Sammy wrote, 'Sam's Bulgar', you'll hear certain harmonic movements which are not Jewish harmonic movements, they're swing harmonic movements. Also, he mixed modes, went from one to the other like changing gears on an 18-speed bicycle. They're not good melodies, he's trying to throw the kitchen sink in there. And he performs them superbly. But I would rather play one of Naftule's or Dave's pieces because it makes more sense from beginning to finish. Sammy goes through all these convolutions, all the keys and up and down the scales, put next to each other, like lightning, so quick, tough to play, some of it awkward, but this is it, this is Sammy's stuff."

Peter gifted me two CDs: *Peysakh Duvid: The Swingin' Klezmer* which features his Original Klezmer Jazz Band, an old-style jazz melange of traditional klezmer, Yiddish theatre, and jokey-Jewish vaudeville tunes; and *Klezmerfats*, Peter performing solo throughout, his stride piano style and side-of-the-mouth Brooklyn vocal mannerisms a happy marriage of Jewish and Fats Waller.

It was with sadness that I learned of Peter's passing at the end of 2022.

· · · ·

Very little klezmer or its jazz derivative was recorded in America between about the late 1950s and the late 1970s. Factors that accounted for this demise include: the embourgeoisement and assimilation of increasing numbers of Jews as social, educational and economic barriers began to erode; the gradual passing of the older generation; and younger Jews gravitating to rock, pop and soul.

Yes, there were those two early sixties albums covered in earlier chapters, one by Terry Gibbs, which juxtaposed bebop and klezmer, the other Shelly Manne's mainstream take on Jewish tunes. Additionally, there was the 1964 release *Cannonball Adderley's Fiddler on the Roof* – Adderley and his sextet's highly enjoyable interpretations of songs from the musical. The tunes are rendered in post-bop mode, the entire band black other than

Austrian pianist Joe Zawinal. 4 "Cannonball saw great potential in the music from this hit show, both in its lyrical content and emotional melodies and in its life affirmation 'in the face of adversity'," Donald Elfman points out on my CD version. Adderley subsequently recorded an extended Fiddler medley at a Chicago club in 1966, captured on the album *Money in the Pocket*. Jewish-jazzwise then, that was pretty much it.

Not quite though because the sixties saw the emergence of three works of Jewish devotional jazz: Jonathan Klein's *Hear O Israel: A Sabbath Service in Jazz*, Gershon Kingsley's *Jazz Psalms*, and Charles Davidson's *And David Danced Before the Lord*.

Perhaps this can be understood in reference to broader concurrent developments in jazz: John Coltrane and other leading improvisers expressing their spirituality through jazz; Duke Ellington's Concerts of Sacred Music; and Lalo Schifrin – whose father was Jewish – composing his Roman Catholic Jazz Suite on the Mass Texts for flautist Paul Horn, a jazz musician of Jewish descent.

It was in 1965 that Jonathan Klein, a jazz-struck high school student from Massachusetts with compositional aspirations, conceived the idea for a jazz sabbath. Encouraged by his reform rabbi father, Klein set an entire Jewish prayer service to various forms of jazz, including modal, and *Hear O Israel* was performed widely throughout New England, Klein at the piano. Some congregants were discomfited by such radical tinkering with the sabbath service. Even so, the reformist North American Federation of Temple Youth, as part of its recruitment drive, decided that Klein's opus should be recorded. With its support, in 1967 he headed to a New York studio with his French horn and baritone sax. Assembled for the session was Rabbi David Davis to read the prayers, soprano and contralto singers, and a pick-up group of leading African American jazz musicians, Herbie Hancock on piano, Ron Carter, bass, Grady Tate, drums, Thad Jones, trumpet and flugelhorn, and Jerome Richardson, flute, tenor and alto sax. A limited-edition album was issued and vanished from sale until its 2008 CD revival.

The composer was never entirely happy with the original recording: the jazz musicians' improvisations, yes, but not his own youthful instrumental contributions, and the choral parts he felt were too classical in form. In 1992, with the collaboration of musicians and students from Berklee College of Music, Klein rearranged *Hear O Israel* for jazzier vocals. The updated version, including excerpts of jazz improvisations from the 1967 session, was issued in a new recording by the Milken Archive of Jewish Music in 1993. In the accompanying notes, Klein explained that he perceived a natural affinity between the improvisatory natures of jazz and cantorial chanting: "The ritual act of creating this music during worship (i.e., improvisation) seemed most appropriate for the Sabbath, when each week, according to Jewish mystical traditions, we re-create the world. While I was not suggesting that this style or mode replace nusaḥ hat'filla [the traditional Ashkenazi prayer modes] as the main musical diet for Jewish worship, I did feel that its occasional use added a unique spirituality."

Milken Archive also issued recordings of those other above-mentioned Judaic-jazz works. Gershon Kingsley's *Jazz Psalms* dates from 1966 and came about when Cantor David Benedict of Temple Israel in Lawrence, New York, commissioned Kingsley to compose three jazz liturgical pieces. Originally titled *Three Hebrew Prayers in a Jazz Idiom*, Kingsley combined the syncopated rhythms of jazz with Jewish modes. Two of these three jazz settings Kingsley later excerpted as a pairing retitled *Jazz Psalms*, as featured on the Milken disc, with soprano vocalist Lisa Vroman and the Kingsley Singers singing in Hebrew, and a quintet of instrumentalists including jazz flautist Harvey Estrin – a veteran of the Tommy Dorsey and Sauter-Finegan bands – given latitude for extended improvisation on the prayer Hashkivenu.

Charles Davidson, like Jonathan Klein, produced a complete Sabbath eve service. His *And David Danced Before the Lord* was first performed in 1966. The work was commissioned by Cantor Richard Botton who, Milken artistic director Neil W Levin explains, "sensed some Jewish interest in further exploration into the contemporaneous experiments in church services". The vocals on *And David* are handled by a cantor given scope to improvise, and by choir. As originally conceived and performed, Davidson scored the instrumentals for a small jazz group, perceiving that the intimacy facilitated improvisation "in much the same way as Indian raga instrumentalists can look at one another as they play and feel the direction and flow of the music as it develops". All manner of devices from jazz and blues interplay with Jewish elements such as Ashkenazi prayer modes in what is a haunting piece that in later revivals was performed for larger orchestration. The Milken recording, with a quintet led by reeds player Ramon Ricker, adheres to Davidson's original template.

These Judaic-jazz works emerged at a time of increased tensions between blacks and Jews, and Dave Brubeck had this in mind when he composed *The Gates of Justice*. Brubeck, neither Jewish nor black, conceived *The Gates* for performance by jazz trio, Jewish cantor, black baritone singer, and choir, "to bring these two cultures together, to show similarities rather than their differences". It was commissioned in 1968 by Rabbi Charles Mintz for the Union of American Hebrew Congregations, premiered a year later and was first recorded, for Decca, in 1971. In his original programme notes, Brubeck explained: "The soloists are composite characters. The cantor tenor, whose melodies are rooted in the Hebraic modes, represents the voice of the Hebrew tradition. The black baritone, whose melodies stem from the blues and spirituals, is the symbol of contemporary man, and a reminder to men of all faiths that divine mandates are still waiting to be fulfilled." A new recording was made for Naxos's American Jewish Music series, in connection with Milken Archive, and released in 2001 to coincide with Black History Month, featuring the Brubeck Trio, cantor Alberto Mizrahi, black vocalist Kevin Deas and the Baltimore Choral Arts Society and Brass Ensemble. 5.

Judaic-jazz, an accompaniment to Jews in their places of worship, is a phenomenon that persists to the present day. 6

• • • •

Dr Tamar Barzel, in her study about the 1990's downtown New York-centred Radical Jewish music scene, grapples with the issue of why, earlier in the century, Jewish musicians active in advanced jazz and rock were so creatively mute about anything ostensibly Jewish in their background. One factor Barzel identifies that pertains to diaspora Jews generally is "the inherited social convention to refrain from too much public Jewishness". As for the musicians, she notes from her interviews that by the 1960s, "American Jews, who did face blatant discrimination in some contexts, nevertheless did not have the same legal and social battles to fight... as did African Americans. This was why, downtown musicians explained, whatever their personal experiences with antisemitism, they felt those problems to be less pressing than the endemic racism and institutionalised discrimination their black colleagues were contending with". 7

While pianist Anthony Coleman told her: "A lot of us, who grew up Jewish in America, we were not in touch with anything rootsy in our culture, because that had been sort of wiped away by the movement after World War II for Jews to become more assimilated into the general American culture... Jews who were interested in becoming musicians... became interested in black musics like jazz and blues. The rootsy side of Jewish music became subterranean, became unknown." 8

It was the klezmer revival, that began a decade or so earlier than the emergence of the Radical Jewish scene, that opened the way for modern Jewish musicians to be far more artistically upfront about their ethnicity. The revival took off in the late seventies as young musicians discovered dusty shellac records of rootsy klezmer that had lain forgotten among grandparental effects. Among them were innovators not content to just replicate the old stuff.

Saxophonist and flautist Lev Liberman, with multi-instrumental ethnomusicologist David Skuse, co-founded The Klezmorim in Berkeley, California in 1975. Liberman maintains that the klezmer revival had its origins in The Klezmorim's early experiments with tight ensemble playing, improvisation, klezmer/jazz fusions, neo-klezmer composition, street music, world beat, and new vaudeville. 10 His search for klezmer music began in 1971 when he deduced that a single unknown genre linked Russian and Romanian folk music to Depression-era cartoon soundtracks, early jazz, and to Gershwin, Weill and Prokofiev.

"I do lay claim to being the first klezmer revivalist to point out reciprocal influences between klezmer music and jazz," Liberman told me. "Way back in the seventies I figured out that many of the two genres' shared attributes must have preceded mutual contact; in other words, the coincident parallel evolution of jazz in America and klezmer in eastern Europe had predisposed musicians to understand one another's musical languages even before widespread contact occurred via emigration, concert tours, recordings, and broadcasts. I'll mention a few such parallels by way of example: underclass status, demographic displacement, bluesy non-Western modes and scales, ensemble playing, improvisation, military-band instrumentation grafted onto folk instrumental tradition, rural musicians and audiences gravitating toward cities, transmission of style and repertoire via apprenticeship and oral tradition, instrumental techniques that mirror vocalisation – the list goes on."

Whatever the provenance of the revival, improvisers such as Ben Goldberg, John Zorn, Frank London, Anthony Coleman and a host of other Jewish musicians, familiar with the jazz of Miles Davis, Ornette Coleman and John Coltrane, and with rock, reggae, funk and other popular and folk forms, have variously sought to integrate all that with their rediscovered Jewish musical heritage.

While this may be seen in the broader context of 'world music' hybridisation of traditional forms with western popular music, my feeling is that for Jews, the neo-Jewish music scene has an additional significance. It is the means by which they are increasingly 'outing' themselves in upfront ways, influenced by all the cultures around them but on their own terms – an assertive Jewishness uncowed by fear of antisemitism. Often, musicians from disparate genres perform together, the permutations endless.

Non-Jewish musicians have also contributed, including black clarinetist Don Byron who caused a stir when he performed klezmer. Yet as Byron, whose résumé includes free jazz, indignantly pointed out, Jews and others had been performing and adapting black-based music for the last hundred and more years so why the fuss? Byron's Mickey Katz interpretations on his 1993 album *Don Byron Plays the Music of Mickey Katz* are typically audacious. The music that inspired Byron's album dates from the late forties and 1950s when clarinetist and comedian Mickey Katz hired a bunch of Jewish musicians to record his jazzy-klez Yinglish song parodies. His personnel included trumpeter Manny Klein, drummer Sammy Weiss, trombonist Si Zentner, violinist Benny Gill, pianist Wally Wechsler, bassist Lenny Breen and arranger Nat Farber, in Katz's estimation "a Who's Who of the greatest jazz musicians in

Hollywood". The tracks they recorded, with Katz doing wacky vocals, included the 'Home on the Range' spoof *Haim Afn Range*. Great comic fun, but musically it was the mischievous adventure in these records that caught Byron's imagination, "all this beautiful voice-leading, four-part harmonies, melodies that go down to 16$^{th}$ notes, four-part fugues, really fancy writing". Byron's participation in Jewish music precedes his Katz album, as a founder member of the Klezmer Conservatory Band, and post-dates it as in his 2005 San Francisco concert that celebrated the clarinet heritage of Sam Musiker and Dave Tarras.

It is not as if the adoption of Jewish music by black jazz artists is unprecedented. Louis Armstrong's origination of scat vocals may have been partly Jewish influenced. Phoebe Jacobs, who we met in the last chapter, claimed: "One day I heard Louis talking with Cab Calloway... about scatting, and Louis said he got it from the Jews 'rockin' – he meant *davening* [swaying while praying]. But Louis never talked about this in public because he feared people would assume he was making fun of the Jews praying." 10 According to Jewish quarterly *Guilt and Pleasure*: "Fans have come up with two interpretations of this: either Armstrong was walking past a synagogue and heard rapid-fire davening... or he heard *nigunim*, Hasidic melodies intended to induce a meditative state." The article continues: "In his writings, Armstrong also recalled lullabies sung by Mrs Karnofsky – a woman whose family befriended and employed him as a kid, and to whom he largely attributes his admiration of Jews and Jewish life. Could Hebrew have inspired the 'heebie jeebies'?" 11 Armstrong, indeed, recorded a tune he titled 'Heebie Jeebies' on which he scats throughout. While the Karnofsky connection is from Armstrong's own writings, the only evidence we have on any Jewish influence on scat remains anecdotal.

Consider too the following tantalising titbit: Sheldon 'Shelly' Hendler, a klezmer musician who worked with Dave Tarras, remembered gigs at the hotel owned by the mother of Jewish bebop musician Allen Eager, and the jazz musicians – Eager's guests – were fascinated by Tarras's klezmer: "Some of the guys I'm talking about included Charlie Parker and Miles Davis... They weren't interested in any of the American stuff we played – they were only interested in the modal stuff Dave played." 12

There are many instances of black musicians' covering Jewish themes, doubtless sometimes simply to gratify Jewish patrons. Cab Calloway, the jazzy singer-entertainer, in 1939 recorded 'Utt Da Zay', a swing version of 'Ot Azoy Neyt a Shnayder' [Yiddish – That's the way a tailor sews] with cantorial vocalising. Other Jewish-inspired songs he sang included Henry Nemo's 'A Bee Gezint' [As long as you're healthy], this with Dizzy Gillespie in his band. Gillespie made jazz with 'Eretz Zavat Halav U'devash' [Hebrew – Land of Milk and Honey], as did pianist Hazel Scott with 'Ich vil zikh shpiln' [Yiddish – I Want to Play for You], while Alberta Hunter recorded 'Ich Hob Dich Tzufil Lieba', singing almost entirely in Yiddish other than two verses enunciating lyrics from Don Raye's 'I Love You Too Much'. Ethel Waters and other black vocalists sang 'Eli, Eli', and Billie Holiday covered 'My Yiddishe Momme'. Ella Fitzgerald, Lionel Hampton, Teddy Wilson, Booker Ervin, Ramsey Lewis, Leroy Jones, Willie the Lion Smith and Slim Gaillard all recorded 'Bei Mir Bist Du Schoen'. Gaillard, a swing-to-bop vocalist, guitarist and pianist, who was half-Jewish, invented the hip nonsensical 'Voutish' language that marked out his songs, several of which have a Jewish schtick – 'Matzoh Balls', 'Dunkin' Bagels', 'Drei Six Cents' [*dreysik* is Yiddish for the number 30]. And Gaillard's 'Vol Vistu Gaily Star' is constructed on a klezmer chord structure.

In recent times, black pianist Warren Byrd has collaborated regularly with Jewish bassist David Chevan in their Afro-Semitic Experience jazz ensemble, a project that accentuates the positives in the black and Jewish American musical and social relationship. David, when I initially contacted him, posted me Afro-Semitic's earliest CDs and answered my questions by email. *Let Us Break Bread Together* (2000) features him and Warren in duo formation, improvising on mainly Jewish prayer tunes. On *This is the Afro-Semitic Experience* (2002), they are supported by a racially mixed band, David the only Jew. Several tunes are again jazz interpretations of Jewish material, Abdullah Ibrahim's 'Water From an Ancient Well' among the other compositions. Adorning the cover is a symbolically historic monochrome photo showing a sign erected outside a US beach club, reading: 'Membership Limited to GENTILES ONLY'. The owners had no need to bar black folks on their sign; in those days, that would have been understood.

So, what had brought David and Warren together for the Afro-Semitic project? Was it at least partly motivated, in these times of strained relations between blacks and Jews in some quarters, by a desire on both their parts to show symbolic solidarity?

The two did not come together specifically for this project, said David: "We had met earlier and played with one another in several groups and settings. This project happened almost by accident. Not that I wasn't already motivated. I was living in Brooklyn when the Crown Heights riots took place in 1991 and was moved even then to make some kind of statement, take some kind of proactive action of reconciliation.

"Though I had many conversations at that time, it wasn't until I met Warren that the germ of the idea emerged and developed. I was late to a gig Warren had booked at Foxwoods Casino [Connecticut]. So when I walked in Warren and the drummer,

Alvin Carter Jr, were already at it, playing a classic gospel number by Andrae Crouch entitled, 'Soon and Very Soon'. I knew that tune and got the joke right away. So, I quickly unpacked my instrument and finished the tune with them. Later that night Warren and I were talking. I asked him about his church playing experiences and whether he'd ever played any Jewish music. I don't think he was quite as enthused as I was but it was my crazy idea to show him some Jewish synagogue music. Before long we'd learned a few tunes. I mentioned what I was doing with Warren to the cantor at my synagogue and a few weeks later he asked me if Warren and I would play at a Martin Luther King service. The service was well attended by the Jewish and African American communities and we were quite surprised by how well we were received. After the service we were approached and asked if we could repeat our performance for another group. Each appearance led to more performances until we realised that we had stumbled onto something for which there was a need. A large number of our performances have been at synagogues or sponsored by Jewish organisations, but not all. We have played at a number of African American churches – and quite a few churches with predominantly white congregations – and count many leaders within the African American community among our supporters."

Not everyone was supportive: "If that was the case we'd be doing something wrong, we'd be watering down our message and turning into the kind of pabulum that Hollywood and other mass culture centres have been feeding the world for far too long. However, we find that our music is appreciated especially by people of all faiths and races who are committed to the ideals of dialogue and community building and good music. There is often an imbalance at our performances of Jewish attendees, but that may have something to do with the venues, often synagogues and Jewish community centres. But when we went to Fisk, a historically

African American University in Nashville and then participated in a service at Vanderbilt University the following night our audiences were a real rainbow. Audiences tend to like what we're doing. It's interesting to watch whose head is nodding to what piece. I often catch church-going African Americans nodding and smiling at the church pieces and a similar response from the Jewish audiences. No matter their faith, people really like to hear the old familiar melodies. I think we hit individuals more than communities. Which, I guess means that eventually we do reach into a community. We have played a number of Catholic churches and institutions where there weren't too many people of Jewish or African descent. Monks, priests and nuns seem to like us a great deal, they understand the idea behind music as a spiritual medium."

Afro-Semitic has since recorded several further albums, including *Further Definitions of The Days of Awe*, captured during Jewish high holy day concerts in New York, New Haven and Massachusetts, with cantors Jack Mendelson, Erik Contzius, Lisa Arbisser and Danny Mendelson: moving, deeply felt, transcendent jazz.

David Chevan is just one manifestation of a significant religiously inspired input in contemporary Jewish-jazz, such that he was moved to write in complaint to *JazzTimes* about Howard Mandel's 'Vibes From the Tribe: Jewish Music, Identity and Jazz' feature on the downtown Radical Jewish Culture music scene, the article focusing mainly on artists whose Jewish identity is secular and cultural. In his letter, Chevan, while commending Mandel on his broad overview, protests: "I was, in the end, disturbed by a picture that Mandel has painted of this resurgence of American Jewish musical culture that highlights artists who work in a sector that is secular and anti-religious and marginalizes the work of Jewish musicians whose work centres around religious music. With few exceptions Mandel's piece was limited to Jewish artists who went to great lengths to distance themselves from their Judaism. Yes, Judaism is a culture – and for many Jews it is the cultural aspect that resonates most strongly, but it is foremost a religion and that element was missing from this article."

Chevan then puts the question: are there any Jewish artists who are addressing the spiritual religious elements of Judaism in musical work that is at all connected to jazz? "The answer is yes and two of these artists, Frank London and Anthony Coleman were mentioned, but not profiled in Mandel's piece. Both Coleman (*Sephardic Tinge* and *Self-Haters*) and London both with the Hasidic New Wave, and on his... *Nigunim* and *Invocations* recordings, have addressed religious themes and concerns head-on... Similarly, pianist Uri Caine's *Zohar/Keter* album is a profound religious statement. Andy Statman, the father of the klezmer revival has made several recordings that include Chassidic sacred songs and veer much closer to jazz than klezmer."

One cannot however assume that because a musician makes jazz with religious material or themes, her or his motivation must be religious too. Quoted in Mandel's article is trumpeter Steven Bernstein whose work includes adaptations of cantorial compositions, who says: "Outrageousness is part of the package, and gets people lined around the block at midnight. That's part of being Jewish, a Lenny Bruce thing, a Mel Brooks thing, my thing. My character, who I am, is not reticent – it's Jewish. Not religiously, but socially. And your music is who you are."

Bernstein's albums for Tzadik's Radical Jewish Culture catalogue – *Diaspora Soul* (1999), *Diaspora Blues* (2002), *Diaspora Hollywood* (2004) and *Diaspora Suite* (2008) – immerse you in parallel universes of Jewish-jazz, each beguilingly different from the others. "That's really the concept of diaspora; it's going to other places and taking the tradition with you," Bernstein has said. 13

When Tzadik's John Zorn first approached him about recording something Jewish, Bernstein was initially reticent, until it struck him that the traditional song 'Heveinu Shalom Aleichem' and the early New Orleans jazz standard 'St James Infirmary' were melodically similar.

That sparked Bernstein's "Gulf Coast epiphany" as he conceptualised *Diaspora Soul*, "thinking not just about the New Orleans sound, but rather the Gulf Coast sound, encompassing Texas and Cuba – and the last part of the Gulf Coast with Miami. And who retired to Miami? The most popular Cuban export of the '50s was the cha-cha. In New Orleans there is a rhythm called the half a cha. And who loves a cha-cha more than the Jews? And the final piece of the grail – the hora bass pattern – one, two-and, and-four-and, is the first half of clave, the heart of Afro-Cuban beat" – hora a rhythmic device much used in klezmer. With a Ziggy Elman-like solo, Bernstein opens the recording on which he is supported by three other Jewish musicians, saxophonists Paul Shapiro and Peter Apfelbaum and bassist Tony Scherr, along with baritone saxophonist Brogan Krauss, Brian Mitchell on Wurlitzer electric piano and organ, and Latino percussionists EJ and Robert J Rodriguez. The piquant mélange of jazz, Jewish, Latin, funky second line New Orleans rhythms and Mitchell's psychedelic/gospel keyboards launched Bernstein's Diaspora series on a high.

His follow-up, *Diaspora Hollywood*, interweaves Jewish traditional and cantorial melodies, and originals, with jazz inspired by two developments from the Los Angeles region. One is the movie music from the early Hollywood composers and orchestrators, many of them Jewish immigrants that made Bernstein "think about the concept of diaspora – people leaving Eastern Europe and coming to Hollywood and the space between these two worlds". And the other was the 1950s' west coast small group jazz arrangers' use of "counterlines, melodic drumming and soft palettes". When Bernstein realised that prominent among them were Jews who "first met playing as teenagers in the east coast borscht belt" – he cites Shelly Manne and Shorty Rogers – "I found the link I didn't know I was looking for." The outcome is captivating: Bernstein, Pablo Clanger on baritone sax and other reeds, DJ Bonebrake on vibes, and a Jewish rhythm team of bassist David Piltch and drummer and percussionist Danny Frankel, create noir-ish soundtracks, bluesy, slightly menacing, vibes chiming away spookily, peppered with spicy Jewish sonorities.

For *Diaspora Suite*, Bernstein leads a ten-piece ensemble. Bernstein's compositions, named after the ancient tribes of Israel, are refracted through sixties-inspired jazz-rock, free jazz, psychedelia and funk; Miles Davis early fusion groups an obvious reference, shades of Weather Report too. Peter Apfelbaum on tenor sax, flute and qarqabas, Ben Goldberg on clarinets, and electric guitarist John Schott are the other Jewish musicians involved.

As for *Diaspora Blues*, featuring Bernstein with the Sam Rivers Trio, its plangent beauty puts me in mind somewhat of Miles Davis's *Sketches of Spain*. Bernstein's trumpet phrasing, if more robust than Miles, carries echoes of the latter in his discernment of the space to leave between the sounds his bell emits, enhancing the dramatic effect. Apart from the occasional flurry of free jazz, the album, which includes covers of compositions by the late Cantor Moshe Koussevitzky, comes over as essentially melancholic. Evidently however, Bernstein does not intend it to be interpreted that way as he quotes Cantor Abraham Idelsohn, the late Jewish musicologist: "The Jew demanded that the chazzan, through his music, make him forget his actual life, and that he elevate him on the wings of his tunes into a fantastical paradisiacal world. The main basis of Semitic and Jewish music is the minor scale which, at a very late date, came to be considered of a melancholy character by the Anglo-Saxon only."

While Bernstein has never created another Jewish-jazz album, in April 2017, as part of a homecoming series of gigs, he presented the Bay Area premiere of his show drawn from *Diaspora Soul*. "When 'Diaspora Soul' came out," he told *Mercury News*, "I started getting emails from people, like, 'My father's a rabbi, and he never liked any of my music. I never thought Jewish music was fun and sexy until this.'"

The vibrancy and multifaceted adventurousness of the new Jewish music, the excellence of the musicianship, attracted many non-Jews, including Cazary Lerski who, when I contacted him via his US-based Polish Jazz Network, responded: "The subject of your book really fascinates me – actually it was [the] Jewish contribution to jazz that brought me back to jazz... and let me rediscover it at its best. Sometime in the mid-nineties when I lived in New York I was hanging around Knitting Factory [the club that was then regularly hosting Radical Jewish events] and getting all the best the downtown scene had to offer then: Zorn, Masada, Klezmatics and much more. I believe that contribution of neo-klezmers to jazz art of the twentieth century should not be underestimated – it changed [the] musical perspective of many people, myself included."

With respect to Cazary, neo-klezmer is far too simplistic a tab. The artists concerned, from diverse musical backgrounds, not only jazz, have synthesised Jewish music in its multifarious manifestations – klezmer, liturgical, Sephardi, Mizrahi, middle eastern, north African – with just about every other kind of music out there.

Take Anthony Coleman, who is associated with experimental jazz. He founded Sephardic Tinge with bassist Greg Cohen and drummer Joey Baron to mine the rich Hispano-Judaic seam of Sephardi music. Growing up in a Dominican neighbourhood of Brooklyn surrounded by Latin sounds profoundly affected the direction took. About his album *Sephardic Tinge* (Tzadik, 1995), he has explained: "I wanted to stay away from Klezmer as a basis for a music reflecting Jewish identity. Poor Klezmer. A music which most of us never heard until the mid to late '70s has to stand for a completely hybrid and fragmented culture – New York Jewish Culture. I started thinking about the music which had accompanied most of my life in some way or another. I thought about the fact that the Mambo and Cha Cha had both been dance crazes in the Borscht Belt during the '40s and '50s. I thought about Sephardic Jews and how strange and mysterious I had always found the idea of their language, Ladino. I added to this the uses that Jazz composers have made of what Jelly Roll Morton called the 'Spanish Tinge', Habanerea and Mambo patterns, montunos."

Sonically more challenging is Coleman's follow-up, *Selfhaters* (Tzadik, 1996). His scores draw on vestiges of klezmer but he and his Selfhaters ensemble subvert the idiom with jagged improvisations: the personnel Coleman on piano, organ, trombone, accordion, sampler and voice, Doug Wieselman, clarinet, Michael Attias, clarinet, alto saxophone and baritone saxophone, Fred Lonberg-Holm, cello and banjo, Jim Pugliese, percussion, and on one track, David Krakauer.

Although jazz informs the music of clarinet virtuoso Krakauer, who in 1995 recorded one of Tzadik's first Radical Jewish Culture albums, *Klezmer Madness*, he has moved beyond it. Conservatory trained, with professional experience in classical music and jazz, Krakauer brings to neo-klezmer improvisational flair and imagination and a contempt for musical boundaries. His entire second Tzadik album, *Klezmer, N.Y.*, showcases 'A Klezmer Tribute To Sidney Bechet', Krakauer's lengthy suite conceived as an imaginary meeting between early jazz legend Bechet and Naftule Brandwein, both of whom were active in 1920s New York. The piece was reprised on Krakauer's album *A New Hot One* for the

French jazz label, Label Bleu, while another track, 'Klezdrix', is a homage to Jimi Hendrix. Krakauer, who views the clarinet as the electric guitar of Jewish music, is in a sense a post-jazz radical conservative. "I want my music to be klezmer, not some sort of a fusion mishmash," he has asserted. 14

The term "Radical Jewish Culture", coined by alto saxophonist John Zorn, came to define an entire movement. In Zorn's own such work, the Jewish component in the music itself is often diffuse but the Jewish identity emphatic. His involvement in Jewish identity music dates from the early nineties by which time groups such as New Klezmer Trio, the Klezmatics, and others were already stretching boundaries.

Zorn's entry, though, proved galvanic and it was his vision that redefined what can be understood as Jewish music. He came with a reputation as an iconoclast of punky New York avant-jazz and experimental music; in jazz writer Stuart Nicholson's estimation, by the end of the 1980s, Zorn was "perhaps the most recognizable, prolific and far-ranging of the downtown musicians". Interviewed by Nicholson back then, Zorn, not yet involved in Jewish music, described his oeuvre as "jazz from Hell... There's a lot of jazz in me, but there's also a lot or rock, a lot of classical, a lot of ethnic music, a lot of blues, a lot of movie soundtracks". 15

He carried over that restlessly exploratory eclecticism to his Jewish-themed music in which he began immersing himself from around 1992. That year Zorn organised the Radical Jewish Culture festival, pointedly held in Munich; on the bill rock stars Lou Reed and Laurie Anderson, guitarist Gary Lucas, the Klezmatics, New Klezmer Trio, a cluster of downtown Jewish jazz musicians, and multi-instrumental experimentalist Elliott Sharp. Also involved were saxophonist John Lurie and his keyboardist brother Evan, cofounders of the cult punk-jazz group Lounge Lizards, whose Jewish lineage stems from their trade union organiser father.

The festival centrepiece was the premiere of Zorn's opus *Kristallnacht*, an extended composition with seven movements and difficult to classify but referencing klezmer, neo-classical and avant-jazz, along with eerie crackly snatches of Nazi radio broadcasts. At Munich, Zorn and his ensemble – Mark Feldman, violin, Marc Ribot, guitar, Anthony Coleman, piano, David Krakauer, clarinet, Frank London, trumpet, Mark Dresser, bass, and the only non-Jew, William Winant, percussion – walked on stage sporting large yellow stars, the badge the Nazis had compelled Jews to wear. "*Kristallnacht* is something else again," wrote *The Wire*, "a search for roots but also a confrontation, a demand, a scream of defiant anger." 16

For Zorn, what began at Munich continued with Radical Jewish events staged at the Knitting Factory in lower Manhattan, the club that Michael Dorf co-founded in 1986 by investing his bar mitzvah money to establish the venue as a performing arts space. Regular sharp-end jazz and rock gigs were held there, including Zorn's Naked City band. Then Dorf witnessed the *Kristallnacht* gig, an experience "that really shook my connection to Jewish culture".

Back in New York, Dorf asked Zorn to organise a Radical Jewish Culture festival at the Knitting Factory modelled on Munich. This, the first of regular Radical Jewish events at the club, took place in October 1992. Knitting Factory had earlier that year hosted a klezmer festival, at the behest, Dorf told an interviewer, of Don Byron – this a year before Byron recorded his Mickey Katz album. It was the klezmer festival's success, Dorf said, that prompted him to approach Zorn. 17

Zorn brought to the movement his creative, organisational and leadership flair and dynamism. In 1993 he launched the Jewish-jazz quartet Masada. Named after the first century hill fortress where Jewish warriors committed suicide rather than surrender to Roman conquerors, Masada comprised Zorn, Dave Douglas, trumpet, Greg Cohen, bass, Joey Baron, drums, all Jews bar Douglas. Musically, Masada's Jewishness was not obvious like klezmer or cantorial, more like trace elements from different aspects of Jewish music that glint in a free-flow stream of jazz reminiscent of Ornette Coleman's *Free Jazz*. Masada's music was not, though, "Ornette Coleman meets klezmer", the way it was frequently, reductively, depicted. "If I read one more time Masada is klezmer meets Ornette Coleman, I'm going to *plotz* [Yiddish – literally, to explode or burst]," Zorn fumed. "It's just simple-minded nonsense." 18 "Of course," Zorn affirmed, "there's klezmer. Of course, there's Ornette, but there are as many influences in that music as went into the composition of Naked City music or any other music I've done – like surf music, movie soundtracks, Sephardic and Arabic music, modern classical, modal jazz."

What Zorn has championed, both in his own work and his support for artists associated with his Tzadik label's Radical Jewish Culture catalogue, is an expansion of the vocabulary of Jewish music. He has written hundreds of tunes for Masada as a basis for improvisation. The first hundred were composed in a big bang burst of creativity before Masada's formation. "The idea with Masada," said Zorn, "is to produce a sort of radical Jewish music, a new Jewish music which is not the traditional one in a different arrangement, but music for the Jews of today. The idea is to put Ornette Coleman and the Jewish scales together." Each Masada composition was based on one of two "Jewish scales", as identified by Zorn, a major scale with the second note flat or a minor scale with the fourth note sharp.

Greg Cohen gave me an insider's take: "The musical language John set up in such a way that every member of the band is given the opportunity to find their own voice. It's not all improvised. He started writing these pieces and tried playing them with an ensemble – his system line allows huge latitude. We played a gig at Knitting Factory and it seemed to be an ensemble that works. It's not always about the level of the musicians, it's certain musicians that think alike – things happen that you didn't expect like quantum theory if you have four musicians who perform without grandstanding. It just took off on that night and spiralled. And there's the importance of Zorn's leadership in putting this together. Part of being a good leader is knowing how much direction to give and when to pull back. It's a process that allowed improvisation within the language of Jewish music that John explored and over the years became very successful and fun to play and all of a sudden, the audience was there. David Douglas's career has blossomed – because of that he's not as available as before, Joey Baron too, and John Zorn tried doing a lot more classical things. I miss it, but there's all the offshoots, including the Masada String Trio."

Zorn intended that his compositions prove adaptable for any type of ensemble, and the Masada String Trio comprising Cohen and two other Jewish downtowners, violinist Mark Feldman and cellist Erik Friedlander, was one such satellite. Other offshoots included jazz-rock fusion group Electric Masada, the chamber sextet Bar Kokhba, and the album *Masada Guitars*, on which Zorn asked three of his favourite guitarists, Mark Ribot, Bill Frisell and Tim Sparks, to play solo versions of his compositions.

The first ten Masada albums were released by the Japanese label DIW. Zorn had spent considerable time in Japan, learned the language and told interviewer Michael Goldberg that "being hit front on with a completely different culture helped me appreciate my own culture. I wouldn't have gotten into Jewishness as much as I did if I hadn't been in Japan". Other factors, he said, were "the death of my father, going to Germany a lot and experiencing *that* whole thing, and then, thinking how many of my close friends and colleagues were Jews... Eventually it came out in my life, like anything else that we think about that's real". 19 Zorn's Jewish identity became manifest in the name of his ensembles, in his onstage attire, in the title of his albums and compositions, in the name of his Tzadik record label and the graphics associated with Radical Jewish Culture albums.

Yet there have been insinuations that his motives may have been mercenary. Fred Kaplan, in *Slate*, kvetched: "The authors of *The Penguin Guide to Jazz on CD* write that the whole Masada project 'raises questions about opportunism' and wonder whether Zorn's sudden 'interest in Hebrew culture' reflects 'an eye to the market strategy.' Apart from the antisemitic undertones (I doubt that the authors would attribute money-grubbing motives to, say, Randy Weston's African ventures or Yo-Yo Ma's *Silk Road* project), the suspicion is way off. To a degree unmatched by nearly any other contemporary artist, Zorn *is* his music." 20

Zorn's advocacy of trailblazing Jewish music proved a boon for the New York clubs most associated with it, and for many downtown musicians, Jewish and otherwise, that have benefited through his Tzadik label, as Bruce Gallanter, founder of the Downtown Music Gallery, testified: "He definitely makes money for those places, he doesn't ask for special treatment and, actually, he pays his musicians really well and he's an incredibly nice guy and his label's helped out a lot of people."

Tzadik was founded by Zorn in 1995 as a non-profit concern to release "the best in avant-garde and experimental music", by no means only Jewish music. Radical Jewish Culture is just part of that, the Tzadik catalogue under which all Masada's post-DIW albums have been released, along with an extensive roster of recordings by other musicians, from jazz and other backgrounds, working with Jewish themes typically across genres.

Clarinetist Ben Goldberg's involvement in Jewish music radicalism pre-dates Zorn's. He studied klezmer in college in the early 1980s and performed at weddings and bar mitzvahs: "I was fascinated by the speedy, lurching, lyrical, exhortatory, digressive, speech-like phrasing and I wanted to find out what it was made of. The ingredients that gave the music its unique character, I discovered, were the microscopically detailed ornamentations and articulations. Each player had his own way of positioning a note in the beat, starting and stopping a note, and getting from one note to the next." 21

Goldberg, previously a member of klez-revivalists Hotzeplotz, joined The Klezmorim in 1984, taking over from the group's original clarinetist David Julian Gray. Rapidly Goldberg gravitated towards a more vanguardist conception, impelled in part, he has explained, by the work of Ziya Aytekin, a non-Jewish traditional zurna player from the Caucasus he met in Sweden. Goldberg was struck by commonalities between Aytekin's music and that of such musicians as John Coltrane, prompting him to wonder if he could similarly deploy klezmer to explore connections between traditional Jewish music and the jazz avant-garde.

The upshot was that in 1987 he formed New Klezmer Trio with bassist Dan Seamans and drummer Kenny Wollesen, not Jews but Goldberg had performed traditional klezmer with them and suggested they see what happened if they cut loose musically: "It was an exhilarating, powerful effect – my first taste of music as a transformative, liberating force... I found that everything I had worked so hard to master – the ornamentation, quirky phrasing, harmonic devices – was now available to me as tools for building my own thing." 22 New Klezmer Trio proved highly influential with the generation of artists that were to form the basis of the Radical Jewish Culture scene, including avant-klez combos Rabbinical School Dropouts and Naftule's Dream, and, critically, Zorn.

Struck by New Klezmer Trio's 1990 debut CD *Masks and Faces*, Zorn invited the group to perform at the Munich *Kristallnacht* festival. As Goldberg recounted: "New Klezmer Trio was the only group at the festival playing a modern version of traditional klezmer music; most of the music did not seem to have 'Jewish' ingredients. By putting so much diverse music under the heading of 'Radical Jewish Culture', Zorn set the stage for a lively and useful debate: what is 'Jewish music?" 23

On *Masks and Faces*, originally issued by Nine Winds in 1991 then re-released by Tzadik, New Klezmer Trio bend and stretch klezmer and freely improvise with it, but on tracks such as 'Hot and Cold' and 'Rebbe's Meal', they are still recognisably in idiom. As too 'Washing Machine Song', with hints of traditional melody but all mangled up. Come the trio's second album, *Melt Zonk Rewire*, their first recorded specifically for Tzadik, they jettison any trace of old klezmer; 'Feedback Doina' opens with a brief klezzy solo from Goldberg, Seamans cuts in with blasting fuzz metal electric bass, Wollesen thrashing around on his kit, before the piece ebbs out in reflective mode.

What is consistently sonically Jewish in Goldberg's output, even on non-Jewish themed albums such as *Ben Goldberg School, Vol. 2: Hard Science,* self-released in 2022, is his klez-inflected voicings and phrasings on a range of clarinets. Or so my ears tell me, so I asked him, and Goldberg confirmed: "For me a significant part of learning the clarinet, and to improvise on the clarinet, took place in the context of Jewish music, so a lot of that is embedded in my sound and how I hear melodies. Also I think that certain skills and habits that I have cultivated are things that first occurred to me as I studied klezmer music – like paying attention to the details of melodic embellishment, etc. So even aspects of my playing that are not idiomatically 'Jewish' sounding can be traced back to my klezmer days."

Jamie Saft's *Borscht Belt Studies* is a standout album in Tzadik's Radical Jewish catalogue, and the six duo tracks on which Ben Goldberg accompanies him are a critical component. The two dovetail beautifully, Saft's piano playing resonant and intense, his touch and acuity, his sense of his instrument's dynamics, putting me in mind of prime Keith Jarrett, while Goldberg's klez-modulated extrapolations add a gritty eastern savour to modern jazz clarinet. The album closes with 'New Zion', a pulsing slow-burn reggae-jazz workout, Saft accompanied by double bassist Larry Garnier and drummer Craig Santiago.

Saft received his first synthesizer as a bar mitzvah present and in Zorn's Electric Masada deployed an armoury of vintage keyboards. Acoustic piano he largely neglected professionally until Zorn persuaded him to record *Astaroth – Book of Angels, Vol 1* (Tzadik 2005), the first album in a series whereby different artists and ensembles were invited to interpret Zorn's Masada Book Two compositions. When Zorn conceived the series, his first compositions for this mammoth undertaking were with a traditional piano trio in mind, so Saft, with bassist Greg Cohen and drummer Ben Perowsky, duly deliver a set that veers from lustrous lyricism to jangly freer passages.

As pianist and organist, Saft also featured on *Filmworks IX* (Tzadik 2000), he and clarinetist Chris Speed conveying the bewitching music Zorn had written and arranged for Sandi Simcha Dubowski's documentary *Trembling Before G-d*. The film is about Jews in Chassidic and Orthodox communities in America, Britain and Israel that outed themselves as gay and lesbian. And Saft played piano on a single track, 'Armistice Swing', with the Masada String Trio on *Filmworks XI* (Tzadik 2002), Zorn's ethereal score for the Aviva Slesin directed documentary *Secret Lives* about Jewish children hidden by non-Jews during the Holocaust.

Uri Caine is yet another enticing contributor to Tzadik's Radical Jewish catalogue. As a pianist, he brings classical technique to jazz, and vice versa as evidenced on his solo album *Moloch, Book of Angels Volume 6* on which he covers nineteen of some of Zorn's most lyrical Masada compositions, such as 'Zophiel', full of dark smouldering eastern savour.

Caine grew up in a left Zionist household in Philadelphia with plentiful exposure to Jewish music but as a professional musician, it was not until Don Byron recruited him that Caine performed anything Jewish, including on Byron's Mickey Katz album.

When that came out in 1993 the Radical Jewish scene was already buzzing but Caine was on the cusp of doing something startlingly original, arranging the music of Gustav Mahler in stunning juxtapositions and fusions with free and straight-on jazz, electro, and Jewish folk and cantorial music. Caine's Mahler project, *Urlicht/Primal Light*, came about at the instigation of Stefan Winter, producer at JMT Records in Germany. The label had released Caine's second album, *Toys*, on which a Caine-led octet performed Herbie Hancock tunes, opening with 'Time Will Tell' that, in Caine's arrangement, features a recurring bass line borrowed from Mahler's *First Symphony*.

Winter, picking up on this, engaged Caine to devise a programme inspired by Mahler's music to accompany Franz Winter's silent movie about the composer. The work was first performed at a screening at the Knitting Factory in November 1995. The Winter brothers subsequently founded the Winter & Winter label with *Urlicht/Primal Light* its first release. Franz Winter, explaining the conception for his biopic, highlighted Mahler's conversion from Judaism to Christianity that enabled Mahler to take up a position as head of the Vienna Opera: "As a converted Jew, he tries his hand at assuming the role of the Ultimate Mystic of the Christian world view, and in the confrontation between that and his musical and cultural heritage – the strains of the 'shtetl', the melodies of the cantor in the synagogue, the plaintive tones of the clarinet – he prophetically articulates the Holocaust of the 20th century."

The project was a game-changer in Caine's career. With Caine as pianist and arranger, his collaborators included cantor Aaron Bensoussan, Don Byron, Dave Douglas and Joey Baron, trombonist Josh Roseman, violinist Mark Feldman, cellist Larry Gold, bassist Michael Formanek, Danny Blume on guitar and electronics, turntablist DJ Olive, and vocalists Dean Bowman and Art Lindsay. Mahler's broodingly magnificent music is not mangled but contemporised – thrilling and moving. The album scooped the 1997 international Best Mahler CD award. Caine has since recorded prolifically for Winter & Winter, including further Mahlers and equally creative adaptations of Bach, Wagner, Mozart, Beethoven and *Rhapsody In Blue*.

Meanwhile, Caine continued recording more overtly Jewish-themed albums. *Zohar Keter*, based on Sephardi-Jewish music, was released by Knitting Factory's JAM (Jewish Alternative Music) label, Cantor Bensoussan and sampler DJ Olive again among Caine's collaborators; it has an intoxicating middle eastern/north African electro-acoustic jazz feel. And for Tzadik, besides *Moloch*, Caine has participated on several recordings as co-leader, including *Nigunim* with trumpeter Frank London and vocalist Loren Sklamberg, this an intimate Yiddish folk-jazz set with Caine on harmonium, Hammond organ and piano.

Two other venerable jazz contributors to Tzadik's Radical Jewish catalogue were Borah Bergman and Glenn Spearman, artists whose careers inclined towards the experimental. Pianist Bergman, whose ambidextrous ability – he could play equally fast with both hands, and cross-handed, opening the way to contrapuntal and polyphonic extemporisation – recorded two Tzadik albums,

*Meditations for Piano* (2003) and *Luminescence* (2009). These differ markedly from the main body of his work in the post-Cecil Taylor free improvisational jazz avant-garde; at Zorn's suggestion, he toned that down and *Meditations* captures Bergman solo on ruminative, cantorial-inspired improvisations, a Jewish-jazz that becalms and beguiles. Similarly, *Luminescence*, only this time with Bergman leading a trio, the perfect platform for his mellifluously mellow compositions influenced by cantorial chants, Bach, Bill Evans and the post-Mahler classicism of Alban Berg.

Glenn Spearman, whose mother was white Jewish, his father black Christian, was a tenor saxophonist, composer and jazz educator who dropped out of college in the sixties to pursue a career in music when, as he remembered it in *European Jazz Journal*, "there was a whole lot of stuff to be dropping out over, the whole sense of Black pride... For me it was a profound time, when I searched for roots and found them in the music". His résumé included writing more than five hundred pieces for tenor sax, four large orchestral works, working extensively in free jazz groups including his own and with Cecil Taylor, and ultimately that search for roots resulted in his Tzadik album *Blues for Falasha*. Released after Spearman's death from cancer, it is a work of profound empathy with the plight of the black Ethiopian Jews sometimes known as Falasha. Facing discrimination in Ethiopia after a "Marxist" coup, Falasha Jews settled in Israel from the late 1970s but struggled to gain full acceptance. Spearman read about them and studied Falasha music, inflections of which inform the album. The recording opens with Spearman's spoken recitation over Falasha tribal chants – "children of Abraham," he intones, "pre-Rabbinic rituals... they are families in exile, separated, forces from outside squeezing them, no home in the motherland, some small chance for a new beginning, they are strangers in a strange, strange land". What follows is a drifting ambient passage that gives way to spiritual free jazz, Spearman at times tender, at times fierce, supported by a quintet of collaborators including Jewish saxophonist Larry Ochs, who has explained: "Glenn seemed intrigued and moved by the fate of the Falasha... Perhaps his own mixed parentage (white Jewish mother, black Christian father) left him feeling equally out of place in the world at large." 24 I asked Ochs if, as *Falasha* was recorded in 1997, the year before Spearman died, did he know he was mortally ill at the time and did that have any bearing on his intent to record such an album. Ochs confirmed that was so.

Afrobeat-inspired Zion80 has proved to be one of the most enduring Radical Jewish ensembles, including three Tzadik releases: *Zion80* (2013), *Adramelech: The Book of Angels vol. 22* (2014), and *The Book Beri'ah Vol 8 – Hod* (2019). The latter two cover John Zorn compositions, Zorn alto saxophonist on both. But the first features instrumental arrangements of Rabbi Shlomo Carlebach songs.

Zion80 was formed by guitarist Jon Madof who, emailing me, explained: "I came across Carlebach's music... just after I moved to New York City. My wife and I had started attending regular synagogue services, and I started to become familiar with the melodies that were used on Shabbat. Only after a while did I find out that many of the songs were written by Carlebach. I started to check out recordings of his music and began performing some of his songs with my trio, Rashanim. I love the beautiful directness and simplicity of his melodies – they have an amazing way of staying in your head."

Around that time, Jon discovered Nigerian Afrobeat music, specifically the politically outspoken Fela Kuti's recordings that combine West African music with funk and jazz. He was instantly hooked: "For me, there's a very specific musical itch that only Afrobeat can scratch. The decision to combine Carlebach and Fela wasn't really a decision at all. I was working at home one Friday in 2011 and listening to Fela all day. The next morning – Shabbat – I was getting ready to bring my kids to synagogue and started humming a Carlebach Shabbat song. Since Fela was stuck in my head from the day before, they just got mashed up in my mind. I started thinking about other Carlebach tunes, and they all worked really well in that style. I began simply by delving into the tunes themselves and experimenting with different ways to bring the Afrobeat sound into the mix."

The instrumentation for Zion80 was largely determined by the Afrobeat sound Jon was striving for: "Fela had several guitars, horns, keyboard, drums and percussion." The original Zion80 ensemble comprised thirteen stalwarts of the downtown scene. The main challenge, said Jon, was getting all the musicians together: "Everyone is really busy. The band kicked off with a residency at The Stone – John Zorn's amazing venue in NYC. We played every Monday night during the summer of 2012. The musicians worked their butts off, not only playing but offering suggestions on the music. I edited and revised the songs a lot during that time, and by the end of the band was in pretty good shape. By the time we got into the studio, the sections of written material and improvisation were pretty much set. A lot of thought went into the specific places where each musician would improvise. It's very important to me to focus on the personalities of the band members and give them space to improvise in musical situations that fit those personalities."

Imminent when I contacted Jon was Zion80's second release, *Adramelech*, volume 22 in Zorn's Book of Angels series: "I started listening to Zorn's music over 20 years ago, so it's a huge honor and privilege to be able to do an album of his Masada music. My trio Rashanim did a previous CD of Masada music in 2005, called *Masada Rock*. Zorn is a huge inspiration to me – as a musician, an artist, a mentor and a friend. The same is true of the other musicians on this scene, from the members of my band to others in the Radical Jewish Culture movement."

Since I contacted him, Jon with bass and oud player Shanir Ezra Blumenkranz has founded Chant Records that, besides issuing further Zion 80 albums, is dedicated to releasing adventurous uncompromising music across the spectrum.

•　•　•　•

Frank London, trumpeter in the Klezmatics, Hasidic New Wave and Zion80, was one of the original klezmer revivalists. I interviewed him in his Greenwich Village apartment.

"When I was nineteen or twenty I went to the New England Conservatory of Music and was a student in the Afro-American music department, in '77 to '80, and got my degree in Afro-American music, which is to say jazz. Before that I grew up on Long Island. I was a trumpet player but all I listened to and ever played was rock and roll, neither jazz nor Jewish music. I went to synagogue, but no active involvement in it. I go to college and start discovering all sorts of music, start getting really freaked out, like jazz just changes my life and I just dive into jazz one hundred per cent. But also around the same time I get involved with what nowadays you would call world music. And what this comes down to in a really practical sense is that I was just trying to learn everything and anything you can do on the trumpet, anything that's traditionally done on the trumpet, anything that's not traditionally done. So I'm studying jazz, classical music, Latin, African, Balkan music – just everything. And actually, my biggest roots are in the sort of AACM, Art Ensemble free improvisation which is coming out of the African American tradition but clearly also very influenced by other traditions – John Cage – very astute, worldly cosmopolitan thinkers. I studied with them, their music and techniques, and the basis of my entire musical aesthetic overall, in whatever genre I might work, comes out of the thinking of people like the Art Ensemble of Chicago and that kind of free improv."

Frank first got involved in Jewish music as a founder member of the Klezmer Conservatory Band, the mainly Jewish ensemble that included Don Byron. The palaver Byron's presence caused is an issue Frank gets heated about: "Don's a genius in many ways, very intelligent, a smart thinker, and what Don likes to do is play with the fact that he knows that people like to think in these ways and so he messes with that. He and I started playing Jewish music at exactly the same time. He was at the conservatory when I was and our first exposure to klezmer was in the same band. So we both played it at exactly the same time but from two different places. He distances himself from it because he became a novelty thing; he saw himself as being, 'Oh, you're the black guy playing Jewish music', and he got sick of that.

"The ideology behind the way people categorise people is reprehensible. Early on in my life as a Jewish musician I got a lot of play very quickly because of being seen as being authentic, and except where people are independently wealthy, we all need to work. If you hang out here among New York musicians, I think for ninety-eight per cent, black, white, men, women, Asian, Latin, Jewish, we're a community. And as a community most of us are really not biased, we're here to play music. But we're also aware that we have to make a living and I'm aware that if I can do a job in a band – and I'm not proud of this but it's practical – if I get called because I'm a white guy and this thing only hires white guys, and I know that my friend Karen works in this band that's a women's big band and they're not going to hire me, and my friend James works in a band that only hires black people, we're not proud of this. But we've got to make a living, we don't begrudge each other that. We would really save our vitriol for the bandleaders who perpetuate that. Or I save my biggest vitriol for players of any type whose key to marketing is that they're authentic because of their race or religion – 'You should hire me over that guy. Why? Because I'm Jewish, black, whatever. And I basically made my reputation by going around saying the obvious, as Don Byron said, 'Hey, anyone can play Jewish music.'"

Such prejudice Frank himself encountered, in reverse: "I got this from the Art Ensemble, from Roscoe Mitchell, I had a clash with him where he said, 'Jazz, African American music'. The form may have been created by people within a certain group; we don't have to take away the ownership of creation from a group. Yes, klezmer is east European Jewish music – does that mean every Jew can play klezmer and every non-Jew can't? No. Does that mean every Jew who plays klezmer is better? No. Does that mean there haven't been some great non-Jews who were influential? Does that mean there haven't been some great white jazz musicians? Does that mean that every innovator in jazz has been African American? No."

Frank put on a recording of the black swing era trumpeter Charlie Shavers playing klezmer jazz licks – making the point that a Jewish musician wouldn't have sounded any more authentic. Then Frank surprised me by saying that he thought another of his favourite trumpeters, Booker Little – who was black – also sounded Jewish on one track, 'Man of Words' on his 1961 album *Out Front.* 25

What first turned Frank on to klezmer could not be more different from what did it for me. In my case, it was the bottle dance wedding scene in the *Fiddler on the Roof* movie: what was this rootsy, sinuous, clarinet-led music that sounded so bittersweet Jewish? I had no name for it but liked it. It was not until I caught Kapelye in London, years later, and bought their *Future & Past* LP, that I encountered the word klezmer for the first time.

Frank also first heard *Fiddler* well before he knew about klezmer but said: "It's one of the reasons why I had absolutely no interest in Jewish music. *Fiddler* was one of a long list of reasons why – it was not interesting to me. If that's what Jewish music is, I don't care. For me, who had no Sam Musiker, no Dave Tarras, no real klezmer stuff, the only thing Jewish in my house would have maybe been *Fiddler* or some Israeli thing, it did nothing for me. I kind of did it the reverse way, it's only obvious to me now, that these guys who wrote *Fiddler* knew the real shit."

What was it, then, that had switched on Frank and his revivalist counterparts to klezmer?

"For me it just meant another in the list of amazing musics that I had never discovered that were blowing my mind. And it all happened at same time, around 1977 and 1982. I would hear a new music and was either not interested or it would blow my mind. I remember the first time I ate Thai food – the same time period up in Boston. And I was like, 'Oh my God, this is unbelievable.' And for me klezmer was like that, but no different than salsa was like that, then Haitian music, then Balkan music. It was just one of the musics that was so unbelievable."

But Frank's Jewish lineage, surely that gave klezmer added significance for him?

"Okay, one answer, one of these amazing musics blowing my mind; two, in terms of how much it's blowing my mind, it doesn't blow my mind as much as jazz, Latin music – it's more on a second tier of mind-blowingness, because the stuff that really blows my mind has to have a lot more improvisation in it, and a lot more rhythmic complexity. So secondly, it's not as deep as Afro-Cuban for me. Third thing, isn't it really nice, isn't it interesting, that I grew up Jewish and I never heard this stuff? But on the other hand, my parents didn't speak Yiddish. I grew up in a suburban working-class household, I'm really assimilated. We were Jewish but we weren't culturally east European Jewish, we were culturally American and religiously Jewish. So yes, it was a point of some interesting pride, wow, this is cool, this is the music from my background, isn't that nice that we're not the only people in the world that didn't have some cool music. Yeah, beyond that, it wasn't like other people will tell you, and they'll mean it, 'I heard my grandmother's voice'. David Krakauer says that; David Harris – Naftule's Dream, the Klezmer Conservatory Band – will not say that, he'll say, 'It's a really fun music to play, really enjoyable and I really got into it.' So I'm not going to argue with someone's experience but neither am I going to say that David Krakauer's music is more authentic, because he hears his grandmother's voice, than mine because I don't."

Were there any common denominators?

"My generalisation is this: among the Jews playing klezmer music, there were three kinds of reactions: I hear this ancestral heritage thing and I will identify with this on a religious basis or on a cultural basis. I know people who fit that and some of those people actually heard it growing up but had forgotten it but went back to it; others hadn't really heard it growing up and they were maybe one jump away from it and they latched on to it; two, this is a really fun music that's fun to play, it means something personal to me in the same way that all the other cool musics that are fun to play are; and, this is especially true for Don Byron although he's not Jewish, but for a lot of the clarinetists, think about it, what were your choices of what you were playing? The clarinetist has always been sort of the outsider in jazz, especially after bebop, but here was a great music for you to play especially if you were a clarinet player. So they just loved playing it. And, you know, 'There's a lot of work playing this stuff so if I get good at it, I can work.'"

Frank gave me a copy of Hasidic New Wave's 2001 JAM [Jewish Alternative Music] label release *From the Belly of Abraham*,

sub-titled *Adventures of the Afro-Semitic Diaspora Episode 5762*, a
Jewish-jazz-rock mash-up with Senegalese drumming. Frank, Greg
Wall on saxes and clarinet, David Fiuczynski, guitar, Fima Ephron,
bass and Aaron Alexander, drums are the HNW personnel, with
organist Jamie Saft guesting, all Jews, and Alioune Faye Yakar
Rhythms contributing the Senegalese beats. As a jazz-rock album
it is on a par with Weather Report and fusion-era Miles, with
arresting compositions and Frank cutting in with beautifully
articulated trumpet and flugelhorn solos. Sadly, that was the last of
HNW's five albums, but Tzadik reissued them as a box set.

For Frank, John Zorn's Radical Jewish Culture conception was
a stroke of genius: "When the klezmer revival first started, it was
like, wow, this is Jewish music and it's not 'Hatikvah' [Israel's
national anthem] and not *Fiddler on the Roof* and not Israeli folk
dancing, wow, that's cool. So it quickly moved from being this
unknown thing, wow, yeah, it's so great and we can love it, it's cool
music and it's Jewish, to being identified as the only thing that was
authentically Jewish. So it went from obscurity to over-saturation
and over-identification way too fast. So Zorn made this cultural
statement saying, wait a second, a lot of things can be Jewish music.
And he just opened the door."

• • • •

Much fascinating work has also emerged outside the Radical
Jewish Culture bubble, so let's drop in on some musicians
concerned, starting with pianist, vocalist and songwriter Ben
Sidran and his 1994 album *Life's A Lesson*, featuring interpretations
of Shabbat songs.

For the recording, Sidran assembled twenty-two Jewish
musicians, mostly jazz artists but also singer-songwriter Carole
King, along with the Gates of Heaven synagogue children's choir.
Actually, make that nineteen Jewish musicians as three involved,

vibraphonist Mike Mainieri, tenor saxophonist Bob Berg and flautist Jeremy Steig, their Jewish lineage is on their father's side – non-Jews then as far as the Judaic authorities are concerned but that didn't worry Sidran and it doesn't worry me.

Or I should say, ultimately it didn't worry Sidran: as he reveals in his book *There Was A Fire: Jews, Music and the American Dream*, when word got out that he was making a recording of Hebrew songs, "one day I received a phone call from the great jazz musician... Mike Mainieri. He said, 'I hear you're making this record of Jewish music. I'd like to play on it.' I said, 'Mike it's for the brothers, you know?'" They discussed it and Sidran relented.

Although Sidran is a jazz musician, on *Life's A Lesson* the songs are straight-on modernisations of Jewish devotional material. I phoned Sidran. He said that with *Life's A Lesson*, he was attempting to do something quite different to the Jewish-jazz avant-garde. "I was not interested in reinterpreting the liturgical songs we recorded, I simply wanted them to sound modern, like the records I listened to. Therefore, we didn't alter the melodic or harmonic structure; we simply expanded the original harmonies. Also, I was not interested in abstracting from the music a new modernism or a synthesis with other forms – jazz, avant-garde, etc. I really wanted to recreate the feeling and the emotional space of the music as I remembered it as a child. I told the soloists, 'This one is for your mother; we aren't here to be hip, we're here to capture a mood.' Zorn and the others in the new Jewish music revival often seem interested in creating a new kind of Jewish music or an abstracted version of more traditional forms."

Fond childhood memories of the synagogue were also what motivated drummer Michael Stephans' album *OM/shalom*, as he told me: "We lived in a community which placed great value upon our synagogue as a religious and cultural centre. I learned a lot about openness and oneness and the importance of family and friends at Temple Zion in West Miami. And I found so much of the Jewish liturgical music sung on Shabbat and on many of our holidays to be intriguing and inspirational. I shared my feelings about what all of that meant to me with another kindred spirit, the great saxophonist Dave Liebman and asked him to be a part of the project. The other great woodwind artist on the date, Bennie Maupin, has been a close friend and musical associate... and we also share a very great spiritual connection outside of – but incredibly similar to – Judaism."

Michael conceived *OM/shalom* while reflecting on the songs remembered from that shul, "the wordless incantations of the old men who would gather each afternoon... and chant prayers that bade farewell to the day and welcomed night", as he expresses it on the sleeve. The atmospheric 'Moon Over Miami' includes his spoken word evocations of those times, while 'Adon Olam/ Resolution Hatikvah' conflates a traditional prayer tune with Coltrane's 'A Love Supreme'. Elsewhere too, Michael picks up on Coltrane's spirituality, working traces of Coltrane's 'Alabama', 'Om' and 'To Be' into Jewish traditional music.

He explained to me: "When you listen to the very beginning of Coltrane's *Ascension*, it sounds a lot like the opening prayer before a *haftorah* is read. The similarity, to me, is alarming; and what follows is no less remarkable: saxophones, trumpets, piano, bass, drums, all *davening* – praising the Creator, bemoaning our transgressions and vulnerabilities – in other words, portraying the human condition through music, just as it was, and is, with the chanting of the old Chassids. It's the musical chanting of those of us who see bringing music into the world as a noble and essential calling. A number of years ago, a young Orthodox rabbi invited me to a small Yizcor service he was giving in his home during the high holidays – he had converted the basement of his home into a small *shul*. At one point in the service, he worked himself up into such a frenzy that, while singing, he was so lost in the moment that he jumped up on the platform and flew into an impassioned solo that was mesmerizing. All I could think of was John Coltrane who, if you've seen him, could *daven* with the best of them."

Presumably, as a rabbi, so can Bob Gluck, but he is also a jazz pianist, and experimentalist composer of what he calls electroacoustic music. With influences that embrace Ornette Coleman, Cecil Taylor, Stockhausen, John Cage, Hendrix, Zappa, Miles fusion, Bach, Stravinsky and Jewish cantorial, Gluck defies categorisation. I quizzed him about the dichotomy between his EMF label electroacoustic releases *Stories Heard & Untold* and *Electric Songs*, which are conceptually Jewish, and his outright FMR-label jazz albums *Sideways*, *Returning* and *Something Quiet*, which are not.

*Stories* opens with a ghostly sound collage of ambient recordings made at synagogues and prayer settings, followed by Gluck's oblique take on Yiddish traditional songs, and the concluding piece 'Jonah Under the Sea' invokes the biblical prophet's sensations in the story of the whale. Although I discern no jazz, it is substantially improvisatory, said Gluck: "The line between various improvisatory forms has never been clear to me. If by jazz is meant a rootedness in traditions emerging from the African diaspora, there is little of that." Gluck however referred me to another EMF release, *Electric Brew*, that he said certainly could be thought of that way, in its treatment of Miles Davis's *Bitches Brew*. It features Gluck on piano, computer-assisted piano, his digitally processed "eShofar", and electronics. "The appearance of a shofar rather than a trumpet may be surprising to some," said Gluck, "but its electronic treatment certainly owes some lineage to the electronic processing concepts that Teo Macero brought to post-production in the original [*Bitches Brew*]. Whether the aesthetic is connected to the original is a matter of discussion, in which I do not take a stand, but see the answer as 'yes and no'. I'm really following my own muse, but certainly that muse has its Jewish and African American sides, both of which go very far back in my life." The single obviously Jewish-themed track is Ofer Ben-Amots' composition 'Akeda' – Hebrew for binding or sacrificial offering as in the biblical tale of Abraham – the main melody based on a liturgical lamentation.

Under a new label, Ictus, Gluck launched his *Tropolet* duo collaboration with soprano saxophonist Andrew Sterman on which the convergence of Jewish with jazz is pronounced. It draws, said Gluck, on the traditional melodies used to chant Torah, haftarah, and Book of Lamentations: "Drawing upon the monophonic, distinctly non-harmonic language of traditional Jewish chant, here I look to Ornette Coleman's harmonologics to consider how in a jazz setting one can play interrelated parallel lines that do not draw upon a conventional harmonic language yet are respectful of both the original source material and the jazz traditions we inhabit. The recording is entirely improvisational, drawing upon pre-selected melodic cells from traditional chant that form the backbone and core material for improvisation; woven within this is some pre-recorded sound collages that I created, introduced in an improvisational manner as an additional layer." Gluck's take on jazz, he said, was not purist: "I think of jazz as having been very much a hybrid art form from its inception."

We remain in leftfield territory with multi-reedist Steven Lugerner's double album *These Are The Words/Narratives*. *Words* is the most obviously Jewish disc in conception, alluding to the Torah – five of the seven tracks identified on the sleeve not only by their English title but also by Hebrew lettering, each corresponding to one of the five books of Moses. "I know the concept is Jewish, but did Jewish music influence you?" I asked Steven. "I mean, if you just listen to the music, without reference to anything else, that wouldn't be obvious."

He emailed back: "Yes, the concept is Jewish, but 'Jewish music' per se didn't really have much of an influence over the album – except for maybe the harmonic progression in 'In The Wilderness'. I was very much influenced by Steve Reich's Tehillim."

Tehillim, minimalist composer Reich's 1981 work reflecting his Jewish heritage, is the setting of Psalms 19:2-5, 34:13-15, 18:26-27 and 150:4-6, with the parts of the work based on these four texts. What Lugerner found particularly interesting is that Reich, by using text as his raw material for composition, ends up writing music that was Jewish by nature but doesn't sound overtly Jewish.

In composing *Words*, Lugerner makes extensive use of Gematria, a method by which medieval Kabbalists derived mystical insights from the Torah by translating certain portions into a series of numbers. He arranged these numbers into music including melodic figures with foreground and background harmony, tempo markings, time signatures and space for improvisation. The other musicians on the album, Darren Johnston, trumpet/flugelhorn, Myra Melford, piano, Matt Wilson, drums, are also Jewish.

I first became aware of multi-instrumental ethnomusicologist Sam Thomas through FourMinusOne's album *Split Decision*, his blowing marking him out as a most distinctive tenor and soprano saxophonist in a trio with bassist Ippei Ichimaru and drummer Eric Platz, the music, partly recorded at Ryles Jazz Club in Cambridge, Massachusetts, veering between post-bop and free form, the players maintaining poise even when taking chances such as on their twelve-minute live spontaneous group composition 'One For Jonny'.

That though was released in the early noughties, since when Dr Sam Toriman Thomas – Torjiman his Sephardi family name – has founded Jewish Awareness Though Music to raise appreciation of

Jewish culture and history through music. His ensembles Asefa – Hebrew for 'collecting' – and Asefa Jazz focus on contemporary approaches to composition, improvisation and fusion, drawing from the global Jewish music heritage.

The original concept for Asefa, Sam told me, was as an informal collection of musicians able to dip into many styles of Jewish music: "This continues to happen in many different settings, however, the main performing group in concert remains focused on jazz and north African Jewish traditions. Naturally, as a saxophonist and clarinetist, I have strong affinities towards playing klezmer as well".

Jazz, said Sam, had been part of his identity since his early youth, along with middle eastern music – Arab and Jewish – and Ashkenazic synagogue music: "My first intermingling of musical elements came in my tenure in 1994 at Berklee College of Music. There I wrote 'Yiddishalach', a synchretic composition and performance. From there, along with my deeper forays into Jewish thought and culture, my playing began to reflect the diversity of musical styles and spiritual feelings about music that I was exploring."

These streams converge on the debut album *Asefa* that captures the ensemble in a trio setup – Sam on soprano sax, clarinet, bendir and ghaita, Eric Platz on percussion and drums and Shanir Blumenkranz, oud and bass, joined on one track by guitarist/vocalist Elie Massias. The music, a multi-fusion of jazz and Jewish middle eastern, north African and east European, feels very natural, very interconnected; a view reinforced with the release of Asefa's second album, *Resonance*, the ensemble augmented now by percussionist Richard Stein, with Rabbi Mihael Kakon contributing poignant vocals on two tracks, and Moroccan violinist Rachid Halihal.

The criss-crossing of Latin-jazz and Jewish song are hallmarks of the work of pianist/arranger Dr Eugene Marlow, and of vocalist Kat Parra. Dr Marlow with his Heritage Ensemble has released three "Hebraic songbook" albums – *Making The Music Our Own* and *Celebrations*, on which most tracks are Chanukah and Purim tunes, and *A Fresh Take*, which reworks the first album. Marlow's deft arrangements – "exploring the jazz chord possibilities under the melodic line" – consistently make for engaging syntheses of jazz, Afro-Cuban, Brazilian and classicism with Jewish folk and liturgical tunes, some of ancient origin. An adroit and sensitive pianist, Marlow is well served by collaborators Michael Hashim on saxes, Frank Wagner, bass, and Nuyoricans Bobby Sanabria on drums and percussionist Cristian Rivera. "I'm the only 'official' Jew in the group," Marlow informed me, "although Maestro Sanabria has been told by an ethnomusicologist that he probably has some Sephardim in his family heritage." Marlow, whom it was my pleasure to meet with his wife over a meal in London where he was born, is also author of an acclaimed study, *Jazz in China: From Dance Hall Music to Individual Freedom of Expression* (University Press of Mississippi, 2018).

As for Kat Parra, her Sephardic Music Experience's *Dos Amantes* covers the songs of the Sephardi Jews whose ancestors perished during, or fled from, the inquisitorial oppression of medieval Spain and Portugal, a lineage that Parra shares. Twice voted best vocalist by Latin Jazz Corner, she has an earthy, soaring purity of voice, somewhat cantorial at times, and, on *Dos Amantes*, sings throughout in Ladino, a blend of old Spanish, Arabic, Hebrew and Turkish, and elements from all these traditions are evident, along with touches of Latin-jazz, rumba, habanera, bossa and funk. The album closes with a joyously rousing modern Sephardi song, 'Hanukia', celebrating the Jewish festival of lights.

When I originally contacted saxophonist and vocalist Jessica Lurie, for this book's predecessor, I observed that it was not so much that she performed and composed specifically Jewish-jazz as that the way she played, sang and wrote was profoundly affected by her exposure to Jewish music.

Jewish on her father's side, she confirmed: "I was raised more culturally Jewish than religiously, but on my own have pursued Jewish studies and moreover the music, both Ashkenzi and Sephardic musics. This as well as a love of Balkan music has definitely influenced my compositions and playing style."

Those influences converge with jazz on the Jessica Lurie Ensemble's debut album *Tiger! Tiger!* on which she is supported by Italian musicians she has regularly collaborated with in Europe. Jewish and Balkan sonorities add exotic savour, but jazz is the liberating medium and Lurie has the gift of always sounding melodious, no matter how far out she improvises, and on tenor and alto saxes, her chief instruments, she frequently veers towards the cantorial in phrasing and timbre. When she sings on 'Surfarara', it is again the chants of the synagogue she evokes, even though, as Jessica informed me, it is an adaptation of a Sicilian mining song. When, however, the lyrics are English – 'Everybody's Got to Eat Sometime', the only other song on the album – she has a vocal quality somewhat reminiscent of Rickie Lee Jones.

When I reached out to Jessica again after my first edition came out, she said: "Lately I am composing more music that is directly Jewish-themed – a new piece 'Der Nister', inspired by *The World to Come* by Dara Horn and her story about Pinchus Kahanovich, music for a performance piece about the Jewish Workman's Circle in NYC, and transcribing nigunim to be used as launching places for improvisation."

'Der Nister' [Yiddish – The Hidden One] is titled after Ukrainian-Yiddish writer Kahanovich's pseudonym; he died in a gulag hospital in 1950 when Jewish culture was suppressed in the Soviet Union. It featured as the longest track on Jessica's *Megaphone Heart*. And for her album *Long Haul*, Jessica composed the liltingly klezmer-ish 'Rare Flares', handling the piece on flute, the tune, she said, a reflection of her father's Jewish heritage.

Another artist then whose Jewish parent was the wrong one for her to be certified kosher by the religious authorities, yet clearly Jessica's sense of Jewishness is a fundamental part of her outlook.

So much so that with Jessica we come full circle, as she has become progressively involved in the Radical Jewish Culture scene, collaborating with the likes of Zorn, Frank London and Zion80.

She told me: "I did a discussion/performance with Mark Ribot, Roy Nathanson, Marty Ehrlich and Greg Cohen about being Jewish musicians who play all kinds of music, coming from secular and religious Jewish households, and how the music we play – which can range from jazz to Latin or funk and experimental free jazz – connects to Judaism, and what do we play when we are asked to play something Jewish – what does that mean? Does it mean the other music we create – not klezmer, or melodically inspired from synagogue/cantors – does it sound Jewish? Is it less so? It was an interesting discussion, and a great set after." 26

. . . .

In interviews, John Zorn has urged Jews to "identify as Jews" and stop trying to "pass for white" – the latter expression borrowed from African American terminology. Black writer Ralph Ellison shared similar feelings about Jews.

Allen Lowe, on the sleeve of his album *Jews in Hell*, cites Ellison. Lowe comes over on the album as a superb wide-ranging jazz saxophonist, plays laconically blistering blues, folk-roots and garage rock on guitar and electric banjo, extracts the most soulful sounds out of a synthesiser since Stevie Wonder, and composes songs with colloquially incisive lyrics that linger in the mind like those of Dylan or Lou Reed.

Although there are no obvious Jewish music influences, *Jews in Hell* is Jewish-jazz in the sense that the thirty-eight tracks are Lowe's angst-ridden ruminations on Jewish identity. These include: 'Leni' – described by Lowe as a "Hate song for an old Nazi (Riefenstahl)"; 'Goyishe World' – "More impotent outrage, with a nod to the Velvet Underground, via the great dobro-ist Stacey Phillips' story about getting beat up on the way home from Yeshiva on Passover eve"; 'Soundtrack Theme From the Film Jews in Hell' – "The film, directed as part of his Community Service by Mel Gibson" – Lowe having a swipe here at the actor/director whose movie *The Passion of Christ* brought accusations of antisemitism. And 'To Dance Beneath the Cuban Sky' is an instrumental featuring pianist Dr Lewis Porter, Jewish founder and director of Rutgers University's jazz history masters degree. In composing it, Lowe says he was trying to evoke the 19th century New Orleans composer and pianist Louis Moreau Gottschalk, and reflects that Jewish musicians – Gottschalk, R&B singer/songwriter Doc Pomus, blues guitarist Mike Bloomfield, and jazz saxophonist Dave Schildkraut are those he cites – represent a movement of permanent post-modernism, "our version of the permanent revolution... a vernacular hybrid musical Fourth Stream of memory, obsession, and aggressive self-interrogation... often mistaken for self-hate". 26

And Lowe quotes Ralph Ellison, thus: "The real guilt of... Jewish intellectuals lies in their facile, perhaps unconscious, but certainly unrealistic identification with what is called the 'power structure'. Negroes call that 'passing for white'. Speaking personally, both as a writer and as Negro American. I would like to see the most positive distinctions between whites and Jewish Americans maintained."

Perhaps there's something of that too in what Captain Beefheart's former guitarist Gary Lucas has said. Asked about the significance of Radical Jewish Culture, Lucas, who cut two Tzadik albums, replied: "I'm a one-worlder, but I think that within that world you have to acknowledge the incredible beauty and diversity of all the people and backgrounds a little more. So for Jewish people, yeah, it's important. It gives many of them a sense of belonging to a community for the first time. They don't feel like they're outsiders encroaching a land that's run by WASP corporations." 27

But as I put the finishing touches to this second edition of my book, I have had cause to wonder about the ongoing longevity of not only Radical Jewish Culture, but also of Jewish-jazz ventures more broadly. Let us backstep in time a few years.

• • • •

In 2013 when John Zorn turned sixty, he celebrated with an extensive series of Zorn@60 gigs, involving well over a hundred of his collaborators, the main action taking place that September at New York venues. And March 2014 saw the premiere of Zorn's Masada Book Three: The Book Beriah, with performances of the first twenty of his latest set of more than ninety new compositions. The concert, at New York Town Hall, involved twenty ensembles, each performing one song from the new book, including Zorn on alto with the Aleph Trio.

Yet scanning the internet, it seems to me there is far less Jewish-jazz activity going on. What particularly raised questions in my mind was a 2018 Seth Rogovoy feature for *Forward*, titled John Zorn's Done With His Masada Project. So, What's Next? It read: "In 1993, John Zorn began composing music based on Jewish themes for a new group, Masada Quartet. Now, 25 years and 613 tunes later, Zorn is closing the book – literally and figuratively – on what evolved into a sprawling, genre-defying series of hundreds of compositions written for dozens of different ensembles, all united by Zorn's restless, melodic sensibility while adhering to a few basic rules that place them as solidly in the world of Jewish music as any cantor's melody or rebbe's nigun."

The occasion for Rogovoy's article was the release, in May 2018, of the final tranche of recordings based on Zorn's Masada Book Three: The Book Beriah compositions that were launched at that Town Hall concert four years earlier. Since when, the ninety-two Book Three pieces had resulted in eleven albums, involving various ensembles. "There's no denying," wrote Rogovoy, "the music's energy or its Jewish feel – all the tunes are based on Jewish scales and employ the essence of Jewish musical DNA: the use of the augmented second interval. The end result is a Jewish sound familiar from klezmer and synagogue music, albeit rendered in styles ranging from death metal to surf rock to free jazz."

As Zorn's next projects were unrelated to anything overtly Jewish, Rogovoy asked if we would hear additional new Jewish music from him at some point? Zorn responded: "I have learned that it is impossible to predict where I may go next, or what my next project may be... At the moment, there isn't a Jewish-based project on the horizon – but tomorrow, who knows?"

Given Zorn's closing comment, I contacted Rogovoy a year on from that article, for some steer on what's happening. Rogovoy is on his side of the Atlantic geographically much closer to the action than I am so I asked him if, given Zorn's pivotal role, the movement as a whole might have run its course, with the artists concerned moving on to non-Jewish related projects.

"I think your final sentence is apt," Rogovoy responded. "While some of the artists in the RJC scene continue to explore that territory, e,g., Paul Shapiro, Frank London, Tim Sparks, it doesn't seem to be to the extent it was in its heyday in the 1990s into the oughts. And with a few exceptions, e.g., Jon Madof's Zion80, I'm not aware of a new or younger generation working in the Jewish downtown avant-garde style of Anthony Coleman, Steven Bernstein, Marc Ribot, et al."

The fact that jazz, folk, Latin and classical acoustic guitarist Tim Sparks remains active on that scene is all the more significant as he is one of several non-Jewish artists that have contributed albums to Tzadik's Radical Jewish roster. It was while travelling around Europe that Sparks developed an interest in east European music and started performing in klezmer bands, then on return to America he joined Voices of Sephard, led by jazz/klezmer trombonist and pianist David Harris. Sparks' RJC albums – he's done four in all – include *Little Princess*, a tribute to klezmer legend Naftule Brandwein.

In March 2020 I contacted John Zorn to get an update on his intentions and he reaffirmed that he had "no plan for more Jewish related works at this time". In fact, just the month before, his Tzadik label released his latest album, *Virtue*, with a triple guitar line-up of Bill Frisell, Gyan Riley and Julian Lage interpreting Zorn compositions "inspired by anchoress Julian of Norwich, a 14th century abbess and one of the founders of Christian mysticism".

About the future of Jewish-jazz more generally, I reconnected with David Chevan. He said: "I have an active life as an openly Jewish-Jazz musician, but I don't know who else continues to lead this path. I'm pretty sure Frank London is still doing something that comes out of his participation in the movement, probably Aaron Alexander and Greg Wall, but no one else comes immediately to mind. As for me, The Afro-Semitic Experience continues to perform quite regularly and I just completed a music theatre work that is a mix of Jewish music and jazz, Letters from the Affair... Whether what I am doing now is radical, I don't know. But

I do know that I continue to create work that comes out of Jewish identity, experience and music."

And Frank London confirmed: "I can't speak for others, but my work in Jewish music is not ending because of John's choices."

I also got in touch with jazz saxophonist Rabbi Greg Wall, a close musical associate of Frank London, and for many years a core participant in downtown RJC activities.

• • • •

Until 2010, one could catch Greg Wall performing every Monday night with some of New York's finest radical Jewish musicians, at The Sixth Street Community Synagogue in Manhattan's east Village where he was the rabbi. Because the synagogue needed to raise cash to shore-up the 150-year-old building, it could no longer afford to fund a permanent rabbi, and in 2013 Wall informed me that he had just been appointed rabbi of Beit Chaverim Synagogue in Westport, Connecticut. He marked his arrival with a gig at Westport Town Hall featuring his group Later Prophets, whose 2009 Tzadik label release *Ha'Orot* celebrates the spiritual writings of Rabbi Avraham Itzchak HaCohen Kook who taught that "heaven can be found in this world". Also lined up at the gig were Zion80, with whom Wall is involved, and the Ayn Sof Arkestra and Bigger Band, a Jewish-jazz orchestra he co-led with Frank London.

Six years later, I Skyped Rabbi Wall to discuss whither Radical Jewish Culture as the new millennium entered its third decade. Also, an opportunity to gain insights on the interconnectedly dual nature of his career, the spark for which, he said, was John Coltrane's spiritual jazz.

"Of course, I was attracted to Coltrane's music – who wasn't, especially if you're into jazz, I mean he's like the *Meshiach* [Messiah] of jazz. The LP version of *Love Supreme* – unfortunately, with the CD generation, people missed out on album covers, which was an experience in itself – and staring me in the face when I opened it up was: 'Dear listener, praise be to God to whom all praise is due.' And I thought, where have I heard that before? I had a bar mitzvah and that was the translation of the *bar'chu* [the call to prayer] in my reform Hebrew Union prayer book. And I said, why is Coltrane spitting back at me from my bar mitzvah what I rejected outright? When I was a student at New England Conservatory in the late seventies, if someone asked me if I was Jewish, I'd say no, my parents are. And now here is Coltrane saying to take this seriously, and when Coltrane says to check it out, I became open to it. Then once I became open to it, things started happening."

Greg thence embarked on his entwined career in jazz and Judaism; so, what did he make of those who perceived affinities between cantorial music and jazz?

"Hogwash. Listen, my rebbe, he's into Duke Ellington music, and he likes the good stuff, and I completely concur. Anything that's good, and if someone's a musician, it becomes part of him, just like you are a product of every book you've ever read and every piece of art you've ever seen, and if it makes an impression, it's stored. And if you go back for repeated reading or viewing or listening then it becomes more accessible to you and you can draw on it. But even if it's in the recesses, it's still there in your subconscious. So, cantorial music is cantorial music, you're not dealing with improvisation, and old klezmer music, there was no improvisation."

I persisted: you do hear people talk about chazzens improvising after a fashion.

"Ah, they have their schtick and they make it work, they apply it. Now you can say, well maybe bebop musicians aren't really improvising, they have their vocabulary and they fit it in. Okay, maybe the art is how they fit it in. But the greats are the ones who are turning it upside down. Anybody who's great in any field is going to be for the most part revolutionary in some way, unless you're talking about the one in a million who's so gifted that their execution of anything just blows you away. But I don't see it. There have been various times that people have made this connection: I remember going to something at Lincoln Center and they wanted to show Cab Calloway completely influenced by Jewish music, and then that klezmer influenced jazz. Or that klezmer was influenced by jazz – well that's actually true; you had people like Sam Musiker and Mickey Katz and these musicians that were playing in both worlds. And Jewish musicians in the 1920s and 30s, there was so much antisemitism in the United States that African Americans were an affinity group for Jews and they were able to make music together, work together and there was a lot of cultural interchange. But I don't read too much into one informing the other so much. But Radical Jewish Culture, now you have people who are multilingual in creating a new language based on these experiences and that's truly a hybrid of cultural influences. And that's far from over."

So now we'd got to the nub of it, from one of the contributors, some thirty years after John Zorn coined the term Radical Jewish Culture.

"I think what's happened," reflected Greg, "is that there's been a maturation, that it's not considered so radical anymore. But the musicians who have been trafficking in those collaborations have not slowed down. I don't think there's been a slow down at all. So Zorn has had an incredible output over the last ten years with his three volumes of the Book of Angels and I've been part of a couple of them.

"Those groups are touring; I just did a tour with Zorn within the past year, and these groups have been touring from the multi-level Volume 3 [Book of Beriah] – it's the best one yet and it's huge – 11 CDs. And even he put it out on vinyl – I want to get a copy. So those groups have been touring. My buddy Brian Marsella has been in Europe... playing music from that project and John Zorn's music, so he might not be recording new stuff under the moniker Radical Jewish Culture right now but these are documentations; they're not studio records that are put together by people coming together for the purpose of making the record, they're projects that are active and living and it's just a snapshot of what happens with Zorn's compositions. The groups are still around, you can hear most of them. I mean Zorn's had a particular role, he's the catalyst, an instigator, he's challenged people. Sometimes out of the challenges that Zorn issues, great things happen, that's part of his talent as an auteur, as a conceptual artist. But it's not dependent on him; Zorn could be going off on any other project, but it doesn't put the brakes on anything."

# Chapter 17: Hip Heebs – an intermission riff

In these final pages of this initial part of my study, some reflections on the role of Jews in American jazz.

The only mention I have come across of an attempt to produce an ethnic breakdown of America's jazz musicians was something jazz writer Martin Williams said, that: "I think it was a sociologist who did some kind of tabulation about the ethnic and national backgrounds of jazz musicians. Of course Negroes were first. And I think next were Jews, next Italians... After that, things came down to such a scarcity that it didn't mean much, as I remember." [1]

Whether Jews really have produced, after African Americans, more jazz musicians than other minorities that I am aware have figured prominently, I would be very hesitant to say.

As Dan Morgenstern told me: "Jazz reflects the idea of America as a melting pot because minorities made such an enormous contribution to this music, it comes out of the encounter between the African and the European – that's a kind of shorthand, it's over-simplified, but what does that European influence mean? It means Irish, Jewish, Italian, Spanish. And if you look at American jazz musicians, minorities really play a dominant role."

Jazz historian Burton Peretti pointed to Artie Shaw's childhood experience of antisemitic taunts to make more a general observation about minorities in jazz, suggesting that Shaw's decision to become a musician had a great deal to do with a "general ethnic passion to overcome marginality... In this respect he seems more intensely alienated than the more optimistically adventurous white players". [2]

Beyond the general ethnic passion to overcome marginality that Peretti correctly identified, is there some more specific Jewish cast of mind we can bring to this issue? Yes, I think so. Those other minorities were endeavouring to find a footing in America, but unlike Jews, they at least had a 'home country' that they could securely identify with. That was not so with Jews in America in the first half of the twentieth century. Whether religious or secular, their sense of Jewishness was supra-national, supra-cultural, and bound up with a sensibility that racial chastisement might come from any quarter, at any time. Since its formation in 1948, Israel has assumed something of a 'home country' status for many Jews who view it as a 'bolt hole' should there be another upsurge of savage antisemitism such as that encountered in Nazi Europe, Tsarist Russia, Soviet Europe, inquisitorial Spain, and elsewhere. No Jew can afford the luxury of complacency – that is part of the lesson of Jewish history, that is at the core of the Jewish mindset, no less so than in the United States which has witnessed periodic upsurges of antisemitism, as during the McCarthy years, and more recently with the spate of murderous attacks on synagogues.

So, to return to Shaw, he conceivably felt even more intensely alienated than non-Jewish minority jazz contemporaries. Those antisemitic episodes spooked him to such an extent that, having Anglicised his name from Arshawsky, for years he avoided disclosing his Jewish roots – that is until his jazz career was almost over: "It took me a long time to get over the impact of it. It gave you a sense of inferiority, so you had to prove you were better. It had something to do with my drive. If you press a spring hard enough, it will jump farther." 3 That is a sensibility that, if you're a creative person in any sphere, must surely affect your work, if it is sincere.

A further consideration is that one frequently comes across testaments from Jews about how the perceived affinities between black and Jewish music attracted them to jazz. The extent of any musicological commonalities can be debated, but what one cannot deny is these Jews' personal experience; it is one way they relate to jazz.

Even Mezz Mezzrow – so infatuated with black music and culture that he considered himself 'colored' rather than Jewish – was struck by certain coincident traits in Jewish and black music. Mezzrow recalled a prison band he performed in while incarcerated in an island penitentiary for drug dealing: "Big John [an Irish band member] tickled about how the band's doing; decides to branch out with more musical activities, starts a choir in the Catholic church on the island... Along came the Jewish holidays and with them a weird situation. The Jewish boys, not to be outdone by the Catholics, organize their own choir and ask me, a colored guy, wouldn't I care to lead it? I find out once more how music of different oppressed peoples blends together. Jewish or Hebrew religious music mostly minor, in a simple form, full of wailing and lament. When I add Negro inflections to it they fit so perfect, it thrills me. I add dominant sevenths to minor chords, sometimes the ninth too; effect colorful and stirring as a bellychord. I just sing 'Oh, oh, oh' over and over again because I don't know the Hebrew chants, but I give it a weepy blues inflection and the guys are all happy about it. They can't understand how a colored guy digs the spirit of their music so good." 4

A real 'colored guy' who did so was Ornette Coleman – one of the most pivotal catalysts in jazz history. In a *New York Times* interview he revealed how Jewish religious music had moved him. Invited to pick records that had impacted on him, Coleman's first request was something by Josef [Jossele] Rosenblatt, the Ukraine-born cantor who settled in New York in 1911: "'I was once in Chicago, about some 20 years ago,' Mr Coleman said. 'A young man said, "I'd like you to come by so I can play something for you". I went down to his basement and he put on Josef Rosenblatt, and I started crying like a baby. The record he had was crying, singing and praying all in the same breath. I said, wait a minute, you can't find those notes. Those are not 'notes', they don't exist."

What Coleman meant was that they do not exist in conventional Western music; as the interviewer Ben Ratliffe observed: "Standard Western notation and harmony is a big problem for him, particularly the fact that the notation for many instruments (including his three instruments – alto saxophone, trumpet and violin) must be transposed to fit the 'concert key' of C in Western music."

About the Rosenblatt recording, Coleman told Ratliffe, "he's singing about something: I don't know what it is, but it's bad". The interviewer wondered how much of Rosenblatt's chanting was improvised, and how much "up-and-down melodic shapes... well practiced" – that is, as in Western music. Coleman responded: "Mm-hmm, I understand what you're saying. But it doesn't sound like it's going up and down; it sounds like it's going out. Which means it's coming from his soul."

One cannot necessarily deduce that Coleman's own art was shaped in any way by his love of cantorial singing, but several Jews mentioned in this book have gravitated to jazz because they discerned affinities with the music they heard in synagogue, among them Nat Hentoff. Readers will remember that as a youth he was turned on to jazz when overhearing Artie Shaw's 'Nightmare' blasting out of a record store – it stopped him in his tracks by reminding him of cantorial chants he had grown up with in shul.

Hentoff, who served jazz as a writer and journalist for more than sixty years, also as a record producer and broadcaster, in a 2014 documentary film about him – *The Pleasures of Being Out of Step: Notes on the Life of Nat Hentoff*, directed by David L Lewis – declared: "The cantor is a basic part of the whole religious experience, and they sing what is called melismatic-ly. That is, they will often take one syllable and use a number of notes on it, and they often improvise with melodies called niguns." He cites the impact of the cantors that so stirred him in shul: "They were so viscerally powerful, I still have a big collection of Jewish cantorial singers. And later on, I told my friend Charles Mingus, the jazz creator... 'I got to play you some of this because this is Jewish blues.' This is what I look for in most music; what most moves me is called the *krechts*, the cry, and that's what you have in all of jazz, one way or the other."

Another draw factor, as jazz/klezmer clarinetist Ben Goldberg sees it, pertains to the Judaic, and by extension secular Jewish, ways of thinking: "Jews are encouraged to ask questions... and we are sceptical of received wisdom. So if you have a musician who's coming from a cultural context, he or she might not be interested in doing things the way they've been told. It strikes me... that in the world of jazz and improvised music, such a disproportional percentage of musicians are Jewish." 5

• • • •

During the first decades of jazz, most Jews who took to it were assimilationists, keen to play down their Jewish identity. Or like Mezzrow, like Artie Shaw, deny it. Most Jewish American jazz musicians, up to the late 1980s, submerged their ethnicity in their creative endeavours, or tried to – the popularisation of 'Bei Mir Bist Du Schoen' was an exception.

Shaw, we have seen, is on record as saying that it was no accident the way he and Benny Goodman played clarinet, that their Russian-Jewish background had something to do with it. Even if they did sound Jewish to a certain extent – and as we've seen that is highly debatable – what they were most trying to do was sound black.

What however are we to make of something that Stan Getz once said, that even though he tried to sound black, it came out sounding Jewish? "Stan might have felt that way, but I don't think anyone listening to him in a blindfold test would know he was Jewish," pianist Roberta Piket said when I corresponded with her. She added: "Lee Konitz once said something similar to me about himself. I think he was referring to that plaintive, modal sound but I'm not sure. In any case I don't think either of them sound particularly Jewish." Neither do I, but that doesn't invalidate how Getz and Konitz felt about their music.

Jazz artists of any originality, besides taking inspiration from other musicians, try to put their own stamp on the music. Jazz educators teach about melody, harmony and rhythm but then urge students to tap into their 'biography'. That would include, for most Jewish musicians, some consciousness of what has happened to Jewish people; that is part of their folk-memory and psychology, their visceral, reflexive response to things, underpinned by personal experiences.

Then there is musical folk memory. Most Jewish musicians will have grown up with experience of synagogue music. Other forms of Jewish music may have helped form their 'inner ear' too. So even if a Jewish musician turned to jazz in rejection of all that, one must allow for the possibility that, subconsciously, some echo might resound in her or his work.

Consider the following quotation: "Sometimes when I'm playing, and I can actually pinpoint it on my records, I feel this influence taking over: it's a kind of Yiddish thing, cantorial. It comes when I play the soprano sax and there is definitely a connection. I don't feel it when I'm on tenor, but the soprano is like an extension of my own hand."

So said David Liebman, as quoted in Mike Williams' book *The Australian Jazz Explosion*, in which Williams acknowledges

Liebman's influence on musicians in Australia. Liebman was there in the late seventies touring with Chick Corea, then stuck around to form the faculty of the first Australian Summer Jazz Camp.

I invited Liebman to elaborate on that Jewish quality he detected in his music: "It's basically the expressive devices that I hear in my soprano, playing a kind of wail and shake and a lot of sliding up and down on the pitch. That's the essence of it and in a way it has become more pronounced over the years. You wouldn't hear this so much when I play straight-ahead jazz, but more in my vamp influenced or ethnic material. The examples are pretty much everywhere. As far as material, I did write and record a string quartet with soprano piece titled *Atonement for Yom Kippur* and I do have a project in mind with cantorial chants and so forth sometime in the future."

Liebman added: "I wouldn't say there is a 'Jewish sound' nor 'Italian' saxophone sound, although we often refer to certain tenor players as being 'Italian stallones' – Carmen Leggio, Sal Nistico, even Charlie Ventura and guys from the swing era. What I would say is that both Italians and Jews are city folks and there is a heritage of music in both cultures. The clarinet and violin of course are big in the Jewish tradition; the trumpet, a la operatic-florid melodies, etc, in Italian, but of course you get on dangerous territory when you generalize."

Absolutely. Still, here's what another tenorist, Lew Tabackin, told me about when he too switches to his other main instrument: "I think there is an eastern European sensibility that sometimes presents itself when I play or compose flute material. This may have something to do with a Jewish experience, or perhaps genetic."

Avant-jazz collaborators pianist Joel Futterman and multi-reedist Ike Levin – whom Michelle Coltman of Charles Lester Music contacted on my behalf – were clear about how Jewish music influences might have seeped into their work. She informed me: "Both grew up hearing cantorial and celebratory Jewish music – they are first cousins and shared similar childhood experiences.... Their family were observant Jews. They said that the heavy minor scale-laden Jewish music, and this combined with the strong emotional expressiveness in cantorial chanting and vocalisations have an influence on them. Both seem to view many cantors as improvising and sort of scatting as they pray. One of both of their major musical influences is John Coltrane who had a strong spirituality, expressiveness and searching in his later playing which they find somewhat similar to cantorial chanting and singing. But they seem to feel that, while they acknowledge the influence of Jewish inspired music, as you suggest the influence is much more diffuse and indirect and blended in with their other experiences growing up in urban environments. Ike's father was a professional musician (violinist) and according to Ike he always had LPs playing at home of mostly Jewish and Yiddish music so Ike heard this music from a very early age."

Loren Schoenberg, when I raised the issue with him, fired back: "These are well worn questions. You're talking about that cry and the chazzans. What you're talking about here goes way beyond Jewish, way beyond African American, you're talking about basic human attributes, basic ways that humans express themselves. And sure, there's a commonality, but you can't get so specific because the singing of La Niña De Los Peines, the famous Spanish singer – I've a lot of her records from the 1930s, 1940s – there's all kinds of people from all kinds of cultures who have this cry and this moan in their voice, and so that's something that's expressed in all kinds of music. I wouldn't make too much of the Jewish cantor and the black blues connection without going into all the various connections. Now having said that, let me really contradict myself. Something that I've always thought, if I've named a jazz player where I've heard something Jewish, it would be one of my favourite tenor saxophone players of all time, Al Cohn. And Al Cohn's style formed a lot of Stan Getz's style. Al Cohn had a certain kind of moaning quality to it that we do associate with a cantor."

So we get back to Getz, via Cohn. It is a pity that no one, to my knowledge, ever sought to pin down Getz on what he perceived as Jewish in his playing.

Fascinatingly though, Roy Nathanson, a very contemporary Jewish American saxophonist, with reference to his own work, has spoken in similar terms: "I know I play in a cantorial, keening way that, hard as I try, isn't black." 6 Nathanson has been deeply involved in the Radical Jewish Culture music scene, about which he was being interviewed by Howard Mandel. But his comments he clearly intended to apply to his work more generally, outside anything overtly Jewish. Nathanson confirmed that was so, when I contacted him: "As I've been doing graduate work in poetry lately, I'm doing a lot of investigation into rhythms of speech. I've always felt that most horn players – and probably any real soloist who has a clearly defined voice – simply speak through their horn with the same inflection that they have with their voice. That is, it's natural it would reflect your cultural background. This is definitely the case with me. I have a nervous keening voice that comes out in a way that is clearly almost cantorial. Me and Anthony Coleman looked at this in an essential way on the Tzadik CD *I Could have Been a Drum*. On 'Soprano Ballad', our premise was that in each simple note, played without any forced Jewish inflection, a kind of common sense of the note itself would be more honestly investigating what cultural language we had in common. We simply played random notes – and followed them. I think the piece actually bears this out. I'm less and less interested in establishing identity differences in people's playing and their lives in general given the tribal nature of the world these days, but I think we breathe, sing and play in patterns that reflect our cultural upbringing. It's the ways we somehow transcend this all that ultimately interests. Another thing to listen to of mine reflecting this question is my 'Spirits of Flatbush' on *Broken Night Red Light* and redone on *Live at the Knitting Factory*."

If Nathanson is right, what he says would apply to any jazz musician whose family background was sufficiently Jewish – a highly contentious point. 7 Violinist Sam Bardfeld, who has worked with Nathanson, and with John Zorn, has been told his playing sounds Jewish. To an extent, he goes along with this, telling me: "I think Harold Bloom in his book on literary influence and literary style talked about the process of trying to write like your influences and in failing, coming up with your own style. I've come to accept that I play Jewish in some way because people and critics keep telling me I do but that's the last thing I aim for. It just comes out this way. The equation people make with new-Jewish improvised music and klezmer drives me nuts. Klezmer music is nice music, it's fine. But Jewish American culture is a real, lived thing – when I read Saul Bellow, Philip Roth, Jonathan Safron-Foer, I see multi-layered contemporary Jewish American characters. The idea that you need to have a *phraigish* scale in Jewish music to make it Jewish is facile."

Sam had just returned, he said, from touring with Bruce Springsteen: "I recently had an interesting experience re Jewishness on the Springsteen tour. My playing is featured on an old gospel tune called 'Oh Mary don't you weep no more'. Bruce played it for us once and then asked the fiddles to improvise an introduction. I instantly heard a Tom Waits-meets-Stuff Smith thing. I went for it and Bruce dug it. A number of critics, mostly in Europe, ended up saying I was playing Jewish or klezmer, which to me was just weird. Part of it was that in some parts of Europe, notably the north, Jewishness is still an exotic category; klezmer has hip exotic cache. In France, Spain and Italy my playing read as 'Gypsy'. On my record

*Periodic Trespasses (The Saul Cycle)*, I created a fictional protagonist named Saul and had seven narrative vignettes throughout the music telling his story. The music is influenced by Andrew Hill/Dolphy-era Blue Note stuff. I didn't set out to make a Jewish record but the character and story – sort of a twenty-first century *shlemiel*-musician-coming-of-age-story does, I think, read as Jewish. Anyways, big topic – that's my two cents."

A profoundly sceptical note was sounded by double-bassist Chuck Israels, who spent several years in the sixties in Bill Evans trio. Larry Bunker, Evans' drummer, told jazz writer Les Tompkins that a quality he appreciated about Israels' playing was that "Chuck gets a kind of a very sonorous, soaring sound – a kind of a melodic sense. Well, sometimes he does sound very Jewish... a very beautiful Jewishness to his solos that I like very, very much. He has the ability to play with the time, to interpolate figures, to get inside the time and then strike off on tangents."

A very beautiful Jewishness? I quizzed Chuck about this, and he said: "Bunker never mentioned it, and I've never thought about it. Most American culture is a little European (with the normal amount of European Jewish culture mixed in, a little west African, and who knows what else. I am a secular Jew, from an urban NY culture informed by a lot of European/American Jewish culture... The particular location and cultural makeup of the people I grew up with had more to do with my musical influences than any kind of generic Jewishness, though my particular upbringing in that culture made me aware of and open to lots of cultural influences and ideas. Many people I knew growing up were black American, Hispanic American, etc, as well as Jewish, and what people think of as more 'normal' Aryan American. Where I grew up, and the influences of my immediate family and friends, had more to do with shaping my music than my Jewishness. As far as the lyricism in my playing goes, it's a direct descendant of Red Mitchell's playing, and his lyricism came from Lester Young. I don't think there was much Jewishness in Red, and that's a direct musical influence, not some imagined cultural relic."

Consider too, what saxophonist Joe Rosenberg told me: "I have played jazz and improvised music with musicians of most religions and all degrees of observance. I can't tell the difference. I've spent a lot of time in Indonesia and played with many Muslim jazz musicians. I've played with a lot of Japanese musicians, many of which are Buddhists. They love the music and most all that goes with it and play great. It seems to be a non-issue from my experience."

What is indisputable is that for most of jazz history, the vast majority of Jewish jazz musicians have taken up this wonderfully supple idiom not to express their Jewishness, but rather their hip American-ness, and a large part of that was and is attempting in some degree to sound black.

In the last forty or so years however, Jewish musicians such as John Zorn, none surely of whom would deny their indebtedness to black music, have deployed jazz, in combination with Jewish music forms and themes, to assert their Jewish identity, producing music that, at its best, has captivated not only Jewish but also many non-Jewish musicians and jazz fans.

Proof of the ongoing, indeed international, impact of Jewish-jazz came at a splendid gig I attended at Cafe OTO in London in November 2021, at which the UK's National Youth Jazz Orchestra performed the music of John Zorn's Masada. The event, under trumpeter Sam Eastmond's musical directorship, was originally scheduled for November 2020 but postponed because of the coronavirus pandemic. 8 Eastmond told me there was never any intention to just do an online replacement performance instead: "I've made two albums of Zorn's Masada music for his series on Tzadik [covering Masada Books two and three compositions] and consider him a friend not just a mentor. He strongly believes in live music being for the people in the room, so without consultation with him I wouldn't feel comfortable moving this into a medium he isn't operating in himself. Especially as this is material originally created for the 'official' Masada releases and stands in most cases as the only versions of these tunes he has released, so have some claim to being 'definitive' or 'original' versions."

. . . .

Let us, for argument's sake, pretend there had never been a single Jewish jazz musician, anywhere. Even were such an absurdity true, Jews would still have profoundly affected jazz in two fundamental ways.

One I covered in Chapter 8 – all those songwriters whose songs have so disproportionately contributed to the jazz standard repertoire, the chord structures alone of which form the basis of many jazz musicians' own compositions.

And the other is the role of the jazz facilitators, in which connection Jews have been omnipresent. I covered some of the most prominent in Chapter 15, among them George Wein, "the godfather of jazz festivals", about whom Stanley Crouch, in an article, acknowledged had "promoted more jazz concerts here and abroad and paid the salaries of more jazz artists than anyone in the history of the music".

In the same piece, Crouch commented more fully on the role of Jewish jazz facilitators, prompted by a visit to the Entertaining America exhibition at the Jewish Museum on Fifth Avenue, New York. The exhibition celebrated the Jewish contribution to American popular entertainment, and Crouch noted: "It is one of the most remarkable stories in American history: Jewish immigrants, most of them from Eastern Europe and Russia, staking claims in the entertainment business and learning the ways and feelings of Americans so well that they produced material that communicated across region, ethnicity, color, religion and class. In something akin to magic, they moved from outsiders to insiders, capturing well the complexity of the American soul in all its humor, melodrama, confusion, dreams and tragedy.

"But the exhibit does not make much of jazz," said Crouch. "That's a serious omission, because it seems to me that one cannot discuss Jews in American entertainment and not talk about the Jewish impresarios, record producers, theater owners and nightclub operators who were so essential to the quality of the business. That's true whether they were hustlers and cheapskates or true lovers of the art who did all that they could to promote the music and the careers of those they loved."

• • • •

"They [the Jews] have a joy of life that's cynical, which is basically the same sensibility as the blues sensibility. That's a greater connection than atrocities... If it was about suffering and atrocities and all that, the American Indians could outplay everybody."

That astute observation, from the ever-quotable Stanley Crouch, I found on avant-jazz multi-instrumentalist Jacob Garchik's *The Heavens: The Atheist Gospel Trombone Album*, in relation to Garchik's composition 'Digression on the History of Jews and Black Music'.

Crouch – whose passing in 2020 was clearly a great loss to jazz criticism – was one of several African Americans I sought out to interview as one of my main underlying themes has been the interrelationship between Jews and blacks in America's jazz. As I have endeavoured to show, there has been much that is positive in that relationship. but I haven't baulked at the tensions inherent in the black/Jewish jazz nexus.

So it was encouraging to note a possible volte-face by Amiri Baraka, formerly LeRoi Jones, not long before he died. Baraka, the reader will remember, faced accusations of being militantly black-centric in his writings about jazz. And I recall that when I was in America conducting research for this book's predecessor, he was facing allegations of antisemitism in connection with comments following the 9/11 attacks.

I was subsequently therefore surprised at Baraka's contribution as one of the interviewees in David L Lewis's aforementioned documentary about Nat Hentoff.

Asked about Hentoff, Baraka observed, "It's interesting, a lot of those critics, they were these immigrant kids who grew up with a similar kind of experience and therefore they could identify with, quote, the outsider."

"A lot of them were Jews," returned the interviewer.

"Yeah, that's what I mean," Baraka confirmed.

Encouraging to learn too that the theme at a ten-day Portland Jazz Festival in Oregon was Bridges and Boundaries: Jews and African Americans Playing Jazz Together. Among the performers were: Joshua Redman, the son of black saxophonist Dewey Redman and Jewish American dancer Renee Shedroff, with his quartet that included black and Jewish musicians; black violinist Regina Carter presenting her project *Reverse Threads* that traces the musical history of African cultures, including that of the tribes of Ugandan Jews; and trumpeter Avishai Cohen, one of the many Israelis on the American jazz scene, leading a jazz collective performing Stevie Wonder songs.

Bill Royston, the festival's artistic director, explained: "The original idea for this festival came from Nat Hentoff's writings about jazz as a meeting place for African and Jewish Americans... Historically, the music drew people together."

On that upbeat note, I draw the curtains on Volume 1. Thus far, in contemplating the jazz Jews story, I've focused solely on the United States, and even then, one notable omission is the proliferation of US-based Israel musicians. They will be covered in Volume 2, in which I expand my study to explore the global ramifications of Jews in jazz, starting in Nazi Europe.

•  •  •  •

## Chapter 1

1. *Creators and Disturbers: Reminiscences by Jewish Intellectuals of New York*, ed Bernard Rosenberg and Ernest Goldstein, Columbia, 1982, p109.

• • • •

## Chapter 2

1. Dr Bruce Raeburn, 'Jewish Jazzmen in New Orleans, 1890-1940: An Overview', *The Jazz Archivist*, May 1997, p1.

2. Raeburn, p4.

3. ibid, p2.

4. Richard M Sudhalter, *Lost Chords*, Oxford, 1999, p79.

5. *Jazzmen*, ed Frederic Ramsay Jr and Charles Edward Smith, The Jazz Book Club, 1958, p45.

6. Raeburn, p4.

7. ibid, p10.

8. Seth Rogovoy, 'Not Your Father's Klezmer – But Neither Was His', *The Jewish Daily Forward*, 9 May 2003.

9. Alec Wilder, *American Popular Song: The Great Innovators 1900-1950*, Oxford, 1972, p87.

10. *Oxford Companion to Jazz*, Oxford, 2000, p36.

11. Stuart Nicholson, *Billie Holiday*, Indigo, 2000, p21.

12. Jeffrey Melnick, *A Right to Sing the Blues: African Americans, Jews and American Popular Song*, Harvard University Press, 2001, p21.

13. *Louis Armstrong: In His Own Words*, Oxford, 2001, p8. The Karnofsky's son Morris, Louis' boyhood friend (aka Nick Karno), started New Orleans' first jazz record store and founded music clubs on Bourbon Street. One black and Jewish New Orleans connection that has withstood any post-civil rights era tensions directly concerns jazz – the famous Preservation Hall, founded by Jewish couple Allan and Sandra Jaffe in 1961 to protect local traditional jazz. Their son Ben runs the venue and plays tuba and bass in the Preservation Hall Jazz Band.

14. Chan Parker, *My Life in E-Flat*, University of South Carolina Press, 1993, p48.

15. James McBride, *The Color of Water: A Black Man's Tribute to His White Mother*, Bloomsbury, 1998, pp66-67.

16. Jewish support for the NAACP continued well into the 1960's struggle for black civil rights.

17. Melnick, p93.

18. ibid, p95.

19. ibid, p62.

20. ibid.

21. *The Jazz Cadence of American Culture*, ed Robert G O'Meally, Columbia, 1998, p405.

22. Noma Faingold, 'Paul Robeson: forgotten hero of Jews', *The Jewish News Weekly of North California*, 19 June 1998.

23. Melnick, p226.

24. *The Duke Ellington Reader*, ed Mark Tucker, Oxford, 1993, pp114-18.

25. *New Grove Dictionary of Jazz*, MacMillan, 1994 edition, pp1177-78.

26. Richard Crawford, *America's Musical Life*, Norton, 2001, p573.

27. Martha Bayles, *Hole in Our Soul*, The Free Press, 1994, p60.

28. Leonard Bernstein, *The Infinite Variety of Music*, Weidenfeld and Nicholson, 1968, p50.

29. Bernstein, p60.

30. Melnick, p78.

31. Crawford, p621.

32. Maurice Waller and Anthony Calabrese, *Fats Waller*, Schirmer, 1997, p136. Waller got his first break while performing at a party at George Gershwin's Brooklyn house. An RCA Victor executive there offered him a recording contract (Jules Stewart, *Gotham Rising*, I.B. Tauris, 2016, p84).

33. David Hadju, *Lush Life*, Granta, 1997.

34. Stuart Nicholson, *Reminiscing in Tempo*, Pan, 2000, pp79-80.

· · · ·

## Chapter 3

1. William Howland Kenney, *Chicago Jazz: A Cultural History 1904-1930*, Oxford, 1994, p99.

2. Bebop-era drummer Stan Levey, when I asked him, dismissed Pollack: "Ben Pollack, that's way back. He couldn't drum, he couldn't carry a tune in a bucket. He was a snare drummer, boom-boom-bass, right off the trees. He had a good band, but he wasn't a drummer."

3. Sudhalter, *Lost Chords*, p304.

4. *Oxford Companion to Jazz*, p684.

5. *Selections from the Gutter: Portraits from the Jazz Record*, ed Art Hodes and Chadwick Hansen, University of California Press, 1997, p203.

6. Mezz Mezzrow, *Really the Blues*, Flamingo, 1993, p42.

7. Saxophonist and composer Charley Gerard, in his study of the racial politics of jazz, comments: "After the 1950s many cosmopolitan Jews were all too familiar with the embarrassing sight of other Jews like Mezzrow pretending not to be Jewish." Gerard, *Jazz in Black & White*, Praeger, 1998, p104.

8. Artie Shaw, *The Trouble with Cinderella*, Da Capo, 1979, p228.

9. Willie the Lion Smith, *Music on My Mind*, Jazz Book Club, 1966, p12.

10. ibid.

11. ibid, p17.

12. ibid, p54.

13. Whitney Balliett, *American Musicians II*, Oxford, 1986, p389.

14. Smith, pp169-70.

15. ibid pp171-72.

• • • •

## Chapter 4

1. Rudi Blesh, *Combo USA*, Chilton, 1971, pp150-51.

2. Robert Walser [ed], *Keeping Time*, Oxford, 1999, p95.

3. ibid.

4. *Creators and Disturbers: Reminiscences by Jewish Intellectuals of New York*, ed Bernard Rosenberg and Ernest Goldstein, Columbia, 1982, p100.

5. *Crescendo*, National Jazz Archive.

6. Consider too Charles Mingus' testimony, also citing other black musicians Goodman later employed: "Benny Goodman came to the Grove with Lionel Hampton and Charlie Christian and Teddy Wilson – came to the front door and they wouldn't let them in. We were all working Hollywood and going in the back doors at the time. I was with Zutty Singleton one time, the drummer in the band I was in. Everybody looked around, 'You mean Benny Goodman walked off the bandstand, eh?' He said, 'You mean they can't come in the front door, right? Fellows, pack up'... And they walked out the front door, man, and that message hit all the clubs at once. Zutty walked in the front door, and nobody said nothing. Black guys used to come in back by the kitchen... So Martin Luther King was just a sample, man. Benny Goodman and Lionel Hampton – that's what started integration... Benny Goodman would take no Jim Crow jobs... He walked off a job that must have cost him twenty thousand that week" – John Goodman, *Mingus Speaks*, University of California Press, 2013, p110.

7. Frank Kofsky, *John Coltrane and the Jazz Revolution of the 1960s*, Pathfinder, 1998, p85. When Fletcher Henderson needed arrangements for his own band, one musician he hired was Jewish guitarist/vocalist Bob Loewy.

8. Lionel Hampton, *Hamp*, Warner, 1989, p68.

9. James Lincoln Collier, *The Making of Jazz*, Papermac, 1981, p223.

10. The museum's president, Leonard Garment, was also Jewish. As a young man Garment had been a saxophonist in Woody Herman's band but decided he wasn't good enough at jazz. He wound up as Richard Nixon's counsellor. Garment, *Crazy Rhythm: From Brooklyn and Jazz to Nixon's White House, Watergate and Beyond*, Da Capo, 1997.

11. John White, *Artie Shaw: Non-Stop Flight*, EastNote, 1998, p41.

12. Billie Holiday, *Lady Sings the Blues*, Penguin, 1984, pp70-71.

13. Jewish bandleader, arranger and violinist Jan Savitt can also be counted among the first non-black swing bandleaders to feature an African American vocalist – George 'Bon Bon' Tunnell.

14. *JazzTimes*, May 2002, p180.

15. 'I'll never sing in a dance band again – Holiday' – Dave Dexter Jr, *DownBeat*, 1 November 1939.

16. Donald Clarke notes, "Lady knew that it was having to listen to advice from hotel managers, sponsors and song-pluggers that had finally disgusted him beyond endurance" – Clarke, *Wishing on the Moon: the Life and Times of Billie Holiday*, Viking, p148.

17. Vladimir Simosko, *Artie Shaw: A Musical Biography and Discography*, Scarecrow Press, 2000, p58.

18. It is Forrest one hears on the Shaw band's delightfully swinging version of 'Deep Purple', recorded in 1939 with Artie's best line-up to that point, and several personnel were Jewish: tenor saxophonist Georgie Auld, pianist Bob Kitsis, bassist Sid Weiss, drummer Buddy Rich and trumpeter Bernie Privin.

19. Joan Peyser, *The Music of My Time*, Pro/Am, 1995, p137.

20. Gene Lees, *Arranging the Scene*, Cassell, 2000, p238.

21. Previn, No Minor Chords, Doubleday, 1992, p97.

22. Roger Segure was another Jewish musician who arranged for black swing bands, including in the 1940s as principal arranger for Jimmy Lunceford. In the 1930s he gigged as piano accompanist to black jazz singer Midge Williams.

23. *Oxford Companion to Jazz*, p281.

24. Peyser, p138.

25. Balliett, *American Musicians II*, Oxford, 1998, pp174-75.

26. Art Hodes and Chadwick Hansen [ed], *Hot Man: The Life of Art Hodes*, University of Illinois, 1992, p22.

27. Ibid, p90.

28. Max Kaminsky, *My Life In Jazz*, Jazz Book Club, 1965, p110.

• • • •

## Chapter 5

1. My spelling of the song, here and elsewhere, is that used on the Carnegie Hall recording. Secunda's original spelling was the Yiddish-Germanic 'Bei Mir Bist Du Schön', but the poster for the 2nd Avenue show, although written mostly in Yiddish, transliterated the song, in English lettering, as 'Bei Mir Bistu Shein', and one encounters other variations.

2. The Apollo was under the ownership and management of Frank Schiffman, a Jew. It remains America's main showcase for black talent.

3. Kenneth Aaron Kanter, *The Jews of Tin Pan Alley*, KTAV, 1982, pp70-71.

4. Peter J Levinson, *Trumpet Blues: The Life of Harry James*, Oxford, 1999, p93.

5. JazzTimes, May 2002, p64.

6. Sudhalter, *Lost Chords*, p605.

7. ibid, p593.

8. ibid.

9. *American Klezmer*, ed Mark Slobin, University of California Press, 2002, p18.

10. Sudhalter, p583.

• • • •

## Chapter 6

1. John White, *Artie Shaw: Non Stop Flight*, East Note, 1998, p119.

• • • •

## Chapter 7

1. In 1952, David Blume, like Josephson Jewish, defied North Carolina segregation laws by founding a bowling alley and jazz club and fully integrating the staff, performers and patrons. – *LA Times* obituary, 24 March 2006.

2. David W Stowe, 'Politics of Café Society', *The Journal of American History*, Vol 84, March 1988, p1388.

• • • •

## Chapter 8

1. Alfred Heisler letter, *New York Times*, 19 December 1999.

2. Charles Hamm, *Yesterdays: Popular Song in America*, Norton, 1983, p329.

3. ibid, p366 and 368.

4. ibid, p372.

5. Jack Gottlieb, *Funny, It Doesn't Sound Jewish*, SUNY, 2004, p43.

6. Richard Rodgers, *Musical Stages: An Autobiography*, Da Capo, 2002, p88.

7. *The Duke Ellington Reader*, p44.

8. *New Grove Dictionary of Jazz*, p1176.

9. Nat Shapiro and Nat Hentoff [eds], *Hear me talkin' to ya*, Penguin, 1962, p232.

10. Harriet Hyman Alonso, *Yip Harburg*, Wesleyan, 2012, p103.

11. Arlen's son, jazz saxophonist Sam Arlen, has recorded an album, *Arlen Plays Arlen*, in dedication to his father.

12. *The Bebop Revolution in Words and Music*, ed Dave Oliphant, Harry Ransom Humanities Research Center, 1994, p169.

13. Michael Burgess, 'Hollywood escapism wins high praise from old guard', *Village News*, 2 August 2000.

14. Richard Crawford, *The American Musical Landscape*, Chapter 7, University of California Press, 2000.

15. Gary Giddins, *Celebrating Bird*, Hodder and Stoughton, 1987, p97.

16. Lennie Tristano made a similar claim, as mentioned by Ira Gitler in sleevenotes for *Sonny Berman: Beautiful Jewish Music* (Onyx 211). Alluding to the harmonic-melodic aspects of jazz, Tristano said: "Jewish cantors and gypsies sound more like it than anything from Africa."

• • • •

## Chapter 9

1. Peter D Goldsmith, *Moe Asch: Making People's Music*, Smithsonian, 1998, p227.

2. *The Bebop Revolution in Words and Music*, ed Dave Oliphant, Harry Ransom Humanities Research Center, 1994, p110.

3. Scott DeVeaux, *The Birth of Bebop: A Social and Musical History*, Picador, 1999, pp146-47.

4. *Oxford Companion to Jazz*, p298.

5. *Jazzways*, ed by George S Rosenthal and Frank Zachary, Musicians Press Ltd, 1946, p35.

6. Marc Myers, *Why Jazz Happened*, University of California Press, 2013.

7. Jews have been heavily involved in America's Latin music scene, as musicians – most famously Larry Harlow, a founder member of the Fania All Stars, affectionately nicknamed *el Judio Maravilloso* (The Marvelous Jew) – and as facilitators and fans. Before he passed in 2017, I was in touch with drummer and percussionist Bobby Matos, who got into Latin music, like many Jews, as a dancer. For my radio show, Bobby sent me his Afro Latin Jazz Ensemble CD *Beautiful As The Moon*, The title track is a lovely Latin take on the old Yiddish theatre song 'Sheyn vidi Levona'. Danny Weinstein, the violinist on this, is another stalwart of Latin music, also as trombonist.

8. Gary Giddins, *Celebrating Bird*, Hodder & Stoughton, 1987, p81.

9. ibid, p100.

10. Arnold Shaw, *52$^{nd}$ St: The Street of Jazz*, Da Capo, 1983, p215.

11. Teddy Reig with Edward Berger, *Reminiscing in Tempo: The Life and Times of a Jazz Hustler*, Scarecrow, 1990, p40.

12. John Szwed, *So What: the life of Miles Davis*, Heinemann, 2002, p92.

13. ibid.

14. Hannah Rothschild, *The Baroness: The search for Nica, the rebellious Rothschild*, Verso, 2012, p88.

15. ibid.

16. ibid, p172.

17. ibid, p188.

18. ibid, p242.

19. ibid, p237.

20. ibid, p195.

21. From an account Nica gave to Robert Reisner, reproduced in *The Picador Book of Blues and Jazz*, Picador, pp283-86.

22. Ross Russell, *Bird Lives!*, Quartet, 1994, p364.

23. Rothschild, p237.

24. ibid, p164.

25. Russell, pp281-82.

26. ibid, p283

27. Gene Lees, *Cats of Any Color*, Oxford, 1995. The chapter 'The Nine Lives of Red Rodney' is an interview in which Rodney recalls his extraordinary and often hilarious exploits.

28. Ian Carr, *Miles Davis*, Harper Collins, 1999, p39.

29. Charley Gerard, *Jazz in Black & White*, Praeger, 1998, p9.

30. Lees, p199.

31. Red Rodney: His Bite is Back', *DownBeat*, February 1981.

32. Gary Giddins, *Faces in the Crowd*, Oxford, 1992, p45.

33. Gerard, p88. Equally unremorseful about his drug habit was the jazz fan father of Susan J Miller. In her book about him, she recalls his close relationship with the jazz musicians he idolised, many of them like him Jewish – "Allen Eager, Tiny Kahn, George Handy, Stan Getz, Johnny Mandel, Georgie Auld – these names resonate in my heart like the Yiddish that I heard so often then... I didn't know what went on between my father and these men. All I know is that for my father, his junkie years were the best of his life... But I couldn't listen. For me, those years of his heroin addiction had been a time of fearful poverty... and terror that my mother would cease to function." – Susan J Miller, *Never Let Me Down*, Bloomsbury, 1999, pp9-10.

34. DeVeaux, p19.

35. Geoffrey C Ward and Ken Burns, *Jazz: A History of America's Music*, Pimlico, 2001, p334.

36. Burt Korall, *Drummin' Men: The Bebop Years*, Oxford, 2002, pp112-13.

37. Ibid, p41.

38. ibid, p42.

39. ibid.

40. Gitler, *Swing to Bop*, p281.

41. ibid, p197

42. Korall, p30.

43. Vladimir Simosko, *Artie Shaw: A Musical Biography and Discography*, Scarecrow Press, 2000, p121.

44. Korall, p217

45. ibid, p213

46. Shaw, incidentally, in my interview with him, enthused about the musicality of Cohn's jazz guitarist son, Joe Cohn.

47. Barry Ulanov, in his *History of Jazz In America*, mentions that in the Herman band, Berman was "one of the leading actors in the band's troupe of Jewish comedians" alongside bandmates Irv Lewis and Sam Marowitz.

48. Gitler, *The Masters of Bebop*, Da Capo, 2001, p94.

49. Also involved was Serge Chaloff, the first musician to successfully adapt Charlie Parker's alto innovations to baritone sax. Chaloff's father was Jewish, but Chaloff's brother disclosed: "Serge and I were brought up in Mother's faith, Presbyterian. Even Dad converted to Christianity eventually, after getting miffed at the rabbi from his synagogue." Vladimir Simosko, *Serge Chaloff: A Musical Biography and Discography*, Scarecrow Press, 1998.

50. From interview in *Chubby Jackson Fan Zine*.

51. Ted Gioia, *West Coast Jazz*, University of California Press, 1998, p164.

52. Lees, p174-75.

53. http://jazzke.org

54. Bret Primak, 'Eddie Daniels: The Real Thing', *JazzTimes* December 1994.

55. Mark Humphrey – sleevenotes to Rounder DVD *Barney Kessel, Rare Performances 1952-1961*.

56. Norman Mongan, *The History of the Guitar in Jazz*, Oak Publications, New York, 1983.

57. Kessel, *Guitar Player*, January 1977.

58. *Guitar Player*, February 1977.

59. Another Marx Brothers jazz link is Harpo's son Bill Marx, a jazz pianist, while Harpo himself played harp on albums with jazz settings – *Harpo at Work* and *Harpo in Hi Fi*.

60. Gitler, *Swing to Bop*, p177.

61. BBC Radio 3 programme, 6 February 2004.

62. Joshua Breakstone – the Musings section of his website, 25 December 2004.

63. *Jazz Journal* interview, October 1987.

64. *Reading Jazz*, editor Robert Gottlieb, Bloomsbury, 1997, p797.

65. Whitney Balliett, *American Musicians II*, Oxford, 1986, pp208-09.

• • • •

## Chapter 10

1. Marc Myers, *Why Jazz Happened*, University of California Press, 2013, p94.

2. ibid, p97.

3. ibid, p111.

4. Andy Hamilton, *Lee Konitz: Conversations on the Improviser's Art*, University of Michigan Press, 2007, p25.

5. Miles Davis: *The Complete Birth of the Cool*, CD sleevenotes.

6. *Miles: The Autobiography*, Picador, 1990, p107.

7. Leonard Feather, *The Jazz Years*, Picador, 1998, p96.

8. *New Grove Dictionary of Jazz*, 1994.

9. In the corresponding footnote in *Jazz Jews*, I indicated that Paul Desmond, Dave Brubeck's lyrical alto player and the composer of 'Take Five', may not in fact have been Jewish. Desmond's family circumstances – real name Brietenfeld – were such that he thought he was Jewish most of his life. Towards

the end an uncle told him he wasn't, Desmond's biographer Doug Ramsey informed me. Yet there remained considerable ambiguity within the wider Brietenfeld family about their ethnicity, as identified by Ted Gioia (*West Coast Jazz*, University of California Press, 1992, p76). I have since discovered that Desmond's instincts about his ethnicity have been posthumously vindicated. In correspondence with a relative of his, Nancy Barton, she told me: "Paul Desmond, born Paul Breitenfeld, was a first cousin of my mother, Ruth Breitenfeld Barton, making him my first-cousin-once-removed. Paul's father, Emil Breitenfeld, was the brother of my mother's father, Frederick Breitenfeld. Paul's father was certainly Jewish by ethnicity, as described in the document I attach. I do not know enough about his mother to say one way or the other." The document Nancy attached, a family tree, describes the origins of the Breitenfeld family back to 1749, as traced through a Czech genealogist. Nancy added: "Doug Ramsey and I have discussed Paul's ethnicity, which did not come fully to light until after Doug's biography was published. It does not surprise me that Paul would have been told by a relative that he was not Jewish, as the Breitenfeld family was secretive about this, undoubtedly due to antisemitism at the time they immigrated into the US, in the 1880s, and thereafter."

10. Konitz was Loren's second saxophone teacher; his first was another Jewish altoist, Hymie Schertzer, Benny Goodman's lead section player.

11. Sudhalter, *Lost Chords*, p565.

12. Benny Green, *Such Sweet Thunder*, Scribner, 2001, p186.

13. Miles Davis, *Miles: The Autobiography*, Picador, 1990, p89.

14. *Keeping Time*, ed Robert Walser, Oxford, 1999, p289.

15. Quoted from the sleeve of *Stan Getz, Early Autumn* (Prism PLATCD 698).

16. Donald L Maggen, *Stan Getz: A Life in Jazz*, William Morrow, 1996, p31.

17. *Focus* CD sleevenotes.

18. Chilton, *Roy Eldridge, Little Jazz Giant*, Continuum, 2002, p154.

19. John Levy, *Men, Women, and Girl Singers*, Beckham, 2000, p79.

20. Oscar Peterson, *A Jazz Odyssey*, Continuum, 2003, p176.

21. Ian Carr, *Miles Davis*, Harper Collins, 1999, p14.

22. Simon, *The Big Bands*, MacMillan, 1967, pp85-86.

23. Mel Tormé, *Traps: The Drum Wonder*, Oxford, 1991, p99.

24. Previn, *No Minor Chords*, pp54-55.

25. Levy, p55.

26. Gitler, *Masters of Bebop*, p189.

27. Ted Gioia, *West Coast Jazz*, p269.

28. Robert Gordon, *Jazz West Coast*, Quartet, 1986, p55.

29. Gioia, p247.

30. Les Tomkins, *Jazz Professional* – National Jazz Archive website.

31. Myers, p63.

32. Similarly, Jewish vibraphonist and composer-arranger Teddy Charles, whose own leftfield propensities were manifest in his New Directions quartet with Rogers, and in their 1956 *Collaboration: West* sessions, in his Tentet, and in his contributions to Charles Mingus's Jazz Composers' Workshop.

• • • •

## Chapter 11

1. André Previn, *No Minor Chords*, Doubleday, 1992, p53. In the LA recording studios in the late fifties, Shelly Manne was first-call drummer, but determined to keep jazz viable, in 1960 he opened Shelly's Manne Hole, one of the great Los Angeles clubs. "From a musician's standpoint, it was very significant because the club was geared to the comfort of the musician, and this was and still is a rarity. The musician was king there and therefore people liked to play there. All the great players of the world passed through," Kirk Silsbee told me.

2. *Oxford Companion to Jazz*, p714. Another film Berg cited is the adaptation of Jewish playwright Jack Gelber's 1959 drama *The Connection* about drug addiction in the bebop world. The play and film featured live jazz musicians as actors, including pianist Freddie Redd who wrote the music.

3. Frank Kofsky, *John Coltrane and Jazz Revolution of the 1960s*, Pathfinder, 1998, p119 and 133.

4. David Amram, *Vibrations*, Chapter 10, Thunder's Mouth Press, 2001.

5. 'Benny Carter, Eight Decades in American Music (Hollywood Jazz and Films, 1940s-1960s)' – Rutgers Institute of Jazz Studies virtual exhibit.

6. Buddy Collette, *Jazz Generations*, Continuum, 2000, pp125-27.

7. ibid.

8. About his *Folk Songs For Far Out Folk* album, Katz explained when it was re-released (Reboot Stereophonic, 2007): "These were the three cultures that were most important to me at the time. The American culture I was very interested in but most as a radical guy who had to learn about folk music and protest songs. And the African element just followed because of the oneness of man. The reason for the Jewish stuff was the mystery." Jewish themed tracks are 'Baal Shem Tov' and 'Rav's Nigun'. Katz told Josh Kun, who wrote the reissue liner notes: "I love the mystery of Judaism... the idea that the Kabbalah

does not answer the final answer – the mystery beyond mystery. It's impossible to ever know what God is" – Katz here alluding to his Kabbalist leanings. In the 1950s, Katz's interest in the Kabbalah inspired beat poet Lawrence Lipton to write a Hebrew poem, 'Trumpets in the Morning'. Katz died in September 2013, just a few months after performing at a 'Jews on Jazz' klezmer summit in San Diego. Katz hadn't come up in my interview with Kirk Silsbee about west coast jazz, but Kirk thought him sufficiently significant to later email me that: "We didn't talk about cellist Fred Katz, who composed and played in the pioneering Chico Hamilton Quintet, of which Buddy Collette was a member. Sure, cello had been employed in some jazz recordings – by Oscar Pettiford, Harry Babison and Mingus – but the use of cello as a regular part of a band's instrumentation was absolutely new in the mid-50s... The texture of cello, flute, Jim Hall's guitar and Hamilton's mallets was something entirely new as well and it had surprising repercussions. On a European festival in the late '70s, members of the Art Ensemble of Chicago commended Collette for the Hamilton recordings (like Buddy's *Blue Sands*), citing them as the precursor to their own work with 'little' instruments."

• • • •

## Chapter 12

1. Wilmer, *As Serious As Your Life: Black Music And The Free Jazz Revolution, 1957–1977*, Serpent's Tail, 1992. ESP-Disk folded in 1994 but Stollman relaunched it in 2005 to bring out reissues, previously unreleased material and new releases. Jason Weiss, for his oral history on ESP-Disk (*Always in Trouble*, Wesleyan, 2010), interviewed Stollman and many of the artists, and remarks: "Complaints have circulated since the original releases about royalties not paid beyond the small advance; Stollman recognizes where proper accounting was lacking and to make up for that lapse is one reason he plunged back into the fray. But he also acknowledges that most of the records never sold very much when the company previously existed." Weiss concludes: "What seems certain is that he never got rich off anyone, far from it.".

2. Frank Kofsky, *John Coltrane and Jazz Revolution of the 1960s*, Pathfinder, 1998, p43.

3. Wilmer, p214.

4. George E Lewis, *A Power Stronger Than Itself*, University of Chicago Press, 2009, 112-14.

5. Marc Myers, *Why Jazz Happened*, University of California Press, 2013, p199. Larry Kart is another Jewish jazz journalist, quoted in Myers' study, that attended sixties AACM gigs.

6. Paul Bley, *Stopping Time*, Vehicule, 1999, p16.

7. Dave Pike, quoted in Laurence Christon's sleeve-notes for Pike's 1976 album *Times Out Of Mind*, Muse MR5092.

8. Quoted from the liner notes to *Solemn Meditation: The Paul Bley Quartet*.

9. Ted Gioia, *A History of Jazz*, Oxford, 1997, p302.

10. *Rough Guide to Jazz*, Penguin, 2004.

11. Lacy, interviewed by Max Harrison, *Jazz Monthly*, March 1966.

• • • •

## Chapter 13

1. Bill Reed, 'Q&A with Ruth Olay', *Songbirds* magazine, 1999.

2. Charles Champlin, 'Ruth Olay – still Jazzy After All These Years', *LA Times*, February 10, 1987.

3. I met Jeremy Kahn in Chicago. He told me about his gig the following evening with Mark Colby's quartet – saxophonist Colby and bassist Eric Hochberg also Jewish. The venue was Jazz Showcase, Chicago's oldest jazz club, founded in 1947 by Joe Segal, another jazz Jew.

4. Spider, it turned out, had a very personal connection to the music, telling me: "I was one of the official acts for the Gershwin centennial in 1998 and I worked very closely with the Gershwin family and had the great pleasure of knowing Frankie Gershwin, George's baby sister. I met her when she was 85 and knew her until she passed away aged 92. She he came out and introduced my concert in New York. She came on stage and sang two of her brother's songs. I loved her very much."

5. Some others include: Barbara Levy Daniels, an excellent interpreter of songbook standards, championed by Ray Charles at the dawn of her career; Janis Siegel, whose vocalese impressed at a Manhattan Transfer gig I was invited to; Deborah Latz – her covers of standards, bossas and blues on *Fig Tree* charming but topped by 'You Are', the atmospheric song she wrote in memory of her late stepmother, on which she shares vocal duties with Griot singer Abdoulaye Diabate; Kathy Kosins from Detroit, where her father supplied clothing for Motown's Berry Gordy and his stable of soul artists, and who besides jazz, has won accolades for her prowess as a soul singer; and Judy Wexler, whose 2019 release *Crowded Heart* covers compositions by contemporary songwriters.

6. Linda Dahl, *Stormy Weather*, Quartet, 1984, p56.

7. Sally Placksin, *Jazzwomen*, Pluto, 1985, p156.

8. Nat Hentoff, *JazzTimes*, May 2005.

9. Sherrie Tucker, *Swing Shift*, Duke, 2000, p152.

10. ibid, pp158-59.

11. ibid, pp180-81.

12. Leslie Gourse, *Madame Jazz: Contemporary Women Instrumentalists*, Oxford, 1995, p4.

13. Nat Hentoff, 'A Thrilling Big Band', *JazzTimes*, November 2003.

14. Sleevenotes, Emily Remler: Retrospective Volume Two.

15. ibid.

16. *DownBeat*, March 1988.

17. ibid.

18. Greg Cooper, 'A Moment With Mimi Fox', *Reverb*, 5th January 2016

19. John Heidt, *Vintage Guitar*, June 2006.

20. ibid.

21. Scott Yanow, The Great Jazz Guitarists, *Backbeat*, 2013, p75.

22. Two other flautists to mention, Andrea Brachfeld and Rebecca Kleinmann, are sort of kindred spirts. Brachfeld is recipient of a Latin-Jazz Lifetime Achievement Award.

23. Shaun Brady, Jazziz, February 2019.

24. Female Jewish jazz instrumentalists also include: pianists Leslie Pintchik, Lynne Arriale and Joan Stiles (Jewish father); violinist/electric violinist Yehudit, a startlingly good musician – her chamber jazz partnership with cellist Beth Snellings yielded the delightful album *Different Strokes ... Live*; saxophonist/ clarinetist Halley Shoenberg, whose *Love Goes 'Round* of mainly standards includes her 'Klezmer Dance' that incorporates elements from traditional Jewish music; alto saxophonist Libby Richman; and trombonist/vocalist Natalie Cressman – daughter of Brazil-style jazz singer Sandy Cressman. A posthumous mention too for Rozanne Levine, who contacted me early in 2012 when, though I didn't realise it, she was battling with cancer. She emailed in gratitude for playing 'Lost Freedoms' from *Chakra Tuning* on my radio show – Rozanne on various clarinets, her husband Mark Whitecage on clarinet, soprano sax and electronics, and both deploying sonic aids such as bird whistles. Their avant-ambient jazz would, I imagine, have received miniscule or zero previous airplay.

25. Gourse, p15.

26. Jewish Montclair members that Jean informed me about included trombonists Sarah Cline and Mara Fox, drummer Kelly Fasman, vocalist Pamela Rose, and occasional contributor percussionist Michaelle Goerlitz.

27. *Leonard Feather Book of Jazz*, Arthur Baker, 1957, p67.

28. Leonard Feather, *The Jazz Years*, Picador, 1988, pp140-41.

29. ibid.

• • • •

## Chapter 14

1. Fred Jung, 'A Fireside Chat with Lew Tabackin', *All About Jazz*, 4 April 2003.

2. W Royal Stokes, *Living the Jazz Life*, Oxford, 2004, pp37-38.

3. ibid, p39.

4. Stuart Nicholson, *Jazz Rock*, Schirmer, 1998, p37.

5. ibid, p44.

6. John Fordham, Obituary, *The Guardian*, 24 October 2005.

7. Quoted from Pike's album *Times Out Of Mind*.

8. Nicholson, p38.

9. *DownBeat*, March 1991.

10. Nicholson, p85.

11. Marc Myers, *Why Jazz Happened*, University of California Press, 2013, p221.

12. ibid, p225.

13. Ian Carr, *Miles Davis*, p281.

14. ibid, p287.

15. Nicholson, p126.

16. ibid, pp68-69.

17. ibid, p147.

18. *JazzTimes*, May 2002, p66.

19. *The Jazz Cadence of American Culture*, ed Robert G O'Meally, Columbia, 1998, p507.

20. *Jazzwise*, June 2002.

21. He is the son of jazz saxophonist Frank Perowsky.

22. *DownBeat: 60 years of Jazz*, Milwaukee, 1995, p213.

• • • •

## Chapter 15

1. Hazel Meyer, *The Gold in Tin Pan Alley*, JB Pippincott, 1958, pp234-35.

2. ibid, p31.

3. Ted Vincent, *Keep Cool: The Black Activists Who Built the Jazz Age*, Pluto, 1995, pp78-79.

4. Duke Ellington, *Music Is My Mistress*, Doubleday, 1973, p72.

5. Stuart Nicholson, *Reminiscing in Tempo*, Pan, 2000, p45.

6. Mark Tucker, *Ellington: The Early Years*, University of Illinois Press, 1991, p171.

7. *Music Is My Mistress*, p72.

8. Don George, *The Real Duke Ellington*, Robson, 1982, p47.

9. James Lincoln Collier, *Duke Ellington*, Pan, 1989, p70.

10. *Music Is My Mistress*, p82.

11. Dave Carey, liner notes – *Irving Mills and His Hotsy Totsy Gang Volume 1*, Retrieval FJ-122.

12. Leonard Feather, *The Jazz Years*, Picador, 1986, p168.

13. 'Joe Glaser & Louis Armstrong – Part 1 Early Days, A memoir by Ernie Anderson', *Storyville* No. 160, December 1994, p124.

14. Richard Meryman, *Louis Armstrong: A Self-Portrait*, Eakins, 1971, p45.

15. Anderson, *Storyville* 160, p127.

16. ibid, p128.

17. ibid.

18. ibid, p124.

19. ibid, pp125-26. These twenties' gems pre-date Glaser's managerial partnership with Armstrong but stengthened the bond between them, as Ernie Anderson learned: "When Louis got the nod for small band record dates, Joe would pack the whole band into one of his big Pierce-Arrow touring cars... and drive them down to the OKeh race records studio in the Loop... Years later when Joe was an agent, and Columbia reissued Louis's early classics, Glaser insisted on them paying Louis Armstrong a 5% royalty."

20. Laurence Bergreen, *Louis Armstrong: An Extravagant Life: An Extraordinary Life*, HarperCollins, 1998, pp451-2.

21. Collier, p278.

22. Anderson, pp132-33.

23. Bergreen, pp477-78.

24. Ricky Riccardi, *What a Wonderful World: The Magic of Louis Armstrong's Later Years*, Pantheon, 2011, p12.

25. Collier, p278.

26. *Louis Armstrong: In His Own Words*, Oxford, 2000, p99.

27. Anderson, *Storyville* 161, p173.

28. ibid.

29. Collier, p330.

30. Bergreen, p450.

31. Anderson, Storyville 161, p179.

32. Collier, p330.

33. Ross Russell, *Bird Lives*, Quartet, 1976, p208.

34. *Eddie Condon's Treasury of Jazz*, P Davies, 1957, p100.

35. ibid, p98.

36. John McDonough, '2001 DownBeat Lifetime Achievement Award MILT GABLER', *DownBeat*, October 2001.

37. Joe Smith, *Off The Record*, Sidgwick & Jackson, 1989, pp24-25

38. Condon, p106-07.

39. *Billy Crystal Presents the Milt Gabler Story*, Verve CD/DVD, 2005. Crystal also recalls the stand Gabler made when, as Decca producer in later years, he encountered resistance to recording left-wing folkies The Weavers: "He recorded the Weavers when they were under scrutiny in the McCarthy era and defended them when the label said you can't record them, they're blacklisted."

40. Barney Josephson (with Terry Trilling-Josephson), *Café Society*, University of Illinois Press, 2009, p51. Gabler also wrote the lyrics to Duke Ellington's 'In a Mellow Tone' and to 'Love' for Nat King Cole.

41. Whitney Balliett, *Goodbyes and Other Messages*, Oxford, 1991, p293.

42. DeVeaux, *The Birth of Bebop*, pp281-82.

43. So Jack Crystal was another Jewish jazz facilitator. His son, Billy Crystal, remembered his father's passion for jazz: "Musicians loved him as much as they loved Milt ... Dad became the voice of the label." His father, said Crystal, started Friday and Saturday jazz night sessions at Central Plaza, New York: "It was a place to dance to Dixieland jazz." *Billy Crystal Presents the Milt Gabler Story* CD/DVD.

44. Frank Kofsky, *Black Music White Business*, Pathfinder, 1998, p31.

45. Teddy Reig with Edward Berger, *Reminiscing in Tempo: The Life and Times of a Jazz Hustler*, Scarecrow, 1990, p29.

46. Dan Morgenstern liner notes, *Miles Davis Chronicles: The Complete Prestige Recordings*, Prestige PCD 012 2.

47. Kofsky, p39.

48. Liner notes, *25 Years of Prestige*, Fantasy/Prestige B00006ZVYR.

49. Michael Cuscuna, Charlie Lourie and Oscar Schnider, *The Blue Note Years: The Jazz Photography of Francis Wolff*, Rizzoli, 1995.

50. Michael Cuscuna and Michel Ruppli, *The Blue Note Label: A Discography*, Greenwood, 2001.

51. Richard Cook, *Blue Note Records: The Biography*, Secker & Warburg, 2002, p10 and 231.

52. Cuscuna/Ruppli, *The Blue Note Label*.

53. Leonard Feather LP sleevenotes, *Sidney Bechet Jazz Classics Volume 1*, Blue Note BLP 1201

54. Gitler, *Swing to Bop*, p227.

55. Bob Porter sleevenotes, *The Best of Blue Note*, Blue Note BLU260545/2.

56. Cuscuna sleevenotes, *Bud Powell Alternate Takes*, Blue Note BST 84430.

57. *Blue Note – A Story of Modern Jazz*, SWR Arte DVD, 1997.

58. Ira Gitler, *The Masters of Bebop*, p117.

59. *Blue Note – A Story of Modern Jazz* DVD.

60. Rudy van Gelder, producer of many jazz classic sessions for Blue Note and other labels, was the son of immigrant parents Louis Van Gelder and the former Sarah Cohen. At the North Sea Jazz Festival awards, he was celebrated as the best recording engineer in jazz history.

61. Lorraine Gordon, *Alive at the Village Vanguard*, Hal Leonard, 2008, p92.

62. Balliett, *Barney, Bradley and Max*, Oxford, 1991, p17.

63. George Goodman, 'Max Gordon now a jazz institution', *New York Times*, 3 September 1982; and Balliett, *Barney, Bradley and Max*, p19.

64. Max Gordon, *Live at the Village Vanguard*, Da Capo, 1988, p11.

65. ibid.

66. ibid, p16.

67. James Gavin, *Intimate Nights*, Grove Weidenfeld, 1991, p83.

68. Balliett, *Goodbye and Other Messages*, p240.

69. Balliett, *Barney, Bradley and Max*, p30.

70. Max Gordon, p91.

71. ibid.

72. Lorraine Gordon, pp192-94.

73. Orrin Keepnews, *The View From Within*, Oxford, 1989, p4.

74. ibid.

75. Rick Kennedy and Randy McNutt, *Little Labels – Big Sound*, Indiana University Press, 2001, pp109-10.

76. ibid, p110.

77. Orrin Keepnews: A jazz producer's legacy'. Interview by Don Heckman, 9 April 2004.

78. Kennedy/McNutt, p111.

79. ibid.

80. ibid, p113.

81. Marc Myers, 'This Jazz Master Is No Musician', *Wall Street Journal*, 11 January 2011.

82. 'Quoted from *Cannonball Adderley's Complete Jazz Fake Book*, Hansen, 1975.

83. 'Orrin Keepnews: A jazz producer's legacy'. Interview by Don Heckman.

84. Ted Gioia writes: "In his autobiography... [altoist Pony] Poindexter lambastes what he perceives as a white/Jewish conspiracy to prevent black musicians from breaking into the Bay Area recording scene and pinpoints the Weiss brothers and Jimmy Lyons as instigators of it. The problem, however, centered less on racism, overt or covert, than on the Fantasy owners' extreme conservatism and their formulaic approach to record producing... This nickel-and-dime philosophy limited their openness to almost any kind of new sound. Once they found marketable artists, like Tjader and Brubeck, the Weisses preferred to record them every few months rather than take chances with new talent." Gioia, *West Coast Jazz*, University of California, 1998, p111.

85. Gioia, p46.

86. Frank Kofsky, *The Jazz Revolution of the 1960s*, Pathfinder, 1998, pp57-58.

87. Gioia, p363.

88. Nat Hentoff, *Speaking Freely*, Knopf, 1997, p48. Hentoff also produced Good Time Jazz sessions for Koenig, recording stride pianists Willie The Lion Smith and Luckey Roberts. They sold poorly but good reviews led to Hentoff's appointment as A&R director of Candid Records for whom he arranged further Cecil Taylor sessions.

89. Ted Hershorn, *Norman Granz: The Man Who Used Jazz for Justice*, University of California Press, 2011, pp42-3.

90. Jim Hopkins, *Ella Fitzgerald: A Life Through Jazz*, New English Library, 1991, p114.

91. ibid, p119.

92. Nat Hentoff, *Listen to the Stories*, Harper Collins, 1995, p100.

93. George Wein, *Myself Among Others*, Da Capo, 2003, p194.

94. ibid, p286.

· · · ·

## Chapter 16

1. Henry Sapoznik, *Klezmer: Jewish Music from Old World to Our World*, Schirmer, 1999, pp79-80.

2. ibid, p111.

3. ibid, p110.

4. David Axelrod, who produced this and other Adderley recordings, was Jewish, and a cult composer. His *Requiem: The Holocaust*, is a dissonant jazz/blues-inflected album issued in 1994.

5. Cantor Mizrahi also participated, with jazz and blues harmonica player Howard Levy, in bridge-building cultural performances in 2007 with Arab and Iranian musicians at venues in the US and Morocco.

6. Bob Applebaum, pianist-composer of three Sabbath services, including for jazz trio and choir, has observed that when the jazz service is presented in synagogue, "many congregants sing along with the choice, in spite of the unusual rhythms and somewhat unexpected harmonies" – I quote his sleeve-notes on *Friday Night Jazz Service*, a 2007 studio recording that features Applebaum-arranged traditional Shabbos melodies.

7. Barzel, *New York Noise: Radical Jewish Music and the Downtown Scene*, p72, Indiana University Press, 2015.

8. ibid.

9. *American Klezmer*, ed Mark Slobin, University of California Press, 2002, p129.

10. Laurence Bergreen, *Louis Armstrong*, Harper Collins, 1998, p267.

11. Jonathan Z S Pollack, 'Who's Yehoodi?: Scat, Jive, and Yiddish 1938-1953', *Guilt and Pleasure*, Winter 2007, pp166-67.

12. Yale Strom, *Dave Tarras: The King of Klezmer*, Or-Tav Music Publications, 2010, p30.

13. Anthony Weiss, 'Composing the Exile: Steve Bernstein's Latest Diaspora Album', *The Jewish Weekly Forward*, 8 February 2008.

14. Howard Mandel, 'Vibes From the Tribe: Jewish Music, Identity and Jazz', *JazzTimes*, September 2001.

15. Stuart Nicholson, *Jazz: the 1980s resurgence*, Da Capo, 1995, p256.

16. *The Wire*, February 1997.

17. Yigal Schleifer, 'Downtown Goes Jewish', *Knit Media*, 1999.

18. *New York Observer*, 14 September 2004.

19. *Bomb*, Summer 2002.

20. Fred Kaplan, 'John Zorn's Joyous Jazz', *Slate*, 3October 2003.

21. Ben Goldberg essay, *New Klezmer Trio And The Origins Of Radical Jewish Culture*.

22. ibid.

23. ibid.

24. The issue of black and Jewish mixed parentage is worthy of further investigation. Other jazz musicians I am aware of from such a family background include electric and acoustic trombonist Josh Roseman and tenor saxophonist

Joshua Redman. Redman is the son of African American tenor saxophonist Dewey Redman but was brought up mainly by his Jewish mother, dancer Rene Shedroff, in a one-bedroom flat in Berkeley. He grew up friends with Dave Ellis, who too is black and Jewish and like Redman, an excellent jazz tenor player. As for Roseman, he was raised in Boston, his mother Jamaican, his father Jewish. On his Josh Roseman Unit albums, electro-acoustic jazz interplays with a swirling vortex of funk, rock, dub and ska. "This music presents a good opportunity to work with and refine notions of identity – your persona comes into focus with the work. Dual heritage gives you that kind of malleability," he told *Jazz Dimensions*.

25. Nat Hentoff, the album's producer, made the following observation about another track, 'Moods in Free Time': "I find Booker's playing here – with its resemblance to a Spanish flamenco singer or a Jewish cantor – exceptionally moving."

26. Altoist Schildkraut performed little after the 1950s. Lowe, who knew him, told me: "Schildkraut had, as Lee Konitz once commented 'a Yiddishe soul'. He was a complete genius and virtuoso – Dizzy Gillespie once told me 'he was the only alto player who captured the rhythmic essence of Bird', and Bill Evans told me there were only two alto players from that era who did not copy Bird – Konitz and Schildkraut. Dave had the most amazing time of any player I have ever heard, and he was a good friend as well, pan-religious in his personal beliefs."

27. Marcus Gammel, *Migration and Identity Politics in New York's Jewish Downtown Scene*, Humboldt-Universität zu Berlin, 2000.

· · · ·

## Chapter 17

1. Martin Williams, *Jazz Changes*, OUP, 1992, pp51-52.

2. Burton Peretti, *The Creation of Jazz: Music Race and Culture in Urban America*, University of Chicago Press, 1992, p90.

3. Charles Levin, 'The art of standing out', *Ventura County Star*, 22 September 2002.

4. Mezzrow, *Really the Blues*, p316.

5. Yigal Schleifer, 'Downtown Goes Jewish', *Knit Media*, 1999.

6. Howard Mandel, *Future Jazz*, Oxford, 1999, p189.

7. Illustrative, in this connection, is the experience of Herbie Mann, as expressed for his final album, the 2002 release *Herbie Mann & Sona Terra: Eastern European Roots*. Mann was a post-war Brooklyn jazz modernist, his parents east European Jews. The album was conceived after Mann had been

diagnosed with inoperable prostate cancer, and on the back of a career that had largely been spent initiating jazz crossovers with Brazilian, African, Latin, Arabian, reggae, Turkish and Arabic music. He reflected: "I've spent my career as a sort of 'assimilado'. I'm not Brazilian, Latin, Japanese, Middle Eastern, Black, etc. My roots are in the culture of Eastern Europe and I am Jewish. Some of the music I'd written in previous years had this Eastern European feeling to it and seemed to come from some mysterious place within me." Music, therefore, that may be said to have manifested itself by some sort of ethno-cultural osmosis. Mann continues: "I set most of it aside because I didn't think it had a place in my musical world. The music always seemed kind of dark and heavy, laden with the suffering of generations... But during the treatment for my cancer, I started thinking about my legacy and those stashed away melodies."

8. Earlier in the pandemic, I was in touch with Philadelphia-based trombonist Dan Blacksberg, whose background is in jazz, klezmer and heavy metal. Like professional musicians the world over, he was contending with the fallout from cancelled bookings. His Tzadik Radical Jewish Culture release *Pillar Without Mercy* with his group Deveykus, promoted as "music that blends the spiritual fire of Hasidic melodies with Albert Ayler and Dark Metal", is with its frontline attack of trombone and twin electric guitars, a smouldering vamp on traditional Jewish wordless *nigunim*.

# Don't miss out!

Visit the website below and you can sign up to receive emails whenever Mike Gerber publishes a new book. There's no charge and no obligation.

https://books2read.com/r/B-A-UGPK-ALEKC

**BOOKS 2 READ**

Connecting independent readers to independent writers.

# About the Author

Mike Gerber, born in 1953, is a London-based journalist, and now also a partner in the Vinyl Vanguard record shop.

Gerber left school at 16 and worked in dead-end jobs before taking a history with Spanish degree in his thirties, and then a post-graduate trainee journalist course.

His career in journalism, as writer and editor, began in the late 1980s. As well as covering a wide range of industries, his features have appeared in the *Guardian*, the *Observer*, *Financial Times*, *New Statesman*, *Lloyds List*, *Jewish Socialist* and on various TV station Channel 4 websites.

Gerber's music journalism includes features in: *We Jazz*, *Cadence*, *fRoots*, *Songlines*, *Long Live Vinyl*, and *IAJRC Journal*. He also presented a regular show on UK Jazz Radio.

Read more at https://www.mikegerberjournalist.co.uk

# About the Publisher

Vinyl Vanguard is a London-based record shop and sometime publisher. If you've enjoyed this book, we would welcome a review via the retailer platform you purchased it from, or via social media.
Read more at https://www.vinylvanguard.com